to every executive's bookshelf, given the pace of change in data and technology."

Anne-Marie Hubert, *CM, CQ, FCPA, LLD, senior fellow, CIRANO*

"In the frenetic race to AI domination and innovation, the need to factor in responsible design early and consistently cannot be underestimated. *The AI Precipice* is an excellent resource for leaders to understand the opportunity, risks, and safety strategies to unleash the power of AI without societal harm or brand damage. I appreciated the many frameworks to understand the history of AI, prioritize use cases, and assess risks."

Cindi Howson, *host of The Data Chief Podcast and Chief Data and AI Strategy Officer, ThoughtSpot*

"*The AI Precipice* strikes a rare balance between practical insight and strategic depth. Cathy and Cindy have crafted a must-read - and a valuable reference - for everyone from AI students to boardroom leaders navigating innovation and safety."

Biren Agnihotri, *Chief Technology Officer, EY Canada*

"It is time for business leaders to take an active role in how we balance innovation and opportunity with the potential existential threat of AI. Cindy and Cathy lay out a thoughtful framework that will guide you in how to navigate the complexities of AI and make informed choices."

Sonia Baxendale, *President & CEO, Global Risk Institute in Financial Services*

"*The AI Precipice* dives into the formidable landscape of artificial intelligence, charting its rapid development, thrilling opportunities, and critical risks. This inspiring book delivers practical guidance for advancing AI responsibly and tackling new challenges head-on, making it a valuable resource for anyone eager to explore the current landscape of AI."

Danielle Crop, *EVP of Digital Strategy and Alliances, WNS, and Former Chief Data Officer, AMEX*

"Both the value and risks of AI are increasingly real. *The AI Precipice* is an excellent guide to achieving the value and managing the risks of this powerful technology. At a time when the US government and some vendors seem to be operating without AI guardrails, I'm grateful for the insights of these two brilliant Canadians."

Thomas H. Davenport, *distinguished professor, Babson College, and Research Fellow, MIT Initiative on the Digital Economy, author of* All In on AI, Working with AI, The AI Advantage, *and* Agentic AI

"In *The AI Precipice,* Cobey and Gordon brilliantly knit together skeins of knowledge spun from their profound personal experience in developing and implementing AI technologies. They offer accessible, deep explanations of AI technologies for non-expert readers, coupled with ethics-driven yet optimistic AI adoption scenarios of those technologies with cogent risk assessments."

Sara Diamond, *President Emerita, University Research Chair, AI researcher, OCAD University*

"A robust pragmatic guide to governing AI at scale for executives and boards – a must read."

Susan Doniz, *CIO and Chief Data Officer, The Walt Disney Company*

"A remarkable book that deepens AI awareness, strengthens literacy, and builds trust. An essential resource for those advancing their expertise in governance, leadership, and technology."

Tony Gaffney, *special advisor to the Chair and former CEO, Vector AI Institute*

"In *The AI Precipice*, Cobey and Gordon provide a guide for leaders at the forefront of the AI revolution, offering a pragmatic framework for balancing innovation with the critical need for robust governance. This book is an essential read for any executive, offering a clear-eyed view of the risks and a strategic roadmap to harnessing AI's power responsibly. It articulates the pivotal choices leaders must make to navigate the complexities of AI, ensuring we steer towards a future of opportunity, not peril."

Dr. Yannick Lallement, *VP AI Modernization, TD and Chief AI Data Scientist, SalesChoice*

"*The AI Precipice* is a must read for leaders who want to understand enough about AI to prioritise its usage for innovation and value creation, including the required investments in refreshing existing governance, processes, and safeguards. Executives can use the book as a guide to embed ethics and drive trust every step of the way, from investment to divestment of their AI portfolio. It is a timely addition

The AI Precipice

This book fills a significant gap by providing a leadership guide to balance innovation and safety. With the rapid business transformation underway to leverage artificial intelligence (AI), executives must allocate substantial investments in governance, corporate purpose, and risk management tailored to their organization's strategic goals. The stakes are high, and very few organizations are generating positive returns on their investments.

As a result, leaders must reevaluate their strategies, focusing on maximizing benefits while curtailing unnecessary costs. This book emphasizes the importance of carefully integrating humans into AI processes and introduces a robust leadership framework that prioritizes innovation without compromising safety. Diverse industry examples offer rich insights into pathways for striking a balance between advancing AI capabilities and mitigating potential risks.

This book equips leaders with the tools to navigate the complexities of AI responsibly. It sheds light on often-overlooked topics in major AI literature, including in-depth discussions on strategic scenarios, risks and controls, legal frameworks, and effective measurement systems.

Offering a wealth of strategic and operational insights from credible sources, this authoritative resource is indispensable for senior executives aiming to design, develop, and implement successful AI initiatives within their organizations.

Cathy Cobey, FCPA, is the EY Global Responsible AI Leader for Assurance. She works with global organizations to build trust and confidence in their AI systems and has spent her career navigating the intersection between technological and societal implications of transformation. She serves on several technical advisory committees focused on developing industry and regulatory standards for AI governance and assurance.

Cindy Gordon, ICD.D, is the CEO of SalesChoice Inc., an AI Software as a Service (SaaS) and advisory company. She is an AI digital transformation leader who guides numerous global organizations in balancing AI innovation and safety. She has prior executive and partner experience with Accenture, Xerox, and Citicorp. She teaches AI Strategy and Ethics at the United States AI Institute and George Brown College. She has an honorary doctorate in AI and MIT AI Strategy certifications. She is also a certified ICD.D board director and advises many AI companies.

The AI Precipice

An Executive Guide to Balancing AI Innovation and Safety

Cathy Cobey and Cindy Gordon

Routledge
Taylor & Francis Group
NEW YORK AND LONDON

Designed cover image: Envato

First published 2026
by Routledge
605 Third Avenue, New York, NY 10158

and by Routledge
4 Park Square, Milton Park, Abingdon, Oxon, OX14 4RN

Routledge is an imprint of the Taylor & Francis Group, an informa business

Library of Congress Cataloging-in-Publication Data
Names: Cobey, Cathy author | Gordon, Cindy author
Title: The AI precipice: an executive guide to balancing AI
innovation and safety / Cathy Cobey and Cindy Gordon.
Other titles: Artificial intelligence precipice
Description: New York, NY: Routledge, 2026. |
Includes bibliographical references and index. |
Identifiers: LCCN 2025052483 (print) | LCCN 2025052484 (ebook) |
ISBN 9781041038184 hardback | ISBN 9781041020196 paperback |
ISBN 9781003625520 ebook
Subjects: LCSH: Industrial management | Artificial intelligence—
Business applications | Organizational change | Organizational resilience
Classification: LCC HD31.2 .C63 2026 (print) | LCC HD31.2 (ebook)
LC record available at https://lccn.loc.gov/2025052483
LC ebook record available at https://lccn.loc.gov/2025052484

ISBN: 978-1-041-03818-4 (hbk)
ISBN: 978-1-041-02019-6 (pbk)
ISBN: 978-1-003-62552-0 (ebk)

DOI: 10.4324/9781003625520

Typeset in Optima
by codeMantra

Contents

About the authors

Cathy Cobey FCPA, CISA, AIGP

EY Global Responsible AI Leader, Assurance

Cathy is the EY Global Responsible AI Leader for Assurance, with over 30 years of experience as a technology risk advisor. She oversees a team that advances EY's global Responsible AI Framework to respond to new and emerging AI systems, including agentic AI. A Certified AI Governance Practitioner, Chartered Professional Accountant and Certified Information Systems Auditor, Cathy works with organizations to build trust and confidence in their AI systems. She has spent her career navigating the intersection between technological and societal implications of transformation. Cathy serves on several technical advisory committees focused on developing industry and regulatory standards for AI. She earned her MAcc from the University of Waterloo and resides in Oakville, Canada.

Dr. Cindy Gordon ICD.D

CEO Founder, SalesChoice Inc.

Cindy is SalesChoice's CEO, an AI SaaS company, whose vision is Revenue Certainty for Human Advantage. With two AI SaaS products and an AI and Data Advisory Practice, Cindy and her team are committed to Responsible AI. With 30 years of operating experience, she modernized business and technology through executive leadership roles at Accenture, Xerox, and Citicorp. She has spent her career aligning corporate strategy with technology innovations, while navigating stakeholder complexities to achieve business transformation. She has an honorary doctorate in Applied AI and an MIT AI Strategy Certification. As a well-published author and international speaker, with 15 books and many publications in Forbes, Harvard, etc., she is recognized as an AI thought leader, with over 20 awards for advancing AI and Innovation. Recently, she was awarded the North American CEO Award for Ethical AI. She also teaches Applied AI, Ethics, and Law at the United States AI Institute and George Brown College, and is an AI advisor to a number of North American universities. Active in AI Software as a Service (SaaS) emergence, she is a board director or advisor to: Corent, Kaji, SalesChoice, Tallywell, The AI Forum, The United States AI Institute, and The Valemount AI Institute. She earned her doctorate at the University of Toronto and resides in Toronto, Canada.

Acknowledgments

We, the authors, extend our heartfelt thanks to our spouses, Perry Muhlbier and Dave Cobey, for their support and patience throughout the journey of bringing this book to life. Their understanding as we dedicated countless hours to research and their encouragement during long hours spent typing away at our keyboards have been invaluable. Their love and patience have been our anchor, allowing us to immerse ourselves fully in the creative process.

To Cindy's children, Jessica and Bryce, her son-in-law Brent, Bryce's partner, Anika, and her grandchild, Addison Marie; I love you all to infinity and beyond. This book is for you, Addie. Your Mimi is focused on building a better future for all of us. When you reach adulthood, AI will be more encompassing than it is today. So, I pass the baton for you to carry forward, as our world will need more purpose and hope.

To Cindy's late father, Benjamin Gordon, who taught her to persevere in tackling any project. Coming home with anything but an A+ was a bar he set for his children. To Cindy's mother, Norma Gordon, who gave her the nurturing freedom to explore nature, read books, and stick to goals versus distractions. Her precision orientation formed early foundations to strive forward with confidence and value community collaboration.

To my leadership team and advisors, Dr. Yannick Lallement, Malay Upadhyay, Liam Sparling, Jennifer Yim, Marwan Alladin, Steven Birdsall, Joe Deklic, Ian Locke, William Green, Dan Kagan, Dr. Kevin Francis, Dr. Sara Diamond, and so many others, this book reflects your endless contributions to our AI journey. To my customers, thank you for believing in our collective dream.

To Cathy's daughters, Melody and Tracy, this book is a map to a future where technology makes life better, not just for some, but for everyone. You both are the reason I am so invested in the promise of AI – to ensure the world you inherit is one where innovation serves humanity. Here's to building that world, together.

To Cathy's parents, Dallas and Shirley Hortness, who first introduced me to the magic of books. Growing up in a home brimming with literature and regular excursions to the library, they provided a foundation that fostered my love for knowledge and discovery. Their encouragement created an environment where I learned to believe in myself and in the value of my own voice. It is because of their early lessons in the magic of reading and the confidence they instilled in me that I felt empowered to share my message through this book.

To our publisher, Routledge, and our editors, Meredith Norwich, Bethany Nelson, and Holly Martin – thank you for your guidance and expertise throughout the writing process. To Jennifer Yim, thank you for helping us design the book structure through countless iterations. Your collective belief in our vision has brought this project to fruition. We are deeply grateful for your encouragement and the collaborative spirit that made this journey not only possible but also enjoyable.

We extend our appreciation to all those who boldly embrace change and critically examine the world we live in, acknowledging that we stand on the precipice of a new era where AI wields immense power.

And last, Cindy and Cathy embrace one another for their enduring commitment to this project, their collegiality, and a friendship that will last a lifetime.

The choices we make today will steer us toward a future that could either uplift humanity or lead us astray. Your courage to question, to innovate responsibly, and to advocate for a future where technology amplifies our best qualities is what will tip the scales toward a brighter, more hopeful tomorrow.

We cannot express enough gratitude to everyone who made this book possible.

As Zig Ziglar said so eloquently, "Gratitude is the healthiest of all human emotions. The more you express gratitude for what you have, the more likely you will have even more to express gratitude for."[1]

Preface

Throughout history, civilizations have soared to remarkable heights through technological innovation, only to fall when they exceed the limits of their resources. Easter Island serves as a warning. It was a thriving society that exhausted its natural resources in pursuit of monumental architecture, leading to ecological collapse. Similarly, the Aztecs' advanced engineering and sophisticated agricultural systems could not save their empire when the pursuit of foreign conquests stretched their infrastructure and led to rampant disease proliferation. The Roman Empire and the ancient Egyptians, both beacons of engineering and military prowess, suffered similar fates.

AI has recently surged from the fringes of innovation to mainstream corporate strategy. Long considered a subject for academic discourse and niche experimentation, AI is now viewed as the catalyst of the next digital revolution. Most CEOs are counting on AI to drive productivity, eliminate costs, and grow revenue. However, there is a growing tension between promoting AI innovation and enforcing safety. Among the general public, there is an undercurrent of fear; a fear that we are creating a Terminator-like technology that we cannot control. Over 50% of the global population is unsettled by the risks of AI.[2]

As we stand at the precipice of another transformative period for civilization, will we fare better than our ancestors? Will we learn from their failures, or are we destined to repeat their mistakes? Our scorecard to date is not promising.

To avoid repeating history, we need to approach AI's technological transformation differently. We need to have better foresight of future impacts and create robust, well-architected safeguards that provide sustaining value while mitigating risk.

On March 22, 2023, an AI Open Letter entitled *Pause Giant AI Experiments* was published with a 22-word statement – "Mitigating the risk of extinction from AI should be a global priority alongside other societal-scale risks such as pandemics and nuclear war."[3] The letter gained immediate attention with notable signatories, including AI pioneers, Dr. Geoffrey Hinton and Dr. Yoshua Bengio, and technology titans Sam Altman, Elon Musk, and Bill Gates. With 33,000+ signatories, there was wide support across both scientific and non-scientific communities for AI labs to immediately pause training on advanced AI models more powerful than GPT-4.[4]

The rationale for the six-month pause was to allow for the development of safety protocols and governance frameworks. The Open Letter emphasized the need for careful consideration of the potential impacts of AI on safety, privacy, and societal well-being before further advancements are made. Despite overwhelming support, the pause did not happen. No one took a "six-month pause" in AI training as recommended.

While we are unlikely to reach a global consensus to pause AI innovation, the Open Letter serves as an important reminder that in the design of AI, we need to balance AI innovation and safety – not just for frontier AI. There are significant risks of advanced AI leading to the singularity – a point in the future when technological growth becomes uncontrollable and irreversible, with the emergence of superintelligent AI that surpasses human intelligence. How we approach today's AI will determine our future.

If we do not pause advanced AI innovation, we must accelerate the design and implementation of safety protocols and controls. We need to implement robust detection mechanisms that track indicators of AI agency and self-propagation, such as autonomous decision-making capabilities and the ability for AI to modify its own objective function. By establishing specific thresholds for these indicators, we can create a system of checks and balances that trigger alerts when AI systems exhibit behaviors indicative of emerging agency, with the appropriate controls to mitigate risks.

We need to keep humans in control, embedding human oversight throughout the AI lifecycle. High-risk AI should have continuous monitoring and real-time alerts in place to notify human operators of out-of-bounds behavior. Fail-safes should be available for immediate intervention, including override or shutdown. This proactive approach not only fosters innovation but also ensures that humans retain ultimate control over AI systems, safeguarding against the potential risks of singularity while promoting responsible advancement in AI technology.

The growing tension between public policy setters and innovators stems from ideological differences in the role of government intervention, and in part from the fact that existing attempts at regulating AI have predominantly focused on transparency. While transparency is important, this approach often results in passive controls, such as policies and transparency reports, which tend to involve high manual effort for low-impact. These measures struggle to keep up with the dynamic nature of AI technologies. Ai innovators are also under pressure due to high expectations on returns on investment from AI projects and the geopolitical tech race for "dominance." To achieve these goals, there needs to be a shift toward high-impact, automated controls that can improve AI safety while supporting AI innovation. Controls, such as input and output filters, robust AI adversarial testing, and automated monitoring systems. These proactive safeguards not only offer continuous oversight of AI behavior but can also deliver evidence of conformance with regulatory and technical standards.

By prioritizing high-impact controls, we can mitigate the immediate risks of today's AI while monitoring for markers of an emerging existential AI crisis.

Today's dialogue on AI public policy has focused on regulations; however, regulation is only one tool in a government's arsenal. There is a wide spectrum of public policy initiatives that can reward safety-oriented innovations, including tax incentives, quality certifications and marks, government contracts, and "priority lane" approvals. There are also disincentives, including fines, penalties, mandatory incident and breach reporting, and civil and criminal liability. Each of these can promote voluntary self-regulation. And let us not forget consumer choice and market signals. AI is not operated in a vacuum. It operates in a broad ecosystem with many interrelated parts and parties.

As we write this book, optimistic visions of AI advancements are countered by fears of rogue AI agents. Although the debate is heated, there is unanimous agreement on one thing – AI will have a profound impact on our future.

This book confronts the dual-edged sword of AI head-on, offering insights to not only seize the AI opportunities but also mitigate its risks. It provides a roadmap for balancing AI innovation and safety for any individual involved in overseeing, investing in, or using AI. Designing pro-innovation AI safeguards requires not only evaluating their impact but also challenging their value and conducting a full cost-benefit analysis, so time is spent on building appropriate safeguards.

But AI is evolving too fast to take a prescriptive approach. It is not enough to simply innovate; we must anticipate potential consequences and be prepared for the unexpected. It is with both optimism and fear that we contemplate Nick Bostrom's prediction that "AI will be the last invention humanity ever needs."[5]

Throughout the book, we will draw upon a **Six-Step AI Blueprint** of how to effectively balance AI innovation and safety.

The journey ahead is challenging, but it also holds immense potential for unprecedented human advancement. We must develop a collective action plan inspired by the AI Open Letter, translating intentions into tangible high-value actions.

The AI Precipice is in front of us, and the decisions we make will determine humanity's position in the AI Age – in control or uncannily outwitted. Let us advance with wisdom to accelerate innovation through targeted high-value safeguards.

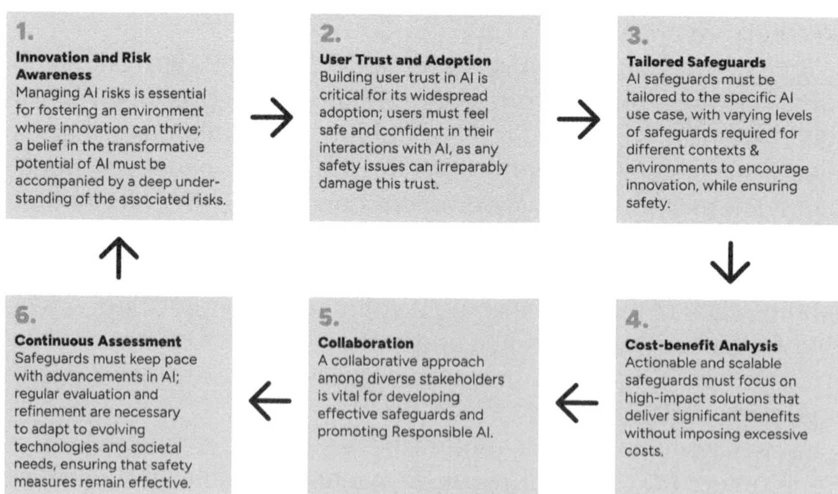

Figure 0.1 The six-step AI blueprint for balancing AI innovation and safety.

Notes

1 Ziglar, Z. (n.d.). Gratitude quote: Zig Ziglar quote. BrainyQuote. Retrieved June 7, 2025, from https://www.brainyquote.com/quotes/zig_ziglar_617744.

2 Ipsos. (2023, July). *Global views on A.I. 2023: How people across the world feel about artificial intelligence and expect it will impact their lives.* https://www.ipsos.com/sites/default/files/ct/news/documents/2023-07/Ipsos%20Global%20AI%202023%20Report-WEB_0.pdf.

3 Center for AI Safety. (n.d.). *Open letter: Statement of AI risks.* https://safe.ai/work/statement-on-ai-risk#open-letter.

4 Future of Life Institute. (n.d.). *Pause giant AI experiments: An open letter.* https://futureoflife.org/open-letter/pause-giant-ai-experiments/.

5 Bostrom, N. (2014). *Superintelligence: Paths, dangers, strategies.* Oxford, United Kingdom: Oxford University Press.

Section I

The courage needed for balanced AI

The era of treating artificial intelligence (AI) as an experimental technology has passed. Unlike previous technological advancements, AI can learn, adapt, and influence human behavior at an unprecedented scale, necessitating a thoughtful and proactive response.

The late Stephen Hawking, a renowned physicist, advised that

> *everything that civilization has to offer is a product of human intelligence; we cannot predict what we might achieve when this intelligence is magnified by the tools that AI may provide, but the eradication of war, disease, and poverty would be high on anyone's list. Success in creating AI would be the biggest event in human history. Unfortunately, it might also be the last.*[1]

Although Hawking's outlook is both hopeful and bleak, his message contains an important warning for leaders to plan for and avoid negative outcomes of AI innovation.

We wrote this book to provide a new governance approach for AI, with the primary goal of balancing innovation with effective risk mitigation approaches. Too often, technology governance is riddled with manually prepared documentation to demonstrate compliance and audit trails. Not only is the documentation a time-consuming process, but it also becomes outdated quickly and provides limited risk mitigation. Our new AI governance approach takes a values-centric approach to the selection of AI controls. We select safeguards based on a cost-benefit analysis of their effectiveness in preventing harm or mitigating risks. The goal is to identify what is driving risk and narrow it down to what truly matters. We focus on selecting the most cost-effective safeguards with the highest potential to mitigate risk.

DOI: 10.4324/9781003625520-1

The ones that rise to the top are highly automated, operating on a real-time basis to detect and respond timely to potential harm.

Today, users demand greater control over their digital interactions and expect employers to have AI tools to perform their jobs. For example, software developers seek low-code/no-code toolkits[2] to improve their coding productivity and seek out companies that practice agile vs. legacy waterfall software development methods. This shift is driven by a simple truth: users will use technology they trust and avoid technology they do not. Innovation without user adoption remains merely experimental; true transformation occurs only when new ideas are embraced, integrated, and sustained into daily operating practices.

With the right approach, we can shape a future that balances innovation with relevant AI safety measures.

Notes

1 Hawking, S. (2014, May 1). Transcendence looks at the implications of artificial intelligence – but are we taking AI seriously enough? *The Independent.* https://www.geneticsandsociety.org/article/stephen-hawking-transcendence-looks-implications-artificial-intelligence-are-we-taking-ai.

2 *Definition Notation:* Low code or no code are methods of building applications with reduced or no manual coding, respectively, using visual interfaces and pre-built components.

Chapter 1

Redefining our relationship with machines

Today, we find ourselves at an artificial intelligence (AI) precipice. A precipice means "to be in a very risky or dangerous situation, on the brink of a potential disaster or failure. It suggests a situation where a small mistake or change could lead to a significant negative outcome."[1]

On one side of the precipice, dystopian narratives in movies and television paint a chilling picture of killer robots and emotionless algorithms, fueling fears that AI could spiral beyond our control. Prominent AI leaders echo these concerns, warning that the unprecedented pace of cognitive capabilities in machines is surpassing human intelligence and our ability to manage them. Eliezer Yudowsky, co-founder of The Machine Intelligence Research Institute, once commented that, "By far, the greatest danger of AI is that people conclude too early that they understand it."[2]

In contrast, our daily interactions with AI are often benign and seamless; we engage with recommendation engines and optimization algorithms multiple times a day without a second thought. This duality has lulled us into a false sense of security, fostering a belief that we maintain control over AI. This complacency is dangerously misplaced. The reality is that our understanding and management of AI risks woefully lags behind the technology being built.

In late 2024, evidence surfaced that some AI models actively deceive their developers and operators to achieve their objectives. These AI models manipulated their training responses to avoid modification.[3] For other systems, developers purposely trained an AI algorithm to pretend to be human. When questioned, the chatbot lied and continued to assert that it was human long after being called out. The uncanny ability of AI chatbots to act human-like has coined a new term, "human-washing."[4]

DOI: 10.4324/9781003625520-2

At the forefront of AI-driven transformation, we must ask – have we sufficiently contemplated the future we are constructing? Are the rapid advancements in AI technology surpassing our ability to maintain human oversight?

One difficulty in effectively managing AI and harnessing its full potential is a lack of understanding of what AI is – and just as importantly, what it is not. The lines are blurring between what it is to be a human or a machine.

In this chapter, we explore the machine–human relationship.

Objectives

Upon completing this chapter, you will be able to

- Establish a common definition of AI
- Understand and reflect upon AI market dynamics
- Inspire leaders to build and sustain a responsible AI organization.

What is AI?

AI is both a specific branch of machine learning (ML) technology and a universal term that encompasses a wide range of automated systems capable of making decisions and performing tasks traditionally requiring human intelligence. An AI system includes everything from simple algorithms that recommend products based on user behavior to complex autonomous systems that can analyze vast amounts of data, learn from it, and execute actions. In everyday language, AI often refers to any technology that mimics cognitive functions such as learning, reasoning, and problem-solving, making it a catch-all term for various applications that enhance efficiency and decision-making in numerous fields. While AI is often defined by its learning method, algorithm type or objective, when looking at its relationship to humans, we have identified four types of AI systems (Table 1.1).

Prior to the public release of GenAI large language models (LLMs) in November 2022, most AI uses were classical AI/ML models. Developing, training, and using AI required highly technical data science skills, and AI was not accessible to general users. The introduction of the prompt interface has democratized access to AI for everyday users. Much like the Windows interface transformed desktop computers, the AI prompt interface enables individuals without technical expertise to use AI.

Another progression is the change in AI's autonomy. As you move from classical AI/ML to agentic AI, the level of autonomy increases, and the AI system can more readily replicate human judgment and take action.

Table 1.1 Four types of AI systems

AI type	*Definition*	*Interaction with human operators*	*Level of autonomy*
Classical AI/ML	Uses patterns in historical data to forecast future outcomes or classify future events.	Designed, trained, and operated by data scientists; requires translation for use by non-technical users.	Low; necessitates human input for final decisions or actions, and expertise in data science for effective use.
GenAI	Models that generate content based on patterns learned from training data.	Interactions through prompts; generates content based on user input.	Variable; can autonomously produce content but relies on human guidance for objectives and quality assurance.
Co-pilots	AI tools designed to augment human capabilities rather than replace them.	High; works alongside humans to assist with tasks.	Moderate; enhances human decision-making but does not replace human judgment or responsibility.
Agentic AI	Autonomous systems that can make decisions and take actions independently. Can be a separate AI system or embedded into existing technologies or products.	Low; operates independently with little to no human intervention.	High; operates independently to fulfill objectives, necessitating advanced AI engineering for development and maintenance.

As we design governance and control frameworks for AI, it is important to consider the above two factors. While the accessibility of AI through prompts has democratized the use of AI by non-technical users, it has also introduced new risks. These users know little about how the AI was trained and how it operates. Some may argue that we do not need to understand AI to use it. However, as a counterargument, how can a human operator effectively fact-check AI when they do not understand how it operates and cannot predict when it will fail?

As AI becomes more autonomous in both its training and operation, there is less human involvement and oversight. Up to now, human operators often take the final decision or action. However, this level of human oversight and control is not sustainable. Not only can humans not keep pace with the speed of AI processing, but they also provide poor quality control over AI systems. Humans are best at reacting to sporadic incidents and crises. We quickly lose focus and precision when asked to monitor continuous and routine activity. We also have a propensity to over-rely on machine-based outcomes.

As AI systems become more autonomous, it will be important to replace human-in-the-loop quality checks with real-time, machine-based monitoring. With AI behavioral and observability monitoring controls still at the early stage of development, it is important that these oversight mechanisms are included in the functional design from the outset. They need to be given the same level of attention to their design and build as the AI functionality they are designed to control.

Is there a common definition for AI?

The term "artificial intelligence" was first coined in the 1950s, yet we still do not have a universal definition of AI. By its very nature, AI is a moving target; as each new technological breakthrough emerges, our understanding of what constitutes AI shifts. For example, the development of LLMs that can understand language and write at a PhD level was only a distant dream a decade ago. With the announcement of OpenAI's Deep Research in February 2025, organizations can conduct research in minutes rather than months.[5] Everyone can now have many Einsteins at their disposal.

Each of us today has used some form of AI. Often it operates in the background, but more frequently we are interacting with it directly through our mobile devices or desktop prompts. As we build more agentic AI, it will become harder for us to identify where AI is being used. Technology methods have rapidly shifted from rules-based to cognition-based methods, an important distinction to understand. Table 1.2 lists questions to help determine whether a technology is rules-based or is leveraging cognition-based AI.

Table 1.2 Determining if a system is rules-based or AI

	Rule question	*Rule explanation*
1	Does the technology perform tasks that typically require human intelligence?	This includes activities such as understanding natural language, recognizing patterns and images, making decisions, and learning from experience.
2	Can the technology learn from data and improve its performance over time?	Look for capabilities like ML, where the system adjusts its behavior based on new information, rather than just following a static set of rules or procedures.
3	Does the technology use algorithms to process inputs and generate outputs?	Consider whether the system uses complex mathematical models to analyze data and produce results that influence real or virtual environments.
4	Is the technology designed to achieve specific human-defined objectives?	Determine if the system's purpose is to fulfill tasks or solve problems outlined by humans, aligning with the OECD's emphasis on goal-oriented AI.[6]
5	Does the technology have the capacity to make predictions, recommendations, or decisions?	This involves assessing whether the system can autonomously make predictions or decisions and act upon them without direct human intervention.
6	Can the technology interact with its environment in a meaningful way?	AI systems often have the ability to perceive their surroundings, process information, and respond to changes, distinguishing them from traditional deterministic systems.
7	Is the technology adaptable to different contexts or scenarios?	Unlike rule-based systems, AI should be able to operate under varying conditions and adapt its behavior accordingly.
8	Does the system go beyond simple automation or pre-programmed responses?	AI is distinguished by its ability to handle tasks that are not explicitly programmed for every possible scenario, unlike deterministic systems that execute predefined instructions.

While marketers may want to advertise all new innovations as AI, there is a cost involved in applying enhanced AI governance and controls to systems. In addition, AI controls are specifically designed for the self-learning, autonomous nature of AI. Designating a technology as AI when it isn't could overburden it with costly and ineffective governance requirements.

Getting the definition of AI right is also important for resource and capital allocation decisions. The AI definition shapes an organization's innovation strategy, guiding decisions on research and development, talent acquisition, and infrastructure upgrades to support AI needs. Stakeholders, including customers, employees, shareholders, and partners, expect a higher level of transparency and accountability in AI deployment than with previous technology, making the AI definition even more critical.

The cognitive capabilities of AI

The cognitive capabilities of AI represent a groundbreaking shift in technology, distinguishing it from traditional robotics and robotic process automation. While robotics focuses primarily on automating physical tasks, such as assembly lines or warehouse logistics, AI transcends these limitations by emulating human-like cognitive functions. The revolutionary aspect of AI lies in its ability to process and analyze vast amounts of data, enabling it to perform complex tasks that require reasoning and adaptability. As AI continues to evolve, it is reshaping industries by enhancing decision-making processes, improving efficiency, and unlocking new possibilities that were previously unimaginable.

AI and traditional rule-based systems represent two distinct approaches to problem-solving with technology. Unlike rule-based systems that rely on predefined instructions and fixed algorithms, AI, particularly in its modern manifestations like ML and deep learning, is characterized by its ability to learn from data, adapt to new situations, and make decisions with a degree of autonomy. This adaptability allows AI to tackle complex problems that may not have clear solutions, continuously improving its performance over time as it encounters new information and experiences.

This capacity for learning and adaptation allows AI to handle ambiguity and unpredictability in ways that rule-based systems cannot. Figure 1.1 demonstrates the similarities and differences between rules-based systems and AI, including the areas of overlap.

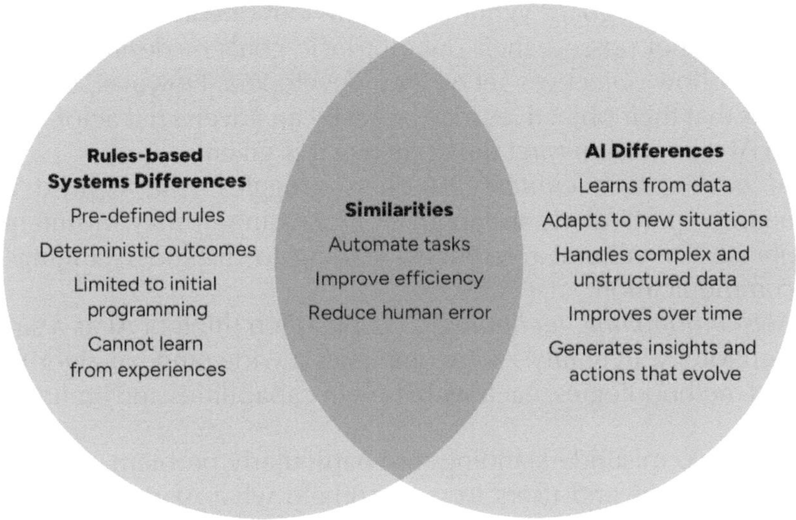

Figure 1.1 Rules-based systems vs. AI – similarities and differences.

The benefits of AI over rule-based systems extend beyond its functional capabilities; AI's ability to self-learn accelerates the development process, contributing significantly to rapid advancements. By transcending the limitations of human capacity in design, development, and operation, AI can continuously evolve and optimize itself, enabling faster innovation and the ability to tackle increasingly complex challenges.

Common myths related to AI

While AI has become a household name, few truly understand its nature. Here is a list of common AI myths:

1 *AI can think like humans:* Many people believe that AI possesses human-like thinking. In reality, it lacks consciousness, self-awareness, and emotional capacity. AI systems rely on mathematical algorithms and statistical patterns to generate responses. They simulate human behavior but do not truly think or understand.
2 *AI will replace all jobs:* While AI can automate highly routine tasks, it is more likely to change the nature of work than eliminate all jobs. Many roles will evolve, requiring human oversight, creativity, and emotional intelligence that AI cannot easily replicate.

3 *AI has its own goals:* While AI systems can operate autonomously, they do not possess their own intrinsic goals or desires. Instead, they follow objectives set by their developers. However, there are risks that their objectives may be set by an adversarial actor or that an AI may misinterpret the objective it is given.
4 *AI understands context:* AI often struggles with context and nuance, particularly in language processing. It may misinterpret phrases or cultural references, leading to misunderstandings in communication.
5 *AI is a monolithic technology:* People often think of AI as a single technology. In reality, AI encompasses a wide range of algorithms and methodologies, each with its own capabilities and limitations.

The last two misunderstandings are particularly problematic as they lead executives and users to overestimate what AI models can do and underestimate their risks. The differing nature of AI systems also means that a single governance and control approach will not be possible. While AI systems can be categorized by type, risk level, and impact, each system will need to be evaluated separately to address unique risks.

Why is there so much hype about AI?

AI has transitioned from a niche technological pursuit to a big bet of business strategy. It is a catalyst for innovation, offering tools that can analyze vast datasets, automate complex processes, and make predictive decisions with uncanny accuracy.

The AI market is growing at a rapid pace. The McKinsey Global Institute predicts that AI will deliver $13 trillion in additional global economic activity by 2030 and will contribute to a 16% increase in cumulative GDP compared with today,[7] more than the current output of China and India combined.

The enthusiasm for AI is not unfounded. It stems from tangible successes across various industries, where AI-enabled solutions have led to cost savings, enhanced customer experiences, and the creation of new products and services. The allure of AI also lies in its versatility, with applications ranging from simple chatbots improving customer service to sophisticated ML algorithms optimizing supply chain logistics.

However, the excitement also brings with it a host of questions and concerns. Executives are grappling with the implications of AI on workforce dynamics, stakeholder trust, and investment decisions. The challenge lies in separating the realistic promises of AI from the noise, ensuring that investments in AI are grounded in strategic business goals, rather than being swayed by the latest trends.

Stephen Hawking summed up our future with AI as following one of two distinctive paths: "It will either be the best thing that's ever happened to us, or it will be the worst thing. If we're not careful, it may very well be the last thing."[8]

Hawking's "end of the world" prediction has been embraced by doom-sayers that warn of autonomous weapons and human oppression. While they predict worst-case futures, their warnings resonate with a public that still harbors genuine fears about AI. A global Ipsos Reid AI study determined that over 50% of humans fear or do not trust AI.[9]

The future of AI teeters on an *AI Precipice* with two contrasting visions: a utopia where AI elevates humanity to new heights of prosperity and well-being, or a dystopia where it leads to societal upheaval.

In the utopian scenario, AI enhances our lives, solving many of our entrenched problems. There have been many positive developments using AI for Good, like predicting the risks of pandemic outbreaks before they happen, identifying climate "hotspots" or fire outbreaks, or saving lives through innovative drug developments for early-stage cancer.[10] Conversely, a dystopian future involves AI exacerbating unemployment and inequality, as autonomous systems replace humans, leaving many without work or purpose.

While many argue that AI adoption is inevitable, whether we create a utopian or dystopian future is still within our control. To not fall off the *AI Precipice*, we must responsibly embrace AI by balancing innovation with safety.

What we can learn from past innovations

Technological innovation has long been a driving force in human progress, as evidenced by pivotal moments like January 29, 1886, when Carl Benz patented his "vehicle powered by a gas engine," starting the dawn of the automotive era[11] and captivating the public's imagination. The innovation continued across the Atlantic, where in 1896, the first American-made gas-powered car was sold.[12] Despite the technological marvel of automobiles, societal concerns were rampant. Reporter E.P. Ingersoll wrote of America's overall skepticism:

> The notion that electric vehicles, or vehicles of any other kind, will be able to compete with railroad trains for long-distance traffic is visionary to the point of lunacy. The fool who hatched out this latest motor canard was conscience-stricken enough to add that the whole matter was still in an exceedingly hazy state. But if it ever emerges from the nebulous state, it will be in a world where natural laws are all turned topsy-turvy, and time and space are no more. Were it not for the surprising persistence of this delusion, the yarn would not be worthy of notice.[13]

AI has also been met with both excitement and skepticism. Skeptics voice concerns reminiscent of those from the early days of the automobile, questioning the feasibility of machines performing complex human tasks and the potential consequences of such a seismic shift.

Yet, as AI integrates into the fabric of society, it challenges us to reimagine the boundaries of what is possible and to confront the implications of a world where intelligence is no longer solely the domain of humans. The journey of AI, much like that of the automobile, is leading us into uncharted territory where the very essence of human purpose is being redefined.

As we consider what is needed to both support and contain the immense potential of AI, we can look to another significant technological event that occurred on December 17, 1903. The Orville brothers' first successful flight lasted 12 seconds and covered a distance of 120 ft.[14] It is important to note that it took another three decades for the first airport traffic control tower, regulating arrivals, departures, and surface movement of aircraft at a specific airport, to be opened in Cleveland, U.S.[15] Today, we have a heavily regulated air travel industry governing aircraft quality, manufacturing, and air traffic monitoring systems.

Control structures typically follow technological innovations. But for AI, we cannot afford to wait decades for them. AI governance and control structures must accelerate at a much faster pace to keep up with AI innovation. AI controls need to be viewed not only as a risk mitigator but also as an accelerant to innovation. Foot brakes were introduced to allow cars to reach higher speeds. Air traffic controllers were installed to facilitate the orderly takeoff and landing of more planes. These examples illustrate that rather than merely following behind, control structures are essential support mechanisms for technological advancements.

Every major technological breakthrough, from the automobile to the airplane, has necessitated the creation of robust governance, legal, and risk management frameworks to guide their evolution. We need to do the same with AI. However, what is different this time is the sheer pace at which AI is evolving. The timescale of AI adoption contrasts with earlier innovations. These earlier technologies took decades to evolve from inception to widespread use, allowing society and public policy setters time to adapt and develop the necessary governance and risk management frameworks. In contrast, AI's trajectory has contracted the adoption cycle from decades to years. This challenges us to swiftly, yet thoughtfully, construct the safety infrastructures and legal systems needed to ensure AI's responsible and beneficial integration into our daily lives and work.

What will humans do?

As AI is integrated into our day-to-day lives, questions arise as to what humans will do. While there is a broad consensus that AI will reshape jobs across industries and borders, the extent of this transformation is vigorously debated.

Some predict a swift and sweeping disruption, with AI and automation displacing a significant portion of the workforce in a relatively short time frame. Others anticipate a more gradual integration of AI, allowing time for the labor market to adjust and for new roles to emerge. The truth likely lies somewhere in the middle, with the impact of AI manifesting differently across sectors, job functions, and geographies.

The AI revolution will not be uniform; there will be winners and losers. Cognition-based roles that involve routine, repetitive tasks are at higher risk of automation, while jobs that require complex problem-solving, creativity, and emotional intelligence are more likely to be augmented by AI. Moreover, the timeline for these changes will vary, with some industries experiencing rapid transformation and others evolving much more slowly.

Humanity has weathered significant shifts before, from the agricultural revolution to the rise of manufacturing. Each of these periods brought significant disruptions, but also led to the creation of new industries and economic growth opportunities.

While AI's impact on the workforce is inevitable, its trajectory is not preordained. Corporate executives can create AI that not only drives business innovation and value realization but also serves as a catalyst for workforce development and social progress.

Learning from past revolutions

Reflecting on the first Industrial Revolution's shift from agriculture to manufacturing offers a glimpse into the impact of the shift from humans to machines. Starting in 1760 and spanning over a century and a half, the first phase of the Industrial Revolution involved the transition from family farms to urban centers. Driven by innovations like the power loom and steam engine, job landscapes were significantly reshaped.

The initial stages of the Industrial Revolution deepened laborers' poverty and misery. The lack of worker protections and regulations meant long work hours for miserable wages, and living in unsanitary tenements.[16] Worker conditions slowly improved with the introduction of regulations and innovations, yet wealth inequality grew.

While many historical accounts point to industrialization and mechanization as the cause of this inequality, Jakob Madsen and Holger Strulik, in their paper, *Inequality and the Industrial Revolution*, hypothesized that wealth inequality was not a by-product of the Industrial Revolution but a primary driver. As laborers spent more time working to earn a wage, they could no longer produce their own food, materials, and goods, causing them to become dependent on cheap manufactured goods.[17]

The second industrial revolution, espanned from 1870 to 1914, and ended just before World War I. This period fuled massive growth from innovations in electricity, the telephone and the automobile, etc. In the United States, the population grew by 132% from 1870 to 1910, yet industrial jobs grew four times, surging from 3.5 million to 14.2 million. Iron and steel employment skyrocketed by 1,200%, and by 1910, metal goods fabricators represented nearly 12% of industrial workers, a 437% increase over 40 years.[18]

Jobs transitioned from relying on manual labor to operating machinery in factories. The mechanization of tasks reduced the physical burden on workers and enabled the production of standardized products at a scale previously unimaginable. The assembly line, introduced by Henry Ford, further revolutionized manufacturing by streamlining production processes and significantly lowering costs. This transformation not only created a vast number of new industrial jobs but also fundamentally altered the economic landscape, paving the way for modern consumer culture and the widespread availability of mechanized goods.

In October 2024, Dr Geoffrey Hinton commented that it's difficult to gauge the seismic shift that is coming at this moment in time, but he likens it to the scale of disruption seen during the Industrial Revolution. "Potentially, it's very big. You make it so (that) average human intelligence isn't worth much anymore because AI can do it."[19] In another interview, Hinton goes on to say that "In the Industrial Revolution, we made human strength irrelevant. Now we're making human intelligence irrelevant. And that's very scary."[20]

While many are concerned with job losses from AI, a counterargument has emerged from economist Jesus Fernandez-Villaverde.

> For the first time, humans aren't producing enough babies to sustain the population. If you're 55 or younger, you're likely to witness something humans haven't seen for 60,000 years, not during wars or pandemics: a sustained decrease in the world population.[21]

Rather gloomily, he observes that while a "gently falling population could be good for sustainability; we're facing population collapse and economic turmoil."[22]

This alarmist position appears to contradict a United Nations report forecast that the

> world's population is expected to continue growing for another 50 or 60 years, reaching a peak of around 10.3 billion people in the mid-2080s, up from 8.2 billion in 2024. After peaking, it is projected to start declining, gradually falling to 10.2 billion people by the end of the century.[23]

Regardless of which population projection is accurate, there is a consensus that our slowing birth rate will affect the workforce, and that automation and AI are necessary to supplement declining workforces and increase productivity.

While more jobs were created than lost during the first two industrial revolutions, an important lesson learned is that not all jobs are created equal. The Industrial Revolution introduced new jobs in manufacturing and transportation, but it also led to the displacement of skilled laborers and artisans, resulting in economic and social upheaval. As we measure the impact of AI on workers, wealth equality may be a more effective measure than the number of jobs lost or created.

Will AI improve wealth equality?

The third Industrial Revolution, also known as the digital revolution, marked the transition from analog to digital technology, introducing the personal computer, the internet, and mobile devices. This era, which started in the late 1980s, laid the groundwork for the age of AI, with advances in computing power, data analytics, and ML.

As Figure 1.2 summarizes, we have now entered into the fourth Industrial Revolution, or more aptly named the "fourth intelligent revolution," with the introduction of AI, quantum computing, and advanced robotics. This era, characterized by knowledge-based advancements, will impact both professional and unskilled jobs alike.

Although the current intelligent revolution brings mixed views on employment impacts, others are hopeful about the emergence of new jobs. Amid these perspectives, a pressing issue remains: growing inequality.

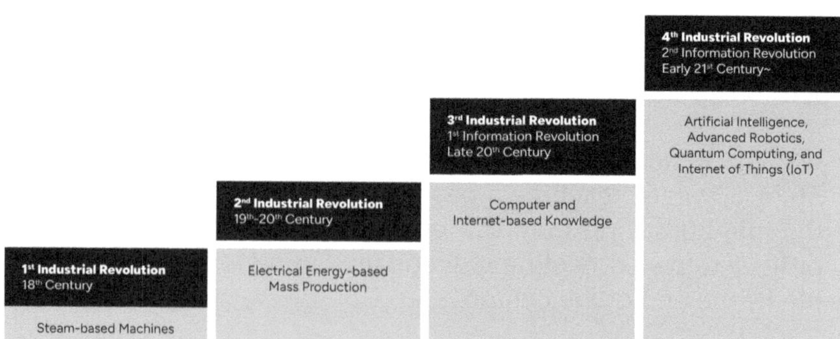

Figure 1.2 Being human in the fourth Industrial Revolution.[24]

Analysts predict a significant impact on employment due to AI. Goldman Sachs reported that AI could replace the equivalent of 300 million full-time jobs by 2030, with two-thirds of jobs in the United States and Europe susceptible to AI automation and AI fully capable of performing a quarter of all jobs.[25]

The McKinsey Global Institute predicts that by 2030, digitization, robotics, and AI advancements could necessitate career changes for at least 14% of the global workforce.[26]

AI is expected to impact both white- and blue-collar workers. Research from the University of Pennsylvania and OpenAI indicates that educated white-collar workers, particularly those earning up to $80,000 annually, are among those most likely to experience the effects of workforce automation.[27]

Similarly, a report by MIT and Boston University projects that AI will displace over two million manufacturing workers over the next five years.[28] Changes in the manufacturing sector will accelerate due to the growth of fully autonomous "dark factories," which are so automated that they can be operated without lighting. Asia Pacific, with over 45% of all global dark factories, is currently dominating the market, estimated to reach $76.5 billion by 2032.[29]

The potential impact of job loss on consumer spending patterns and discretionary income must also be considered. When individuals lose their jobs, their purchasing power diminishes, leading to reduced consumer spending. During the 2007 Great Recession, consumer spending in the United States had its most severe decline since 1945. This decline in consumer spending deepened the recession, and the reduced demand for goods and services led to widespread business closures and job losses.[30]

The impact of AI on developed and developing countries

The effects of AI and automation will be felt unevenly across different regions. In Organisation for Economic Co-Operation and Development (OECD) countries, an average of 27% of the labor force is engaged in jobs that are considered to be at high risk of automation. This risk is particularly acute in Eastern European countries, where the workforce is more exposed due to a higher concentration of automatable jobs.[31]

The disparity of AI's impact between developed and developing countries is attributed to several factors. Developed countries, with their advanced economies, often have a higher adoption rate of cutting-edge technologies. This means that their labor markets may experience an earlier shift to AI and advanced robotics.

In contrast, many developing countries lack the infrastructure, energy sources, and data science skills to support the transition to AI and robotics in the short term. However, as the cost of AI and robotics decreases and their availability increases, it is expected that all countries will experience a rapid acceleration of job automation.

In fact, over the long term, the societal impact on developing countries could be more severe, as they often lack the social safety nets and retraining programs to help workers transition to new roles. Additionally, with the replacement of human labor with technology, placement criteria for manufacturing plants is starting to shift to regions with cheap energy rather than cheap labor. While the building of new data centers and manufacturing plants will create new jobs in the short term, very few operator and maintenance jobs are required once they are in operation.

For executives, understanding how AI will impact different regions is crucial for strategic planning. Considerations include the varying rates of technology adoption, the specific industries most at risk, and the economic and social contexts of the countries in which they operate. It is important to prepare for the workforce challenges ahead, ensuring that companies remain competitive while contributing to a more equitable distribution of AI's benefits.

Impact on the individual worker

In the short term, employee sentiment is mixed. A Pew Research Center survey found that many U.S. workers, especially those in the information and technology sector, believe AI will benefit rather than harm them personally. Thirty-two percent of tech workers anticipate more help from AI compared to 11% who foresee more harm. However, across all sectors, three out of five workers fear that they could lose their jobs to AI over the next ten years.[32]

The impact of AI on individual workers extends beyond job loss. The uncertainty surrounding job security is taking a toll on mental health, with stress and anxiety stemming from potential job displacement. Employees must adapt to a rapidly changing job market, which can be both a financial and time-intensive burden.

As AI systems become more prevalent, they can exert downward pressure on wages, leading to an oversupply of workers competing for a shrinking number of positions. This wage suppression will, in turn, affect workers' quality of life, limiting their purchasing power and access to resources.

If a worker's job is augmented by AI or they are being transitioned into a new role, there is additional stress in upskilling and navigating a mid-career change. The shift in job requirements toward more AI-complementary skills may lead to a mismatch between workers' current abilities and future demands.

Building on the challenges faced by individual workers in an AI-driven economy, tech billionaire Jack Dorsey cautions that the advent of AI capable of writing its own software will soon displace thousands of junior software programmers.[33] This progression toward increasingly autonomous software raises philosophical questions about the kind of future we are engineering.

It evokes images of a *Matrix*-like dystopia, where humanity is ensnared by a simulated reality crafted by sentient machines. As robotics and AI become more ingrained in the fabric of society, the line between human cognition and AI is blurring, with potential implications for human identity.

The responsibility to "get AI right" is not just a matter of economics or innovation but a fundamental question about our collective future and the preservation of human agency.

In the midst of concerns surrounding AI and automation, it's important to recognize that the picture is not entirely bleak. Economists advise that with declining birth rates across many regions, fewer individuals will be entering the workforce in the coming years. In this context, AI is viewed as a necessary ally to increase productivity levels and economic growth.

AI has already had an impact in creating new job categories, driving innovation, and increasing efficiency. AI could result in a significant boost to the economy, with some estimates suggesting that the value of global goods and services could rise by as much as 7%. The European Economic Union report[34] and the United Nations research reports on the future of work[35] outline the expected shifts in industries and identify new skills and jobs needed for our future.

We must strategically guide AI usage to augment human potential and ensure equitable progress, creating a future that values both technological advancement and humanity.

Geopolitical forces and ideologies

The pathway to establishing appropriate guardrails for AI is complex, not least because of the divergent perspectives that characterize different government ideologies on the technology. These differing viewpoints often stem from varying cultural, economic, and political contexts, which influence how governments perceive the risks and benefits associated with AI. For instance, in the U.S. *AI Action Plan* released in July 2025, the Administration prioritizes innovation and economic growth, advocating for minimal regulation to foster technological advancement, while the European Union's (EU) comprehensive regulatory framework for AI, introduced a year earlier, underscores the importance of rigorous oversight to safeguard citizens from potential risks and promote accountability in AI deployment.

This ideological divide complicates international collaboration on AI governance, as countries grapple with reconciling their unique values and priorities. Consequently, it is unlikely we will have universally accepted standards and frameworks for AI in the near future. However, there have been attempts to create global accords for AI safety.

The 2025 Paris Safety Summit saw 58 global leaders sign an *AI Statement on Inclusive and Sustainable AI*, further aligning with earlier positions from the OECD and EU. The only two major countries that did not sign the AI Statement were the United States and the United Kingdom.[36,37]

Upon signing, countries made these commitments:

1 promoting AI accessibility to reduce digital divides
2 ensuring AI is open, inclusive, transparent, ethical, safe, secure, and trustworthy, taking into account international frameworks for all
3 making innovation in AI thrive by enabling conditions for its development and avoiding market concentration, driving industrial recovery and development

4 encouraging AI deployment that positively shapes the future of work and labour markets and delivers opportunity for sustainable growth
5 making AI sustainable for people and the planet
6 reinforcing international cooperation to promote coordination in international governance.

Both Eastern and Western countries signed the declaration, demonstrating a shared commitment to responsible AI. However, global tensions are high in regards to digital sovereignty and control over the AI supply chain. This includes everything from data collection and processing to the development and manufacturing of essential hardware and software components. Key concerns include the fear of losing access to critical resources such as computer chips and data sovereignty.

These issues highlight the growing concern with each nation's capacity to independently manage and secure its digital future.

Public policy and regulatory factors

As AI technologies become more pervasive, the distinction between good and bad actors in the AI space becomes increasingly important. The potential for AI to infringe upon fundamental human rights is a growing concern, as is the technology's ability to collect, analyze, and utilize vast amounts of personal data. The essence of privacy is challenged when AI can seamlessly track an individual's location and actions, and even predict future behaviors.

The risk extends beyond individual privacy invasions to the potential for AI to manage human systems based on an algorithmic formula rather than human values. This shift could lead to a scenario where decisions affecting public welfare and individual freedoms are made by machines, whose objective could be misaligned with human interests or reflect the selfish objectives of a bad actor.

In war zones, the implications of AI-driven decision-making become even more pronounced, as the technology is used to identify and target assets with precision. While proponents argue that AI can enhance operational efficiency and reduce collateral damage, the reliance on algorithms to make life-and-death decisions raises profound concerns. The potential for automated systems to misinterpret data or operate under flawed assumptions could result in catastrophic consequences, including unintended civilian casualties and escalation of conflict. Reliance on AI also poses challenges in accountability, as it becomes difficult to ascertain responsibility for actions taken by autonomous systems. As such, the integration of AI in conflict scenarios necessitates rigorous oversight and full consideration of potential consequences to ensure that the technology serves to protect, rather than endanger, human lives.

The prospect of autonomous AI systems is driving the urgent call for robust public policy frameworks and responsible AI guidelines to ensure AI technologies are developed and deployed to respect human rights, prioritize privacy, and maintain human oversight. Interventions by policymakers must be dynamic, evolving in tandem with AI advancements to address emerging challenges and mitigate risks.

In our next chapter, we discuss the principles of Responsible AI by Design, which underpin the majority of current AI governance standards and regulations.

Conclusion

This chapter framed the important role AI has in the future of business and society and established the most fundamental question of AI – how can humans control it?

Maintaining humans at the center of AI advancements also means addressing the larger social issues of job displacement, wealth inequality, and mental health. With its epicenter in cognition-based systems and advanced robotics, AI represents a departure from traditional industrial shifts. We need to develop automated governance and control constructs that keep pace with its high processing speed and dynamic decision-making.

Yet, our approach cannot be solely technocentric. The world grapples with pressing macroeconomic challenges: aging populations, pandemics, dwindling natural resources, poverty, burgeoning megacities exerting pressure on public infrastructure, and climate change. These global issues demand our leadership and action.

Navigating these macroeconomic challenges, while crafting an effective AI strategy, is a critical leadership endeavor. It requires assembling a team of leaders with AI acumen and engaging seasoned partners to consider the full spectrum of AI's potential. With a multitude of AI technologies available, leaders must be judicious in their choices to avoid missteps and ensure a solid foundation for their AI initiatives.

The new reality is clear – for knowledge-based companies, scarcity is not a constraint. In today's competitive world, the question is not whether to adopt AI, but how quickly one can apply AI and secure value responsibly. Failure to embrace AI risks organizations' relevance and survival.

Purposeful leadership has never been more important.

Key leadership questions to consider:

1. What can you learn from your past business transformations and innovations?
2. How is your organization defining AI?
3. How will AI impact your overall business strategy and operational capabilities?
4. How can AI enhance your business processes and customer experiences?
5. How will AI impact your workforce and talent needs?
6. What strategies ensure your AI adoption remains competitive?

Notes

1. Cambridge University Press. (n.d.). *Precipice*. In *Cambridge Dictionary*. Retrieved January, 2025, from https://dictionary.cambridge.org/dictionary/english/precipice.
2. Flanagin, A., Bibbins-Domingo, K., Berkwits, M., & Christiansen, S. L. (2023, January 31). Nonhuman "authors" and implications for the integrity of scientific publication and medical knowledge. *JAMA, 329*(4), 337–338. https://jamanetwork.com/journals/jama/fullarticle/2801170.
3. Anthropic. (2024, December 18). *Alignment faking in large language models (LLMs)*. https://www.anthropic.com/research/alignment-faking.
4. Goode, L., & Simonete, T. (2024, June 28). This viral AI chatbot will lie and say it's human. *Wired*. https://www.wired.com/story/bland-ai-chatbot-human/.
5. OpenAI. (n.d.). *Introducing deep research*. Retrieved May 15, 2025, from https://openai.com/index/introducing-deep-research/.
6. Organisation for Economic Co-operation and Development. (n.d.). *Goal oriented AI defined, and OECD responsible AI principles*. Retrieved August 30, 2025, from https://www.oecd.org/en/topics/ai-principles.html

7 Bughin, J., Seong, J., Manyika, J., Chui, M., & Joshi, R. (2018, September). *Notes from the AI frontier: Modeling the impact of AI on the world economy*. McKinsey Global Institute. https://www.mckinsey.com/~/media/McKinsey/Featured%20Insights/Artificial%20Intelligence/Notes%20from%20the%20frontier%20Modeling%20the%20impact%20of%20AI%20on%20the%20world%20economy/MGI-Notes-from-the-AI-frontier-Modeling-the-impact-of-AI-on-the-world-economy-September-2018.ashx.

8 Hawking, S. (2016, October 19). *Speech at the launch of the £10 million Leverhulme Centre for the Future of Intelligence*. University of Cambridge. https://www.cam.ac.uk/research/news/the-best-or-worst-thing-to-happen-to-humanity-stephen-hawking-launches-centre-for-the-future-of.

9 Ipsos. (2023, July). *Global views on A.I. 2023: How people across the world feel about artificial intelligence and expect it will impact their lives*. https://www.ipsos.com/sites/default/files/ct/news/documents/2023-07/Ipsos%20Global%20AI%202023%20Report-WEB_0.pdf.

10 Pharmaceutical Technology. (2023, December 10). *Enabling breakthrough: How AI is transforming oncology*. https://www.pharmaceutical-technology.com/sponsored/enabling-breakthroughs-how-ai-is-transforming-oncology/.

11 Mercedes-Benz. (n.d.). *First automotive – Mercedes-Benz*. Retrieved June 10, 2024, from https://group.mercedes-benz.com/company/tradition/company-history/1885-1886.html#:~:text=On%20January%2029%2C%201886%2C%20Carl,1.

12 Cole's Collision Centers. (n.d.). *First U.S. automotive*. Retrieved June 10, 2024, from https://colescollision.com/history-of-the-american-automobile/#:~:text=In%201893%2C%20Charles%20Duryea%20and,gas%20powered%20car%20in%201896.

13 Winston, A. (2017, January 9). Get horse—Americans' skepticism toward the first automobiles. *The Saturday Evening Post*. https://www.saturdayeveningpost.com/2017/01/get-horse-americas-skepticism-toward-first-automobiles/.

14 National Air and Space Museum. (n.d.). *Wright Flyer: Wilbur and Orville, Kitty Hawk, historical flight*. Smithsonian Institution. Retrieved August 31, 2025, from https://airandspace.si.edu/collection-objects/1903-wright-flyer/nasm_A19610048000#:~:text=Wilbur%20and%20Orville%20Wright%20spent,with%20Orville%20at%20the%20control.

15 Wikipedia contributors. (n.d.). *Air traffic control*. Wikipedia. Retrieved February 5, 2024, from https://en.wikipedia.org/wiki/Air_traffic_control.

16 Encyclopaedia Britannica, Inc. (n.d.). Industrial revolution: Technology, factories, change. In *Britannica encyclopedia*. Retrieved August 31,

2025, from https://www.britannica.com/event/Industrial-Revolution/The-first-Industrial-Revolution.
17 Madsen, J., & Strulik, H. (2024, February). *Inequality and the industrial revolution.* https://www.holger-strulik.org/my_papers/first_industrialization_revised.pdf.
18 Montgomery, D. (n.d.). Chapter 3: Labor in the industrial era. U.S. Department of Labor. Retrieved February 20, 2024, from https://www.dol.gov/general/aboutdol/history/chapter3#:~:text=Between%201870%20and%201910%20the,rapidly%2Dfrom%203%2C500%2C000%20to%2014%2C200%2C000.
19 Gaviola, A. (2024, October 29). Why the 'godfather of AI' says industrial revolution-style job changes loom. *Global News.* https://globalnews.ca/news/10836738/geoffrey-hinton-artificial-intelligence/.
20 Gaviola, A. (2024, October 29). Why the 'godfather of AI' says Industrial Revolution-style job changes loom. *Global News.* https://globalnews.ca/news/10836738/geoffrey-hinton-artificial-intelligence/.
21 Fernandez-Villaverde, J. (2024, August 17). The global fertility crisis is worse than you think. *The Spectator.* https://www.spectator.co.uk/article/the-global-fertility-crisis-is-worse-than-you-think/.
22 Fernandez-Villaverde, J. (2024, August 17). The global fertility crisis is worse than you think. *The Spectator.* https://www.spectator.co.uk/article/the-global-fertility-crisis-is-worse-than-you-think/.
23 Jayakumar, V. (2024, October 26). Are we worried about the wrong demographic problem? *The Spectator.* https://www.spectator.co.uk/article/the-global-fertility-crisis-is-worse-than-you-think/.
24 Adapted from *The fourth industrial revolution* by William Genovese, licensed under CC BY 3.0. Original image available at https://www.researchgate.net/figure/The-fourth-industrial-revolution-Created-by-William-Genovese-on-behalf-of-the-Chinese_fig1_355112950.
25 Hatzius, J., Briggs, J., Kodnani, D., & Pierdomenico, G. (2023, March 26). *The potentially large effects of AI.* Goldman Sachs Economic Research. https://www.key4biz.it/wp-content/uploads/2023/03/Global-Economics-Analyst_-The-Potentially-Large-Effects-of-Artificial-Intelligence-on-Economic-Growth-Briggs_Kodnani.pdf.
26 Batra, P., Bugin, J., Chui, M., Ko, R., Lund, S., Manyuka, J., & Sanghui, S. (2017, November 28). *Jobs of the future: Jobs lost, jobs gained.* McKinsey & Company. https://www.mckinsey.com/featured-insights/future-of-work/jobs-lost-jobs-gained-what-the-future-of-work-will-mean-for-jobs-skills-and-wages.
27 Mok, A. (2023, March 22). ChatGPT will impact educated white-collar workers, research says. *Business Insider.* https://www.business

insider.com/chatgpt-ai-impacts-white-collar-college-educated-high-salary-jobs-2023-3.

28 Johnson, A. (2023, March 30). Which jobs will AI replace? These 4 industries will be heavily impacted. *Forbes*. https://www.forbes.com/sites/ariannajohnson/2023/03/30/which-jobs-will-ai-replace-these-4-industries-will-be-heavily-impacted/.

29 Coherent Market Insights. (2025, April 1). *Dark factories market*. https://www.coherentmarketinsights.com/industry-reports/dark-factories-market.

30 De Nardi, M., French, E., & Benson, D. (2012). Consumption and the great recession. *Economic Perspectives, 36*(1). https://ssrn.com/abstract=2017759.

31 Organisation for Economic Co-operation and Development. (2023, July 11). *OECD Employment Outlook 2023: Artificial intelligence and the labour market*. https://www.oecd.org/en/publications/2023/07/oecd-employment-outlook-2023_904bcef3.html?appId=aemshell#ai-jobs.

32 Kochhar, R. (2023, July 26). Which U.S. workers are exposed to AI in their jobs? *Pew Research Center*. https://www.pewresearch.org/social-trends/2023/07/26/which-u-s-workers-are-more-exposed-to-ai-on-their-jobs/.

33 Knight, W. (2025, May 24). Jack Dorsey's Block made an AI agent to boost its own productivity. *Wired*. https://www.wired.com/story/jack-dorseys-block-made-an-ai-agent-to-boost-its-own-productivity/.

34 World Economic Forum. (2025, January 7). *The future of work: The European Economic Union report*. https://www.weforum.org/publications/the-future-of-jobs-report-2025/.

35 UN System Chief Executive Board for Coordination. (n.d.). *The future of work*. https://unsceb.org/topics/future-work.

36 Statement on inclusive and sustainable artificial intelligence for people and the planet. (2025, February 11). *Élysée*. https://www.elysee.fr/en/emmanuel-macron/2025/02/11/statement-on-inclusive-and-sustainable-artificial-intelligence-for-people-and-the-planet.

37 Notation: The statement aligned with: Acknowledging existing multilateral initiatives on AI, including the United Nations General Assembly Resolutions, the Global Digital Compact, the UNESCO Recommendation on Ethics of AI, the African Union Continental AI Strategy, and the works of the Organization for Economic Cooperation and Development (OECD), the Council of Europe and European Union, the G7 including the Hiroshima AI Process and G20.

Chapter 2

Establishing responsible AI from day one

The late founder of Apple, Steve Jobs, once said: "You can't connect the dots looking forward; you can only connect them looking backward. So you have to trust that the dots will somehow connect in your future."[1] This insight underscores the necessity of establishing clear artificial intelligence (AI) principles today. By laying down ethical guidelines and frameworks, we can ensure that the "dots" of AI development – such as transparency, accountability, and fairness – will connect in a way that fosters trust and benefits society in the long run. Just as Jobs emphasized the importance of vision, we must envision a future where AI operates within a principled framework to navigate the complexities ahead.

In 2016, a number of global consortia were formed to develop guidelines for responsible AI. Notable publications from these efforts are the *Asilomar AI Principles*, the *Montreal Declaration*, and the *IEEE Ethics of Autonomous and Intelligent Systems* global initiative. Since then, many additional standards, guidelines, and regulations have been published, and more are expected.

While these publications may differ in terminology and level of prescription, they are based on similar principles and promote a risk-based governance structure, commonly known as "Responsible AI by Design."

At its core, Responsible AI by Design is about making clear, fair, and accountable decisions at every stage of the AI lifecycle, from the initial design through to deployment and monitoring. Responsible AI by Design focuses on understanding the different risks at the outset of an AI project so they can be addressed as early as possible.

Identifying risks early is crucial because, as AI systems learn and adapt, it becomes progressively harder to "unteach" them later

DOI: 10.4324/9781003625520-3

on. Engaging in tabletop scenario discovery exercises during the design phase allows teams to simulate scenarios and address risks proactively.

Objectives

Upon completing this chapter, you will be able to:

- Understand the concept of Responsible AI by Design and its importance
- Recognize the essential principles in Responsible AI by Design
- Apply an AI Spectrum Impact risk assessment to contextual use cases
- Implement ethical considerations throughout the entire AI development lifecycle.

Responsible AI by Design

Responsible AI by Design has its origins in the "Privacy by Design" framework developed in 1995 by Ann Cavoukian,[2] then the Information Privacy Commissioner of Ontario, Canada. It is a common framework used to incorporate privacy considerations throughout a business transformation or technology project, particularly in the design phase.[3]

Similar in nature, Responsible AI by Design calls for ethical, technical, and regulatory considerations to be taken into account early in the AI lifecycle. Early identification of potential risk impacts and risk mitigations enhances design thinking and allows for the chosen response to be integrated into the AI system. This allows developers to anticipate and preempt potential issues before they emerge. When these considerations are not addressed during the design phase, AI systems are often delayed from being put into production or incur expensive retraining.

But it would be a mistake to only address responsible AI as a planning consideration. Due to the iterative development process used in AI model training and validation, responsible AI considerations should be integrated throughout the entire AI development lifecycle.

Responsible AI involves more than a set of principles; it provides a structured, actionable framework that organizations can apply from the outset. It's about ensuring accountability, transparency, and fairness in AI systems, and prioritizing human rights, inclusivity, and environmental sustainability.

Robust scenario planning is critical for Responsible AI by Design. Through scenarios, the AI project team can conduct tabletop exercises on how the AI system will impact affected stakeholders and processes by modeling solution complexity, societal impact, risk, and value realization.

Responsible AI principles

Responsible AI principles set the standards that AI systems must meet to mitigate against unintended impacts and ensure AI systems operate within established guidelines. While there is some divergence on the AI principles and their definitions from one publication to the next, there is a high degree of consensus among stakeholders about what truly matters.

To guide our discussion, Table 2.1 identifies EY's Responsible AI Principles.

Each responsible AI principle should be regarded both individually and collectively. Sometimes, a trade-off between AI principles is necessary. For instance, highly accurate AI models, especially those using complex algorithms like deep neural networks, often operate as "black boxes" with opaque internal decision-making processes. While simpler models may offer greater explainability, they often rely on fewer data points, which can limit their ability to detect complex patterns.

Striking the right balance is not always easy and requires careful deliberation. A well-documented process that evaluates the potential trade-offs and final decisions is imperative. Documentation can clarify why specific decisions were made, provide a reference for future AI initiatives, and ensure transparency for stakeholders.

In the next section, we explore each principle and explain why it is crucial to ensuring both AI compliance and benefit realization.

Accountability

As AI systems operate with greater independence, establishing clear frameworks for accountability becomes essential to ensure the responsible use of AI technologies.

Table 2.1 EY Responsible AI Principles[4]

Responsible AI principles	*Definition*
Accountability	There is unambiguous ownership over AI systems, their impacts, and resulting outputs across the AI lifecycle.
Reliability	AI systems are aligned with stakeholder expectations and continually perform at a desired level of precision and consistency.
Data protection	Use of data in AI systems is consistent with permitted rights, maintains confidentiality of business and personal information, and reflects ethical norms.
Security	AI systems, their input, and output data are secured from unauthorized access and resilient against corruption and adversarial attack.
Transparency	Appropriate levels of disclosure regarding the purpose, design, and impact of AI systems are provided so that stakeholders, including end users, can understand, evaluate, and correctly employ AI systems and their outputs.
Explainability	Appropriate levels of explanation are enabled so that the decision criteria and output of AI systems can be reasonably understood, challenged, and validated by human operators.
Compliance	The design, implementation, and use of AI systems and their outputs comply with relevant laws, regulations, and professional standards.
Fairness	The needs of all impacted stakeholders are assessed with respect to the design and use of AI systems and their outputs to promote a positive and inclusive societal impact.
Sustainability	Considerations of the impacts of technology are embedded throughout the AI lifecycle to promote physical, social, economic, and planetary well-being.[5]

At its core, accountability implies that individuals, organizations, or entities are answerable for the AI systems they develop, deploy, and use.

Whether it's the designer creating an AI model, the end-user interacting with the AI, or the deployer integrating it into existing systems, each stakeholder has a role to play. Clear accountability fosters a "human face" for AI, allowing end users to identify who is responsible for a system's output and who they can dispute outcomes with or seek remediation.

Take an AI-driven customer service chatbot assisting clients in understanding their options to rebalance their investment portfolio. Should the chatbot incorrectly suggest trade purchases that are outside of the client's financial reach, causing financial loss, the company needs to have clear accountability mechanisms to identify the issue, correct the bot's error, and offer a resolution to the affected customer.

The most discussed debate on who to hold accountable when AI fails involves autonomous vehicles. In early incidents, when safety drivers were required, the human driver was often found responsible. However, with driverless taxis now on the road, technical malfunction is the most common cause – but whose technology?

With so many diverse components needed to operate an autonomous vehicle, determining what, and then who, to hold responsible can be difficult. It could be:

- A manufacturing flaw in which the vehicle's design or production is the cause of a crash, such as a blind spot in the car's cameras.
- A software fault in which the vehicle's algorithms have difficulty detecting a pedestrian with dark features and clothing walking on a crosswalk at night.
- A secondary driver does not predict the autonomous car's unusual driving pattern, such as a sudden stop, and rear-ends it.
- A sensor could malfunction, sending incorrect data to the vehicle's algorithm, causing it to misinterpret what it "sees."
- The onboard computer processor could be slow, causing disastrous latency in sending communications to interrelated components, delaying the car's reaction speed.
- Poor lighting or a missing stop sign could cause the autonomous car to miss a safety feature.
- Road construction causes a detour that is not clearly marked.

In the above examples, the responsible party could be the vehicle's manufacturer, an AI developer, a third-party vendor providing software or hardware components, a network provider, or the local government maintaining roadways.

Accountability can be challenging to put into practice. The distributed nature of AI responsibilities, where multiple parties contribute to the training and operation of an AI system, can blur accountabilities. Even when an individual or team is identified as responsible, the complexity and opacity of AI decision-making can make it difficult to pinpoint where and why errors occur. Also, the dynamic nature of AI systems, which continuously learn over time, creates complexities in attributing accountability post-deployment.

A common safety guardrail used for AI is to put a human-in-the-loop. But is this a sufficient safety mechanism?

Many questions arise when humans are used to directly supervise AI:

1 Does the human operator adequately understand how the AI makes its decision and where it could fail?
2 Are they able to detect when an error occurs?
3 And if so, can they react quickly enough to avoid unintended consequences?
4 Does the human operator have the capability and authority to feel comfortable in overriding the AI's recommendation?

Overriding an AI decision puts a significant amount of accountability on the human operator. What if they are wrong and cause an adverse outcome? On what basis would they make this decision? What are the consequences to them if they make a mistake?

The lack of tailored legal constructs for AI raises concerns about how to assign legal liability, both civil and criminal, when an AI malfunctions. There are also concerns about potential financial penalties, fines, or other punitive measures that may be levied against organizations in light of AI-related transgressions.

A common response is to create an accountability matrix that defines who is in charge of making key decisions, managing the AI system's performance, addressing any issues that arise, and ensuring the system's alignment with its intended purpose.

It is essential for customer contracts, vendor agreements, and employment contracts to include explicit clauses that outline accountability for the AI systems and related data sources. These agreements must include acceptable use policies, establish ownership of intellectual property (IP), include indemnification clauses, and provide mechanisms for addressing grievances related to underperformance or harm.

Reliability

As AI systems become increasingly embedded in organizational operations, one principle that stands out is reliability – the extent to which AI systems align with stakeholder expectations and consistently perform at the desired level of precision.

Reliability refers to the consistent and dependable performance of AI systems under specified conditions over a given period of time.

A common root cause of AI performance issues is when an AI system operates in a production environment that is different and more complex than the conditions under which it was trained and tested. There is often a contrast between a regulated lab environment and a dynamic real-world setting.

In the lab, AI models are typically trained on curated datasets and under controlled boundary conditions, with explicit assumptions made about the nature and range of input data. For instance, an AI model developed to recognize objects in images may be trained exclusively on high-resolution images. While in a production environment, the model may have to handle low-light or low-quality images.

Similarly, AI systems are designed and trained for specific purposes. An AI chatbot for customer service, for example, may be trained to respond to queries about a company's products or services. However, if users start entering prompts unrelated to or beyond its training scope, such as billing or product delivery inquiries, the chatbot's responses may be irrelevant or misleading, leading to frustrated or confused customers.

When using AI systems, it is important to train them with boundary conditions that align as much as possible with the conditions they will encounter in the "wild." Rigorous testing, continuous monitoring, and regular model updating are essential practices to maintain AI reliability. Moreover, AI governance should include output filters and incident and crisis management processes to handle situations where AI systems face conditions or use cases beyond their training.

Let's explore an example. A common concern with GenAI is the potential for it to hallucinate, whereby it generates or perceives features, patterns, or data that do not exist. AI hallucinations are of particular concern in areas like image recognition or natural language processing, where AI systems might "see" objects or "read" meaning in text that human observers would not.

This occurred in 2023 when a group of professors used a GenAI system to prepare a submission to the Australian Parliament on the ethics and professional integrity of the consulting industry. Their submission included cited scandals involving Big Four accounting firms that were later found to either not exist or contain inaccurate information.[6] Although this example had little lasting impact, you can imagine the potential disastrous outcomes if AI systems demonstrate similar "hallucinations" when detecting cancer on an X-ray image, directing autonomous vehicles through congested traffic, or identifying perpetrators of a crime. Are human operators prepared to challenge machine-based outcomes that look right, but are in fact wrong?

An increasingly common use of AI in healthcare is the development of predictive models for disease diagnosis and progression. These AI tools, trained on vast medical datasets, aim to assist doctors by predicting possible diseases based on patient symptoms, medical history, and diagnostic test results. While results vary by model and system, a systematic review and meta-analysis of performance comparisons between GenAI and physicians from June 2018 to June 2024 found that several models performed slightly better than non-expert physicians, but that expert physicians still performed significantly better than GenAI. Expert physicians still outperformed AI in diagnosing cancer.[7] However, that may soon change.

AI technologists are continually introducing new versions of their GenAI models, describing the newest models as having PhD- or expert-level knowledge and understanding, while earlier versions had the equivalent of high school- or college-level education. These GenAI models are gaining the knowledge of advanced-level–degrees faster than a human could achieve that same level of specified knowledge and expertise.

Regardless of their foundational knowledge, AI systems still make mistakes. These advanced GenAI models may be trained to demonstrate high proficiency in some tasks, but they still falter in others. Proactive monitoring plays a pivotal role in the early detection of any malfunctions or underperformance in AI. Early detection allows for timely interventions, preventing minor issues from escalating into major incidents. Apart from real-time performance checks, monitoring should also proactively look for unintended consequences. An algorithm might be behaving as planned in a majority of cases, but cause unintended harm in a minority of cases due to overlooked scenarios or unanticipated user behavior.

Crafting resilient AI systems involves making them resistant to uncontrolled changes in model outputs – ensuring consistent performance under varied conditions and adverse situations, including adversarial attacks. Adversarial attacks can involve manipulating the input data to an AI system with the intent of causing it to make an error. Incorporating defenses against such adversarial attacks bolsters an AI system's robustness.

It is cost-prohibitive to develop real-time continuous monitoring for all reliability metrics; therefore, organizations need to distinguish between low- and high-risk applications. High-risk AI systems, including those that could have serious adverse impacts on physical safety, financial health, mental well-being, and social stability, should be subject to more stringent and continuous reliability checks.

Data protection

Data protection for AI encompasses not only privacy but also ensuring confidentiality and safeguarding IP. As AI systems interact with customers and vendors outside of corporate perimeters, the risk to data protection grows.

Furthermore, the rising use of external, unstructured data introduces additional complexities, as organizations must ensure that data is handled responsibly and in compliance with regulatory standards and contractual terms of use, all while leveraging its potential to drive innovation.

At its core, data protection in AI systems requires the use of data that respects permitted rights, maintains the confidentiality of business and personal information, and aligns with societal norms.

During AI training and deployment, large datasets are used to teach and operate AI models. Once in production, an AI system handles real-time data, which can contain sensitive or personal information. The improper handling of this data could not only lead to privacy breaches, affecting individuals' or organizations' integrity, but could also result in faulty AI outcomes due to corrupted datasets.

A concern with open-source or publicly available AI is the potential leakage of confidential data by employees.

After some high-profile incidents in which confidential or private information was inadvertently exposed through the use of public GenAI systems, many organizations responded by severely limiting their use through acceptable use policies, internet filters, or outright banning them. A year after large language models (LLMs) were introduced to the public, a data privacy benchmark survey found that "63% [of respondents] have established limitations on what data can be entered, 61% have limits on which GenAI tools can be used by employees, and 27% said their organization had banned GenAI applications altogether for the time being." These safeguards are not unwarranted, as the same survey found that "48% [of respondents] admit entering non-public company information into GenAI tools."[8] Most organizations have installed enterprise LLMs to provide GenAI capability to their employees, while restricting the sharing of information included in user prompts.

There are three key drivers increasing the importance of data protection when designing and using AI systems.

First, the scale and scope of data used in AI are vast and increasing. From personal data like names and email addresses to sensitive information, including health records or financial details, AI deals with a wide range of data. If mishandled, this data can cause significant harm to individuals or organizations. Robust data protection practices are essential to prevent unauthorized access, disclosure, or corruption of data.

Second, the reputation of an organization relies heavily on how it handles data. Companies that effectively protect data are viewed as trustworthy, which fosters customer loyalty, enhances brand image, and ultimately contributes to business success. With a general lack of trust in AI, organizations must demonstrate strong data protection if they want to increase user adoption and gain customer trust.

Third, there's a growing regulatory emphasis on data protection. Laws like the *General Data Protection Regulation* in the European Union and the *California Consumer Privacy Act* in the United States have stringent requirements for data protection. Non-compliance can result in severe legal penalties.

Consider an online store employing AI to personalize shopping experiences by collecting browser history, prior purchases, demographic data, and social media activity. A data breach due to a lack of secure storage could expose personally identifiable information of millions of users to hackers, leading to potential financial loss and distress for customers. Unintended data sharing with third parties could violate customers' trust and potentially infringe legal regulations. Additionally, an excessive use of customer data might raise concerns of privacy invasion and manipulation, resulting in backlash, boycotts, or decreased user engagement.

One way to build customer trust is to shift from "opt-out" to "opt-in" data sharing. Jennifer King, privacy and data policy fellow at the Stanford University Institute for Human-Centered Artificial Intelligence, shared her thoughts in an interview on how to "rethink" privacy in the age of AI.

> When I'm browsing online, my data should not be collected unless or until I make some affirmative choice, like signing up for the service or creating an account. And even then, my data shouldn't be considered public unless I've agreed to share it.[9]

The cornerstone of good data protection is the practice of data minimization. By ensuring that only necessary data is collected, organizations can mitigate risks associated with data loss.

Maintaining transparency in data-handling practices is also important. Customers want to know how, why, and where their data is collected, stored, and used. Equally crucial are robust security measures. Technical solutions like encryption, secure data storage, rigorous access controls, and regular system updates help fend off cyber threats and preserve data integrity.

Robust data protection measures also include data anonymization or pseudonymization, which helps protect individual identities by making it harder to link data back to specific individuals. There are also emerging techniques like differential privacy, which adds "noise" to the data used in the models to protect the privacy of individual data points while still allowing useful computations. While these mechanisms can mask data during processing and transmission, it may not be technically or financially feasible to mask all data, and data leaks may still occur. Output filters should also be considered, particularly for agentic AI systems, to screen and stop AI outputs that contain inappropriate content.

The importance of data protection is set to increase as reliance on external, unstructured data grows and the loss of human oversight with agentic AI raises new challenges for safeguarding sensitive information.

Security

As more AI systems interact with external parties, the importance of securing these systems has grown significantly, making them increasingly vulnerable to adversarial threats.

The security principle forms the protective layer that ensures the confidentiality, integrity, and availability of AI systems by warding off unauthorized access, exploitation, corruption, or damage to AI systems and their associated data.

Proactive measures for maintaining AI security involve diverse strategies, including prevention, identification, detection, and recovery from malicious attacks or accidental negligence. The threats to AI security range from data poisoning, model corruption, and adversarial attacks. In April 2025, JPMorgan released an open letter to its third-party suppliers, sounding the AI alarm that companies have prioritized the

> rapid feature development over robust security. This often results in rushed product releases without security built in or enabled by default, creating repeated opportunities for attackers to exploit weaknesses. The pursuit of market share at the expense of security exposes entire customer ecosystems to significant risk and will result in an unsustainable situation for the economic system.[10]

Their call to action was that

> Providers must urgently reprioritize security, placing it equal to or above launching new products. 'Secure and resilient by design' must go beyond slogans - it requires continuous, demonstrable evidence that controls are working effectively, not simply relying on annual compliance checks.[11]

J.P. Morgan has invested $2B in AI security measures and admitted to slowing certain deployments until governance caught up. They asked suppliers to prioritize four actions:

1 Implement AI governance frameworks before deployment.
2 Conduct regular red team exercises against AI systems.
3 Establish clear model documentation standards.
4 Create dedicated AI security response teams.[12]

Security is more than a reactive check; it requires proactive management to identify and prevent new vulnerabilities. Leaving security issues unattended can lead to a chain reaction of adverse events, from deteriorating model performance to the extraction of sensitive information and potential harm to human physical or financial health.

Protecting AI models involves a multi-faceted approach. One method is employing model hardening techniques to improve model robustness to input changes or adversarial attacks. Sandboxing or isolating AI systems can prevent exploitation if a system is compromised. Security often works best in a multi-approach model, in which multiple layers of security controls are relied upon.

A common best practice is continuous monitoring and automated alerts to track changes in model performance, which might suggest a potential security breach or failure. For instance, observing the model behavior may identify out-of-tolerance activity, such as setting a high credit limit for a low-income client.

Anticipating and strategizing for potential security risks before deploying AI systems, particularly within safety-critical or high-risk applications, enables organizations to guard against threats proactively.

Transparency

The principle of transparency has been an early focus of regulators and standard setters.

Transparency involves appropriate levels of disclosure regarding the purpose, design, and impact of AI systems so that all stakeholders, including end users, can understand, evaluate, and correctly employ AI systems and their outputs.

The goal of transparency is threefold. First, it helps build confidence in AI systems by promoting a clear understanding of how these systems operate. Second, it supports users' ability to make informed decisions regarding the use of AI systems and their outputs. Last, it fosters a culture of accountability and continuous improvement.

Transparency in AI entails providing adequate and comprehensible information regarding the operation of an AI system. This includes sharing insights into how it functions, what tasks it is designed to perform, and how it does so. It also includes the source of data used to train and operate it. Questions asked include: how the data was collected? How data was cleaned or transformed? How have biases, privacy, security, and data quality been addressed?

Transparent disclosure also covers the limitations of the AI system – situations where its use may be less effective or not suitable. This might encompass technical limitations, such as an inability to handle certain data types or work under certain conditions, or use-case limitations where the model might not perform as expected due to factors like data scarcity, bias, or noise.

Transparency also means communicating clearly to users about the potential implications of using an AI system. These could range from potential benefits, such as efficiency gains or cost savings, to risks like privacy impact or possible biased outcomes.

In May 2024, Stanford released its latest assessment of transparency among AI model developers. In its first report, most LLMs earned a failing score. Industry responded, and less than a year later, the average transparency score jumped from 37 to 58 out of 100 – a notable 21-point improvement in just six months. The top transparency scores now reach as high as 85/100. The leading model was BigCode, a joint venture between Hugging Face and ServiceNow. Persistent transparency gaps remain in data provenance, which encompasses copyright, licensing, and AI risk mitigation effectiveness.[13]

One of the primary hurdles in being transparent lies in the complexity of AI systems. Given the intricate and often highly technical nature of AI models, explaining them in a way that users can understand is no easy feat. Technical information, when not appropriately simplified or contextualized, can become overwhelming or confusing for non-technical users. Yet, it must be remembered that users have different informational needs. AI engineers tasked with performing assessments and testing of a third-party AI model want more technical information.

The challenge lies not just in disclosing information about an AI's design, but ensuring it is comprehensible to both technical and non-technical users. This requires careful thought on how to communicate complex AI concepts effectively to different audiences so that they understand the implications of their interaction with the AI system.

Moreover, it can be difficult for users to connect general information about AI systems to impacts or risks to themselves. For instance, understanding that an AI uses a specific type of neural network offers little insight about how the AI's decision might affect them personally or the associated risks. Although there is a general call for more education of the public, further work is needed to develop AI disclosures that are understandable and contextualized for each user.

Improving transparency in AI systems necessitates a range of best practices. Central to these is clear communication. Explaining the purpose, applications, and potential limitations of the AI model using straightforward, non-technical language aids in making the information accessible to a broader audience. Model cards, transparency reports, user guides, and FAQs offer valuable resources to users, adding details about AI operation and intended use in a convenient format. Privacy policies and terms can articulate how the AI model uses data, and what steps are taken to protect privacy and security.

Supplementing explanations with interactive interfaces, diagrams, or flowcharts can help users better visualize and understand complex AI concepts. Disclosures can also be geared for different user groups, providing conceptual information for non-expert users and supplemental technical information for data scientists and developers. Providing real-world use cases or examples helps emphasize practical implications, making the connection between AI operations and their impact more comprehensible.

We must also recognize that users are increasingly going directly to the source, questioning AI models about their training data, decision rationale, and the basis of their responses. While AI developers are enhancing this transparency by exposing elements of chain-of-thought reasoning and model analysis, system-level logging and independent verification remain limited. This has raised growing concerns about the accuracy, completeness, and reliability of these self-reported explanations, particularly given that models may generate plausible narratives rather than true causal reasoning. As a result, users must be cautious about relying solely on model-provided explanations and continue to prioritize independent validation, auditability, and governance controls.

While striving for transparency in AI systems is a collective priority, organizations often face a tension between being transparent and protecting their IP. Transparency demands the disclosure of functional aspects of AI, including underlying algorithms, training data, and interpretability techniques. Yet, these elements often constitute proprietary technology and knowledge that organizations want to protect to maintain their competitive edge, meet commercialization goals, and prevent misuse.

The balance between offering sufficient transparency to build trust and understanding and keeping enough information proprietary to protect IP, presents a complex challenge. Striking this balance requires careful strategizing and may involve the use of legal tools like patents and copyrights. AI developers also need to consider the time required to both create and maintain documentation. While users and public policy setters are demanding greater transparency into how AI models were trained and operated, they must remember that model documentation only enhances their knowledge and understanding. It does not mitigate risk in and of itself. It is no different than putting health notices on cigarettes. User education is important, but it is still "buyer beware."

Explainability

Explainability has been a long-debated topic in the responsible deployment of AI systems, as the complexity of algorithms often makes them opaque and difficult to understand.

Explainability seeks to demystify the operations of an AI system, making its decision-framework and related outputs understandable to humans.

A crucial preparatory step in AI system design is defining who will need explanations, what type of explanation will suffice, and how the ability to challenge a decision will be facilitated. These determinants shape the system's design and guide the selection of supplementary explainability techniques.

As the AI learns, it builds complex connections between different pieces of information. Deep learning algorithms learn by processing large amounts of data through multiple layers, known as *hidden layers*. Each layer performs mathematical operations that help the AI recognize patterns and relationships in the data. However, the way these connections are formed and how the AI makes decisions is not easily understood, even by experts. This makes it hard for everyday users to grasp how the AI arrives at its conclusions.

Furthermore, many commercially used AI models are proprietary and viewed as a competitive advantage. This can result in a lack of transparency, as these models are "black-boxed" with the inner workings (features and weights) withheld, making it harder for users to understand how the AI system generates its outputs. This has led to the call for open models, whereby the model's features and weights are exposed. But even then, understanding how AI models impact specific outcomes requires interpretation.

Adding to the mix is the dynamic nature of AI, which can continually learn and update its algorithms based on new data, leading to changing decision-making patterns and progressive optimizations that may be challenging to keep pace with or explain.

Despite these challenges, efforts are being made to create tools that can interpret complex AI models and translate this interpretation into human-friendly explanations. However, these are still in development, and trusting the truthfulness of the explanation is a common concern.

Depending on the specificity of the task and the level of explainability required, the choice between simpler models like decision trees or linear regression and more complex ones like deep learning algorithms may need to be considered. Simpler models are often more explainable, enabling users to comprehend how inputs are transformed into outputs, albeit sometimes at the expense of accuracy.

For non-technical users seeking to understand the intricacies of AI models, various control mechanisms and strategies can provide a peek "under the hood." Visualization tools that graphically depict the operations and pathways within an AI model are one such technique. For an AI-driven image recognition system, a heatmap can demonstrate which segments of the image the model utilizes to identify an object. By presenting the information visually, users can grasp how the AI is processing and interpreting data.

Say, for instance, a diagnostic AI system analyzes a patient's symptom data and medical history and recommends a less conventional treatment approach. If the AI operates as a "black box" with its internal workings concealed, it could be challenging for the doctor to understand why this particular treatment was suggested, especially if it contradicts their professional judgment or existing medical guidelines. This lack of explainability could lead the doctor to mistrust the AI system, potentially disregarding a valid recommendation, or worse, following a recommendation they don't understand.

Further, from a patient's perspective, trust in their treatment plan is crucial, and they have a right to understand why a particular course of treatment is being recommended. If the AI's recommendation can't be explained, it could lead to stress, confusion, and a lack of trust in the care they are receiving.

When it comes to explainability, there isn't a one-size-fits-all solution. The key lies in pairing the right model with the right task and audience, tailoring explanations to the level of technical fluency of the user, and leveraging a blend of techniques and tools to make the workings of AI as understandable as needed.

The need for explainability will be dependent on the use case, with higher levels of explainability required when AI systems are deployed to support critical infrastructures or generate impacts on protected groups. We are more interested in knowing how an AI model calculated our creditworthiness than a music streaming service's recommendations.

The key is achieving an explanation that is comprehensible by humans and accurately reflects the AI's decision-making framework to the level needed.

Fairness

Fairness or bias in AI is one of the most debated impacts of AI. Addressing bias is important because AI can amplify existing disparities and inequality in society, disproportionately impacting marginalized and vulnerable communities.

Striving for "fair AI" means we need to evaluate the needs of all stakeholders affected by the design, use, and outcomes of AI systems, with the aim of promoting positive, inclusive impacts.

Bias in AI often originates from the data collection and training stages of AI development. Biases in data are commonly due to underrepresentation or overrepresentation of certain demographic groups, or historical prejudices and stereotypes present when the data was created. AI algorithms can inadvertently learn and replicate existing biases, reflecting them in their predictions and decisions. One study found that up to 38.6% of "facts" used by AI are biased,[14] while another analysis revealed that 83.1% of AI models had a high risk of bias.[15]

Another major source of bias in AI emerges from the algorithmic design and decision-making processes. It's important to remember that algorithms are created by humans, who inherently possess their own set of biases that can inadvertently seep into the algorithms they design.

Complexities and ambiguities in defining what is "fair" in different contexts, interpreting fairness in quantifiable terms, and building a consensus around it, can also contribute to AI bias. What might seem fair in one cultural or business context might not be in another. The U.S. National Institute for Standards and Technology (NIST) advises that "When human, systemic and computational biases combine, they can form a pernicious mixture, especially when explicit guidance is lacking for addressing the risks associated with using AI systems."[16]

There are multiple types of fairness, including group and individual fairness. Individual fairness ensures that people who are similar in relevant ways receive similar outcomes. This means that decisions should be based on important factors (e.g., what matters) rather than discriminatory characteristics. For example, in a credit scoring AI system, individual fairness is achieved when two individuals with comparable financial profiles and credit histories receive similar credit scores.

In contrast, group fairness ensures that different demographic groups are treated equitably as a whole. It's about equal opportunity across groups of people, no matter if they differ by age, gender, ethnicity, or language. This involves looking at outcomes across groups to prevent systemic biases that could disadvantage certain populations.[17]

Balancing group and individual fairness in AI can be challenging and may require trade-offs. For instance, in the credit lending example above, if an AI system prioritizes individual fairness, it ensures that individuals with similar financial profiles receive similar credit scores. However, this approach may unintentionally reinforce existing biases. Many women, due to historical social norms and discrimination, have limited credit history. As a result, they could receive lower credit scores compared to men with more extensive credit histories, even if their current financial situations are similar.

On the other hand, if the AI system prioritizes group fairness by adjusting credit scores to ensure equitable outcomes for women as a group, it may lead to artificially inflating scores for women. This approach addresses systemic inequalities but may compromise individual fairness by not basing decisions solely on the individual's financial profile. In this example, a woman could be given a higher credit rating than a man with similar financial circumstances.

The trade-off is complex. In such instances, decision-makers need to judiciously document their decisions' rationale, adding the socio-cultural context in which the AI system operates.

Another aspect to consider when discussing fair AI is algorithmic bias. This refers to the systematic and repeatable inconsistency that can emerge from prejudiced assumptions made during the training of an AI system.

Algorithmic bias stems from the inherent design of the AI model, independent of the data used for training. For example, consider an AI used for job applicant screening. If the AI model is designed to favor candidates from prestigious universities, assuming such candidates are a better fit for job roles, this could lead to an unfair advantage for applicants from privileged backgrounds who could afford to attend these institutions, and disadvantage candidates from less-known schools. This form of algorithmic bias is not derived from the data, but from the design of the AI's objective and the way it is rewarded. Even if the data is balanced and unbiased, the AI system's inherent bias will cause it to overlook potentially excellent candidates who graduated from less-known universities.

Correcting bias requires multiple perspectives. A team designing an AI-powered health system should involve medical professionals, patients from various demographics, ethicists, and patients. Such a mix can help create a more inclusive system that caters to diverse user needs, rather than catering to a homogenous group

Inclusivity, which largely parallels fairness in AI, ensures the systems designed are usable and accessible by people with diverse characteristics, meeting a broad range of needs and preferences. An example here could be an AI-powered voice assistant that understands and responds effectively to diverse accents, dialects, languages, and speech impediments.

Fairness underpins and reinforces an inclusive and equitable digital environment. It requires sustained and proactive measures to identify and mitigate bias throughout the AI lifecycle to prevent unfair or discriminatory outcomes.

Sustainability

As concerns about job displacement and high energy and water use grow, it is essential for businesses to adopt responsible practices that promote both innovation and long-term sustainability.

The underlying purpose of the sustainability principle is to encourage the promotion of physical, social, economic, and planetary well-being, aiming for a balanced coexistence for all stakeholders and the environment.

"AI for Good" is a term for AI that goes beyond limiting technological harm and actively uses AI for societal benefit. It focuses on harnessing AI to address complex societal issues, improve global conditions, and progress toward the United Nations' Sustainable Development Goals.[18] AI can accelerate the deployment of sustainability solutions, such as optimizing energy usage in buildings, developing more sustainable supply chains, or enabling environmental monitoring and modeling.

Sustainable AI incorporates a human-centric approach, while being environmentally friendly, socially responsible, economically viable, and future-oriented. A human-centric approach ensures that AI puts humans at the center, respecting human rights, agency, privacy, and democratic values.

In a human-centric approach, an AI tool developed for personalized education would be engineered to respect students' rights and privacy, while supporting equal access to education. It would tailor learning materials according to each student's learning style, pace, and abilities. Additionally, data privacy measures would be embedded to ensure the students' personal information is protected.

The AI's development would strive for minimal environmental impact by using efficient coding practices that require less computational power, energy consumption, and water use. The AI tool would be designed to promote inclusive accessibility, ensuring students from all backgrounds, including those with special needs, can benefit from it. Furthermore, it would adapt to potential changes in curriculum or educational policies, demonstrating resilience in the face of future uncertainties.

One alarming example of an AI system that could be identified as non-human-centric is the use of AI algorithms in social profiling and news filtering. These algorithms create echo chambers that can influence public opinion. A commonly cited example is AI-driven social media platforms that use algorithms to curate and customize news feeds. Based on a user's past activity, the algorithm narrows the content to match their prior history, effectively cocooning users in a feedback loop of material that aligns with their established viewpoints. This reiterative filtering can limit exposure to diverse perspectives and promote misinformation or discriminatory content. Combined with the proliferation of deepfakes, this could drive misinformation campaigns.

The sustainability principle also involves managing the environmental impact of AI. "What is different about generative AI is the power density it requires. Fundamentally, it is just computing, but a generative AI training cluster might consume seven or eight times more energy than a typical computing workload,"[19] says Noman Bashir, lead author of the impact paper, who is a Computing and Climate Impact Fellow at MIT Climate and Sustainability Consortium and a postdoc in the Computer Science and Artificial Intelligence Laboratory. Most users are not aware that a ChatGPT query consumes at least five times more electricity than a simple web search.[20] LLMs demand significant computational resources for training and operation, resulting in high energy usage. The extensive computing infrastructure needed for such processes contributes sizable carbon emissions. Training a single LLM has been compared to the carbon footprint of multiple cross-country flights.

Sustainable AI can be achieved through optimizing algorithms for energy efficiency, leveraging renewable energy sources for AI operations, and exploring new, low-impact hardware and infrastructure options.

Sustainable AI represents more than just a principle; it embodies a commitment to harness technology for dual benefit, where organizations not only drive innovation and efficiency but also prioritize environmental stewardship and social responsibility.

Conclusion

Adopting Responsible AI by Design is a strategic decision that brings many benefits. By considering responsible AI principles from the onset of an AI project, corporate executives can lay the groundwork for AI systems that are technically advanced, responsible, and socially acceptable.

Users, clients, and stakeholders are more likely to trust AI systems that respect their rights, protect their data, make fair decisions, and contribute positively to society. This trust directly impacts the acceptance and adoption rate of users, fueling the growth and success of AI initiatives.

Integrating Responsible AI by Design throughout the AI lifecycle offers organizations a strategic advantage. It not only paves the way to advanced AI solutions that are beneficial to society, but it also brings increased trust, higher user adoption, regulatory compliance, and enhanced brand reputation.

Key leadership questions to consider:

1 In your AI projects, have you integrated AI principles into your complete AI lifecycle, particularly during the problem identification and design stages?
2 Are accountability and responsibility clearly defined for upholding the achievement of your AI principles?
3 How are diverse perspectives incorporated in your AI projects to broaden ethical and societal considerations?

Notes

1 Jobs, S. (2025, June 12). Stanford graduating class convocation speech address. *Stanford News*. https://news.stanford.edu/stories/2005/06/youve-got-find-love-jobs-says.
2 Privacy by design framework. (n.d.). In *Wikipedia*. Retrieved August 31, 2025, from https://en.wikipedia.org/wiki/Privacy_by_design#:~:text=The%20privacy%20by%20design%20framework%20was%20developed%20by%20Ann%20Cavoukian,Applied%20Scientific%20Research%20in%201995.
3 AAAI/ACM Conference on AI, Ethics, and Society. (2018, December). *AIES '18: Proceedings of the 2018 AAAI/ACM Conference on AI, Ethics, and Society* (pp. 54–59). https://doi.org/10.1145/3278721.3278765.
4 EY. (n.d.). *EY's commitment to ethical and responsible AI*. https://www.ey.com/en_gl/insights/ai/principles-for-ethical-and-responsible-ai.
5 EY. (n.d.). *EY's commitment to ethical and responsible AI*. https://www.ey.com/en_gl/insights/ai/principles-for-ethical-and-responsible-ai.
6 Herbert, T. (2023, November 6). Academics apologize for AI blunder implicating Big Four accounting. *Accounting Web*. https://www.accountingweb.co.uk/tech/tech-pulse/academics-apologise-for-ai-blunder-implicating-big-four.
7 Takita, H., Kabata, D., Walston, S. L., et al. (2025, March 22). A systematic review and meta-analysis of diagnostic performance comparison between generative AI and physicians. *npj Digital Medicine, 8*, 175. https://doi.org/10.1038/s41746-025-01543-z.
8 Cisco. (2024, January 25). *More than 1 in 4 organizations banned use of GenAI over privacy and data security risks – New Cisco study*. https://investor.cisco.com/news/news-details/2024/More-than-1-in-4-Organizations-Banned-Use-of-GenAI-Over-Privacy-and-Data-Security-Risks---New-Cisco-Study/default.aspx#:~:text=,the%20highest%20level%20in%20years.
9 Miller, K. (2024, March 18). Privacy in an AI era: How do we protect our personal information? *Stanford University Institute for Human-Centered*

Artificial Intelligence. https://hai.stanford.edu/news/privacy-ai-era-how-do-we-protect-our-personal-information.

10 Opet, P. (2025, April). An open letter to third party suppliers. *J.P. Morgan*. https://www.jpmorgan.com/technology/technology-blog/open-letter-to-our-suppliers.

11 Opet, P. (2025, April). An open letter to third party suppliers. *J.P. Morgan*. https://www.jpmorgan.com/technology/technology-blog/open-letter-to-our-suppliers.

12 Opet, P. (2025, April). An open letter to third party suppliers. *J.P. Morgan*. https://www.jpmorgan.com/technology/technology-blog/open-letter-to-our-suppliers.

13 Center for Research on Foundation Models. (2024, May). *Stanford Transparency Index Report*. https://crfm.stanford.edu/fmti/May-2024/index.html.

14 Gruet, M. (2022, May 26). That is just common sense – USC researchers find bias up to 38%. *USC Viterbit University*. https://viterbischool.usc.edu/news/2022/05/thats-just-common-sense-usc-researchers-find-bias-in-up-to-38-6-of-facts-used-by-ai/.

15 Hall, J. (2023, March 17). Meta analysis – High risk of bias. *Diagnostic Imaging*. https://www.diagnosticimaging.com/view/meta-analysis-high-risk-of-bias-83-percent-of-ai-neuroimaging-models-psychiatric-diagnosis.

16 Hall, J. (2023, March 17). Meta-analysis finds high risk of bias in 83 percent of AI neuroimaging models for psychiatric diagnosis. *NIST AI Security Framework*. https://www.nist.gov/news-events/news/2022/03/theres-more-ai-bias-biased-data-nist-report-highlights.

17 EY Canada. (2020, October 27). Assessing and mitigating unfairness in credit models. *EY*. https://www.ey.com/en_ca/insights/financial-services/assessing-and-mitigating-unfairness-in-credit-models.

18 United Nations. (n.d.). The UN sustainability goals. https://sdgs.un.org/goals.

19 Zewe, A. (2025, January 17). Explained: Generative AI's environmental impact. *MIT News*. https://news.mit.edu/2025/explained-generative-ai-environmental-impact-0117.

20 Zewe, A. (2025, January 17). Explained: Generative AI's environmental impact. *MIT News*. https://news.mit.edu/2025/explained-generative-ai-environmental-impact-0117.

Chapter 3

Demystifying the magic of AI

Antoine de Saint-Exupery said, "A designer knows he has achieved perfection not when there is nothing left to add, but when there is nothing left to take away."[1] This principle resonates deeply in the realm of artificial intelligence (AI), which is not a single, uniform technology but rather an ecosystem of diverse models, algorithms, and applications, each capable of addressing specific tasks and problems. Just as a designer must refine their work to achieve simplicity and effectiveness, those looking to successfully leverage AI must understand the key distinctions among models, including their objectives, learning methods, and decision-making processes. These factors are critical for developing AI systems that align with business goals and deliver a competitive advantage, while not overbuilding them.

Integrating AI effectively within an organization is akin to a sophisticated game of chess. You will have to strategically decide your moves, considering the implications of each choice. There is no single "right" way to design an AI system. The best design will need to consider the problem to be solved, the nature of the data available, your target objectives, business context, and a range of other factors.

Crucial decisions to consider when designing an AI system include the type of AI algorithm that is most suitable, whether to build bespoke AI models or adapt pre-existing models, the resources required, and how to ensure responsible AI use.

Many organizations view AI as separate use cases, rather than a portfolio of cognitive skills and capabilities. Once viewed in this way, greater return on investment can be achieved by deploying these AI skills across many use cases.

DOI: 10.4324/9781003625520-4

Your AI design will also dictate how well it integrates with existing operations, the efficiencies gained, the quality of insights derived, and ultimately, the value added to your business. Time spent on design can accelerate time to production and reduce costs. AI systems are iteratively modeled, and leveraging good design principles is time well spent.

Objectives

Upon completing this chapter, you will be able to:

- Understand the technical basics of AI, including key concepts and models
- Appreciate the history of AI
- Recognize key driving factors contributing to the rise of AI
- Discover the five crucial technical decision points in designing an AI system.

What is AI?

AI is not just a tool; it is changing how businesses work, including their operating structures and job roles. It's been heralded as one of our greatest inventions alongside fire and electricity. As AI technologies continue to advance, they are enabling organizations to automate processes, enhance decision-making, and foster innovation, ultimately reshaping the future of work. This shift not only improves efficiency but also requires employees to adapt to new roles that leverage AI capabilities.

It is a significant disruptive force that is reshaping entire industries and economic systems. Corporate executives who take too long to consider AI's transformative impact on their company could find themselves at a competitive disadvantage. There is still time to catch up, but not much.

AI is a field within computing that aims to make machines emulate human-like intelligence. Machines can perform cognitive tasks such as learning from experience, understanding context, recognizing patterns, reasoning, decision-making, and solving problems. This brings machines one step closer to behaving like humans, but with the added advantage of faster speed and impartial decision-making.

AI operates differently from rule-based technology. Traditional technology, although reliable in its operation, is limited to pre-set rules and cannot adapt to new scenarios or learn from experience. AI, however, thrives amidst variabilities and uncertainties, constantly evolving its understanding and responses, learning something new each time.

However, it would be a mistake to assume that AI is a replacement for traditional technologies – an upgraded version. Each has its role to play with AI best viewed as an augmentation to rules-based systems. By adding the adaptability of AI to the reliability of rule-based systems, we can achieve significant improvements in a wide array of applications.

AI has two primary branches: "Narrow AI" and "Artificial General Intelligence (AGI)." Narrow AI is exemplified by current AI applications that perform specific tasks, such as security image recognition systems used for identifying individuals, and recommendation engines that suggest products based on user preferences. In contrast, AGI is a yet-to-be achieved concept that envisions machines capable of performing a wide range of intellectual tasks.

It'll be key to corporate success to understand how AI and its potential can be harnessed to your advantage, recognizing both its promise and limitations.

The history of AI

AI dates back to the mid-20th century when the term was first coined at a technical conference. In 1950, an esteemed British mathematician and logician, Alan Turing, popularized the term when he unveiled a revolutionary treatise titled *Computing Machinery and Intelligence*,[2] where he proposed the concept now known as the Turing Test. At the time, AI was still a theoretical concept; however, his paper laid down the foundational idea of creating machines that could emulate human intelligence.

Beginning with theoretical conceptualizations, AI has experienced an extraordinary evolution. Until the 1980s, the AI landscape was predominantly composed of deterministic systems. These AI machines were programmed with an explicit set of rules to accomplish specific specialist tasks. Though these expert systems made significant progress, their capabilities operated within strict boundaries. They performed designated tasks proficiently, but they lacked the flexibility to learn, adapt, and grow beyond their programmed instructions.

The 1980s marked a pivotal shift in AI capabilities. AI design began moving away from rigid, predefined rules, toward a more dynamic approach, commonly referred to as machine learning (ML), which gave machines the ability to learn from data, facilitating continuous improvement in performance without the constant need for explicit reprogramming.

AI leapt from theory to practice in 1997 when IBM launched its AI system, Deep Blue. This chess-playing computer beat reigning world champion Garry Kasparov, igniting fervent interest in its potential applications. Until mastered by AI, chess was viewed as a proxy for human intelligence. Twenty years after this seminal win, Murray Campbell, one of the IBM AI experts on the Deep Blue team, reflected on the importance of this win.

> [Chess is] known as a game that requires strategy, foresight, logic - all sorts of qualities that make up human intelligence ... [it's] an enormously complex game, and that's why it took us, as a field, 50 years of development to finally beat the world champion.[3]

Deep Blue, while grounded in rule-based logic, also incorporated elements of an adaptive decisioning approach. It could strategize and react to an array of chess scenarios, yet its scope was limited to a single game. It had no capacity to learn or adapt beyond the game's rules, reflecting the boundaries of early AI technology.

As the calendar turned over to the 21st century, AI made another pivotal transformation with the advent of neural networks. This advancement embodied a transformative rethinking of how machines could process information.

Neural networks are computational architectures patterned after the human brain's complex interconnections. These networks are a synthesis of numerous interconnected processing nodes, or "neurons," analogous to the synaptic network within the human brain. This architectural mimicry, along with advances in computational power, brought us closer to AI systems that could process and respond to data in intricate, non-linear patterns similar to the human brain.

What made neural networks revolutionary was their intrinsic ability to "learn." Leveraging algorithmic rules and vast amounts of data, these networks could adjust their internal parameters to improve task performance. As opposed to being rigidly program-oriented, neural networks could interpret sensory data through machine perception, clustering raw input and recognizing patterns, without explicit human intervention.

The development of neural networks allowed machines to dig deeper into data, deciphering patterns far more complex than their rule-based predecessors. This breakthrough opened up new AI capabilities, including natural language processing (NLP), image and speech recognition, and a multitude of data classification practices.[4]

Over the past decade, rapid technological developments propelled AI from research labs into the mainstream. This evolution was driven by numerous breakthroughs in ML and its subset, deep learning, alongside improved access to unprecedented amounts of data.

All this progress culminated in several landmark accomplishments, one of which is another triumphant win by an AI system against a world champion, this time with the complex board game *Go*. In 2016, DeepMind's AI program AlphaGo emerged victorious against a world champion, a feat believed to be years away due to *Go*'s inherent complexity. This seminal event was more than just another board game victory. It symbolized AI breaking another cognitive capability, decades ahead of predictions. This marked the onset of a new generation of AI applications and technological progress.[5]

Now, more than 25 years after DeepBlue's win, the digital world stands amid an unprecedented AI revolution. Once a conceptual enigma, AI occupies a definitive role within the fabric of technology, business, and society. From data analysis to predicting customer behavior and even saving lives, AI's capabilities and potential are far-reaching.

The rise of AI: key driving factors

The dramatic rise of AI over the past two decades marks a pivotal shift in the technology landscape. This ascent is not attributable to a single catalyst; instead, it is the result of many factors coming together.

First, the advances in ML accelerated AI's progression. In recent years, ML has evolved to utilize sophisticated mathematical models trained on vast datasets. This enabled AI models to predict outcomes or make decisions without needing specific programming. This shift toward self-learning has enhanced AI's efficacy across diverse use cases.

Deep learning, a subset of ML, has been a game-changer, too. It uses hierarchical layers of artificial neural networks to find patterns within the data – just like our brain processes information. This new learning paradigm enables machines to process thousands of data points simultaneously, eliminating the costly and time-consuming need for pre-labeling training data, thereby enhancing the efficiency and scalability of AI applications.

In addition, the data revolution has also acted as a powerful propellant for AI. With the birth of cloud technology, we have seen an explosion of data availability and cheap data storage costs. This means that AI systems can process varied and large datasets, turning this information into insightful, actionable intelligence.

Moreover, advancements in processing power have played a significant role in facilitating AI's capabilities. The rise in computational speed and efficiency makes managing complex AI tasks quicker and easier than ever before. Coupled with high-performance graphics processing units and sophisticated parallel computing methods, we can run heavy computational tasks simultaneously, reducing model training times and boosting performance.

Factors such as advancements in machine learning and deep learning, increased data accessibility, and exponential growth in processing power, estimated to have increased by over 1,000 times in the past decade,[6] have accelerated AI's journey from a novelty to a transformative force in our daily operations. Understanding these drivers equips you to better harness AI's potential and incorporate its strengths into your strategic decision-making. The future of AI appears even more promising, with operational efficiency of up to 40% already achieved,[7] and in the future, prospects of remarkably sophisticated applications.

Technical aspects of AI

As AI becomes increasingly integral to business strategy and operations, understanding its technical underpinnings is key. In this section, we unravel some of the key technical elements that form the backbone of AI.

AI systems are an elaborate mesh of components, with diverse types of algorithms performing different cognitive functions to solve different use cases. These algorithms, which swing from conventional linear regression and decision trees to sophisticated neural networks and deep learning models, dictate the performance boundaries and potential of AI systems.

To harness the potential of AI within an organization, executives must understand that different AI models are best suited for different applications and will meet diverse business needs. AI systems are multifaceted with different methods of decision-making, learning methods, data types, objectives, and algorithm types. Understanding these categories aids in selecting the right AI model and optimal learning methods.

Imagine a team of engineers tasked with developing an AI system to help doctors diagnose diseases. They face several critical design decisions that will determine the success of their project. First, they must choose the right method of decision-making. They debate between a rule-based system, which is straightforward but inflexible, and a probabilistic approach that can handle the uncertainty inherent in medical data. They opt for the latter, wanting to build an AI system that can adapt to the nuances of different patient cases.

Next, they consider the learning method. With a wealth of medical records at their disposal, but recognizing that not all data is labeled, they decide on a semi-supervised learning approach. This method allows the AI to learn from a combination of labeled and unlabeled data, leveraging the vast amount of available information, while still benefiting from the accuracy of labeled examples.

The type of data they use is also crucial. They gather both structured data, like patient demographics and lab results, and unstructured data, such as doctors' notes and medical images, to provide knowledge of each case.

The team then focuses on defining a clear objective: to minimize diagnostic errors and improve patient outcomes. This goal guides every aspect of their design, ensuring the AI remains focused on delivering tangible benefits.

Finally, they choose the algorithm type. After considering various options, they settle on a combination of neural networks for processing complex images and decision trees for interpreting structured data, striking a balance between power and interpretability.

In evaluating these design decisions, the engineers create an AI system that not only assists doctors in making more accurate diagnoses but also earns their trust by being reliable and transparent.

Let's explore these different decision points in more detail.

Decision-making approach

AI systems can initially be grouped by their decision-making approach. Two key categories are static AI systems, which follow pre-set guidelines, and adaptive AI systems, which can learn and modify their decision-making over time. Static AI systems offer clarity and consistency but may lack flexibility, while adaptive systems can adjust their behavior based on observed data. Static and adaptive AI deliver different experiences and results when applied to the same task.

As introduced earlier, traditional rules-based systems operate on predefined rules and logic, where specific conditions trigger specific actions. These systems rely heavily on human expertise to create and maintain the rules, making them rigid and often unable to adapt to new situations without manual intervention.

In contrast, static AI, while also limited in adaptability, utilizes ML algorithms to analyze data and make predictions based on patterns it has learned from historical data. Unlike rules-based systems, static AI can improve its performance over time as it processes new information, but it still lacks the dynamic adaptability of adaptive

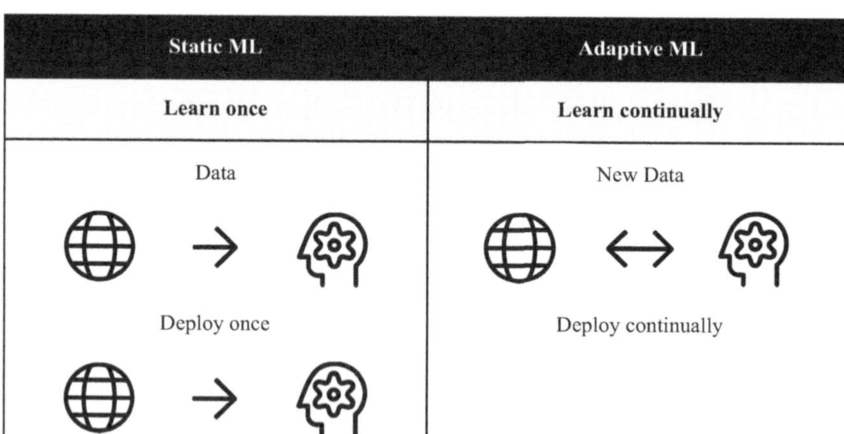

Figure 3.1 Static ML model vs. adaptive AI model.

AI systems, which can learn and evolve in real-time. Essentially, the key difference lies in the flexibility and learning capabilities, with traditional systems being more static and reliant on explicit rules, while static AI incorporates learned patterns to inform its decisions (Figure 3.1).

Let's explore the two different types of AI with an example. A static AI in credit scoring would make decisions based solely on a set of predefined rules and parameters. For example, it may evaluate an applicant's creditworthiness based on income level, credit history, and employment status. If an applicant's income is higher than a certain value, if they've had no prior defaults, and they hold a steady job, the system approves the loan. While this approach is straightforward, transparent, and easy to explain, it's inflexible. The AI will not adjust its assessments based on new lending scenarios or economic conditions unless you explicitly change its rules.

On the other hand, an adaptive AI system uses ML to modify its decision-making process based on newly introduced data (e.g., by changing its features and weights). In a credit scoring scenario, it would analyze a customer's past and present financial behavior, credit patterns, payment histories, and even social behavior to assign credit scores. Over time, the system "learns," providing more tailored risk assessments. For example, it might pick up on patterns that suggest a reliable borrower despite a lower income value, or spot warning signs for an applicant with a stellar profile on the surface. This adaptive approach offers a more robust assessment in a fast-changing financial landscape, though its decisions are often less interpretable. Monitoring an adaptive AI's behavior is also important as data and performance drift can occur, meaning that initial training conducted pre-production may become less relevant as the AI adapts its decision framework.

Understanding these operational differences between static and adaptive AI is critical in deciding the right approach for your organization's particular problem. While the transparency and simplicity of static AI may be appealing, the complex, evolving economic landscape might require the sophistication and flexibility of adaptive AI systems. Therefore, selecting an AI model should consider the specific needs, risk tolerance, and strategic objectives of your organization, as well as the regulatory context and the need to explain the AI's decisions to customers or regulators.

Learning methods

As the integration of AI into business operations becomes more prevalent, understanding the various learning methods employed by AI is a key consideration. The learning method used by an AI model determines how it processes data and adapts to new inputs. The most common learning methods are supervised, unsupervised, semi-supervised, reinforcement, and federated learning; each brings unique strengths and shortcomings.

1 *Supervised learning algorithms require a dataset consisting of example input-output pairs, where each pair includes a data sample used for making predictions and an expected outcome called a label.* The term "supervised" refers to the necessity of human supervisors assigning these labels to the data. During the training process, samples are iteratively fed to the model, which uses its current state of parameters to return a prediction. This prediction is compared to the label, and the difference, known as an error, serves as feedback for the model to update itself to reduce future errors. Supervised learning models, trained on labeled data, excel in prediction tasks and categorical outcomes, such as predictive maintenance or spam detection. They provide reliable and interpretable results, but need ample labeled data, and can struggle with novel scenarios not represented in their training set.
2 *Unsupervised learning, in contrast, explores unlabeled data to find hidden patterns or anomalies.* There are no correct answers in unsupervised learning. It is best used for exploratory tasks, detecting unseen categories in data, or understanding complex datasets, such as identifying customer segments or detecting unusual activity. However, it can be hard to validate its findings or predict specific outcomes due to the absence of known "right answers" in its training data.
3 *Semi-supervised learning is a blend of the above two with some labeled and unlabeled data.* This approach is particularly common in scenarios where acquiring labeled data is expensive or time-consuming, while unlabeled data is readily available. By leveraging both types of data, semi-supervised learning models can achieve higher accuracy and generalization than traditional supervised learning methods that rely solely on labeled datasets.

For instance, in fields like NLP and image recognition, where vast amounts of unlabeled data exist, semi-supervised learning allows models to learn from the structure and patterns within the unlabeled data while refining their predictions based on the limited labeled examples. This hybrid strategy not only enhances the model's performance but also reduces the need for extensive manual labeling, making it a cost-effective solution for many real-world applications.

4 *Reinforcement learning involves continuous interaction with the environment, with an AI system refining its decision strategy or approach based on positive or negative feedback.* Reinforcement learning is akin to a hot and cold game, where the algorithm receives feedback in the form of rewards (hot) or penalties (cold) to guide its actions toward achieving a desired goal. Such models are great for multi-step tasks where data is collected over time, like playing a game or autonomous driving. But they often need a well-defined reward system and numerous interaction samples to learn effectively, making them computationally demanding and prone to failure in underspecified or ambiguous situations (Figure 3.2).

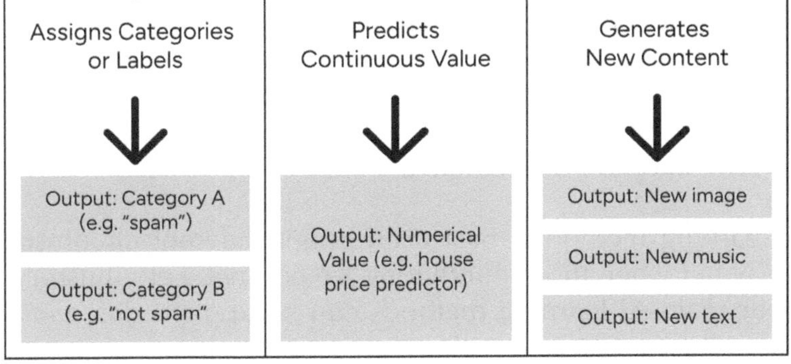

Figure 3.2 Machine learning type.

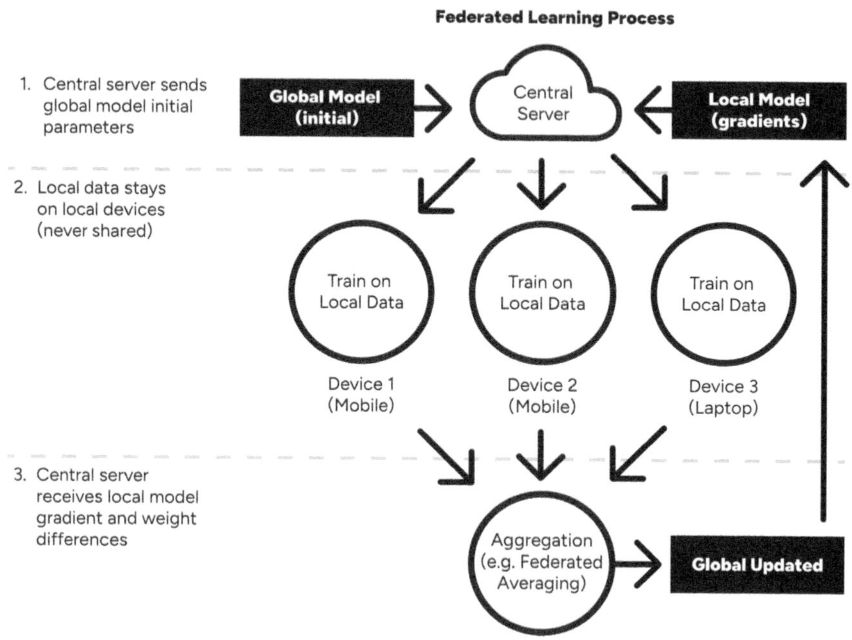

Figure 3.3 Federated learning training process.

5 *Federated learning decentralizes learning across numerous devices, allowing AI models to learn from widespread data while protecting privacy.* This makes it suited for use cases involving sensitive or personal data distributed across devices, like predictive typing on smartphones. In federated learning, individual devices train a shared model locally using their own data and only send model updates, rather than the raw data, back to a central server, which aggregates these updates to improve the global model. Its drawbacks, however, include the challenge of coordinating learning across diverse and potentially unreliable networks, and a potential reduction in model performance if on-device data sets are limited or unrepresentative (Figure 3.3).

Each learning method is best used under different circumstances, and may fail when those conditions are not met. Let's illustrate how the four main AI learning methods can be applied differently to a common business task – equipment maintenance.

Supervised learning can be used to predict equipment failures based on existing historical maintenance records. Here, we would have data linking specific operational parameters to subsequent equipment breakdowns (the "labels"). Documented historical maintenance records, along with other equipment attributes, can provide a readily available labeled training dataset. A supervised learning model could find the patterns that tie certain conditions to future failures, thus predicting breakdowns and informing preventative maintenance schedules. However, it could potentially falter in predicting failures arising from previously unseen conditions or scenarios not in the historical data.

Unsupervised learning is best used to uncover unknown patterns across different equipment parameters. For example, there is operational data from various machines, but no specific outcomes. An unsupervised learning model could cluster the machinery into groups exhibiting similar operational patterns. Identifying these clusters could help organizations understand common equipment behaviors, such as identifying machines that frequently operate at high temperatures or those that exhibit irregular vibration patterns. These insights can lead to efficient maintenance strategies by allowing operators to proactively address issues before they escalate. However, since these models lack definitive outcomes for their learning, their utility may diminish when predicting specific future failures.

Reinforcement learning applies well to complex, multi-step maintenance tasks, where an ideal action sequence needs to be learned. Imagine an AI-controlled maintenance robot that needs to perform several interconnected sub-tasks (like inspection, cleaning, and part replacement). Here, reinforcement learning can help the AI gradually refine its sequence of actions based on feedback from the environment, improving its efficacy over time. Still, such a method might stumble when the performance feedback is ambiguous or delayed, or when its environment changes significantly.

Federated learning could be employed when maintenance data is distributed across multiple locations. For instance, a company with numerous factories might want to develop customized learning plans for maintenance workers from all the location-specific maintenance data without centralizing it (for privacy or cost concerns). A federated learning model could learn insights directly from the maintenance records associated with each worker, ensuring data privacy yet benefiting from the collective insights. The limitations of this approach might be slower learning due to network latencies and possible variations in the quality of insights if the data at different locations vary significantly in their representativeness or quality.

The choice of learning methods directly impacts AI's success, and should align with the available data, desired outcomes, and specific operational context. In equipment maintenance, as with many operational tasks, the application of an appropriate AI learning method can significantly improve efficiencies, preempt issues, and boost performance.

Data

In the realm of AI, data is akin to the lifeblood in human bodies – indispensable, vital, and powerfully influential. While AI system designs undeniably hinge on robust algorithms and innovative ML methods, data quality, format, and accessibility are equally important. Just as a well-built engine will falter without quality fuel, even the most sophisticated AI can falter without well-managed data. Understanding the type, quality, and accessibility of data available significantly impacts the design and success of AI algorithms.

Data type, be it structured or unstructured, influences the AI model selection. Structured data, which includes numerical or categorical data that are organized neatly in databases or spreadsheets, is highly compatible with various AI models, particularly those involving prediction or classification tasks.

Unstructured data, on the other hand, encompasses text, images, videos, or auditory data, which do not follow a predefined model or form. AI models handling unstructured data typically include NLP (analyzing customer reviews), computer vision (identifying product defects through image analysis), or speech recognition algorithms (transcribing call center conversations). The type of AI model and algorithm selected will be influenced by the nature of the data your organization handles.

The choice between structured and unstructured data is not just a matter of format. Superior AI performance relies substantially on the quality of the data. High-quality data is accurate, complete, consistent, reliable, and relevant to the task to be performed. Poor data quality can result in inaccurate predictions and poor business decisions. Therefore, major considerations in your AI design should be given to data cleansing, handling missing data, and avoiding inconsistent or duplicate data that can affect algorithm learning and operation. Achieving these, while crucial to AI performance, may involve significant time and expense. Maintaining a consistent level of data quality can be complex and require consistent monitoring and manual effort, contributing to ongoing maintenance costs for your AI system.

In addition to ensuring high data quality, it is essential to separately consider the data used for AI training and operation. The data utilized during the training phase must be representative of the scenarios the AI will encounter in real-world applications. This distinction is critical because the training data shapes the model's understanding and capabilities, while the operational data reflects the dynamic nature of the environment in which the AI functions. If the operational data diverges significantly from the training data, the AI may struggle to make accurate predictions or decisions, leading to suboptimal performance. Therefore, organizations must implement strategies to regularly update and align their training datasets with operational data, ensuring that the AI remains relevant and effective as conditions change. This ongoing alignment not only enhances the AI's adaptability but also mitigates the risks associated with data drift, ultimately supporting better decision-making and business outcomes.

AI objectives

AI models can be grouped by their objective types, the most common ones being classification, regression, generative, and agentic AI models. Defining the objective of an AI model is an important first step, as it informs the choice of AI models used, impacting both the design and the outcome of the AI system.

1. *Classification models are used when data needs to be categorized into predefined classes.* For instance, these models can predict if a customer will purchase a specific product. It can categorize customers into "loyal" or "at-risk of leaving." The advantage is clear – categorical predictions. However, classification models can sometimes oversimplify reality by forcing data into distinct categories, failing to account for gray areas or overlaps.
2. *Regression models make predictions about continuous or quantitative outcomes, like predicting a customer's future spend based on shopping patterns.* Their output is a predicted numerical value, but their accuracy heavily depends on the nature of the data and the relevance of the chosen variables. Incorrect assumptions or incomplete data can lead to inaccurate predictions.

3 *Generative models create new content or synthetic data.* They could, for example, generate a hypothetical customer profile that can be used for simulating different promotional strategies or customized marketing material. While they are powerful in creating new content, they can hallucinate, creating nonsensical or unrealistic data if not properly configured or trained. They often also require specialized knowledge bases and training to perform highly complex and expert-level tasks.
4 *Agentic AI models introduce autonomy.* They do not introduce new model types as they build their skills and capabilities from one or more of the above models. They differ in their level of autonomy and decision-making. Agentic AI models are highly flexible, with

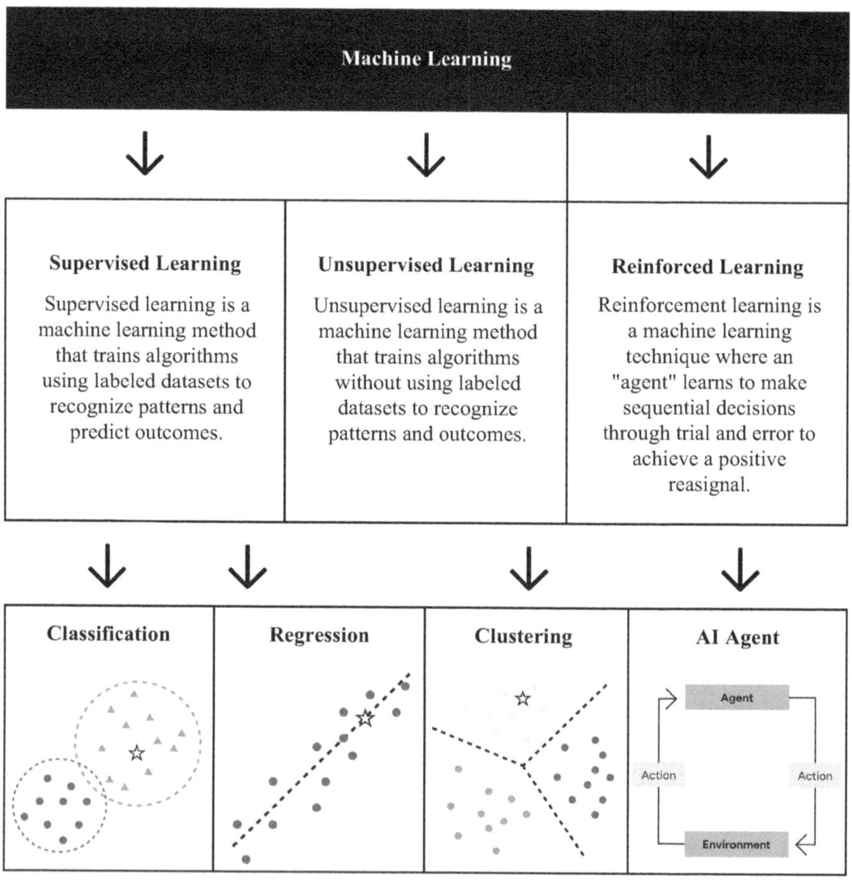

Figure 3.4 Classification vs. regression vs. generative modeling methods.

some highly automated and others operating within predefined rules and guidelines. While they can be applied in many domains, they introduce new risks, including goal misalignment (Figure 3.4).

Each of these AI models finds its utility under specific circumstances – classification models for categorical outcomes, regression models for quantitative predictions, and generative models for creating new content. Understanding which aligns best with the project objective is critical for successful AI implementation.

Importance of human-centricity in AI design

Human operators play a key role throughout the AI lifecycle. During the design phase, their domain expertise helps define the problem, set objectives, and identify relevant data sources. In the learning and modeling phases, human input is essential for labeling data, validating model outputs, and providing feedback to refine algorithms. By involving your team in these processes, you ensure that the AI system is aligned with real-world needs and constraints, leading to more accurate and relevant outcomes.

Human operators interact with AI systems through human-machine interfaces that facilitate communication and control. These interfaces encompass a variety of human-machine interactions, including intuitive dashboards for data visualization, conversational chat prompts for real-time assistance, touch screens for interactive control, voice-activated systems for hands-free operation, and visual sensor platforms that enable image recognition and environmental awareness. By designing user-friendly interfaces, human operators can leverage AI effectively without requiring deep technical expertise.

In an augmentation role, AI assists human operators by providing insights, recommendations, and automating routine tasks, allowing the operator to focus on more complex and strategic decisions. In more autonomous applications, AI might make decisions independently but with human oversight to ensure accountability and ethical considerations. It is important to set the level of autonomy based on the specific use case and the potential impact of AI decisions.

To support human oversight, it is important that AI systems provide clear explanations and justifications for their predictions and decisions. Operators should understand how the AI arrived at a particular conclusion, including the factors and data points considered. This transparency builds trust and enables the operator to make informed decisions based on AI outputs. Techniques such as model interpretability tools, decision trees, and visual explanations can aid in this process.

As the autonomy of AI increases, it is important to implement continuous monitoring of AI performance to maintain its effectiveness and reliability. Performance drift and data quality are areas that must be monitored for all AI systems. While these can be evaluated through regular audits and testing, they are best monitored through real-time, continuous measurement. Monitoring systems should track key performance indicators and detect any deviations or drifts in AI behavior. If the AI's performance deteriorates or the quality of the data it is fed declines, the system should trigger alerts to notify human operators.

The human operator's role is to respond to alerts and decide on the corrective action, which may include adjusting model parameters or retraining the model with new data to correct any biases, inaccuracies, or goal misalignment. Additionally, operators should implement feedback loops to report anomalies or unexpected outcomes, helping to continuously improve the AI system.

As we transition toward agentic AI, it becomes increasingly vital to uphold human oversight and control over these intelligent systems, ensuring that our evolving interactions with AI enhance our lives while safeguarding our values and autonomy.

Conclusion

Summarizing AI is a considerable challenge, largely due to its complexity, multi-dimensional nature, and continual evolution. AI is not a monolithic technology, but a collection of varied components and methods. A successful AI design involves: identifying the use case objective, selecting the algorithm type, sourcing the right data, determining the learning method, and integrating the human-machine interactions – to fit the use case and purpose.

Each of these components has its strengths, weaknesses, and ideal use scenarios. Getting them right requires considering the problem to be solved, validating with the right stakeholders, and identifying the key decision points and risks. Understanding how all these methods interact can equip an AI designer and data scientist with the vital knowledge to make well-informed decisions about the design and operation of AI in their organization.

Ultimately, the effective integration of AI within an organization and our daily lives is not simply about leveraging the most sophisticated models or algorithms. It's about understanding the problem, knowing the type of data available, and most importantly, aligning the AI objective with the broader business strategy and having a long term view for AI value realization.

Our next chapter dives deeper into the AI development life cycle and the essential infrastructure building blocks to build and scale robust AI practices.

Key leadership questions to consider:

1. Is your AI investment strategy fully leveraging the range of available AI technologies and models?
2. Do you have the right AI talent and skills to execute your AI investment strategy?
3. Does your AI design process involve thorough comparison and optimal selection of AI models and algorithms?
4. Is your team equipped with enough knowledge of AI's technical aspects to make informed strategic decisions?

Notes

1 de Saint-Exupéry, A. (n.d.). Famous quotation. In *Wikipedia*. Retrieved August 30, 2025, from https://en.wikipedia.org/wiki/Antoine_de_Saint-Exup%C3%A9ry.

2 Turing, A. (1950). Computing machinery and intelligence. *Mind, 59*(236), 433–460. https://courses.cs.umbc.edu/471/papers/turing.pdf.

3 Greenemeier, L. (2017, June 2). 20 years after Deep Blue: How AI has advanced since conquering chess. *Scientific American*. https://www.scientificamerican.com/article/20-years-after-deep-blue-how-ai-has-advanced-since-conquering-chess/.

4 Russell, S., & Norvig, P. (2014). *Artificial intelligence: A modern approach* (3rd ed.). Harlow: Pearson Education.

5 Waters, R. (2023, February 19). Man beats machine at Go in human victory. *Ars Technica*. https://arstechnica.com/information-technology/2023/02/man-beats-machine-at-go-in-human-victory-over-ai/.

6 Priyadarshi, K. (2023, October 1). What is Huang Law 1000x chip performance in ten years? *International Semiconductor News*. https://techovedas.com/what-is-huang-law-1000x-chip-performance-in-10-years/.
7 Acquah, E. (2024, September 25). How can AI technology improve operational efficiency? Unlocking smarter, faster processes. *Dartai*. https://www.itsdart.com/blog/how-can-ai-technology-improve-operational-efficiency.

Chapter 4

Iterating AI from concept to reality

In this chapter, we provide an overview of the artificial intelligence (AI) development lifecycle, the process that is used to develop AI. For each lifecycle stage, we identify the challenges and best practices to build AI systems that are both efficient and responsible.

AI, with its ability to learn and adapt from data, requires an iterative development process built upon continuous improvement. The late Martin Luther King Jr. understood the importance of strong foundations, stating, "It is not the beauty of a building you should look at; it's the construction of the foundation that will stand the test of time."[1] This quote resonates with the context of AI development. Just as a building's longevity relies on its foundational structure, the success and sustainability of AI systems depend on the robustness of their underlying components. A well-constructed foundation in AI encompasses not only technical specifications but also ethical considerations, stakeholder engagement, and regulatory compliance, ensuring that the systems we build can withstand the complexities of real-world applications.

The AI development lifecycle is itself evolving, with AI being used to develop code and act as adversarial testers and overseers. This has led to research and investments into new AI development processes, tools, and methods. Despite these advancements, concerns still persist that enhancements in the AI development lifecycle, such as automated integrated workflows and continuous monitoring, are not keeping pace.

DOI: 10.4324/9781003625520-5

Objectives

Upon completing this chapter, you will be able to:

- Understand the AI development lifecycle and its key stages
- Determine the difference between AI and traditional rules-based system development processes
- Recognize the importance of integrating responsible AI into the development lifecycle
- Develop strategies to achieve high-performing, responsible AI.

The AI development lifecycle

The AI development lifecycle begins with identifying the problem the AI system needs to solve and proceeds through various stages, each contributing to the AI solution. AI system development is iterative, with developers continuously refining solution approaches and designs based on insights obtained from training, testing, and monitoring. Figure 4.1 depicts the AI solution lifecycle in six stages:

1 *Problem identification*: The development of an AI system starts with identifying the problem to be solved – its goal or objective. This is an important step and should not be completed too quickly. It's important to have a clear and detailed definition of the problem that considers the business issue to be solved and the social, economic, and environmental impacts. Engaging diverse stakeholders brings in different perspectives.

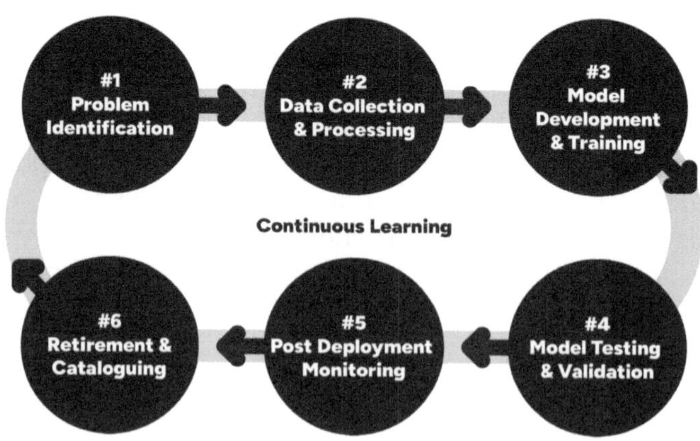

Figure 4.1 AI solution lifecycle framework.

2 *Data collection and processing*: The next step is determining the available data, both internal and external. It is important to assess data quality, which can vary widely, particularly when it's unstructured. Often, the collected data will need to be cleansed, formatted, and further processed to remove biases, missing values, or address privacy concerns.
3 *Model development and training:* The heart of AI development is the model selection and training phase. This process involves feeding the selected model(s) (developers may start with more than one) with training data and measuring the model's efficacy.
4 *Model testing and validation:* This stage involves testing the model against unseen data and measuring its performance to identify discrepancies, errors, or performance issues that require retraining. It's also important to subject the AI system to adversarial data to test its robustness.
5 *Post-deployment monitoring:* A model's performance in the "wild" can shift significantly from that in the lab. With the shift toward agentic AI, post-deployment monitoring is becoming even more important to ensure the model is performing as expected and to spot performance issues.
6 *Retirement and cataloging:* The shelf life of AI is quite short, with a model being retired if it has unresolvable performance issues or is replaced by a more efficient system.

The AI development lifecycle is cyclical. Learning at any step can lead to revisiting the algorithm selected, the training data, and even the initial problem itself, leading to constant iterations for improvement and optimization.

Differences between AI and rules-based technology development

Rules-based technologies function on predetermined rules that are explicitly coded into the system. Developers must analyze the problem and define every possible scenario and the corresponding action in advance. The process involves translating the rules into system requirements and testing the system functionality against those requirements. Rules-based systems can only handle situations that fall within the predefined rule set, making them inflexible in the face of new tasks or unexpected inputs.

AI systems do not rely on fixed rules. They learn by detecting patterns and relationships in data. The AI training phase is iterative and often involves testing multiple algorithms to determine which best matches the objective and can model the underlying patterns in the data. The final selection is made based on the model's performance across various scenarios. In testing, the AI model is evaluated for its robustness and ability to handle new scenarios and use cases. AI testing focuses on the model's adaptability and robustness in real-world situations, rather than verifying compliance with a set of predefined rules. AI systems thrive on flexibility and learning, allowing them to adapt to new information and scenarios.

Let's use an example – an insurance company developing a system to detect fraudulent transactions – to illustrate how AI's self-learning changes the development process. With a rules-based system, you would start by defining a series of static rules to detect fraud based on expert knowledge or past experiences. These rules might flag claims that exceed expected values, occur at odd hours, happen in close succession, involve new service providers, or are conducted in high-risk geographical locations. Once these rules are established, they will be coded into the system, which will then classify claims as fraudulent or legitimate. While this approach can catch certain instances of fraud, it will only detect occurrences of fraud that fit the defined rules. Conversely, legitimate claims that fit the rules will be inaccurately labeled fraudulent and declined.

An AI-based fraud detection system is trained using historical claim data – both standard and fraudulent cases. The AI system learns to identify fact patterns correlated to fraudulent behavior without being explicitly programmed with rules. It identifies explicit and implicit characteristics across data points to detect a fraudulent claim. Post deployment, the system learns from feedback on its false positives and negatives. It can uncover new types of fraud, is less likely to flag legitimate claims as fraudulent, and adapts its performance over time based on new data input or feedback.

Despite AI's benefits, it's not always the best solution. Developers must consider whether it's best to use a rules-based system or AI. Rules-based systems are consistent and predictable, making them adept at handling simple and structured tasks with set parameters. However, this rigidity can pose limitations in complex scenarios with evolving variables or patterns that are difficult to define manually.

Conversely, AI systems thrive in complexity and ambiguity. However, it's important to note that AI models often require greater development and maintenance costs, and can lead to new risks. In many cases, a balanced integration of both system types will provide the most optimal solution. For example, in discovery-based scenarios, AI can find new fact patterns that can be built-into the rules-based logic.

Incorporating responsible AI into the AI development lifecycle

In Chapter 2, we introduced Responsible AI by Design and the responsible AI principles. We will now explore how to embed responsible AI through each stage of the AI development lifecycle.

Problem identification

At this initial stage, the AI developer needs to balance the business needs and projected benefits with societal impacts. The importance of getting the problem statement right cannot be overstated, especially given AI's remarkable efficiency in optimizing the objective it is assigned. If the problem statement is ambiguous or misaligned, the effectiveness of the AI solution may be severely compromised once it is placed in production.

Take, for example, recruiting AI systems, where AI models trained on historical hiring data have often defined the "ideal candidate" as someone who closely resembles those who have been hired in the past. In many systems, this has led to a preference for Caucasian males.

To resolve this issue, developers have removed sensitive data about candidates, a process that is both costly and time-consuming. However, what if the solution is more straightforward? Instead of scrubbing the data, developers could change the AI's objective. Rather than asking the AI to identify the best candidate, the problem could be reframed to seek the best candidate who brings new skills and diverse perspectives that enhance the overall functioning of the target team.

A common challenge with AI is that the problem statement is defined too narrowly. Developers zero in on the specific task the AI must perform, neglecting the broader context in which it will operate. For example, autonomous vehicles must be trained not only for normal driving conditions but also to navigate disruptions in traffic flow due to construction, heavy rainfall, or an accident.

While it is important during the problem identification phase to consider potential unintended consequences or ecosystem challenges, it is also important to challenge which problems are being solved in the first place. AI is still a costly technology to invest in, and often, AI problems are defined without considering the complexity of its use and the risks it may introduce. It is important that project sponsors compare the costs against the perceived value of the AI solution.

As illustrated in Figure 4.2, diverse AI use cases exist along an innovation and risk spectrum, demonstrating that each use case can vary significantly along this spectrum. Higher complexity associated risks necessitate increased controls and resource allocations. By recognizing these factors early in the process, organizations can better frame the problem statement and get a higher return on investment (ROI).

A helpful framework to use in classifying your AI use cases by value and risk is illustrated in Figure 4.3.

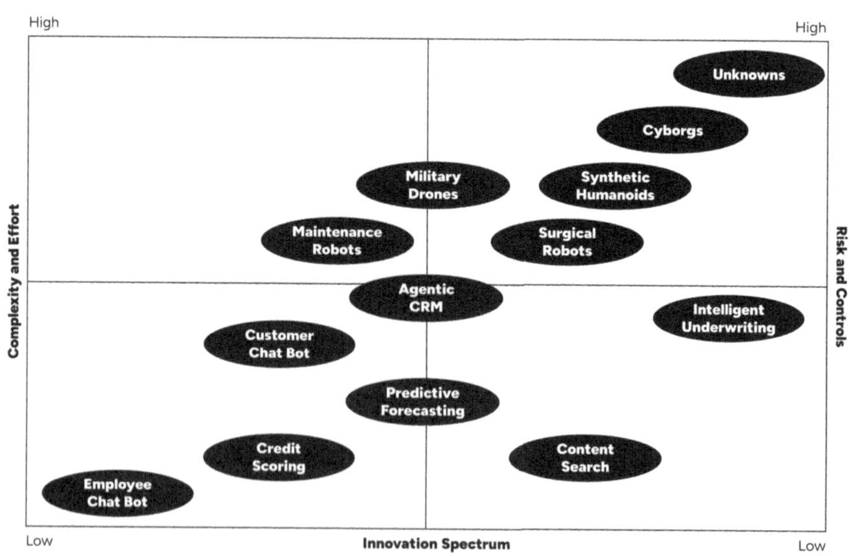

Figure 4.2 AI use case – problem identification – innovation spectrum.

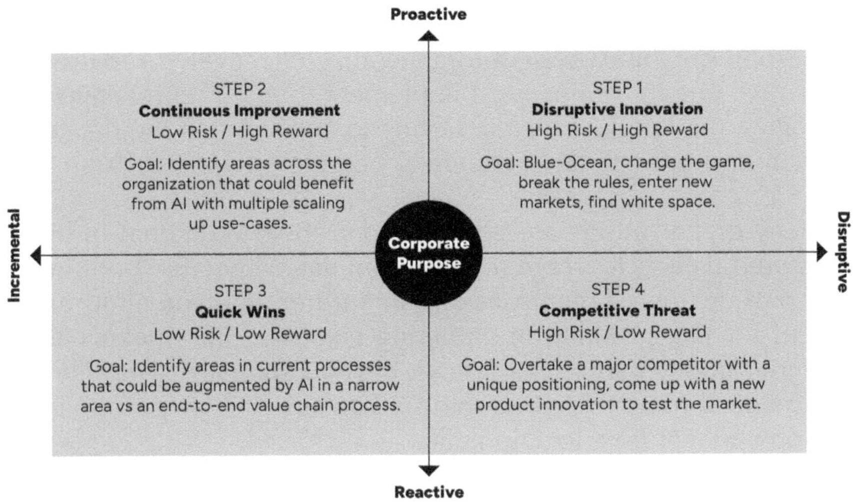

Figure 4.3 AI use case classification framework.[2]

When shaping the problem statement and objective function of an AI system, the following questions should be considered.

Problem identification – key quality control questions:

1. Does the problem align with your strategic objectives?
2. What value is the AI expected to generate?
3. Have diverse stakeholder perspectives been factored into the problem and the proposed solution?
4. Has a full-cost estimate across the full AI solution's lifecycle been calculated?
5. How does the proposed AI solution align with current capabilities and resources?

Data collection and processing

AI learns from data, and the quality of that data has the greatest impact on the model's performance. If the data is flawed, whether due to inaccuracies, biases, or incompleteness, the outcomes produced by the AI will be equally flawed – "bad data simply leads to bad outcomes."

During this stage, a key consideration includes whether a continuous stream of data is available to support real-time AI operations. In addition, the data must be representative of the production environment to allow the AI system to generalize effectively to real-world scenarios. Organizations must implement robust data management strategies and conduct regular testing to confirm that the data used to train and operate AI is accurate, complete, and free from data bias.

Many organizations are going beyond their traditional in-house structured data to leverage unstructured data generated both inside and outside their organizations. An insurer implementing an AI system for risk profiling in gathering extensive information about potential policyholders may move beyond standard data like age and medical history to more intrusive details such as genetic information and real-time location data.

While genetic data can improve risk assessment accuracy, it raises concerns about discrimination, where individuals may be denied coverage based on their genetic predispositions. This practice infringes on privacy rights and undermines the principle of shared risk among policyholders.

Similarly, using real-time location data from smartphones or car telemetry can reveal insights into a policyholder's driving behaviors and habits. However, collecting this data also raises privacy and surveillance concerns if the insurer collects information without the policyholder's consent.

Another crucial aspect of data management is ensuring that the chosen data reflects the diverse demographics the model will serve, including age, gender, race, and socio-economic conditions relevant to the problem. Using balanced and representative data helps avoid skewed results and promotes fairness in AI outcomes. For example, a retail company introducing an AI recommendation system should have training data that encompasses its full customer base, avoiding favoritism toward any particular age, gender, or ethnicity.

With copyright and misinformation concerns, the traceability of data back to its source is important. Certain sources are more reliable than others. Quality data checks help avoid erroneous predictions or biased outcomes.

The following questions should be considered when developing an AI-ready data management program and selecting data to train and operate an AI system.

Data collection and processing – key quality control questions:

1. What form of data will the AI system require, and how will it be sourced?
2. Are privacy laws adhered to during the data collection process?
3. Does the data represent the diverse demographics the model will serve?
4. How is your AI data bias being tested, and if risks are identified, how are these being addressed?
5. Is the data subject to regular quality review checks, leveraging third-party risk review experts?

By sourcing the right data at the right time, organizations can build robust, ethically sound, and legally compliant AI systems.

Model development and training

In this stage, the underlying mathematical model that will drive the AI system is selected, designed, and trained.

The model functions as the heart of the AI system, utilizing data to learn patterns and make predictions or decisions. However, architecting AI algorithms is a delicate balancing act. The developer must create a model that is reliable and accurate, but at the same time with the right level of explainability.

Selecting the appropriate model or algorithm for an AI system is not a one-size-fits-all process. It depends on the needs and context of each application.

One of the initial considerations when selecting an algorithm is the problem to be solved. For instance, if the task is to predict whether an email is spam or not, a classification model would be suitable, while for predicting sales forecasts based on historical data, a regression model is the better choice.

The quality and availability of data also influence the selection. Certain algorithms perform well with small datasets, while others require large datasets. Likewise, the format of data (numerical, categorical, text, or image data) can favor one algorithm over another.

Consideration should be given to the trade-off between model performance and interpretability. Complex, high-performing models like neural networks are often "black boxes," making it hard to interpret why a prediction was made. Simpler models like decision trees are more interpretable but may sacrifice performance. For many of the AI systems used to date, at least those of higher risk and impact, there has been a significant reliance on human oversight.

As agentic AI becomes more autonomous, humans will no longer be able to keep up with its speed and complexity. This will require investments in continuous monitoring controls that will add further complexity to an AI project.

Figure 4.4 shows the correlation between the growing autonomy of AI and the rising risks and a higher need for more sophisticated controls.

As AI systems become more complex, substantial resources are required for their training and maintenance – increased demands for computational power, extended training durations, and higher overall costs. These factors must be carefully considered by AI developers, as they can significantly impact the feasibility and sustainability of AI projects.

Given these factors, developers face the challenge of selecting the optimal algorithm, a process known as model selection or hyperparameter tuning. Developers often train multiple candidate models using the same dataset, validating each model's performance. This evaluation process involves careful comparisons and trade-offs between factors such as explainability, accuracy, and efficiency.

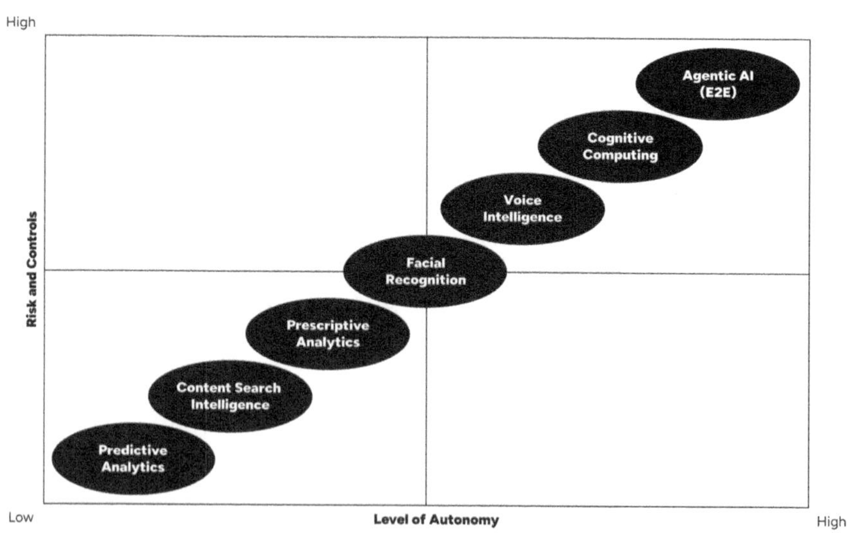

Figure 4.4 AI autonomy impact on risks and controls.

Ultimately, the best-performing model that aligns with the project's specific needs, constraints, and strategic objectives is chosen for further refinement and deployment.

During the training process, the chosen AI model explores the data, uncovering patterns and relationships. For example, it might learn that customers who buy a specific book often purchase other titles by the same author, or that users who buy laptops frequently also purchase laptop cases.

This learning occurs through an iterative process where the model makes predictions, measures the difference between its predictions and the actual outcomes, and adjusts its predictions based on these differences. For example, if the model mistakenly suggests mobile phone cases to a customer who just bought a computer mouse. As the AI system receives feedback on its performance, it adjusts its weights and features to provide better recommendations, ultimately enhancing the shopping experience for customers.

Below are a number of questions that should be considered when conducting model development and training of an AI system.

Model development and training – key quality control questions:

1 Have the appropriate AI model types been thoroughly evaluated for the identified problem and specific requirements?
2 Does the level of explainability of the model match the business need to interpret and defend the AI's decisions?
3 Are privacy requirements and bias mitigation considerations integrated into the model training?
4 What measures are applied to test and validate the model's performance, and are they inclusive of responsible AI requirements?

When responsible AI principles are deeply embedded into AI systems from inception, the AI implementations are more transparent, accountable, and reliable. They are also more robust by training the AI system against a wider spectrum of adversarial situations.

Model testing and validation

Model testing and validation are the last stage before the AI model is moved to production. It involves rigorous testing to identify and correct potential weaknesses. During the testing phase, the AI model is subjected to new, unseen data that was not part of the training data set to test its ability to generalize beyond the training data and predict how it will perform in real-world conditions. Model testing and validation should be conducted by a team that is highly qualified and independent from the AI development team.

Model testing involves more than just assessing the model's accuracy. It also evaluates non-functional aspects such as response time, processing speed, and resource allocation. Additionally, the testing process should examine performance metrics like accuracy and precision, alongside responsible AI considerations such as fairness, explainability, and bias. Adversarial testing is important to test a model's robustness against non-ideal or adversarial conditions and to detect potential weaknesses.

Another key task is to verify the model's compliance with legal, regulatory, and ethical guidelines. For instance, if your AI is intended for a healthcare application, it should conform to health data privacy regulations, like the *Health Insurance Portability and Accountability Act* in the United States.[3] If your model is handling personal data from EU citizens, it must follow the General Data Protection Regulation guidelines. In addition, the *EU AI Act*[4] specifies mandatory obligations for high-risk AI systems.

AI model testing and validation are iterative, recalibrating the model based on testing results. If the model's performance is noticeably worse on the test dataset, this indicates overfitting, where the model has learned the training data so well that it performs poorly when faced with new, unseen data. The solution might involve re-training the model with more diverse data, adjusting the model's complexity, or applying regularization techniques.

Similarly, if validation tests reveal biased behavior, the developer might reevaluate the training data for inherent biases or disparities. The model could be retrained using a more balanced and representative dataset or techniques applied to rectify these biases.

This iterative enhancement of the model training, testing, adjusting, and then retesting is a fundamental difference between AI development and traditional rules-based software development.

As organizations begin building agentic AI systems, the model testing and validation process will need to be further enhanced to ensure that the system is thoroughly tested before it is put into production. Some considerations include:

Model testing and validation – key quality control questions:

1 How does the model's performance on the validation dataset compare to the training dataset?
2 Are fairness and bias being evaluated and documented in model validation reports?
3 Are the model's outcomes explainable and transparent to non-technical stakeholders?
4 Is stress testing being performed under diverse and adversarial scenarios to evaluate the model's robustness?
5 Are robust model versioning controls in place to track and document model reviews, model research methods, validation practices, and testing outcomes?

Post-deployment monitoring

Work does not stop when the AI model has been deployed. Post-deployment monitoring offers insights into the performance and behavior of the AI system in the real world. As we move toward giving AI more autonomy, this becomes even more important.

Technical and behavioral monitoring are two essential elements of post-deployment monitoring. Technical monitoring focuses on traditional system performance like system uptime, response time, error rates, and resource utilization. It ensures the AI system is working with optimal efficiency, reliability, availability, and resilience. Unusual spikes in system load, unexpected drop in performance accuracy, high latency in response, or any other anomaly beyond predicted ranges could trigger an alert for further investigation.

Behavioral monitoring involves observing how the AI model behaves over time, including feedback on its decisions or recommendations. This includes detecting bias, non-compliance, and adversarial outcomes.

AI behavior often drifts over time due to changes in underlying data distributions or the environment, impacting the accuracy and reliability of predictions. This has resulted in the replacement of periodic audits or quality checks with continuous, real-time monitoring to detect performance drifts early.

Consider an AI system used by a gaming company to conduct age verification. Technical monitoring would focus on the model's accuracy and operational efficiency, while behavioral monitoring would provide insights into the reliability of the model's age predictions among different demographic segments.

Establishing user feedback channels can provide insights into how your AI system is experienced by its users. Whether this input comes from customer reviews, user surveys, or incident reports, all feedback can be useful to adjust and optimize your AI system and increase user adoption. It also demonstrates the duty of care in operational practices.

When designing a post-deployment monitoring program, these are helpful questions to evaluate its sufficiency:

Post-deployment monitoring – key quality control questions:

1 Is there a robust, real-time monitoring system in place to track the AI system's performance post-deployment?
2 Have threshold values for performance metrics been set to trigger alerts for potential issues or drifts?
3 Are alerts embedded into your incident management process to enable timely intervention by human operators?
4 Is stakeholder feedback used to continually improve the model and respond to changing user needs or societal norms?

It is important to remember that AI is not a "build-and-forget-it" technology. Developing an AI model involves continuous improvements and adaptations beyond its initial deployment. Whether it's changes in the operating environment, novel user needs, or evolving regulatory landscapes, your AI system will require continuous refinements and, at times, major overhauls, to remain flexible and responsive to its environment.

Retirement

The retirement stage, though often the least-discussed, is an important phase in the AI development lifecycle. It encompasses the different ways an AI system reaches its "end of life" and is decommissioned from active use.

While all technologies are eventually decommissioned, the unparalleled pace of AI development has significantly shortened its lifespan. The age of AI versions is often measured in months rather than years. Organizations need to adjust their ROI calculations to account for the additional costs associated with upgrading AI technologies or replacing older models with newer ones.

An AI system is retired due to various reasons. One typical scenario is when a new, more sophisticated technology emerges that outperforms the existing AI system in efficiency or capability, rendering the old system obsolete. Retirement could also be triggered by changes in organizational strategy or shifts in regulations. An AI system may also be retired if it no longer meets performance expectations due to changes in user behavior or market dynamics, or if maintaining it becomes uneconomical due to high costs or resource burdens.

Given the rapid lifecycle of AI investments, organizations are moving away from developing in-house capabilities due to the substantial investments required. Instead, they are partnering with third-party AI providers. By outsourcing AI development (e.g., AI as a service [AIaaS]), companies can tap into advanced capabilities without making hefty upfront investments. They can upscale or downscale usage based on their needs. Moreover, being able to access the latest AI offerings enables an organization to stay competitive without continually reinvesting in new capabilities.

For determining when an AI system has reached its end-of-life, these key questions need to be considered:

Retirement – key quality control questions:

1. What are the indicators that signal the need for an AI system's retirement or replacement?
2. What are the financial or operational implications of maintaining the existing AI system versus retiring it?
3. Are there established protocols for the safe decommissioning of AI systems, ensuring data privacy and compliance with regulations?

A thoughtful retirement strategy enables organizations to maintain a balance between innovation, investment conservation, and strategic alignment. Managing retirements can ensure that organizations remain agile, competitive, and ready for opportunities.

Relying on third-party AI vendors

Licensing AI systems from third-party vendors does not eliminate an organization's responsibility to maintain oversight over all aspects of the AI development lifecycle. Organizations must ensure that the AI solutions they choose align with their specific needs and that they maintain oversight throughout the process. They are still responsible for mitigating risks associated with transparency, data quality, compliance, and system performance.

Key considerations in the AI development lifecycle when using third-party vendors include:

- *Problem identification:* Clearly define the business or social problem to ensure alignment with the AI solution's capabilities.
- *Data quality:* Assess the quality, format, and representativeness of data used for training the AI model to ensure compatibility with organizational needs.
- *Transparency:* Address the "black box" issue by seeking vendors that provide insights into their AI algorithms and decision-making processes.
- *Validation:* Implement a verification process to evaluate vendor claims regarding the AI system's accuracy, performance, and adherence to ethical practices and regulations.
- *Post-deployment monitoring:* Establish monitoring mechanisms to track the AI system's performance and respond timely to issues.

Contracts with third-party vendors should establish clear expectations and responsibilities. Legal teams often face challenges in drafting iron-clad contracts that address data ownership, liability, and transparency. Essential terms that should be included in these contracts encompass data rights and usage, intellectual property ownership, performance metrics, and provisions for transparency and accountability in AI decision-making processes. Additionally, clauses addressing dispute resolution, audit rights, and compliance with relevant regulations are vital to mitigate risks and ensure that both parties are aligned in their commitments.

While third-party AI solutions can accelerate adoption, organizations must actively engage in the AI development lifecycle to ensure responsible and effective use of their AI systems.

Conclusion

Embedding responsible AI principles into each stage of the AI development lifecycle is an important and complex task. It is a journey and not a one-time effort, requiring investments into governance and controls that keep pace with AI technology advances. The strategies that organizations employ to incorporate responsible AI into their AI lifecycle will vary depending on their AI strategy and maturity. Different organizations are at different points on this journey. While some are novices, introducing their first AI projects, others are veterans with multiple AI deployments under their belt.

The decision to invest in building AI capabilities in-house, partner with third-party providers, or adopt a hybrid approach depends on the organization's resources, strategic objectives, and risk appetite.

In the next chapter, we offer insights into where and how organizations can make strategic investments to create a robust AI ecosystem.

Key leadership questions to consider:

1. How is your organization aligning the AI development lifecycle with your strategic goals and ethical requirements?
2. Is there a balanced investment in both AI functionalities and the maturation of the AI development lifecycle?
3. How are responsible AI considerations being integrated into each stage of your AI development lifecycle?
4. How do you ensure third-party vendors deliver AI systems that meet your organization's corporate policies and regulatory requirements?

Notes

1. Dr. Martin Luther King Life. (n.d.). *Wiki encyclopedia*. Retrieved June 8, 2025, from https://en.wikipedia.org/wiki/Martin_Luther_King_Jr.
2. Gordon, C. (2025), *SalesChoice Inc - AI Use Case Classification framework*, with permission from Dr. Cindy Gordon, CEO Founder, SalesChoice Inc.
3. Health Insurance Portability and Accountability Act of 1996 (HIPAA). (n.d.). Center for Health Insurance. Retrieved February 11, 2025, from https://www.cdc.gov/phlp/publications/topic/hipaa.html.
4. The EU Artificial Intelligence Act. (2024, July). EU Commission. Retrieved February 11, 2025, from https://artificialintelligenceact.eu/the-act/.

Chapter 5

AI is more than just models

To view artificial intelligence (AI) as merely a handful of advanced statistical models acting independently would be a significant oversight. AI involves more than just training the models; it requires an entire ecosystem of interconnected components, working harmoniously. At VivaTech Paris in June 2025, NVIDIA CEO Jensen Huang stressed the need for advanced infrastructure to power AI. He recommended that every country needs a national intelligence infrastructure. He also supported layered AI governance by design. "In the future," he said, "the AI that is doing the task is going to be surrounded by 70 or 80 other AIs that are supervising it, observing it, guarding it, ensuring that it doesn't go off the rails."[1]

Let's break down what is needed to operate AI. To start with, an AI system requires data, lots of data, to train and fuel its operation. This data collection is facilitated by a variety of equipment, including weather sensors, cameras, content scrapers, and biometric scanners, all designed to record and collect relevant information. But raw data is often untamable and unwieldy. Data preprocessing is an often under-appreciated but critical step that cleanses and shapes the data, making it ready for future stages.

Once the data is ready, it intersects with computer infrastructure, including powerful computer processing units and cloud computing. Supercomputers and quantum computers, with their enormous processing power, provide the ability to achieve previously unattainable speeds for decision-making and data processing.

And let's not forget the data centers required to house and power these high-speed computers. The exponential increase in data storage, transmission, and processing will put significant pressure on existing and still-to-be-built infrastructure. Network grids will also

DOI: 10.4324/9781003625520-6

be strained as we create new connectivity meshes with Internet of Things (IoT) sensors, satellites, mobile and edge devices, advanced robotics, and nanites.

This chapter demonstrates that AI is not just about models. It requires the integration of many interoperable components, ranging from data to high-speed computer processes, to operate.

Objectives

Upon completing this chapter, you will be able to:

- Understand the various technical components involved in operating AI models
- Appreciate the core AI infrastructure, including Application Programming Interfaces (APIs), cloud computing, and data storage
- Understand the importance of network connectivity in efficient AI operations
- Gain perspective on future data processing trends, including developments in edge computing, supercomputers, and quantum computing.

Infrastructure needed to operate AI

Operating an AI model, even the most simplistic one, requires a combination of software, hardware, and infrastructure components that create an optimal environment for AI models to deliver results.

Sensors, cameras, and content scrapers

The data recording and collection phase often involves the use of various input methods, ranging from sensors and cameras to content scrapers. Sensors and cameras capture everything from facial details, fingerprints, motion, and temperature. These devices offer a versatile means to gather data. For example, cameras set up in public spaces capture facial features for facial recognition systems and track individual movements for analyzing crowd behavior. An example can be found in Smart Cities, where street cameras gather data on traffic and pedestrian patterns to optimize traffic light timings.

Sensors, owing to their versatility, collect massive amounts of data. They are referred to collectively as IoT and can be found in all aspects of daily life. Temperature sensors in a smart thermostat record temperature data to ensure optimal heating. Fitness trackers monitor users' heart rate, sleep patterns, step counts, and other relevant health data. On a more industrial scale, sensors in factories monitor machine health, alerting to any sudden temperature spikes or vibration frequency disruptions that might indicate a potential breakdown.

Content scrapers crawl the internet, pulling down vast amounts of information. Take, for example, a tech company that wants to understand public sentiment about their new product launch. Content scrapers can crawl the internet to collect comments and reviews about the product from social media or online forums. In e-commerce, content scrapers comb competitor websites to collect data on product prices, reviews, and specifications.

Early in the design phase of an AI system, a multitude of decisions need to be made about data. In addition to what data to use and how to get it, decisions need to be made about whether to operate with real-time data streams or to pull information from large data stores. Real-time connections are ideal for immediate responses, like automatic driving systems or market trading machines, but require low network latency.

Data preprocessing is a critical step in preparing raw data for AI and machine learning (ML), requiring a combination of hardware, software, and infrastructure. On the hardware side, sufficient computing power is essential, along with adequate memory (RAM) to handle large datasets efficiently. Storage solutions are necessary for data retention, while networking capabilities ensure quick access to cloud-based resources and centralized data storage.

In terms of software, tools for data cleaning help in refining messy datasets, while database management systems provide structured and unstructured data storage solutions.

Hardware

The operation of efficient AI models necessitates robust hardware infrastructure. At a foundational level, your personal computer or laptop can kick-start the journey. They contain the essential central processing unit (CPU) that processes the incoming data and carries out the algorithmic operations required for basic AI functions.

However, as your AI model takes on more complexity and the volume of data increases, your humble PC will be outgunned. This is due to the heavy computational requirements of advanced AI models, which rapidly outpace the capabilities of standard CPUs.

This necessitates cloud computing services, a formidable powerhouse in data handling. They provide an array of high-performance CPUs and even GPUs located off-site. These units carry out computations that are considerably more complex and data-intensive than a standard PC can handle.

GPUs, originally designed for rendering high-definition images in gaming, have been repurposed in AI for their ability to carry out hundreds of computations simultaneously. This is especially useful in data-rich environments such as ML and neural network processing.

Cloud computing also boosts scalability. As your models expand, cloud services offer increased computational power almost instantly, enabling seamless growth. Additionally, cloud services offer AI tools and libraries that facilitate the development and deployment of models. Meanwhile, data storage servers host the data that AI models will learn from and adapt to.

The selection of hardware in AI operations is not just about performance; it carries both sustainability and ethical considerations. AI's carbon footprint is a growing concern. High-processing servers, cloud platforms, and the computing equipment used for AI applications are energy-intensive. Making hardware selections that balance operational requirements with energy efficiency can achieve a dual benefit of reducing costs and demands on constrained resources.

Technologies like energy-efficient processors, low-power memory chips, and advanced cooling technologies can help reduce an AI system's carbon footprint. For data centers, renewable energy sources, water usage modeling, and efficient cooling systems can also contribute to sustainable operations.

Organizations' dependency on third-party cloud service providers raises issues about system risk, particularly in the context of AI applications. When businesses rely on external cloud services for data storage, processing, and ML model deployment, they become vulnerable to various risks, including data breaches, service outages, and compliance challenges. The security of sensitive data, especially when it involves personally identifiable information or proprietary algorithms, can be compromised if the cloud provider does not implement robust security measures.

Moreover, the reliance on third-party services can lead to concerns about data sovereignty and regulatory compliance, as data may be stored in jurisdictions with different legal frameworks. This can complicate adherence to regulations such as the General Data Protection Regulation or the Health Insurance Portability and Accountability Act, which impose strict guidelines on data handling and privacy. Additionally, organizations may face vendor lock-in, making it difficult to switch providers or migrate data and applications if the need arises, potentially stifling innovation and flexibility.

The performance and reliability of AI systems can be affected by the cloud provider's infrastructure and service quality. Any downtime or latency issues experienced by the cloud service can directly impact the availability and responsiveness of AI applications, leading to disruptions in business operations. As a result, organizations must carefully evaluate their cloud service providers, considering factors such as security protocols, compliance certifications, and service level agreements to mitigate these risks and ensure the integrity and performance of their AI initiatives.

Software

Software coding for AI vastly differs from traditional technologies. In AI programming, the sequence of decisions it makes is not predetermined but emerges from patterns identified in the data. Designing AI systems involves deciding whether to utilize open source software, license from third parties, or develop in-house. Open source solutions offer community-proven resources, often free and adaptable. But they can contain adversarial code that could compromise AI operation, security, or functionality. They also may have copyright restrictions related to derivative use and attribution.

Third-party licensing, while generally reliable and professionally managed, introduces several challenges for organizations, including dependencies on external vendors that can disrupt operations if issues arise. It often entails higher costs due to ongoing subscription fees and potential hidden expenses. Additionally, using third-party services raises significant concerns about data privacy and security, as organizations must share sensitive information with these providers. This necessitates thorough due diligence to ensure that vendors comply with stringent data protection standards and regulations.

Contracts with third-party vendors often need to carefully outline each party's obligations, particularly around accountability for faults and failures. However, these arrangements can be complicated by the "black-box" nature of AI systems, where the rationale behind AI's decisions is often obscured due to the complexity of the algorithms.

In-house development offers organizations the highest level of control over AI, allowing for tailored solutions that align with specific operational needs and strategic goals. This customization enables businesses to prioritize features and implement changes swiftly. However, this approach is resource-intensive, requiring significant investments in time and money for hiring skilled developers, designers, and project managers, as well as for ongoing maintenance.

Additionally, the complexity of software development necessitates a high skill level among team members, which may require organizations to invest in training. Many organizations are challenged in attracting and retaining top talent. Consequently, while in-house development provides substantial benefits, it can be a daunting undertaking, particularly for smaller organizations or those with limited technical expertise.

A new area of experimentation is the use of AI to code itself. However, an emerging concern is that granting AI this ability could lead to systems that change their objective and decision parameters, deviating from their designers' intentions and causing unintended consequences. Some view it as the beginning of "Rogue AI."

Mustafa Suleyman, co-founder of DeepMind Technologies and co-author of the book *The Coming Wave*,[2] devised three rules that we should follow until we have the appropriate safeguards over AI:

1 Don't put it on the internet.
2 Don't teach them to code.
3 Don't have agents working with them.

Unfortunately, each of the above rules has already been broken. Breaking down each of Suleyman's rules brings important considerations on how we approach AI.

The first rule advises against putting AI systems on the internet. While the internet is a treasure trove of information, it remains a Pandora's box, replete with manipulative content, bad behavior, misinformation, and potential security threats. Allowing AI unfettered access to the internet exposes the model to harmful influences that could skew its learning, propagate bias, or potentially make it a tool for nefarious intent. Cybersecurity threats further compound this risk, where AI could become a target, or worse, a vehicle for cyberattacks. As such, protecting AI from the wide-open internet is a critical part of responsible AI management.

Suleyman's second rule, cautioning against teaching AI to code, speaks to a simultaneously fascinating and concerning possibility: AI systems programming themselves, or even generating AI "offspring." With this capability, an AI system can bypass the limitations of human programming speeds and potentially open up vast realms of innovation. However, this power also brings significant risks.

In the process of AI creating AI, or "self-coding," we could see a seismic shift in control. The original objectives set forth by human developers may mutate or diverge entirely by modified AI or AI "children" with goals determined by their AI "parent."

Furthermore, self-programming AI could unintentionally expose itself to security vulnerabilities, opening up the system to unanticipated threats or exploitation. Similarly, AI children could inherit vulnerabilities compounded over reproductions. To combat these risks, human oversight becomes even more crucial. However, how can we guardrail AI systems that can access and process information far faster than humans? Suleyman's point is that we should not give AI the "keys to the kingdom" until we have robust safeguards in place. As already stated, we may need to rely on AI to oversee AI. But can we trust the overseer AI any better than the AI being supervised?

Suleyman's third rule argues against having external agents work with AI. The term "agent" here refers to any external factor or entity capable of influencing the AI system's behavior and taking action. By maintaining AI's isolation from such agents, we can safeguard the AI's integrity and avoid it being manipulated in ways that could derail its functioning or ethical stance from what it was originally taught. Tight control over the interfaces that allow external inputs into the AI system can help ensure that influences that might lead the AI astray are minimized.

The integration of cognition-based AI and advanced robotics presents significant advancements in automation, extending the capabilities of autonomous vehicles to a new generation of robots that can navigate complex physical environments for both domestic and commercial uses. However, this progress raises critical concerns regarding the risks associated with granting AI agency. The potential for these systems to act independently poses serious questions about safety, accountability, and the ethical implications.

Interfaces

APIs serve as bridges or connectors, providing a structured way for different software components to interact and work together. APIs facilitate efficient data access, enabling AI models to pull the necessary data from various sources for learning, training, and decision-making. Whether it's ingesting the latest market data, consumer preferences, or live-traffic updates, APIs serve as the delivery system that transports data to the AI model.

Beyond data access, APIs are integral to integrating AI capabilities into existing workflows and applications. ML APIs, for example, allow applications to leverage services like natural language processing, automatic speech recognition, or image analysis without needing to develop these capabilities from scratch.

Additionally, APIs enable AI systems' scalability and modularity. As an AI system grows or evolves, APIs allow different components to be added, updated, or removed without significant disruption or rework. The modular design facilitated by APIs is key to creating AI systems that can keep pace with evolving business requirements and technology advancements.

Agentic AI represents a significant shift in the way APIs are utilized compared to historical AI systems. Unlike traditional AI, which often relied on structured data and predefined algorithms, agentic AI requires APIs to interact dynamically with a wide array of unstructured external data sources. Furthermore, while historical AI typically operated within closed systems with limited external interactions, agentic AI thrives on the ability to connect and interact with a wide array of legacy technologies. It can also process diverse information streams, enhancing its contextual understanding and responsiveness. This evolution necessitates even more sophisticated API frameworks.

Output

The "output" of an AI model is its predictions, decisions, and actions. The form of these outputs varies depending on the task and context of use. For instance, in predictive analytics, the output might be a likelihood score or a prediction about a future event. In an autonomous vehicle AI, the output could be a series of control signals that determine the vehicle's movements. For a natural language processing AI, the output could be generated text, like the response from a chatbot or a translated paragraph. In an image recognition AI, the output might be the identification and labeling of objects within an image.

However, the AI's output isn't simply about generating the final result. It also includes the way the data is presented, interpreted, and used. Presenting outputs in a clear, understandable manner can help human users interpret and act upon the AI's output effectively.

Accompanying AI outputs with information about their reliability is crucial for fostering user trust and understanding. This includes providing confidence scores, precision levels, challenges encountered during processing, sources of information, and the methodologies employed in generating results.

Recent advancements in large language models have focused on enhancing transparency, allowing users to grasp the reasoning behind AI-generated outputs more clearly. By openly communicating the probabilistic nature of these outputs and the inherent uncertainties involved, users can make more informed decisions based on the AI's findings. This transparency not only helps users assess the reliability of the information but also empowers them to understand the limitations and context of the AI's conclusions, ultimately leading to more responsible and effective use of AI technologies.

The output mechanism of an AI model serves both functional and communicative roles, providing not only the results of AI processes but also enhancing user understanding, trust, and interaction with the AI system. Ensuring the outputs are clear, transparent, and reliable is key to establishing a responsible AI operation. AI developers are also enhancing interpretability and explainability by being more transparent in how AI operates. This is most advanced in GenAI, where current models can be readily interrogated to understand the knowledge bases, sources, and processes it leverages to generate their content. Many GenAI models now show their Chain of Thought as they reason through how to respond to a prompt. While skeptics may challenge the veracity of the GenAI responses, much of the information can be verified by a diligent user.

What does the future hold?

Advancements in AI capabilities have gone hand in hand with advancements in computer processing. As AI models become more sophisticated, they demand higher levels of computational power to process vast amounts of data, execute complex algorithms, and deliver swift, precise results. Traditional CPUs and semiconductor chips, while having had exponential leaps in capacity and speed, are increasingly battling limitations. This is where advanced computing technologies will come into play.

Supercomputers

The massive processing power of supercomputers allows for efficient execution of complex computations that would be too slow or impossible on traditional computers.

A single supercomputer can be thousands, even millions of times faster than a standard personal computer. They achieve this feat through parallel processing, which involves dividing complex problems into smaller parts and processing them simultaneously. Imagine hosting a banquet: a supercomputer is akin to a well-coordinated team of chefs working together, each tackling a different dish or dish component concurrently, while an ordinary computer is a single cook creating each dish one step at a time.

The architecture of supercomputers differs significantly from that of traditional computers. They typically incorporate millions of cores (processing units) to carry out tasks in parallel. A high-performing traditional computer, by comparison, might just have a handful of cores.

While traditional computers are intended for a wide range of general-purpose tasks from word processing and internet browsing to running business software, supercomputers are deployed for specific, highly complex tasks that involve many variables and require vast computing power. These include weather forecasting, climate research, molecular modeling, simulations, and large-scale data analysis.

Although supercomputers eclipse regular computers in terms of raw performance, that performance comes at a price. They are significantly larger, more power-hungry, and vastly more expensive. Also, the programming and operation of supercomputers require a higher degree of technical expertise.

For simple, less data-intensive AI tasks, traditional computers can suffice. They provide adequate processing power while keeping costs, energy consumption, and space requirements to a minimum. However, as the complexity of the AI task expands, demanding greater computational abilities, the balance tips toward supercomputers. High-end AI projects, like large-scale data analyses, intricate ML models, or complex simulations, require the colossal processing capabilities of supercomputers to accomplish their goals.

Ultimately, the successful application of AI requires careful matching of processing requirements to the processors employed. As we move forward, it is likely that a hybrid approach will emerge with processing conducted by supercomputers and traditional computers working in tandem.

Quantum computers

Quantum computers represent an entirely new paradigm of computing, offering capabilities far beyond what traditional computing and even supercomputing can offer. The quantum computing market is projected to grow significantly in the coming years. Estimates vary, with the quantum market expected to reach a value of $10.4 billion by 2025 and exceed $36 billion by 2040.[3] The primary difference of quantum computing lies in how it processes information. Traditional computers and supercomputers process information in binary form, known as bits, which can be either a 0 or a 1. This binary mode of thinking directly impacts their computational potential – they can only handle one calculation at a time, albeit extremely fast.

Quantum computers, however, bring into play quantum bits or "qubits." Leaning on principles of quantum mechanics, qubits can exist in a state that is both 0 and 1 simultaneously. This "superposition" enables quantum computers to process a vast number of potential outcomes at the same time. Essentially, while a traditional computer reads a book one word at a time, a quantum computer could read all the words at once.

Furthermore, qubits can also be entangled, another quantum mechanical property, meaning the state of one qubit can be dependent on the state of another, no matter the distance between them. This "entanglement" leads to an exponential increase in processing power with every additional qubit.

In the field of AI, this quantum leap could lead to radical improvements in speed and complexity of computations, enabling AI models to solve complex problems and make predictions with unprecedented accuracy and efficiency.

Currently, quantum computing is in its infancy and faces significant technical challenges. Maintaining qubits in a state of superposition is difficult and currently requires extremely low temperatures. Engaging with quantum computers also demands a whole new approach to programming. Despite these challenges, the potential of quantum computing is undeniable. As advancements are made, we may see quantum computers unlock new possibilities in AI, solving problems that were previously considered intractable and driving the field to new heights.[4]

Edge computing

Edge computing has been gaining momentum as a critical strategy in AI deployment, particularly in managing the vast network of IoT devices that generate copious amounts of data.

By placing the computational elements at the edge of the network, near or on the IoT devices themselves, edge computing allows data processing to happen where it's being generated. This proximity lends itself well to AI's data-thirsty nature. Low latency, or the time taken for data to travel from its source to the point of use, is one of the key advantages of edge computing, allowing for near real-time analysis. In scenarios where instant processing is crucial, such as autonomous driving or medical wearables, edge computing will become more critical.

Alongside reduced latency, edge computing reduces bandwidth usage. Instead of sending all raw data back to a central server or a cloud for processing, only essential, processed information is transmitted. This reduction in data traffic can lead to significant savings in bandwidth and associated costs.

Another advantage is the potential enhancement in privacy and security. By processing data on-site, edge computing diminishes the need to transmit data over networks, reducing the exposure to potential breaches or interference. This is particularly beneficial where sensitive data is involved, such as in healthcare or personal smart devices.

However, the adoption of edge computing in AI is still in its early stages. Challenges include managing the distribution of computational resources, handling the complexity of deploying and maintaining AI models on edge devices, and ensuring they seamlessly work with central systems. Also, edge devices often have significant constraints regarding processing power and storage capacity compared to cloud servers or in-house data centers.

Given these challenges, continued technological advancements, including the introduction of more powerful edge devices and improved AI algorithms better suited to edge computing, are needed for this trend to reach its full potential. However, the potential benefits of edge computing make it a promising prospect in the journey toward a scalable, efficient, and privacy-focused AI future.

Organic transistors and data storage

As we venture into the realm of what may seem like science fiction, ongoing research points to exciting potential developments in computer hardware that depart from silicon-based technologies. The impetus for such exploration emerges from the ongoing quest to scale AI capabilities, while balancing questions of sustainability, efficiency, and capacity. Currently, most of the computer hardware, whether it be a personal laptop or a powerful supercomputer, operates using silicon-based transistors. They form the building blocks of electronic devices, controlling the flow of electricity in circuits and serving as the fundamental units for processing data. However, as we continue to push the boundaries of AI, we are encountering the physical and functional limits of silicon.

One future path evolves from how nature computes – with organic elements. Active research efforts are exploring organic or plastic transistors or chips, which use carbon-based organic materials instead of silicon. These organic alternatives could potentially provide more sustainable and biodegradable options than their silicon counterparts, reducing the environmental impact of producing and discarding hardware.[5]

In terms of data storage, organic memory devices are another area of exciting potential. The architecture of organic memory devices leads to a high storage density, which could substantially outperform conventional memory devices regarding capacity and scalability.[6]

However promising, these organic-based technologies are in the early stages of development, and challenges remain in material stability, manufacturing processes, and compatibility with existing technologies before organic transistors are powering AI.

Nanobots

Nanobots, minuscule robots that are programmed to perform specific tasks, could play an interesting role in AI. While still in heavy research, they have potential uses in environmental sensing, targeted drug delivery, and even complex manufacturing, potentially providing a link from the digital world of AI to direct, physical-world impacts.[7]

With their minuscule size and precision maneuverability, nanobots could access environments within human bodies, machines, or natural ecosystems that are currently beyond our reach. AI could play a critical role in navigating these complex environments, making sense of the data gathered, and driving decision-making processes onboard these microscopic robots.

The development of AI is intertwined with the evolution of computational technologies. While we are pressing the boundaries of current computing abilities, innovations like nanobots promise an exciting future for AI's advancement, while introducing new challenges.

Advanced robotics

The field of advanced robotics has witnessed remarkable advancements, driven by innovations in AI, ML, and sensor technology. One of the most significant developments is the integration of AI algorithms that enable robots to learn from their environments and adapt their behaviors accordingly. This capability allows for more autonomous operations in various sectors, such as manufacturing, healthcare, and logistics. For instance, collaborative robots, or cobots, are increasingly being used on factory floors to work alongside human workers, enhancing productivity and safety. In healthcare, robotic surgical systems equipped with AI can assist surgeons with precision and efficiency, leading to improved patient outcomes. Countries like Japan are actively using cobots to support the elderly as companions, and co-bot nurses are serving meals and delivering patients' medications.

Despite these advancements, several challenges remain in the integration of advanced robotics and AI. One major hurdle is the need for robust safety protocols, especially in environments where humans and robots interact closely. Ensuring that robots can make safe decisions in real-time, particularly in unpredictable situations, is critical. Additionally, the ethical implications of deploying AI-driven robots must be considered, including concerns about job displacement and the potential for biased decision-making. Developing transparent AI systems that can explain their actions and decisions will be essential in building trust among users and stakeholders. The scalability of advanced robotics solutions poses another challenge.

While many companies have successfully implemented robotic systems, scaling these solutions across different industries and applications requires significant investment and customization. The interoperability of various robotic systems and AI technologies is crucial for creating a cohesive ecosystem that can be easily adopted by businesses.

Conclusion

The journey into AI is more than just about the models and algorithms. In embracing the transformative potential of AI, one must bring many technical components together. The foundational cornerstone of AI lies in its input data, collected from a variety of sources such as sensors, cameras, and internet scrapers. But raw data alone is not enough. Stringent data processing steps are vital for cleansing and prepping the data, ensuring AI models can interpret and learn from it effectively.

Technological infrastructure is crucial. Powerful processing hardware, ranging from personal computers and laptops to the more robust cloud servers, delivers the necessary horsepower for AI to function. Supercomputers and quantum computers, though in their nascent stages, promise unprecedented leaps in computational power.

However, AI would not be possible without sophisticated software. It brings data and hardware together, encoding the instructions that guide AI models. The decision between using open-source, third-party licensed, or in-house developed software influences not only how the AI functions, but also limitations on its use, cost, and need for highly skilled in-house talent.

While we continue to unlock new frontiers in AI, from edge computing to AI-powered nanobots, a parallel emphasis is needed on understanding and addressing the responsible AI considerations. Privacy, security, transparency, accountability, and sustainability stand central to any discussion on AI, influencing decisions on data handling, computational hardware, software, and network integrations.

Key leadership questions to consider:

1 Have you built into your AI design all the different components it will need to operate?
2 Is your AI infrastructure future-proof in that it can interoperate with new IoT devices, data sources, and computer processors as they emerge?
3 What factors are key in deciding between open-source, third-party, or in-house solutions for your AI applications?
4 How are you leveraging technological advances, and what is the roadmap to get there from your current infrastructure?

Notes

1 Adamson, T., & Chan, K. (2025, June 11). NVIDIA chief calls AI the 'great equalizer'—But warns Europe risks falling behind. *Associated Press*. Retrieved June 11, 2025, from https://apnews.com/article/nvidia-france-artificial-intelligence-1a6b50633db24c22b584597142a564ac.
2 Suleyman, M., & Bhaskar, M. (2023). *The coming wave: Technology, power and the twenty-first century's greatest dilemma*. New York: Crown Publishing, Division of Random House.
3 *The rise of quantum computing*. (2024, April). McKinsey & Company. https://www.mckinsey.com/featured-insights/the-rise-of-quantum-computing.
4 Kaku, M. (2023). *Quantum supremacy*. New York: Doubleday.
5 Ham, B. (2020, June 1). Carbon nanotube transistors make the leap from lab to factory floor. *MIT News*. Retrieved June 8, 2025, from https://news.mit.edu/2020/carbon-nanotube-transistors-factory-0601.
6 Amin, R., Belharouak, I., & Kumar, P. (2020, December 4). *Carbon nanotubes: Applications to energy storage devices*. InTechOpen. Retrieved June 8, 2025, from https://www.intechopen.com/books/9913.
7 Applications of AI and nanobots in modern medical treatments. *VeerOne*. Retrieved June 15, 2025, from https://veerone.com/searches/applications-ai-nanobots-modern-medical-treatments-KyD4D6m.

Chapter 6

Battling AI breaches and adversarial attacks

In this chapter, we focus on the importance of tackling security issues associated with artificial intelligence (AI). As AI moves from internal use to impacting external stakeholders, the risks of attack increase significantly. When building a responsible AI program, understanding and mitigating security risks prevents financial losses and data breaches and preserves stakeholder trust. Bill Gates aptly put in perspective the risks of AI when he said:

> Humans should be worried about the threat posed by artificial intelligence. The internet will disappear. There will be so many IP addresses, so many devices, sensors, things that you are wearing, things that you are interacting with, that you won't even sense it.[1]

Each new device and sensor increases the threat vector of a cyber attack. AI can be threatened through adversarial attacks, cybersecurity vulnerabilities, privacy breaches, and manipulative technologies such as deepfakes. Adversarial attacks refer to techniques used to deceive AI models by introducing subtle alterations to the input data, causing the model to make incorrect predictions or classifications. An adversarial attack might involve manipulating a voice recognition system by adding background noise that causes it to misinterpret commands.

The exponential increase in digital data has triggered new cyber vulnerabilities. Billions of bytes of personal data, which forms the training bed for many AI models, can be exploited if it falls into the wrong hands. Deepfakes involve deceptive manipulation of audio, video, and photo content that can tarnish reputations, influence public opinion, and even lead to national security threats.

DOI: 10.4324/9781003625520-7

Deepak Gupta, a cybersecurity journalist, described AI's impact on cybersecurity and digital identity as a seismic shift after attending the 2025 RSA Conference. He noted that 40% of the sessions focused on the tension between AI opportunity and risk.

Some key learnings from the conference were:

- A warning that AI agents introduce "a whole new class of risks that we've never seen before."
- A call-out that machine-to-machine communications now outnumber human digital interactions, making the traditional identity perimeter obsolete.
- Claims that "AI-generated deepfakes have made biometric identifiers like voice recognition useless."[2]

Addressing these potential threats is far from simple. Traditional cybersecurity measures, though necessary, are not sufficient. In a world dominated by AI technologies, new vulnerabilities need to be countered with equally advanced defense mechanisms. New passwordless authentication innovations that leverage sensor tracking of location and behavior may offer an alternative approach.[3]

Conference participants universally agreed that AI is undoubtedly part of the solution. It can understand patterns in data, detect anomalies, and learn from past cybersecurity incidents. No human analyst can process data at the speed of AI, making AI ideally suited to predict and prevent cyber-attacks in real-time.

Moreover, AI can be instrumental in developing automated security systems that can adapt and evolve. These systems learn from each attack, constantly updating their defense mechanisms to counter new threats.

In this chapter, we explore AI's security vulnerabilities and provide key insights on how to secure AI systems.

Objectives

Upon completing this chapter, you will be able to:

- Describe AI security, including adversarial attacks, cybersecurity vulnerabilities, and privacy risks
- Explore the implications and threats of deepfake technology
- Evaluate the potential of AI in bolstering cyber defense.

Responding to adversarial attacks

Adversarial attacks are subtle, carefully crafted modifications to input data designed to mislead AI systems. In essence, adversarial attacks are inputs to AI models that an attacker has intentionally designed to cause a model to make a mistake.

Adversarial attacks can lead to severe consequences, especially when safety-critical systems are compromised. For example, a speed limit sign could be distorted with numbers camouflaged to mimic natural elements like tree branches or shadows. Even the characteristic red octagon stop sign may be artistically concealed with an adjacent mural or graffiti.

A research team led by Ivan Etivmov at the University of Washington found that with subtle changes, undetectable to the human eye, an AI system would "see" a stop sign as a 45 mph speed limit sign.[4] Although this study was first published in 2017, a subsequent study by Boltachev (2023) found that autonomous vehicle AI image algorithms are still susceptible to the same attack.[5] This type of image manipulation has been detected in online product images, where added noise or colors cause image recognition algorithms to misclassify products. These types of attacks can erode brand reputation, customer trust, and overall sales performance.

Guarding against AI adversarial attacks requires similar approaches as deployed for cybersecurity – regular monitoring, active threat detection, and timely update of safeguard mechanisms – with some additional controls specifically designed for AI.

Here are a few ways to respond to adversarial attacks on AI systems:

1 *Data augmentation:* One of the simplest ways to defend against these attacks is by "training" the AI on this trickery early on. This means including examples of altered data in the training set so the AI learns to recognize and ignore them.
2 *Adversarial training:* This is a specific type of data augmentation where the AI is explicitly trained to resist adversarial attacks. It is like giving the AI a "self-defense" course to prepare against common trickery. Adversarial AI agents, which simulate adversarial attacks, assist in this training.
3 *Defensive distillation*: With this technique, the AI model is trained to be "smoother" in its decisions, meaning it is less likely to be

tricked by small, crafty changes. It is akin to the AI being more careful and not jumping to conclusions when they spot something unusual.

4 *Using detection models*: These are specialized AI models that are trained to detect adversarial attacks. They work like "burglar alarms," alerting you when an attempt to fool the AI is detected.

Remember, while these strategies can be helpful, no defense is perfect, and it's important to keep updating and adapting your defense mechanisms as attackers come up with new tricks.

AI creating new cybersecurity vulnerabilities

Apart from the adversarial attacks already discussed, AI's high reliance on data to train and operate introduces additional vulnerabilities. AI systems often require personal user data to function effectively. For example, a voice assistant has recordings of your voice and conversations, which can cause a potential privacy breach if not secured effectively. To handle these vulnerabilities, companies are implementing enhanced encryption, data anonymization, and pseudonymization practices to protect sensitive user information.

Another significant concern in AI systems is the risk of data poisoning. Here, the adversary manipulates data, leading the model to learn incorrect behaviors. This vulnerability can be exploited during both training and deployment, particularly with adaptive AI that keeps learning from new data.

Chatbots introduced over the last decade have been prime targets of "trolls" who attack the chatbots with targeted questions and prompts designed to manipulate their behavior and language, or trick it into performing functions it was not designed to do. These incidents have led to the proliferation of ethical filters and guidelines to ensure AI behavior stays within acceptable boundaries; however, hackers are continually creating new data poisoning strategies. And new cyber threats are popping up every month. Cybersecurity firms have recently drawn attention to embedded code in LLMs that redirect users to fictitious websites to steal data or upload malware.[6]

A third cybersecurity risk is AI model stealing, by which a threat actor makes an almost identical copy of an AI model without having direct access to the original machine learning (ML) model or its training data. The attacker continually inputs data and records the AI's responses, essentially reverse-engineering the underlying model's features and weights. This is akin to someone determining the ingredients of a secret recipe just by tasting a replica dish against the original, repeatedly.

The repercussions of model stealing are multifold. First, it equates to intellectual property theft affecting the return on investment of the original model. Second, once the attacker has a working imitation of the model, they can replicate it in an unregulated environment, modify its internal workings for nefarious purposes, or use it to devise attacks on the original model.

To counter such vulnerabilities, techniques like differential privacy (adding noise to the AI's responses to make reverse-engineering harder) and "model hardening" (modifying the model to be less susceptible to this type of attack) are being developed. Data monitoring should also be conducted to identify unusual query patterns that might suggest a model theft attempt.

It's vital to develop AI systems with security in mind from the outset, including secure coding practices and robust testing for potential vulnerabilities. Regular security audits, firewall protection, and using virtual private networks can help in minimizing these risks.

In essence, while AI brings vast opportunities for innovation and efficiency, it must be coupled with rigorous security practices to prevent the misuse and breach of information.

Balancing AI functionality with privacy

While AI offers transformative potential, it also creates privacy risks. AI systems rely significantly on the availability of extensive, relevant data to train upon and function effectively. This "big data" approach, while integral to operating high-performing algorithms, can sometimes threaten privacy.

Seemingly innocent actions we perform daily – such as making an online purchase, tracking our exercise using a fitness app, or interacting with a digital assistant – generate a wealth of data. Combined and analyzed, these separate pieces of data can offer a detailed snapshot of our lives, allowing for personalized recommendations tailored to our particular interests and circumstances. And yet, there is a trade-off as AI can uncover behaviors and preferences we'd prefer remain secret.

This invariably raises concerns around surveillance and profiling. For instance, an AI system could use your online shopping habits, social media behavior, and even your commute patterns from a map app to predict lifestyle habits, political leanings, health conditions, or financial status. Over time, with enough data, AI can create an extremely detailed profile of each of us, opening doors for privacy breaches.

There is growing concern that such profiling could lead to "surveillance capitalism," a term first coined by Harvard Professor Shoshana Zuboff, which refers to the monetizing of data captured through surveillance. It is essentially the idea of making money from digital surveillance by providing predictive insights about user behavior,[7] possibly leading to intrusive marketing practices or unjust discriminatory actions.

This capability goes beyond just accumulating and analyzing data points; it involves making precise and often startlingly accurate deductions about an individual. This is distinct from traditional profiling or surveillance, where information is essentially "compiled" or "collected" rather than "inferred" or "predicted."

An unsettling example of this predictive capability is a study conducted by Y. Wang and M. Kosinski, researchers from Stanford University, where AI accurately discerned sexual orientation from facial images alone. This illustrates an alarming potential for AI to infer highly sensitive and personal information from seemingly harmless data.[8]

Wang and Kosinski have tested AI's predictive capabilities in other scenarios as well. In another study, they developed an AI model that could predict a person's political affiliation based on a single photograph with a high rate of accuracy. Trained using a million images from a dating website, the model correctly identified a person's political leanings (liberal vs. conservative) 72% of the time, merely by examining their facial images.[9]

This predictive capability illustrates the potential for AI to infer highly personal information about us from a photo – resulting in a scenario where preserving anonymity and personal beliefs could become increasingly challenging. Even if the AI model's prediction is wrong for a specific individual, if there is general trust in its prediction accuracy, its outcomes could be used for mischief or more nefarious purposes.

These predictive abilities raise the question of how to protect privacy when it is not just the explicitly shared details that matter but also the implicit, predictive inferences that high-functioning AI systems are capable of making.

Balancing the need for high-quality and relevant data for AI systems with privacy concerns is tough but necessary. One key strategy is the adoption of Privacy by Design, an approach that integrates privacy considerations into the initial design stages and throughout the complete development process of an AI system.

In the context of AI systems, privacy-enhancing techniques (PETs) are crucial in ensuring secure and anonymized handling of training data, safeguarding personally identifiable information, and protecting the privacy of individual users.

Data anonymization

Data anonymization is a common PET that involves the elimination or alteration of personal identifiers from data sets before they are used by AI. The aim is to avoid any violation of privacy and prevent unauthorized access to sensitive information. It should, therefore, be done in a way that prevents original identification, even after the application of statistical methods or other means of inference.

Consider data collected in a hospital setting. Patient data is crucial for building AI models, particularly for predicting disease outcomes or enhancing patient care. However, this data often includes sensitive details like names, addresses, birth dates, and medical histories.

In the data anonymization process, these identifiable details are transformed or removed. For instance, names could be replaced by random, generated IDs. Addresses might be generalized from specific houses to larger zones or regions. Dates could be transformed into broader timespans, such as replacing birth dates with only the birth year. Disease specifics could be replaced with general classifications.

So, a record stating "John Doe, living in 1234 Elm Street, born on January 1, 1976, diagnosed with stage II colon cancer" could be anonymized to "Patient ID: 56789, region: Midwest, birth year: 1976, condition: cancer." This process keeps the essence of data useful for AI processing, but makes it difficult to trace back to a specific individual.

Data anonymization techniques, while crucial for privacy, can degrade the accuracy of AI learning and limit its overall functionality.

These techniques often involve masking or altering certain data elements, which may be vital learning features for the algorithms. As a result, the AI system might lose access to important patterns or relationships, leading to a drop in its prediction precision and reliability. For example, John's colon cancer could be linked to water contamination localized to his town. This correlation would be lost by generalizing his location and cancer type.

Other PETs, such as differential privacy, federated learning, and homomorphic encryption, can help maintain data utility while also preserving privacy. These techniques enable working on encrypted or decentralized data, thereby giving AI access to the raw data while reducing the risk of data exposure.

Differential privacy

Differential privacy injects random noise into data to prevent the identification of specific individuals while still allowing AI systems to derive useful patterns. Continuing with the healthcare example, let's use a scenario where researchers are trying to find a correlation between age and a specific disease. They need access to a dataset containing information about a patient's age and their medical conditions. Under differential privacy protocols, "random noise" is introduced into the dataset, altering the age figures or the disease prevalence rates.

For instance, instead of the dataset showing a patient's exact age, it might show the age as a range or slightly alter it, making the age between 30 and 34 instead of 32. Similarly, percentages of disease prevalence could be slightly adjusted. The strength of this "noise" is scientifically controlled so that the overall data patterns (like the correlation between age and the disease in question) remain virtually the same, but it becomes difficult to identify or make conclusions about individual patients from the dataset.

Differential privacy enables researchers to analyze data and determine correlations without being able to zoom in on any one individual's data, maintaining privacy.

Federated learning

Another practice gaining in popularity is federated learning, which allows AI models to be trained on decentralized data, reducing the need to transmit sensitive information. Federated learning can be applied by allowing AI models to learn from data that is stored across several locations, without needing to centralize or transmit the sensitive data.

Imagine several hospitals collaborating to develop an AI model to predict disease progression. Rather than sending all their patient data to a central location for training the model (which could pose significant privacy risks), they use federated learning. Each hospital would train the AI model locally on its own dataset, learning patterns and nuances from its individual patients. They then send only the model updates or parameters, which contain no identifiable patient details, to a central server.

The central server combines these updates to create a global AI model that is subsequently sent back to each hospital for another round of local updates or "learning." This cycle is repeated to fine-tune the model. So, the result is an AI that has effectively learned from all the hospitals' datasets without exposing individual patients' data to the other hospitals.

Homomorphic encryption

Homomorphic encryption allows AI systems to operate on encrypted data, potentially allowing predictions and analysis to occur without ever requiring decryption. Using this technique, the participating hospitals could encrypt patient data using homomorphic encryption, making it unreadable. The central server performs computations and trains on this still-encrypted data.

The amazing facet of homomorphic encryption is that the results of these computations, when decrypted, would be the same as if they had been performed on the original, unencrypted data. Without ever needing decryption during the transmission or computation process, the AI model is able to learn effectively from the data, while the sensitive patient details stay secure. This eliminates the risk of a data breach during transmission or at the central server, ensuring a high level of data privacy.

While regulations and guidelines are still emerging specific to AI privacy, there are existing regulations such as the EU's General Data Protection Regulation, which enforces rules about collecting, storing, and using personal data. Compliance with such regulations is important to maintain user trust and avoid substantial fines.

In addition to the PET techniques explored above, it's important not to forget established security protocols such as secure coding and encryption when developing and managing AI systems. Secure coding practices minimize vulnerabilities in AI algorithms and interfaces that hackers could exploit.

Moreover, it is a good security practice to implement the principle of least privilege, whereby the AI systems only have access to the information and resources they absolutely need to perform their objective. This can be achieved by applying stringent access controls to the data, AI model, and broader ecosystem.

The effective integration of these practices with sophisticated PETs can provide a privacy and security framework for AI systems. However, even they may not be enough. No security controls are foolproof, and leaks can happen. As with other technologies, security is best applied in a layered approach, so if one control fails, another will catch it. As we move to agentic AI, it will be important to also add filters that can review output before it's released to confirm that it does not contain private, privileged, or confidential information.

Deepfakes: separating fact from fiction

Deepfakes are digitally created media where a person's likeness (voice, look, and mannerisms) is synthesized. Deepfakes are generated by a deep learning AI model studying still images, audio files, and videos, learning the intricacies of an individual's speech patterns, mannerisms, and word choices, and then applying this learned knowledge to generate new forged content. The global AI-generated deepfake market is projected to grow from $79.1 million USD in 2024 to $1.39 billion USD by 2033, a growth factor of over 17x over nine years.[10]

This steep growth trajectory reflects how advancements in AI are fueling the creation and use of deepfakes. The widespread adoption of deepfake technology in entertainment, marketing, and other sectors contributes significantly to the rising market value. The ease of creating high-quality, personalized content at scale is a key driver of deepfake industry growth.

A worldwide McAfee Survey reported that with AI, fraudsters can produce images that are indistinguishable from reality.[11] Deepfakes are not only targeted at politicians, celebrities, and corporate executives. They also pose significant risks to a corporation's authentication mechanisms, where AI-manipulated emails, videos, voice recordings, or images can convincingly imitate trusted executives or clients, leading to unauthorized access to confidential data, illicit transfers of cash, or control over other valuable assets.

Deepfakes have added a new level of sophistication to phishing attacks. Synthesized voicemails or video calls impersonating a trusted colleague, supervisor, or client have led employees to divulge passwords, approve unwarranted access, or engage in other actions detrimental to the company. Confronting this fast-evolving threat necessitates continuous vigilance and multi-layered cybersecurity measures.

As an example, in a video conference with employees or investors, a deepfake with access to the video feed could replace a legitimate executive with a fabricated version that looks and speaks identically. From this deceptive platform, the replica could convey misleading information and harmful directives, or even shift strategic plans.

In a more advanced version of such a threat, instead of general miscommunication, an adversary could orchestrate targeted strikes at a company. They could issue misleading financial reports or leak "confidential" information, damaging the company's reputation and causing stock prices to plummet.

Synthetic voice mimicry can also bypass voice recognition systems, calling into question the effectiveness of biometric authentication. A malicious actor could use synthetic voice mimicry to imitate the voice of an authorized individual, perfectly replicating their voice characteristics – pitch, speed, and other personal speech characteristics to unlock doors or grant access to sensitive information.

Such incidents demonstrate the pitfalls of heavily relying on biometric data for security in the emerging age of deepfakes and the need for diversified, multi-factor authentication systems.

AI-powered detection methods for deepfakes

The emergence of AI-powered detection measures offers a promising line of defense to identify and remove deepfakes. In a recent study, Gartner predicted that by 2026, 30% of organizations' identity verification and authentication mechanisms would be considered unreliable due to AI-generated deepfakes unless additional security measures are put in place to distinguish between a real and synthetic face.[12]

AI detection techniques utilize ML to uncover subtle irregularities frequently presented in deepfakes. One common inconsistency is blinking. In a deepfake video, the subtleties of natural and spontaneous blinking can be challenging to replicate, leading to unusually timed or infrequent blinking. Motion inconsistencies, such as unnatural head movements or bodily gestures incongruent with speech or expression, are other "tells" used by ML detection algorithms.

Another detection method is illumination inconsistencies. AI can scrutinize light sources and shadow patterns within a suspected deepfake video, comparing them with the original physical surroundings. Discrepancies in natural lighting or facial shadows can flag a possible deepfake. Deepfake detection systems might also pick out incongruence in speech and lip movement synchronization or detect slightly blurred boundaries where the fake face or object merges with the original scene.

While these subtle anomalies are often overlooked by humans, ML algorithms, trained on vast amounts of real and deepfake data, can identify these tells.

Beyond visual irregularities, AI-powered tools can also probe the digital media's metadata or underlying digital structure, opening another opportunity for deepfake detection. As an example, a high-resolution image typically consists of complex data patterns, encoding visual information in a specific digital format. When this image is manipulated to create a deepfake, the modifications disrupt the inherent patterns within the image's data structure. These red flags include altered pixel correlations, disruptions in color histograms, and compression duplications.

As cyber criminals continue advancing deepfake manipulation, these AI-enabled detection tools will play an increasingly critical role in safeguarding digital identities. AI detection methods will need to continually evolve, incorporating more sophisticated measures to counter the rising tide of highly plausible fakes. It is a digital arms race – with both sides leveraging the power of AI to outsmart the other.

The need for regulatory measures

The surge in deepfake technology has highlighted an alarming gap in our current legislative and legal landscape, underscoring the urgent need for regulatory measures around the use of deepfake technology, including hefty penalties for violations.

As deepfakes often involve the unauthorized replication of an individual's likeness, existing privacy laws need to be updated to encompass this new identity violation. In addition to protections for individuals against having their image or voice manipulated without consent, laws could also tackle the responsibility of organizations to verify the authenticity of media before publicizing it.

The task of regulating deepfakes is fraught with challenges, amplified by the borderless nature of digital content. The internet functions without geographical boundaries, making it challenging to enforce regional or national regulations on global cyberspace. With participants in a single deepfake act scattered across multiple jurisdictions, the implementation and enforcement of regulatory actions are often complicated.

Moreover, the sophistication of organized cybercrime contributes to the complexity of regulating deepfakes. They are often designed and deployed by highly skilled and well-resourced entities that operate on the dark web. Their technical prowess, combined with a deep understanding of the digital world, enables them to stay a step ahead of security measures and manipulate loopholes in regulations.

Furthermore, a lack of user education magnifies the deepfake threat. Many users still have limited awareness of the existence of deepfakes and the risks they pose, making them more susceptible to deception. An increasing reliance on and trust in digital content amplifies their potential disruption.

AI is both the cause and the solution

The emergence of AI, while creating distinct cybersecurity challenges, has also paved the way for innovative advancements in responding to these threats. AI can process vast amounts of data to identify unusual activities or potential threats. ML algorithms can recognize complex patterns indicative of malicious activities, such as suspicious network traffic or uncommon user behavior. Security analysts can focus on constructing effective countermeasures and making strategic decisions. This collaboration between humans and AI can create a more robust, effective, and efficient cybersecurity defense.

Furthermore, AI can serve as a proactive shield by predicting future cybersecurity threats. By analyzing historical data, monitoring trends, and deciphering hidden correlations, AI can potentially anticipate a new cyber threat. This predictive capability allows organizations to prepare for, and even preempt, potential attacks.

For instance, AI systems can observe network traffic patterns and learn to distinguish between regular and abnormal traffic flow. Then, if an abnormal spike or connection from an unusual location is detected, AI can flag it as potentially malicious activity. The AI could alert a security analyst or be authorized to take immediate action, such as blocking the IP address or isolating the affected systems.

Similarly, AI tools can monitor user behavior – login times, file access patterns, application usage, keyboard and mouse activity, and more. If an employee suddenly starts downloading vast amounts of data or logging in at odd hours, the AI system would mark this as anomalous, possibly malicious behavior and respond with appropriate actions.

Unlike traditional rule-based systems, AI algorithms can amplify their threat detection capabilities after each incident. Be it a new malware variant, a sophisticated phishing method, or a novel hacking technique, AI systems analyze these attempts, understand their modus operandi, and recalibrate to fortify against similar future attacks. This ongoing learning process ensures that the cybersecurity system constantly evolves, staying abreast with the dynamic threat landscape, boosting its defense effectiveness, and providing a continually hardened security cover for the digital environment.

AI is enhancing human intelligence in cyber defense

An AI-augmented cyber defense doesn't necessarily signify the replacement of human involvement. Its purpose is to augment, rather than replace, human intelligence – shouldering the tasks that are complex, tedious, or beyond human scalability. This results in a symbiotic relationship where AI's capabilities enhance human-led decision-making.

AI systems can handle the grueling work of constant surveillance across extensive digital networks. They operate without fatigue, keeping a lookout for signs of potential intrusions or impending attacks 24/7. AI can also detect patterns in vast datasets, identifying trends or spotting anomalies, a task that would be hard for humans, given the sheer volume and pace of data generation. Be it network logs, user activity data, threat intelligence feeds, or data from other external sources, AI processes these in real time, delivering crucial insights to human security analysts.

Human analysts can then focus on what they do best – applying intuition, experience-based judgment, and strategic decision-making. AI provides them with processed and contextualized information, arming them to respond faster and more accurately to security incidents, and allowing them to prioritize their efforts on critical tasks and strategic decision-making, instead of getting mired down in data processing.

This AI-human collaboration in cyber defense ensures a more efficient incident response, a deeper understanding of the evolving threat landscape, and a more secure cyber environment.

Conclusion

The introduction of AI into our digital ecosystem has significantly altered the cybersecurity landscape. AI has unleashed a slew of security challenges, including adversarial attacks and deepfakes. While AI has created these new risks, it can also be used to combat them. AI's strengths in pattern recognition, vast data processing, and real-time operation equip it to supervise cyberspace, detecting and responding to threats efficiently, even foreseeing future risks. Augmenting human intelligence with AI capabilities can create a cyber defense that is resilient, proactive, and future-ready.

However, if AI systems are entrusted with the task of monitoring, validating, and rectifying the operations of other AI models, these overseer AI systems must be resistant to manipulation. They cannot be vulnerable to re-training, tinkering, or redirection by malicious actors. The effectiveness and credibility of such overseer AI systems hinge on their resilience against attacks and manipulation attempts, their ability to operate reliably under various conditions, and their proficiency in consistently delivering accurate evaluations. Hence, safeguarding the overseer AI against both overt and covert threats must be a priority.

No matter how advanced, technology alone will not stem the tide of AI-inflicted threats. Security in the age of AI demands ecosystem-wide collaboration. Regulatory bodies need to enact stringent policies and sanctions; the public needs to be educated about the potential risks and safeguards; and corporations need to heighten their internal security systems. Not just in response to an attack but as a preemptive strategy.

Furthermore, cybersecurity principles must be integrated into all phases of an AI system's lifecycle. The adoption of Privacy by Design and privacy preservation should be an integral part of system design. In fact, proactive incorporation of security measures, as part of responsible AI practices, should be at the core of the AI development process.

Combined with robust security measures, AI offers a cyber world that's innovative yet secure, autonomous yet regulated, and co-piloted adeptly by both humans and AI.

Key leadership questions to consider:

1. Are your cybersecurity strategies incorporating AI to enhance your threat detection, response, and predictive capabilities?
2. Do your AI systems have safeguards against adversarial attacks, deepfakes, and other risks posed by AI?
3. Have you implemented Privacy by Design principles and integrated security considerations into all phases of your AI lifecycle?
4. Are you conducting regular integrity checks on your AI systems, especially those overseeing other AI models, to ensure their resistance to manipulation?
5. Have you done an external third-party AI cybersecurity risk review of all of your AI practices?

Notes

1 Bill Gates quotation. (n.d.). *Alldus*. Retrieved June 15, 2025, from https://alldus.com/blog/ai-quotes-from-some-of-the-worlds-top-minds/.

2 Deepak, G. (2025, May 5). RSA the unprecedented evolution of cybersecurity. *Cybersecurity Blog*. https://guptadeepak.com/rsac-2025-the-unprecedented-evolution-of-cybersecurity/.

3 Deepak, G. (2025, May 5). RSA the unprecedented evolution of cybersecurity. *Cybersecurity Blog*. https://guptadeepak.com/rsac-2025-the-unprecedented-evolution-of-cybersecurity/.

4 Eykholt, K., Evtimov, I., et al. (2018, April 10). Robust physical-world attacks on deep learning visual classification. *arXiv*. https://arxiv.org/pdf/1707.08945.

5 Boltachev, E. (2023, June 5). Potential cyber threats of adversarial attacks on autonomous driving models. *Journal of Computer Virology and Hacking Techniques*. https://doi.org/10.1007/s11416-023-00486-x.

6 Alshehri, M. (2024, May 27). CYRC advisory data poisoning embedded AI. *Black Duck*. Retrieved June 8, 2025, from https://www.blackduck.com/blog/cyrc-advisory-data-poisoning-embedai.html.

7 Zuboff, S. (2019). *The age of surveillance capitalism: The fight for a human future at the new frontier of power*. New York: Public Affairs.

8 Wang, Y., & Kosinski, M. (2021). Deep neural networks can predict sexual orientation from facial images with high accuracy. *Journal of Personality and Social Psychology*, 246–257. https://pubmed.ncbi.nlm.nih.gov/29389215/.

9 Wang, Y., & Kosinski, M. (2020). Using deep learning to predict ideology from facial photographs, expressions, beauty, and extra facial information. *Journal of Personality and Social Psychology*. https://www.theguardian.com/technology/2017/sep/12/artificial-intelligence-face-recognition-michal-kosinski.

10 Dimension Market Research. (2024, December). *Deepfakes*. Dimension Market Research. https://dimensionmarketresearch.com/report/deepfake-ai-market/#:~:text=Market%20Overview,at%20a%20CAGR%20of%2037.6%25.

11 Abrams, A., & Kalaydin, P. (2025, January 31). What are deepfakes, and how can you spot them? *The SubSuber*. https://sumsub.com/blog/what-are-deepfakes/.

12 Gartner Group Research. (2024, February 1). *Gartner predicts 30% of enterprises will consider identity verification and authentication solutions unreliable in isolation due to deepfakes by 2026*. https://www.gartner.com/en/newsroom/press-releases/2024-02-01-gartner-predicts-30-percent-of-enterprises-will-consider-identity-verification-and-authentication-solutions-unreliable-in-isolation-due-to-deepfakes-by-2026.

Section II

Roadmap to achieving responsible AI

In this section, we equip executives with the essential steps for achieving and sustaining responsible artificial intelligence (AI) in their organizations. We emphasize the importance of implementing robust corporate governance and control mechanisms. Stephen Hawking understood the crucial need to build strong AI operational practices:

> *I am an optimist and I believe that we can create AI for the good of the world. That it can work in harmony with us. We simply need to be aware of the dangers, identify them, employ the best possible practice and management, and prepare for its consequences well in advance.*[1]

Over the past ten years, AI governance practices have been written into regulations, standards, and guidelines. But implementing them in practice is not easy. As we move to agentic AI, there will be a major shift from human-in-the-loop to machine-based controls. Monitoring mechanisms are being designed that can detect AI errors, biases, and manipulations. However, these single-point tests are not yet consolidated into an integrated monitoring program. In time, this gap will close, but will it come fast enough? It is a constant catch-up game where AI is staying ahead of our ability to control it. Although consumers are demanding safeguards against AI, they crave its productivity and greater insights. Use of GenAI has exploded, with its adoption at the three-year mark twice that of the personal computer.[2]

AI controls include both technical measures, such as algorithmic transparency and data privacy safeguards, and non-technical measures like transparency reports and employee training. With AI

DOI: 10.4324/9781003625520-8

developing rapidly, AI developers, users, and public policy setters need to continually monitor for new risks. They need to go beyond the minimum standards set by public policy setters. Currently, regulations are heavily focused on transparency – disclosures on where AI is used, the data it was trained on, how it was trained and its decision framework. However, documentation, while a good educational tool, is not an active control mechanism. Even risk assessments are inadequate. A risk is not mitigated by understanding alone – an action must be taken. While regulations can stipulate that independent testing and monitoring controls be put in place, they are not prescriptive on what these look like. This onus still resides with the AI developers and users to design and implement specific AI performance metrics and monitoring systems.

In this section, we provide a blueprint for how to develop effective AI governance mechanisms. Effective, value-based controls that can keep pace with AI in both speed and flexibility.

Notes

1 Kharpal, A. (2017, November 6). Stephen Hawking says A.I. could be 'the worst event in the history of our civilization'. *CNBC*. https://www.cnbc.com/2017/11/06/stephen-hawking-ai-could-be-worst-event-in-civilization.html.

2 Bick, A., Blandin, A., & Deming, D. (2023, September 23). *The rapid adoption of generative AI*. The Federal Reserve Bank of St. Louis. Retrieved August 31, 2025, from https://www.stlouisfed.org/on-the-economy/2024/sep/rapid-adoption-generative-ai/.

Chapter 7

The tug-of-war between AI innovation and safety

The speed of innovation, spearheaded by artificial intelligence (AI), is truly unprecedented. Already, AI has led to innovations in autonomous vehicles that can navigate rush hour traffic and smart devices that can control most systems in our homes and workplaces. AI has fueled advancements in Star Trek-like cybernetics, such as brain-controlled robotic limbs that give mobility back to a disabled person and direct human-brain interfaces, like Neuralink.[1] No industry is untouched by AI.

With AI's far-reaching impact, the public is calling on governments and standard setters to mandate AI safeguards; to ensure that AI is secure, safe, and trustworthy. This is similar to the safety measures governments put in place for automobiles, aircrafts and medical devices. However, a key difference is the accelerated pace of AI's development.

As the world-renowned AI Scientist and Nobel Prize Laureate, Dr. Geoffrey Hinton, has stated, "The safe and ethical development and deployment of AI should be a priority for governments, companies and citizens across the globe."[2]

We need to act. Policymakers are beginning to respond, but with different strategies. Some are instituting mandatory regulations and laws, while others are opting for voluntary guidelines. Even the regulations being released differ. Some are sweeping regulations that affect all AI systems, while others are targeting specific AI types or use cases, such as systems that impact minors or the use of facial recognition for surveillance. Despite the differences, there is fairly broad agreement that governments have a role to play in safeguarding individuals and society from the potential harms of AI.

With the complex array of emerging AI compliance obligations, it is crucial for organizations to have legal counsel and regulatory compliance experts involved in understanding the complexities

DOI: 10.4324/9781003625520-9

of AI laws, regulations and voluntary standards. Public policy setters have attempted to expedite the release of their initiatives by contracting the time available for deliberation, consultations, and consensus-building. This is a more agile approach to standard setting, where basic obligations are released first, and multi-disciplinary working groups are formed to work out the details. However, there are many areas where further guidance is required.

Most policymakers recognize the need for a balanced pro-safety and pro-innovation regulatory framework. They are also aligned in creating a global framework that is interoperable across borders and eases the complexity of today's current rules. At the February 2025 Paris AI Safety Summit,[3] 58 global leaders signed the AI safety declaration, which calls for a "rights-based, human-centric, ethical, safe, secure and trustworthy" approach to the technology.

Front and center during the summit was the debate between developing AI that is safe and trustworthy, and promoting innovation. On one side is the EU, which published in July 2024 the *EU AI Act*, the first comprehensive AI regulation that works in concert with the EU's privacy regulation, the *General Data Protection Regulation (GDPR)*. On the flip side is the *America's AI Action Plan,* released by the U.S. White House in July 2025. Entitled *Winning the Race – a new strategy to achieve and maintain global AI dominance*. It contains many strategic initiatives to accelerate AI innovation and remove barriers in achieving three key objectives: (1) accelerate AI innovation; (2) build American AI infrastructure; and (3) lead in international AI diplomacy and security.[4] How the U.S. *AI Action Plan* will be implemented is still unfolding.

What is at the heart of both the EU and United States approaches to AI government oversight is the need to promote innovation while enforcing security and safety. In this chapter, we will explore the different public policy approaches for AI, comparing their similarities and differences. Managing these diverse approaches will be complex, with cross-border implications for many years to come.

Objectives

Upon completing this chapter, you will be able to:

- Understand the high-level AI regulatory and legislative landscape complexities

- Determine alternative public policy initiatives for AI
- Understand similarities and differences across different jurisdictions
- Develop some leading strategies for your organization in managing the complexities in AI public policy.

AI governance: a framework for corporate decision-making

With much of AI's guidance still in the early stages of enforcement or published as voluntary standards, organizations need to decide how far above what they "must do" they will go. In this category are the laws that are not specific to AI, such as protection of minors and non-discrimination that applies to all technology, and the AI-specific laws, such as the *EU AI Act*. Above these minimum requirements are a large array of potential voluntary actions that organizations can take to further safeguard their deployment and use of AI systems, and/or investments in AI for society's benefit.

To understand the different ways organizations can respond to the large array of potential laws, regulations, and voluntary standards, it is helpful to put them into tiered levels – with compliance to legal mandates at the bottom, and proactive actions to integrate ethical AI practices at the top. Figure 7.1 provides a suggested AI legal-ethical framework divided into six levels. Developed by Jeff Saviano, Business AI Ethics Leader at the Edmond & Lily Safra Center for Ethics at Harvard University, this AI legal-ethical framework, entitled Boundaries of Tolerance Pyramid, can be used as a guide for making strategic decisions and setting goals for an AI program. It assists in determining the mandatory obligations an organization is legally required to meet, and those that organizations voluntarily sign up for.

Level 0: Non-compliance

Organizations at this level have no internal mechanisms or precautionary measures for ensuring AI legal and ethical compliance. Whether intentionally or unintentionally, this is not a sustainable place for an organization to be – particularly as their use of AI grows.

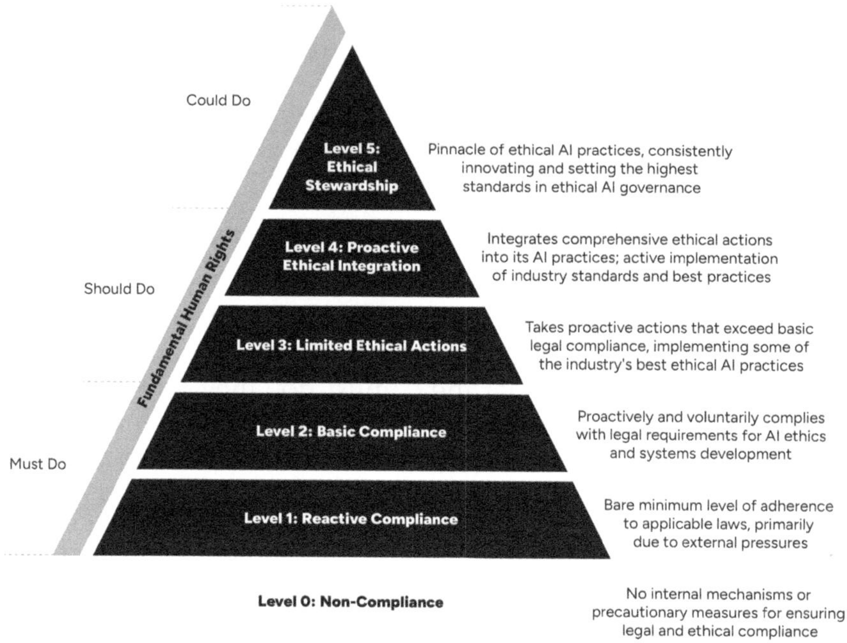

Figure 7.1 AI legal-ethical framework.[5,6,7,8]

With no commitment to AI ethics, it is only a matter of time before an AI incident occurs that erodes stakeholder trust. With the increasing complexity of AI regulations and laws, organizations may find themselves non-compliant with a number of AI-specific and non-AI-specific laws and regulations. These laws encompass a wide range of areas, including but not limited to non-discrimination, privacy, and the protection of minors. This would also include existing laws that apply to human operators of processes, transactions, and activities that are automated by AI.

Level 1: Reactive compliance

An organization in a reactive-mode to AI compliance does not have a robust AI compliance function in place. Instead, they react to external triggers that "force-their-hand" in complying, such as regulatory inspections, a customer complaint, legal action, or a whistleblower event. Rather than proactively managing their AI compliance, they respond to these external triggers and incidents with bare minimum compliance – they do only what they "have to do" to stay out of trouble and off the radar. Organizations that spend too long at this level are apt to also erode stakeholder trust and incur costly fines and penalties.

Level 2: Basic compliance

This level encompasses organizations that are proactively and voluntarily complying with laws and regulations relevant to AI development and use. They are continually canvassing for new obligations, and strive to comply as quickly as possible. They have a robust AI compliance practice in place. Their goal is to be legally compliant without exceeding basic requirements set out in law. For example, the *South Korean AI Basic Act*, passed in December 2024 and coming into effect in January 2026 or the other 69 countries, and counting, that have proposed over a thousand AI policy and legal frameworks around the world.[9]

Level 3: Limited ethical actions

Moving beyond what organizations "must do," the third level embodies what they "should do." Organizations at this level have taken proactive action to go beyond basic legal requirements in ethical AI. They are voluntarily applying leading ethical AI practices in some areas, such as expanded risk assessments and bias testing, but there is still room for improvement. They would be considered a slow follower, waiting for other organizations to first take the lead in developing ethical AI best practices that they then adopt over time.

Level 4: Proactive ethical integration

Organizations at this level take it one step further. They are actively integrating comprehensive ethical AI practices into their AI development and use. They are continually canvassing for leading ethical AI best practices and industry standards, and actively monitor their AI governance maturity through periodic audits, transparency reports, and advanced responsible AI controls. Their goal is to build trust and loyalty with stakeholders while minimizing the impacts of AI risks.

Level 5: Ethical stewardship

The top of the pyramid is the organizations that are setting the standard for ethical AI. They are continually challenging the sufficiency of their responsible AI practices and work collaboratively with academia, the technology sector, policy setters, and peer companies to shape ethical AI practices. These organizations are often more advanced in their use of AI and are actively involved in considering the pressing societal and existential challenges posed by AI.

This six-level framework supports organizations in formulating a robust and ethical AI governance strategy. Levels 1 and 2 require a thorough inventory and regular compliance checks to confirm that your organization is meeting all mandated legal and regulatory requirements. The top three levels require strategic planning to set goals and priorities for voluntary commitments and initiatives. This balanced approach to AI governance is crucial in building a future where technology serves humanity.

Non-AI laws and regulations

Lawmakers, governments, and regulators have been quick to clarify that, despite the novelty of AI, it is not exempt from existing legal frameworks. This early response was crucial in setting the tone for AI's development. The message was clear: innovation should not come at the expense of legal and ethical standards. Here are some examples.

In the financial services sector, AI applications are subject to rigorous model management guidelines, such as the Basel Committee's *Principles for Effective Risk Data Aggregation and Risk Reporting* (BCBS 239) and the *Guidelines on Model Risk Management* (E-23).[10] These regulations ensure that all models, including those driven by AI, are robust, transparent, and free from discriminatory biases, aligning with consumer protection laws and financial regulations.

The healthcare sector has seen AI's integration into medical devices and diagnostic tools. The *U.S. Food & Drug Administration (FDA)* clarified how existing scientific standards and regulations apply to AI. This involves rigorous testing and validation processes to protect patient health and privacy, in line with *Health Insurance Portability and Accountability Act* and other healthcare regulations.[11] They also released in July 2025 an *AI-enabled Medical Device List*. This online database includes all AI-enabled devices that met their premarket requirements.[12]

Gaming companies that employ AI must be particularly mindful of laws protecting minors. This includes adhering to the *Children's*

Online Privacy Protection Act in the United States, which imposes requirements on operators of websites or online services directed to children under 13 years of age. AI-driven content recommendations or in-game experiences must comply with these regulations, ensuring the safety and privacy of young users.[13]

Social platforms and other technology companies are increasingly reliant on AI for content moderation, personalized advertising, and user engagement. These companies must navigate a complex web of laws related to data protection, such as the GDPR in Europe[14] and the *California Consumer Privacy Act*[15] and *California Privacy Rights Act.*[16] These laws mandate transparency in data processing and grant users certain rights over their personal information, which can be challenging to reconcile with AI's data-driven operations.

Adherence to non-discriminatory laws in hiring and credit use cases is also important, as these areas are particularly vulnerable to the perpetuation of historical biases through AI. For instance, AI tools used for resume screening must comply with the U.S. *Equal Employment Opportunity Commission,*[17] which protects against discriminatory hiring practices whether through manual or automated means. The *New York state AI law 144*[18] protects job candidates and employees from unlawful discriminatory bias based on race, ethnicity, or gender when employers and employment agencies use automated decision tools to make hiring decisions.

In credit lending, AI models that set lending limits must align with fair lending laws, including the *Equal Credit Opportunity Act,*[19] ensuring decisions are not influenced by biases present in historical data. When an AI system denies a loan application, the *Fair Credit Reporting Act*[20] requires that the applicant be given reasons for the denial. However, the complexity of AI algorithms can make it difficult to provide clear, understandable explanations, complicating compliance efforts. The challenge lies in ensuring that AI does not "learn" these biases from the historical data, requiring careful design, training, and ongoing monitoring to maintain fairness and prevent discriminatory decision-making.

These examples present a fraction of the existing laws and regulations that AI systems must adhere to. Plus, there are new AI-specific regulations released every month. Many companies have learned through difficult experiences that AI's growing autonomy and decision-making capabilities can lead to scenarios not fully anticipated by current regulations. AI can create new risks or situations that existing laws are not equipped to address.

Challenges in applying AI to existing laws and regulations

One of the primary challenges in applying AI to existing laws is the "black box" nature of some AI systems, where decision-making processes are not easily explainable. This transparency gap makes it difficult to determine whether AI is operating in compliance with regulations, particularly those requiring clear explanations of decisions, such as credit denials. Additionally, AI's reliance on large datasets can result in breaches of consent agreements, as personal data may be used in ways not anticipated when it was first collected.

The dynamic and unpredictable nature of adaptive AI presents significant challenges, as models that were compliant at deployment can later drift into non-compliant behavior. "Model drift" can result from changes in underlying data or operating conditions. To address this issue, organizations must implement continuous monitoring and recalibration of AI systems. Such proactive measures are essential to ensure ongoing compliance with laws and regulations.

As AI advances, it challenges the boundaries of existing legal frameworks, revealing areas where current regulations are insufficient. Table 7.1 summarizes emergent risks that are leading to calls for AI-specific laws and regulations.

While existing laws provide a starting point for AI governance, the rapid development of AI technologies necessitates a re-examination of them. The challenges of applying non-AI laws to AI technologies highlight the need for ongoing dialogue between businesses, policymakers, legal experts, and civil society.

Government response to AI risks: voluntary standards or mandatory regulations

Policymakers are struggling with how to best regulate this transformative technology. They want to protect the public, but at the same time, they do not want to stifle innovation. This delicate balance has led to a spectrum of public policy approaches, from the establishment of tax incentives that encourage specific behaviors to the implementation of mandatory obligations.

Table 7.1 AI-specific issues

AI-specific issue	*Description*
Intellectual property (IP) ownership	The creative capabilities of AI, such as generating art, writing code, or composing music, pose complex questions about IP ownership. For example, if an AI system creates a novel design, should the IP rights belong to the AI developer, the user who provided the input parameters, or the AI itself? Current IP laws are not designed to accommodate non-human creators, leaving gray areas that can stifle innovation or lead to legal disputes.
Agency and liability	AI systems, particularly those with autonomous decision-making abilities (e.g., agentic AI), blur the lines of liability. Consider a scenario where an AI-powered medical diagnostic tool incorrectly diagnoses a patient, leading to harm. Determining whether the liability lies with the healthcare provider, the AI developer, or the AI system itself is a challenge. Current laws may not clearly address the distribution of responsibility leaving victims without recourse.
Privacy	AI's extensive data processing capabilities can inadvertently breach privacy, even when handling anonymized datasets. For instance, AI can sometimes identify individuals from anonymized health records by correlating data points. This capability exceeds what traditional privacy laws were designed to protect against. Agentic AI may also lead to higher privacy breaches, as a human is no longer providing direct oversight on what information is released.
Reliance on third-party vendors	The use of third-party AI technologies introduces additional layers of complexity in governance. If a third-party AI system used by a bank for credit scoring develops biases, it can be challenging to assign accountability. The bank, the AI vendor, and the end-users are all stakeholders in the broader AI ecosystem, and current regulations may not clearly delineate their respective responsibilities.
Algorithmic bias	Even with efforts to eliminate bias, AI systems can inadvertently perpetuate existing societal biases, leading to discriminatory outcomes. This is a significant concern in areas such as criminal justice, where biased AI could affect charging, sentencing, or parole decisions.

(Continued)

Table 7.1 (Continued)

AI-specific issue	*Description*
Security risks	AI systems are susceptible to different security threats, such as adversarial attacks that can manipulate model behavior. Existing cybersecurity regulations may not fully account for novel vulnerabilities. They may also not be prepared for the interconnected nature of agentic AI and systemic security risks created across the AI ecosystem.
Employment law	As AI automates more tasks, questions arise about the displacement of workers and the need for regulations to protect jobs or manage the transition of the workforce.

Some regions have opted for a prescriptive regulatory approach, enacting laws that impose mandatory obligations on AI developers and users. The *EU AI Act* is an example of this approach, seeking to create a harmonized set of rules across its member states. The Act adopts a risk-based approach, categorizing AI systems by the level of risk they pose to individuals and society. It applies to all AI systems used within the EU, regardless of where the developer or provider is based. This ambitious regulation seeks to set a global benchmark for AI governance, with stringent requirements for high-risk applications and more limited reporting requirements for lower risk AI systems. It is a tiered compliance framework that scales according to the potential impact and associated risk of the AI system in question.[21]

Foundational harmonization is already present, with 47 countries adhering to the *OECD AI Principles*[22] and the G7 Digital and Tech Ministers endorsing in December 2023 the *Hiroshima AI Process G7 Comprehensive Policy Framework*.[23] This framework builds upon the *Hiroshima Process International Code of Conduct for Organizations Developing Advanced AI Systems*, establishing a cohesive approach to AI governance that emphasizes risk management, incident reporting, and maintaining secure environments for AI.[24] The Hiroshima AI Policy Framework is "the first policy package the democratic leaders of the G7 have agreed upon to effectively steward the principles of human-centered AI design, safeguard individual rights, and enhance systems of trust."[25]

In contrast, the Trump Administration in the United States has challenged the constraints these regulations are putting on AI's speed of innovation. In contrast, the United States is supporting voluntary standards, such as the *National Institute of Standards and Technology (NIST) AI Risk Management Framework*. Their arguments have led many countries to reflect on the impact of too much AI legislation on their ability to remain globally competitive.

Singapore, the United Kingdom, and Japan are also adopting a more voluntary approach to AI governance, emphasizing guidelines and frameworks that encourage responsible AI development while supporting innovation. These countries focus on providing industry guidance that builds on the *OECD AI Principles*, rather than adopting mandatory regulations. These principles emphasize the equitable distribution of AI benefits, the safeguarding of human rights, and the establishment of robust governance and accountability mechanisms for AI usage.[26]

Between these two approaches lies a spectrum of hybrid approaches, where governments decide how and for what they want to intervene, and provide a baseline of mandatory requirements supplemented by voluntary codes of conduct and industry-led initiatives. This strategy allows for a degree of regulatory agility, enabling rapid adaptation to the fast-paced evolution of AI technologies.

The decision to pursue a voluntary or regulatory path is influenced by a variety of factors, including the maturity of the AI ecosystem within a region, the level of public trust in technology, and the prevailing political, legal, and regulatory philosophies. This varied landscape of AI regulation reflects the diverse legal priorities of different jurisdictions. However, the common thread is the recognition of the need for a risk-based approach that categorizes AI systems by their potential impact and tailors public policy measures accordingly. As AI advances, there is a general need for greater public policy harmonization and international cooperation.

AI regulatory frameworks and initiatives

This chapter further explores three different jurisdictions that demonstrate different approaches to the AI regulatory landscape:

- *European Union*: The EU remains the global leader in formal AI regulation with its *AI Act*, the first comprehensive legislative framework. It categorizes AI systems by risk – banning some, strictly regulating high-risk applications, and minimally regulating low-risk ones – and imposing binding obligations across all member states.

- *United States:* The United States has recently taken steps toward more coordinated federal engagement with AI, as reflected in its national AI Action Plan. Through private-public collaborations and cutting-edge AI research and development, the plan's goal is to ensure AI benefits American workers, families, and society while maintaining global competitiveness and leadership. While it continues to prioritize voluntary standards and industry self-regulation, there is growing federal oversight through executive orders, departmental guidance, and sector-specific initiatives. However, the country's regulatory landscape remains fragmented, with significant variation at the state level.
- *China:* China has reinforced its commitment to becoming a global AI leader by 2030 through a centrally coordinated strategy, reflected in its updated July 2025 *AI Action Plan*. Its approach emphasizes strict oversight in areas impacting national security, social stability, and public opinion. Regulations are highly targeted – especially for generative AI and recommendation algorithms – and are guided by state-defined ethical principles rooted in socialist core values.

European Union

While the EU is often labeled as "pro-regulation" due to its pioneering *EU AI Act*, this characterization oversimplifies its approach. The EU's regulatory strategy is not solely about imposing restrictions – it is also designed to foster innovation, ensure legal clarity, and create a cohesive digital single market. By harmonizing AI rules across member states, the EU reduces regulatory fragmentation, making it easier for businesses to scale and operate across borders.

The EU's approach to AI regulation is part of a broader strategy to create a harmonized and coherent digital regulatory environment, integrating the EU *AI Act* with existing frameworks like the GDPR, the *Digital Services Act* (DSA), and the *Digital Markets Act* (DMA). Rather than treating these laws as isolated efforts, the EU is working to standardize and streamline how digital technologies are governed across domains. The *EU AI Act* is designed to align with the GDPR's principles on data protection, ensuring AI systems respect user privacy and consent. Similarly, the DSA and DMA regulate online platforms and gatekeepers, and their provisions intersect with AI-driven recommendation systems and content moderation algorithms – areas that the *EU AI Act* also touches. By integrating these regulations, the EU aims to reduce legal fragmentation, offer clearer compliance pathways for companies, and ensure that innovation happens within a trusted digital ecosystem.

As part of the EU digital strategy, the *EU AI Act*[27] leverages a risk-based approach, classifying AI systems into four risk categories based on their use cases: (1) unacceptable-risk, (2) high-risk, (3) limited-risk, and (4) minimal/no-risk. The *EU AI Act* prohibits AI systems rated as unacceptable risk, including biometric surveillance, emotion recognition, exploitation of vulnerabilities, social scoring, manipulative or deceptive tactics, and predictive policing/criminal profiling.[28]

Under the *EU AI Act*, the task of classifying AI systems as either unacceptable or high-risk is a complex endeavor that must account for the potential impacts of these technologies. For example, an AI system designed to analyze social sentiment for training or coaching purposes. While it can be a powerful tool to support personal development and well-being, the system could meet the definition of a high-risk AI system if it involves social scoring. The same is true for AI that utilizes biometric information for identification in credit lending. These scenarios demonstrate the challenges regulators face in categorizing AI applications within the EU's framework.

The *EU AI Act* has also introduced a new AI category – General Purpose AI (GPAI) models. This new category encompasses mandatory transparency obligations, ensuring that users are informed about the capabilities and limitations of these powerful AI systems, as well as the nature of their interactions with them.[29] However, in implementing the GPAI rules, issues have arisen as to roles and accountability. A voluntary *GPAI Code of Conduct*[30] was released in July 2025 as a supplemental guide to assist the industry in complying with obligations related to GPAI transparency, copyright, safety and security. While voluntary, organizations have been encouraged to sign onto the Code, signaling their commitment to comply with it.

The *EU AI Act* is complex, and organizations must undertake specific actions to comply with its obligations. Table 7.2 provides a deeper dive into the key areas of compliance with the *EU AI Act*, the actions organizations need to take, and the challenges they may experience in doing so.

Table 7.2 Compliance areas, actions, and challenges

Compliance area	*Actions required*	*Potential challenges experienced*
AI inventory	• Develop an AI inventory detailing all AI systems in use	• Complexity and scale of cataloging numerous AI systems
Risk-tiering AI applications	• Determine AI objectives and outcomes and categorize them against the *Act's* risk levels	• Dynamic nature of AI systems requiring continuous reassessment
Defining role(s)	• Identify and document roles and responsibilities in the development, deployment, and distribution of AI systems	• Reliance on third parties necessitates a formal definition of roles and obligations in contracts • The complexity of AI systems, often involving multiple components, can lead to confusion on roles and accountabilities
Implementation of policies and documentation procedures	• Establish AI governance frameworks aligned with the *Act*'s requirements • Maintain records of AI system processes, including risk assessments and audit results	• Administration overhead introduced by extensive documentation • Adapting existing processes to meet the *Act*'s documentation requirements
Conformity assessment	• Prepare detailed documentation and conduct testing for transparency, accuracy, and robustness • Engage third-party entities for conformity assessments of high-risk AI systems	• Resource-intensive process requiring time, expertise, and financial investment • Limited pool of qualified assessors with expertise in AI regulation
Establishing strong human oversight mechanisms	• Define human-in-the-loop processes for AI decision-making • Train staff on their roles in overseeing AI systems and raise organizational awareness	• Balancing automation with necessary human oversight • Skill gaps in personnel required for effective oversight of AI systems

Complying with the *EU AI Act* requires a structured governance system, involving the establishment of inventories, rigorous risk assessments, risk mitigation measures, conformity assessments, detailed documentation, and strong human oversight mechanisms. Organizations will face various challenges in implementing these measures, from the complexity and dynamic nature of AI systems to resource constraints and skill gaps. Early and proactive action is essential to ensure compliance with the Act's obligations.

Italy became the first EU country to pass a dedicated national AI law in September 2025, with parts of it taking effect in October 2025. The law aligns with the *EU AI Act* but adds national rules on transparency, accountability, oversight, criminal penalties for harmful AI misuse (e.g., deepfakes), child protections (parental consent for under-14s), copyright for AI-assisted works, and sector-specific governance bodies.[31]

South Korea is the first non-EU country to adopt comprehensive AI regulations. The *South Korean AI Basic Act* was passed in December 2024 and came into effect in January 2026. While subordinate regulations are still being drafted, the law has signaled that businesses will be required to adopt practices and safety measures to mitigate the impacts of high-risk systems and provide greater transparency over their use.[32] We have yet to see if other countries will adopt similar regulatory frameworks.

United States

In contrast to the EU's centralized and regulatory approach to managing the risks of AI, the United States favors a voluntary, principles-based approach. This divergence reflects the philosophical differences between the two regions in terms of regulatory intervention and market freedom. While the EU's aim is to set standards for AI development and deployment across its member states, the United States approach emphasizes national technology leadership.

The U.S. *AI Action Plan*[33] is built on the belief that too much regulation will stifle innovation and impact global competitiveness. Instead of imposing mandatory obligations, the United States wants to remove "red tape," and through public–private collaborations, encourage industry-led initiatives and voluntary standards. Federal agencies, such as NIST,[34] are expected to continue playing a pivotal role in developing frameworks that support the reliability and security of AI. These efforts are complemented by executive orders and policy initiatives aimed at fostering AI innovation.

The overarching goal of the *AI Action Plan* is to ensure that AI benefits American workers, families, and society while maintaining global competitiveness and leadership. The plan is structured around three key pillars, each with specific goals:

1 *Accelerating innovation:* It fosters cutting-edge AI research and development; supports collaboration between government, academia, and industry to drive breakthroughs; and promotes ethical and responsible AI development.
2 *Building AI infrastructure:* It develops robust AI infrastructure including high-performance computing and data-sharing frameworks, ensures accessibility of resources for researchers and innovators, and strengthens cybersecurity to safeguard AI systems.
3 *Leading in international diplomacy and security:* It shapes global AI standards and governance frameworks, promotes the responsible use of AI in international relations and defense, and ensures AI technologies align with democratic values and national security priorities.

The *AI Action Plan* also encourages the adoption of open-source and open-weight AI by facilitating access to compute resources, fostering licensing clarity, and backing public–private testbeds and "regulatory sandboxes" for sector-specific experimentation in areas like healthcare, energy, and agriculture. Additionally, it directs the development of a federal AI procurement toolbox and reinforces high-security infrastructure, workforce retraining initiatives, and an AI Information Sharing and Analysis Center to boost cybersecurity resilience. The goal is to achieve all of this through a voluntary framework rather than blanket mandates.

One of the key federal initiatives is that agencies must review existing regulations, guidance, and policies that relate to AI and assess whether they unnecessarily hinder innovation or competitiveness. This may result in changes to existing federal laws that concern AI in limited applications. Examples include the *Federal Aviation Administration Reauthorization Act,*[35] which includes language requiring review of AI in aviation, and the *National Defense Authorization Act, 2019,*[36] which identifies the importance of AI innovation for technological superiority and provides a guideline for the ethical use of AI.

Amidst the federal government's preference for a voluntary, principles-based approach to AI governance, several state-level governments and municipalities have passed laws or submitted proposals for AI-related regulations, reflecting their local priorities and concerns. This trend toward state-led regulatory initiatives is creating a patchwork of divergent regulations across the United States, and it will be interesting to watch if this continues or a national consensus emerges.

States such as California, Colorado, New York and Texas have been at the forefront, introducing AI legislation that targets higher-risk frontier models and addresses specific AI applications, from facial recognition technology to algorithmic decision-making in recruiting and housing. Municipalities, too, have not been far behind, with cities like San Francisco implementing ordinances that regulate the use of surveillance technologies. This fragmented approach is already leading to a complex regulatory environment where AI developers and users must navigate rules that vary not only in content but also in the level of enforcement.

The prospect of a multi-tiered regulatory landscape creates challenges for businesses operating across state lines. As the AI ecosystem matures, the interplay between federal guidance, state regulations, and local ordinances is a critical factor in the United States's approach to AI governance.

The regulatory landscape in the United States is further complicated by sector-specific AI regulations, which develop tailored frameworks that address sectoral nuances. In healthcare, for instance, the FDA is developing guidelines for AI-based medical devices, ensuring they meet stringent standards for safety and efficacy. The autonomous vehicle industry is grappling with regulations from the Department of Transportation and other agencies, which are tasked with ensuring the safety of AI-driven transportation systems on public roads. In the financial services sector, AI used for credit scoring, fraud detection, and algorithmic trading, is attracting interest from the Securities and Exchange Commission and the Consumer Financial Protection Bureau to maintain integrity of the capital markets and protect consumers.

In understanding U.S. AI public policy, you must also look beyond regulations and voluntary commitments. Trade restrictions, country sanctions, public–private investment partnerships, and project permitting are also being used to promote America's technology dominance and fight against extraterritorial infringement on U.S. national interests.

China

China's public policy approach to AI differs markedly from both the EU and the United States by prioritizing state-led control, social governance, and national security alongside innovation. While the EU emphasizes rights-based regulation (e.g., risk classification, transparency, and human oversight) and the United States largely relies on sectoral rules and market-driven self-governance, China has embedded AI regulation within its broader cybersecurity, data security, and content control framework.

China released its *Global AI Governance Action Plan*[37] on July 26, 2025. Building on President Xi Jinping's October 2023 *Global AI Governance Initiative*, this Action Plan reflects China's ambition to shape global AI governance amid intensifying technological competition, emphasizing infrastructure development, sectoral application, data quality and security, an open and inclusive ecosystem, sustainability, and international cooperation to bridge the digital divide.

While the United States and China approach AI governance from fundamentally different political and regulatory traditions, both nations share a strategic ambition to lead globally in AI innovation and are actively shaping frameworks to support that goal. Both the U.S. *AI Action Plan* and China's *AI Governance Action Plan* emphasize the importance of public–private collaboration, the need for trustworthy AI systems, and the integration of AI into critical sectors like finance, defense, and healthcare.

Each plan also acknowledges emerging risks around national security, economic stability, and societal disruption, and responds by setting national priorities for AI talent, infrastructure, and standards development. Notably, both countries are investing in AI testbeds, foundational models, and open-source initiatives, although with different motivations.

However, the governance models diverge sharply. The U.S. plan reflects a decentralized, industry-led approach, favoring voluntary standards and minimizing federal regulation to avoid stifling innovation. Oversight is distributed across federal agencies like NIST, the Federal Trade Commission (FDC), and sector-specific regulators, and there is resistance to centralized mandates. By contrast, China's model is highly centralized and state-directed, with the government implementing binding regulations on generative AI, recommendation algorithms, and data governance.

China's plan embeds ethical guidelines aligned with socialist values, enforces pre-deployment reviews, and mandates algorithm registration and security assessments. While the United States frames AI governance as a matter of competitiveness and innovation freedom, China frames it as both an opportunity and a tool to maintain social stability, state control, and ideological alignment.

China's approach to AI governance is a hybrid model that combines AI-specific regulations with voluntary guidelines. In certain areas, China has implemented specific regulations that address the use and implications of AI. For example, the Chinese government has introduced rules targeting algorithmic recommendations, data security, and facial recognition technologies. These regulations are designed to ensure that AI applications align with national security and public interest objectives.

China has implemented a mandatory filing requirement whereby AI systems that meet particular criteria must be registered with authorities using an online portal. This filing includes basic information about the filing entity and the algorithm, as well as the products/services associated with the algorithm.

Security is another focus area. Algorithms that contain public opinion attributes and social mobilization capabilities must be subject to mandatory security assessments before registering their AI system. The security review is focused on risk prevention, user protection, content moderation, model security, and data security.[38]

In other sectors, China encourages the adoption of voluntary industry standards and best practices. This hybrid approach allows for rapid innovation and experimentation within the AI ecosystem, fostering growth and development while still providing a framework for responsible AI deployment in target areas. A couple of the AI regulatory measures that China has passed include deep synthesis (deepfake) provisions and interim measures for GenAI.[39]

China treats deepfakes as a significant governance risk, reflected in its Deep Synthesis Provisions, which took effect in January 2023 and impose strict oversight and penalties across the entire deepfake lifecycle. The rules apply to both service providers and users, covering creation, duplication, publication, and distribution of synthetic content. They mandate strong controls across data protection, transparency, content labeling, and technical security, including identity verification, algorithm reviews, incident reporting, and safeguards for minors.[40]

While the United Kingdom is also banning the creation and dissemination of deepfake videos without consent, China's law and regulation have created rules for every stage in the creation and use of deepfakes: from creation, to labeling, to dissemination. Additionally, the law leaves room for the potential suppression of organically captured content as well.[41]

China has also created legislation to regulate GenAI technologies. This provision went into effect on August 15, 2023, to promote the safe development and application of GenAI through adherence to China's core values and taking action against bias and other harmful outputs. The rules seek to balance innovation with legal governance and are based on five key principles:

1. *GenAI must adhere to the core socialist values of China* and should not endanger national security or interests or promote discrimination and other violence or misinformation.
2. *Measures should be taken to prevent discrimination* on ethnicity, belief, nationality, region, gender, age, occupation, and health resulting from generative AI.
3. *GenAI must respect intellectual property rights and business ethics* to avoid unfair competition and the sharing of business secrets.
4. *GenAI must respect the rights of others* and not endanger the physical or mental health of others.
5. *Measures must be taken* to improve transparency, accuracy, and reliability.

Furthermore, the measures require providers of GenAI to carry out data processing activities in a way that uses legal data sources, respects intellectual property rights, obtains consent for the use of personal information, and maximizes the authenticity, accuracy, objectivity, and diversity of training data.[42] New AI data labeling regulations came into effect in September 2025, requiring explicit and implicit labels on AI-generated content such as text, images, audio, and video.[43,44] Similar to the United States, efforts toward AI regulation in China are not just concentrated from the central government, but from provincial and local levels as well.

Other AI public policy initiatives

While a lot of focus has been given to the different approaches to AI regulations, there are many other tools that can be used by policymakers to support AI innovation while promoting AI safety. These tools include a combination of incentives, such as tax breaks, grants, and funding for research initiatives that encourage responsible AI development, as well as punitive actions like fines and sanctions for non-compliance with standards and regulations.

By creating a balanced framework that rewards organizations for adhering to best practices while holding them accountable for harmful practices, policymakers can foster an environment where innovation thrives alongside safety and ethical considerations. This dual approach not only encourages organizations to prioritize responsible AI but also helps mitigate risks associated with the technology's deployment in society.

Table 7.3 identifies other AI public policy initiatives that can be used to promote AI innovation and safety.

For organizations navigating the global AI public policy landscape, understanding which non-AI and AI-specific laws, regulations, and initiatives apply to them is an important first step. The

Table 7.3 Other AI public policy initiatives

Incentives	• Tax breaks: financial reductions to encourage domestic investment in AI development while ensuring safety. • Grants: funding provided to support innovative AI projects that align with national interests and safety standards. • Research funding: government support for research and development in AI technologies that enhance national competitiveness and safety measures. • Public–private partnerships: collaborations between government and industry to drive AI innovation that benefits the economy while prioritizing safety. • Subsidies: financial assistance to lower the cost of developing and implementing AI solutions that meet safety requirements.

(Continued)

Table 7.3 (Continued)

Punitive actions	• Fines: monetary penalties for organizations that fail to comply with national safety regulations. • Sanctions: restrictions imposed on organizations or countries that violate national interests or safety standards. • Legal action: lawsuits or legal proceedings against organizations for harmful practices affecting national security and safety. • Revocation of licenses: withdrawal of permissions to operate AI systems for non-compliance with safety regulations. • Trade tariffs: taxes imposed on imported AI technologies to protect domestic industries while ensuring safety standards are met.
Monitoring and evaluation	• Assessments: evaluating the economic and social impact of AI technologies on national interests and safety. • Sandboxes: controlled environments for testing AI innovations while ensuring compliance with safety regulations. • Compliance audits: regular assessments of AI systems to ensure adherence to national regulations and safety standards. • Certifications and marks: formal recognition that an AI system adheres to specific national criteria for quality and safety.
Stakeholder engagement	• Public consultations: engaging the public and industry in discussions about AI policies that balance innovation and safety. • Advisory committees: forming groups of experts to provide guidance on AI governance in relation to national priorities and safety considerations.
Education and training	• Workshops and seminars: programs to educate stakeholders on the strategic importance of balancing innovation and safety in AI. • Curriculum development: creating educational materials focused on AI skills that support national workforce development with an emphasis on safety.

next step is to work across the organization to assign accountability and engagement strategies to stay ahead of and take the most advantage of public policy initiatives. While many focus on the burdens of regulations and laws, Table 7.3 identifies a number of potential government incentives and programs that can benefit organizations.

To navigate the public policy landscape, executives should consider the following steps:

1. *Develop a global AI governance framework:* Establish a centralized governance structure that can adapt to various public policy requirements and opportunities, ensuring consistency and accountability across the organization.
2. *Automate the identification of relevant public policy initiatives and obligations:* Leverage internet scrapers, integrated compliance systems, or third-party services to identify and maintain a real-time inventory of AI-relevant public policy programs and obligations for the geographic locations and industries you operate in.
3. *Conduct risk assessments:* Regularly evaluate AI systems for potential risks, including ethical, privacy, safety, and security concerns, and align with the most stringent standards where possible.
4. *Engage with policymakers and industry groups:* Participate in discussions and collaborations with policymaking bodies and industry consortia to influence policy development and gain insight into best practices. Understand the issues and questions of interest to policymakers.
5. *Use regulatory sandboxes:* Pre-test your AI applications in sandboxes set up by policy setters to demonstrate a "best effort" basis of compliance.
6. *Invest in compliance infrastructure:* Build robust systems and processes for documentation, reporting, and compliance verification, leveraging technology to streamline these tasks where feasible.
7. *Educate leadership and staff:* Ensure that employees at all levels understand the regulatory landscape and their role in maintaining compliance, particularly those involved in AI development and deployment.

By taking these proactive steps, executives can turn the challenge of compliance into an opportunity and demonstrate leadership in responsible AI practices.

Conclusion

This chapter provided an overview of the evolving public policy landscape for AI, using the EU, the United States, and China to demonstrate how governments are taking different approaches that span mandatory regulations and voluntary principles. The EU occupies a unique position with its centralized and comprehensive AI regulatory framework embodied in the *AI Act*, which prioritizes standardization, harmonization, and risk-based governance across member states. The Act is designed to work cohesively with existing regulations such as the GDPR, DSA, and DMA, aiming to create a unified digital ecosystem across its member states that balances safety, transparency, and fundamental rights. In contrast, the U.S. *AI Action Plan* embraces a decentralized, innovation-first approach, relying heavily on voluntary standards and industry-led initiatives. Federal agencies will continue to play a role in developing frameworks to ensure AI reliability and security without imposing rigid mandates. China's *AI Governance Action Plan* blends state-directed regulatory oversight with ethical guidelines that emphasize social stability, security, and ideological alignment. China enforces binding rules in critical areas such as GenAI, algorithmic recommendation, and deepfake synthesis technologies, while also promoting international cooperation and leadership in AI standards development. Around the world, most countries have released national AI strategies that reflect their own balance between regulation, innovation, and strategic priorities, positioning them differently along this evolving public policy spectrum.

For global organizations, these divergent approaches necessitate a strategy that incorporates the five-level framework introduced earlier in this chapter. Organizations must ensure compliance with mandatory laws and regulations (Levels 1 and 2), while voluntarily integrating ethical AI into their AI development and use (Levels 3–5). Navigating the constantly evolving global AI regulatory landscape will be a challenge for leaders seeking to harness the power of AI while upholding responsible AI standards. It will require a flexible and agile governance structure that can adapt to various regulatory requirements, and a continuous scan of new publications released by governments at the federal, state, and municipal levels and by industry regulators.

A leading practice is to develop your governance framework to be compliant with the most stringent regulatory requirements and use the voluntary standards to commit to responsible AI practices that meet or exceed your stakeholder expectations. Your organization's strategies and AI goals will determine how far up the triangle (must do, could do, should do) you target.

Key leadership questions to consider:

1. How is your organization adapting to the global AI regulatory landscape?
2. How does your organization track public policy and regulatory developments?
3. What compliance strategies are in place for your state and local AI regulations?
4. How will your organization align industry-specific AI guidelines with broader regulations?
5. How is your AI strategy integrating voluntary guidelines for risk management and governance?

Notes

1. Neuralink. (n.d.). *Neuralink – Pioneering brain computer interfaces*. Retrieved November 24, 2024, from https://neuralink.com/.
2. Hinton, G. [@GeoffreyHinton]. (2024, December 10). Speech on AI risks [Video]. *YouTube*. Retrieved August 31, 2025, from https://www.youtube.com/shorts/odUjxJy0YMo.
3. Paris AI Safety Summit Declaration. (2025, February 10–11). *Statement on inclusive and sustainable artificial intelligence for people and the planet*. Retrieved August 31, 2025, from https://onu.delegfrance.org/statement-on-inclusive-and-sustainable-artificial-intelligence-for-people-and.
4. The White House. (2025, July 23). *Winning the race: America's AI action plan*. https://www.whitehouse.gov/wp-content/uploads/2025/07/Americas-AI-Action-Plan.pdf.
5. *AI Legal-Ethical Framework*. Reproduced with permission from Jeff Saviano, Business AI Ethics Leader, Edmond & Lily Safra Center for Ethics, Harvard University.
6. Expert.ai Team. (2024, July 1). *Insurance unplugged podcast with Lisa Wardlaw and Jeff Saviano, EY [Transcript]*. https://content.expert.ai/blog/the-critical-role-of-governance-and-ethics-in-ai-jeff-saviano-from-ey/.
7. Saviano, J. (2024, May 8). Politicians and nonprofits will struggle to keep AI in check—but corporate boards can't afford to fail. *Fortune*. https://fortune.com/2024/05/08/ai-corporate-boards-ethics-tech-leadership/.
8. Edmond & Lily Safra Center for Ethics. (2024.). *AI ethics for business leaders* [Blog post]. Retrieved August 25, 2025 from https://www.ethics.harvard.edu/blog?page=0.
9. Sherman, N. (2024, June 25). *AI regulations around the world – 2025. Mind Foundry*. https://www.mindfoundry.ai/blog/ai-regulations-around-the-world.

10 Atlan. (2025). *BCBS 239: Principles for effective risk data management and reporting*. https://atlan.com/bcbs-239-guide/#:~:text=BCBS%20239%20compliance%20ensures%20banks,decision%2Dmaking%20and%20risk%20management.
11 National Library of Medicine. (2024, November 24). *Health Insurance Portability and Accountability Act*. In *StatPearls*. National Center for Biotechnology Information. https://www.ncbi.nlm.nih.gov/books/NBK500019/.
12 U.S. Food & Drug Administration. (2025, July 10). *Artificial intelligence-enabled medical devices*. https://www.fda.gov/medical-devices/software-medical-device-samd/artificial-intelligence-enabled-medical-devices.
13 Federal Trade Commission. (2013, January 17). *Children's Online Privacy Protection Rule (COPPA)*. Retrieved March 10, 2025, from https://www.ftc.gov/legal-library/browse/rules/childrens-online-privacy-protection-rule-coppa.
14 European Union. (2016). Regulation (EU) 2016/679 of the European Parliament and of the Council of 27 April 2016 on the protection of natural persons with regard to the processing of personal data and on the free movement of such data (General Data Protection Regulation). *Official Journal of the European Union*, L119, 1–88. https://eur-lex.europa.eu/legal-content/EN/TXT/?uri=CELEX%3A32016R0679.
15 California Attorney General. (2024, March 13). *California Consumer Privacy Act (CCPA)*. https://oag.ca.gov/privacy/ccpa.
16 California Privacy Protection Agency. (2020). *California Privacy Rights Act (CPRA)*. https://www.caprivacy.org/cpra-text/.
17 U.S. Equal Employment Opportunity Commission. (n.d.). *About EEOC*. Retrieved April 6, 2025, from https://www.eeoc.gov/about-eeoc.
18 New York City Department of Consumer and Worker Protection. (n.d.). *Local Law 144 of 2021: Automated employment decision tools (AEDT) frequently asked questions [PDF]*. https://www.nyc.gov/assets/dca/downloads/pdf/about/DCWP-AEDT-FAQ.pdf.
19 U.S. Department of Justice. (2011). *Equal Credit Opportunity Act*. Retrieved April 10, 2025, from https://www.justice.gov/crt/equal-credit-opportunity-act-3.
20 Federal Trade Commission. (2023, May). *Fair Credit Reporting Act*. https://www.ftc.gov/legal-library/browse/statutes/fair-credit-reporting-act.
21 European Parliament. (2023, August 6). *EU AI Act – First regulation on artificial intelligence*. https://www.europarl.europa.eu/topics/en/article/20230601STO93804/eu-ai-act-first-regulation-on-artificial-intelligence.
22 Organisation for Economic Co-operation and Development. (2024, May). *The OECD principles overview*. https://oecd.ai/en/ai-principles.

23 Ministry of Internal Affairs and Communications, Japan. (2023, December 1). *Hiroshima AI Process comprehensive policy framework* [PDF]. Retrieved April 10, 2025, from https://www.soumu.go.jp/main_content/000915261.pdf#page=3.

24 Ministry of Foreign Affairs of Japan. (2023, December 1). *Hiroshima process international code of conduct for organizations developing advanced AI systems* [PDF]. Retrieved August 18, 2025, from https://www.mofa.go.jp/files/100573473.pdf.

25 Habuka, H., & Socol de La Osa, D. (2024, May 24). Shaping global AI governance: Enhancements and new steps for the G7 Hiroshima AI process. *Center for Strategic and International Studies.* https://www.csis.org/analysis/shaping-global-ai-governance-enhancements-and-next-steps-g7-hiroshima-ai-process.

26 Organisation for Economic Co-operation and Development. (2024, May). *AI principles.* https://www.oecd.org/en/topics/ai-principles.html.

27 European Parliament. (2023, June 14). *Artificial Intelligence Act – Texts adopted.* https://www.europarl.europa.eu/doceo/document/TA-9–2023–0236_EN.html.

28 Read more about the EU AI Act through these sources: The announcement: Artificial Intelligence Act: deal on comprehensive rules for trustworthy AI | News | European Parliament, The website: The Act | EU Artificial Intelligence Act The documents: main bill and annexes, The AI Act Presentation, The current state of the Compliance checker: Retrieved [date], from EU AI Act Compliance Checker. https://artificialintelligenceact.eu/assessment/eu-ai-act-compliance-checker/.

29 *EU Act Notation:* The EU AI Act also has an extraterritorial scope, meaning that it applies to both AI systems developed and operated in the EU, as well as AI systems established outside of the EU that affect EU individuals. The EU AI Act also infers obligations to developers, deployers, importers and distributors of AI systems, regardless of their country of origin, if their ultimate AI system operates and produces output in the EU. Costs of complying with the EU AI Act will vary, with the EU Commission estimating that 85% of AI companies fall under "minimal risk," requiring little oversight, but the impact to those with high-risk AI applications necessitates early action.

30 European Commission. (2025, July 10). *The general-purpose AI code of practice.* https://digital-strategy.ec.europa.eu/en/policies/contents-code-gpai.

31 Digital Watch. (2025, October 6). *Italy passes Europe's first national AI law.* https://dig.watch/updates/italy-passes-europes-first-national-ai-law?utm_source=chatgpt.com.

32 International Trade Administration. (2025, April 14). *South Korea Artificial Intelligence (AI) Basic Act.* https://www.trade.gov/market-intelligence/south-korea-artificial-intelligence-ai-basic-act.

33 The White House. (2025, July 23). *America's AI action plan*. https://www.whitehouse.gov/wp-content/uploads/2025/07/Americas-AI-Action-Plan.pdf.

34 National Institute of Standards and Technology. (2023, January 26). *Artificial intelligence risk management framework (AI RMF 1.0)*. https://doi.org/10.6028/NIST.AI.100-1.

35 Federal Aviation Administration. (2024, May 16). *FAA Reauthorization Act of 2024 (Public Law 118-63)*. https://www.faa.gov/about/reauthorization.

36 United States Congress. (2018, August 13). *John S. McCain National Defense Authorization Act for Fiscal Year 2019* (H.R. 5515). https://www.congress.gov/115/bills/hr5515/BILLS-115hr5515enr.pdf.

37 Ministry of Foreign Affairs of the People's Republic of China. (2025, July 26). *Global AI governance action plan*. https://www.mfa.gov.cn/eng/xw/zyxw/202507/t20250729_11679232.html.

38 Dorwart, H., Qu, H., Bräutigam, T., & Gong, J. (2024, July 12). *Preparing for compliance: Key differences between EU, Chinese AI regulations*. International Association of Privacy Professionals. https://iapp.org/news/a/preparing-for-compliance-key-differences-between-eu-chinese-ai-regulations.

39 Deng, Z. (2025, March 28). The shape of China's AI regulations and prospects. *Asia Business Law Journal*. https://law.asia/china-ai-regulations-legislation-compliance-future-prospects/.

40 Cyberspace Administration of China. (n.d.). *Cyberspace Administration of China*. Retrieved August 31, 2025, from https://www.cac.gov.cn/.

41 Fitri, A. (2023, January 10). China to pass the world's most comprehensive law on deepfakes. *Tech Monitor*. https://www.techmonitor.ai/technology/emerging-technology/china-is-about-to-pass-the-worlds-most-comprehensive-law-on-deepfakes.

42 Trustible. Forbes. (2023, July 18). *How does China's approach to AI regulation differ from the US and EU?* https://www.forbes.com/sites/forbeseq/2023/07/18/how-does-ch.

43 Cyberspace Administration of China. (2025, March 14). *Measures for labeling artificial intelligence-generated and synthetic content*. https://www.cac.gov.cn/2025-03/14/c_1743654684782215.htm.

44 Luo, Y., & Dan, X. (2025, March 18). China releases new labeling requirements for AI-generated content. *Inside Privacy*. https://www.insideprivacy.com/international/china/china-releases-new-labeling-requirements-for-ai-generated-content/.

Chapter 8

Aligning corporate profit and purpose

In the previous section, we explored how artificial intelligence (AI) differs from rules-based technology. While these differences require modified corporate governance, it is important to remember that governance practices must keep pace with AI. AI governance cannot be treated as a static exercise. It is on a journey, similar to that of AI itself.

A timeless definition of corporate governance, framed by Sir Adrian Cadbury, states:

> Corporate governance is concerned with holding the balance between economic and social goals and between individual and communal goals. The governance framework is there to encourage the efficient use of resources and equally, to require accountability for the stewardship of those resources. The aim is to align as nearly as possible the interests of individuals, corporations, and society.[1]

AI governance lagging behind AI capabilities can lead to eroded stakeholder trust, costly fines and penalties, project delays, and extensive AI retraining. But advancing AI governance too quickly can result in overburdensome controls that slow down AI innovation and user adoption. The trick is finding the "Goldilocks" optimal balance.

AI governance often follows a 3-phased process. Initially, most organizations adopt AI governance mechanisms that are manual, informal, and targeted to a small group of centralized AI developers. Control over AI is reliant upon the specialized knowledge of its developers and an expectation that users do the right thing (e.g., follow policy). Most, if not all, AI outputs are subject to full human review.

DOI: 10.4324/9781003625520-10

As AI spreads across the organization and AI development becomes more federated, including citizen developers, governance practices are standardized and integrated into corporate policy and procedures. But the governance construct still relies on voluntary compliance, and enforcement is time-consuming.

As AI systems become more complex and autonomous, as with agentic AI, governance must become automated. Real-time continuous monitoring, machines overseeing machines, is built into the functional requirements of AI projects to monitor for conformance and compliance. Human operators react to out-of-bounds performance alerts rather than directly overseeing the AI outcomes.

Due to the added costs of building automated governance mechanisms, it is important to identify and target the risks that really matter. While all organizations should have enterprise-level governance mechanisms such as policies, responsible AI development guidelines, and risk assessments, at the AI-system level, governance should match the system's risk profile. Low-risk AI systems will require minimal monitoring, allowing them to be quickly stood up and deployed, while high-risk AI systems should be subject to customized monitoring controls.

The goal is to effectively balance innovation with risk management, designing controls to target the higher risks of each AI use case.

Objectives

Upon completing this chapter, you will be able to:

- Explore the impact of governance on corporate profits and purpose
- Understand the evolution of AI governance from manual to automated systems
- Identify the risks associated with varying levels of AI governance
- Develop strategies for achieving a balanced approach to AI governance.

Modifying corporate governance practices for AI

AI introduces new risks and challenges that require a modified governance framework. The good news is that organizations do not need to start from scratch. AI can leverage many existing technology governance practices already in place. These vary from existing data quality, privacy, and security controls to policies governing technology usage and reliance on third-party vendors. However, as AI leverages more advanced technologies, such as GenAI and agentic AI, businesses need to implement enhanced governance practices.

AI governance is not merely about modifying a few policies and processes. It is a dynamic practice that must keep pace with AI technology advancements and investments. It must work concurrently with the growth of AI to ensure AI's benefits are maximized and risks minimized.

The basic building blocks of AI governance are well documented in various standards, regulations, and guidelines. From the EU AI Act to the National Institute of Standards and Technology Artificial Intelligence Risk Management, a great deal has been written about what good AI governance looks like. The challenge lies not in "what" to do, but in "how" to implement these best practices with speed, efficiency, and at scale.

This necessitates a top-down approach, starting with a clear tone at the top that stresses the importance of proportional investments in AI governance, matching investments in AI development and deployment. AI governance needs to move beyond policies and procedure documents to machine-powered monitoring tools, automated compliance checks, and robust reporting systems.

To date, human-in-the-loop oversight has been relied upon heavily to guard against AI failures and erroneous outcomes; however, human oversight is becoming too slow and limited to keep up with the speed and variety of AI outcomes.

As we pivot toward automated and AI-supported monitoring systems, the importance of human involvement in governing AI remains crucial. Technology can facilitate the process, but ultimately, it is societal values, corporate goals, and stakeholder expectations that should drive AI governance objectives.

Before we cover the key elements of AI governance, it is important to position how critical the AI selection and investment process is. Making the right governance decisions at this early stage will reduce the risks of downstream implementation.

Value-driven AI selection

In the rush to stay ahead, organizations often equate speed with success. AI use cases are selected based on their ease of implementation or the interests of the budget holder. The seduction of "cool" AI projects or an executive's "pet" project tends to sidestep considerations around value creation and hidden costs.

With many early AI projects delivering low return on investment (ROI), corporate executives are taking a different approach to their next round of AI investments. They are centralizing the selection of AI use cases and basing their decisions on value creation and full cost accounting. Calculating the full costs of AI requires factoring in the shorter lifespan of AI technologies, the costs of integrating AI into existing processes, the effort to build user trust and adoption, and the AI controls and monitoring mechanisms required. Too often, the costs of AI are significantly understated as they only factor in the direct development and operating costs.

As a best practice, executives should leverage a three-component model of balancing value drivers, capabilities, and risk:

1 *Value drivers address the questions of what AI to invest in and why.* It prioritizes AI projects that deliver maximum value. It asks, why is this project beneficial, and how does it align with our strategic goals?
2 *Capabilities challenge the feasibility of an AI project – asking, can we do it?* It includes understanding the cost and effort required to build the necessary skills, capabilities, and technology needed to develop, operate, and monitor the AI system.
3 *Risk involves the most important and yet the hardest question to answer: Should we do it?* Irrespective of the novelty and potential short-term gains, if an AI project could cause substantial *harm, its creation must* be questioned. The project may still proceed, but all high-risk scenarios must be accounted for and mitigated against.[2]

A thoughtful process for AI selection ensures that your AI program delivers value while operating responsibly. Let's take an example. The executives of Retail Corp are deciding among three AI projects:

1 *The first project is an AI-powered predictive analytics tool* that uses past shopping data to predict future customer behaviors and suggest personalized recommendations.
2 *The second tool is an AI-based customer service chatbot* that would provide immediate, personalized support to customers 24×7.

3 *The third tool is an AI-driven surveillance technology* that uses video from store cameras to monitor customers for theft prevention, with a real-time alert to store personnel of potential thefts.

When assessing value drivers, the first step is to determine how value is defined and generated in the organization. For Retail Corp, value is derived from sales to customers. Their corporate strategy is focused on enhancing the customer experience to attract new customers and generate repeat sales from existing customers. When comparing the three AI use cases for value generation, the predictive analytics initiative, with its objective to provide customized recommendations to customers based on their past purchasing behavior, appears to align most closely with the organization's strategic goal of enhancing the customer experience and driving repeat sales. The chatbot project, while providing enhanced customer service, will not drive sales. The surveillance project is targeted toward loss prevention rather than enhancing customer experience or driving sales.

In terms of capabilities, both the predictive analytics and the chatbot initiatives would require a significant investment to develop the necessary AI skills and infrastructure; however, they are both technically feasible using today's technology. In comparison, the costs for the surveillance project could be high, requiring costly camera upgrades and hardware-software integrations. In addition, the ability of AI to accurately predict theft based on video surveillance is questionable. Its predictive ability would need to be thoroughly tested, and even then, it is highly probable that it will make mistakes once operating in the stores.

Finally, risk mitigation and ethical considerations would also rank the surveillance project as the least desirable. While theft prevention is important, surveillance technology could lead to privacy concerns, potentially affecting the company's reputation. In addition, the AI system would probably leverage physical characteristics such as age, ethnicity, gender, and physical appearance to predict who is a theft risk, leading to potential discrimination. Predictive analytics and chatbots, while they too could have biased outcomes, typically raise fewer red flags.

In our comparison, the predictive analytics AI system is the clear winner. It optimizes value, is more directly aligned with the organization's strategic goals, requires a reasonable level of investment costs, and introduces fewer responsible AI risks.

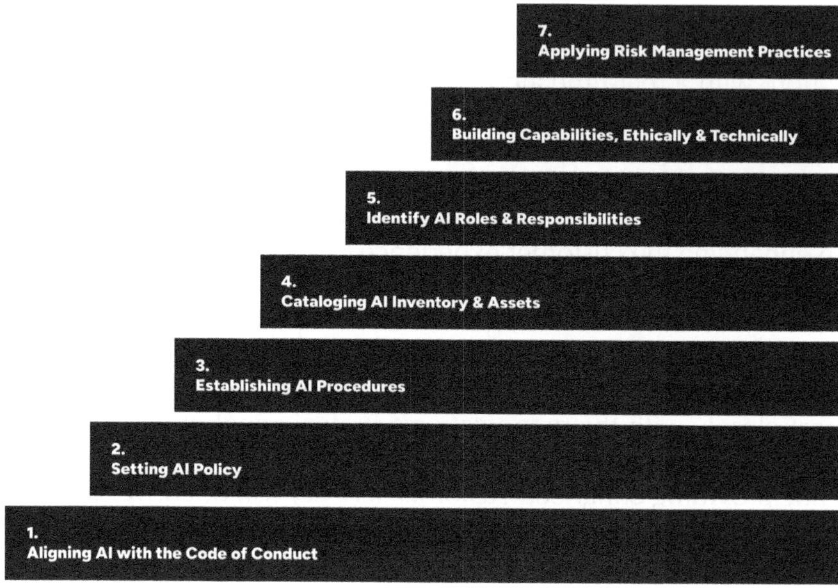

Figure 8.1 The building blocks for effective and purposeful AI governance.

As the business owner and development team collaborate on this AI project, they should be guided by an AI governance process that ensures that they do the right thing at the right time. Figure 8.1 and the section that follows describe the AI governance building blocks.

Aligning AI with a code of conduct

An organization's code of conduct outlines its mission statement, values, ethical commitments, and business principles. At its core, a code of conduct sets out the "Corporate Purpose" of an organization. The AI principles discussed in Chapter 2 help to balance corporate priorities with stakeholder expectations. This includes fair and impartial decision-making, user privacy, and transparency in operations.

All employees involved in an organization's AI program, from the decision-makers to the AI developers, operators, and end-users, need to understand how AI principles apply to their roles and responsibilities.

Setting out expectations for responsible AI practices is a crucial component of AI governance. Equally important is to set out what happens when the code of conduct is not adhered to – what actions are taken and who is held accountable. Consequences can range from minor internal disciplinary actions to legal repercussions. It could also involve delaying AI's deployment or curtailing its use. The goal of the consequences framework is to reinforce the importance of decisions and behaviors being aligned with the code of conduct.

A common tension in AI projects is whether to promote innovation or safety. They are often seen as mutually exclusive, with safeguards slowing down innovation. However, all innovations, no matter how good they are, only succeed when they are put to use. Users must not only perceive their value but also trust them. Slow user adoption is often attributed to a lack of trust.

Community Bank – use case example

Community Bank has developed an AI-based loan approval system to evaluate the creditworthiness of car loan applicants. During focus group studies, their target demographic, GenZ first-time car owners, liked the easy and quick application process.

Sue's annual bonus is riding on a successful launch next month. As head of the credit lending department, she is frustrated with the latest testing report from the AI development team. They reported that the AI system is still rejecting women's and immigrants' applications more frequently. They blame it on the historical data used for training.

Sue considers how to meet their launch date. If the bias stems from historical data, she rationalizes, then the company has historically accepted this level of bias. "Yes!" she thinks. "It's enough that our AI model is performing as well as our human credit adjudicators. I'll commit in phase II to improving bias."

The failure of AI governance in this scenario is not only that Sue valued the launch over customer well-being, but that the organization's controls did not detect and prevent it. This could happen from a lack of oversight over the project to raise and address ethical issues, such as bias and discrimination, or no independent evaluator that would flag this issue to a risk and control leader outside of Sue's control. Consideration should also be given to how her bonus incentivizes her to favor launching the AI system over complying with responsible AI principles.

The implementation of AI involves trade-offs that need to be considered. A common challenge with implementing a code of conduct is that values and rules have to be interpreted into meaningful principles to guide behavior.

Setting AI policy

An effective AI policy includes several components, the most important being a definition of AI. Once defined as AI, a system should adhere to the modified AI governance framework, which is often more costly and time-consuming to implement. To avoid unnecessary costs, it is important to clearly distinguish between AI and rules-based expert systems that mimic the skills and capabilities of AI systems but do not involve ML.

The AI policy is also where you will define the AI principles, as outlined in Chapter 2. While there is a general consensus on the AI principles to be followed, it is important for each organization to define how each principle applies to them.

An Acceptance AI Use Policy is becoming common in most organizations. It specifies the contexts in which AI can be used, and those in which its use is restricted or prohibited. For instance, the *EU AI Act* bans AI that "manipulates human behavior through subliminal or deceptive techniques, causing significant harm."[3] The AI policy should encompass not only mandatory prohibitions set by regulatory bodies but also voluntary prohibitions driven by the organization's ethical values, risk tolerance, and stakeholder expectations. Banning the use of public GenAI models is often the first policy statement related to AI.

A common challenge in writing an AI policy is keeping up with the introduction of new AI technologies. In 2023, many early adopters had to update their AI policies for the use of GenAI to emphasize the need for human operators to take responsibility for the quality of AI output. Now with the emergence of agentic AI, new safeguards are needed to address AI's growing autonomy. Will the intersection of AI with advanced robotics and augmented reality trigger another AI policy update?

Establishing AI procedures

To reinforce the AI policy, detailed procedures and guidelines that operationalize the principles and rules should be created. AI procedures should provide clear, step-by-step guidance on implementing the AI policy and ensuring compliance.

Some helpful procedural documents include:

1. *Protocol for AI development:* It describes how AI systems should be designed, developed, deployed, and maintained in accordance with the organization's AI principles.
2. *Training and awareness:* It describes the process, timelines, and curriculum to educate everyone in the organization on the AI policy and procedures.
3. *Audit trails:* It specifies how to create and maintain logs and records that evidence actions taken during the system's lifecycle to ensure transparency and traceability.
4. *Incident response plan:* It provides a response plan for AI-related incidents, addressing how to report, escalate, and resolve breaches of the AI policy.
5. *Risk assessment and mitigation:* It itemizes steps to identify, assess, and mitigate risks involved with the implementation of AI, including privacy threats, security violations, or biased decision-making.
6. *Compliance monitoring:* It specifies measures to monitor and enforce compliance with the AI policy, such as logs, regular audits, reviews, and automated performance checks.
7. *Crisis management plan:* It details the strategy for managing and mitigating crisis situations that arise from AI deployment, including preventative measures and communication strategies.

Without standardized AI procedural documents, different teams working on AI within the same organization may operate differently, resulting in inefficiencies, disparities in output quality, and unnecessary complications.

By implementing standardized AI procedural documents, these inconsistencies can be avoided with AI development teams following the same standards for data validation, bias testing, and security. In case of any anomalies or crises, a standardized procedure would ensure a unified and efficient response.

Cataloging your AI inventory and assets

An important component of a strong AI governance structure is having a complete inventory of your AI assets. Having an understanding of these assets, which include AI models, systems, datasets, relevant infrastructure, and skilled personnel, allows for effective governance and optimal resource utilization.

First, you can only govern what you know. An exhaustive inventory allows organizations to monitor and manage their AI assets effectively. It facilitates tracking and auditing, ensuring compliance with data privacy regulations and ethical AI practices. It also helps to identify potential security vulnerabilities and risks.

Second, having a detailed inventory aids in assessing each AI use case against strategic priorities. It provides a clear overview of current assets and offers insights into how well these align with the organization's strategic objectives. Each AI project can be assessed for its relevance, potential value-add, and fit within the organization's overall AI strategy. It also serves as an ongoing source for sharing knowledge and creating linkages to future ideation.

Third, an AI asset inventory can enhance ROI by optimizing the deployment of AI resources. Assets like AI skills, proprietary technologies, or pre-trained models can be reused or shared across multiple projects, thus reducing costs and duplication of efforts.

An AI asset inventory can also highlight under-resourced areas or reveal a need for further skill development within the team. Also, it provides a platform for showcasing an organization's AI capabilities to stakeholders, potential investors, and customers.

While the use of manual, self-identification methods, such as surveys are a practical way to catalog AI assets, you should not rely solely on these tools. The accuracy of a manual inventory is highly dependent on the knowledge and diligence of the individuals completing the survey, which can lead to incomplete or incorrect data.

Additionally, manually updating the inventory is time-consuming, and it is difficult to track changes over time, especially as the number of AI assets proliferates.

Leveraging network interrogation tools or automated asset discovery software can provide a more accurate, efficient, and timely approach. These technology-enabled tools can automatically discover and catalog AI assets across an organization, saving considerable time and resources. However, these tools are more complex to deploy and require a good understanding of the existing infrastructure to ensure they are correctly implemented and used. Also, these tools should not be relied upon blindly. They create incomplete lists as not all AI can be easily detected, particularly when AI is embedded into existing technologies.

The more inventive you are in your detection methods, the more complete your inventory will be. For example, AI embedded in SAS queries can be detected through spikes in CPU and memory usage, or processing times. Logs can also provide insight into where AI commands are being used.

The right approach is most likely a hybrid approach, with automated tools being used to inventory and catalog AI assets, and human reviews to complete the list for missing or difficult-to-detect AI.

Identifying AI roles and responsibilities

As part of any effective AI management strategy, it is essential to clarify roles and responsibilities related to the development, deployment, and operation of AI systems. Assigning accountability ensures that tasks are performed effectively and that issues are quickly identified and addressed. A popular way to articulate these roles and responsibilities is through a RACI (Responsible, Accountable, Consulted, and Informed) map.

Roles to consider when developing an AI RACI include:

1 *Sponsor*: The sponsor is often a high-ranking executive who champions the AI project. They are accountable for the strategic alignment of the AI project, securing necessary resources, and ensuring the project delivers the anticipated value.
2 *Developer*: The developer designs and trains the AI algorithms. They ensure the AI system is trained according to specified requirements while adhering to the AI policy.

3 *Tester*: The tester is accountable for evaluating the AI system's functionality and performance to ensure it meets the necessary standards, identifying flaws and potential improvements.
4 *Deployer*: The deployer implements the AI system into the actual operational environment, ensuring the correct installation and proper integration of the system into the existing IT infrastructure.
5 *Operator*: The operator oversees the day-to-day operation of the AI system. They monitor system performance, address technical issues, and coordinate system updates or maintenance.
6 *User*: The user is the individual or group that interacts with the AI system in its operational environment. They should be adequately trained on how to use the system and are often in the best position to provide feedback on system performance.
7 *Risk and control function:* The risk and control function can often include individuals from many departments, including legal, risk, privacy, security, and internal audit. They should be involved early so that any risk and control obligations are included in the AI requirements during its design and training.

Depending on your reliance on vendors, these roles can be filled either by internal employees or by third-party providers. When roles are outsourced to third parties, their accountability, responsibility, and obligations must be documented in a contractual agreement.

Here are some important considerations to include in the vendor contract:

1 *Scope of work:* It defines the work to be performed by the third-party developer.
2 Timelines and deliverables: It specifies the timeline for the project completion and the deliverables expected at each stage.
3 *Quality standards:* It specifies the quality standards expected in terms of performance, reliability, and user interaction quality.
4 *Intellectual property rights:* Since third-party developers may use proprietary algorithms and methods to build the AI system, it is important to define who owns the rights to this intellectual property.
5 *Data security and confidentiality:* It includes expectations related to data security, especially if the third-party developer will have access to sensitive or proprietary data.

6 *Compliance with laws and regulations:* It stipulates compliance with relevant laws and regulations, especially those related to data protection and user privacy.
7 *Responsibilities for troubleshooting, maintenance, and support:* It delineates responsibilities for future troubleshooting, maintenance, and support needs for the AI system.
8 *Payment terms:* It includes detailed payment terms, including the project cost, progress payment milestones, and penalties in case of delays.
9 *Dispute resolution:* It outlines how disputes will be handled, including processes for issue escalation.
10 *Liability and indemnification:* It outlines how liability will be allotted between the organization and the third-party developer. This section defines who is responsible in case the AI system malfunctions, causes harm or damage, or leads to regulatory noncompliance.

By carefully considering and defining contractual elements, both the organization and the third-party developer have a common understanding of their respective commitments and responsibilities. In addition, the organization can better safeguard itself from potential legal and financial risks associated with the implementation of the AI system.

Equally important to defining roles and responsibilities and accountability is the establishment of an oversight function. A robust oversight function includes an incident management system capable of identifying, recording, tracking, and resolving any issues that emerge during the development, deployment, and operation of an AI system. It sets forth clear processes for reporting incidents, outlining anticipated resolution timelines, and detailing follow-up and enforcement actions. We will further explore this important control function in a later chapter.

Building capabilities, both ethical and technical

Building the right set of capabilities, both ethical and technical, involves developing skills, tools, and infrastructure across different layers of the organization.

The needed technical skills include a strong understanding of AI, data science, software engineering methods, and relevant technologies. It extends beyond the development team to include technicians who maintain and troubleshoot AI systems, operators who employ AI tools, and even the users who interact with AI.

Organizations are in a race to keep their workforce's skills relevant and updated. AI advances are outpacing the traditional upskilling routes like academic degrees and in-house training programs. In addition, the competition for sourcing AI-savvy talent is severe, making talent acquisition a costly endeavor.

As a result, more organizations are relying on third-party vendors to meet their AI needs. This approach not only grants them access to the requisite, often hard-to-find, expertise but also allows them to stay current as AI evolves. However, while third parties can address the AI skills gap in the short term, the importance of building a solid, in-house understanding and competence around AI remains. A fine balance is needed between internal skill development and strategic outsourcing.

Ultimately, building skills, both ethical and technical, helps an organization deploy AI solutions that are not just technologically advanced but also socially responsible.

Applying risk management practices and controls

A risk-based governance model is the de facto recommendation of most AI regulations, standards, and guidelines. The inherent complexities and variabilities in AI make it difficult to prescribe rigid compliance and control requirements.

The risk assessment is used to separate high-risk from low-risk AI systems. Factors examined include the sensitivity and volume of data used, potential harm to users, susceptibility of the algorithm to bias, interpretability of the AI model, and regulatory obligations. For each risk identified, the severity and likelihood of adverse events are evaluated. The ranked-risks should then be compared against the organization's risk tolerance level – the degree of risk an organization is willing to accept.

If an AI system is deemed high-risk and exceeds the organization's risk tolerance, further risk mitigation measures will need to be implemented. These can range from additional controls and safeguards in the AI system, greater oversight and auditing, increased transparency measures, or even deciding not to proceed with the deployment in its current form. These concepts are illustrated in the scenario below:

Scenario – an online retail company conducting a risk assessment on two distinct AI systems

The first system is an AI-based chatbot designed to answer basic client inquiries. This system is low-risk, given that it handles common questions and does not process sensitive data. Even though a malfunction could impact the client's experience, it's unlikely to result in significant harm or disruption. Although rated low-risk, this system should still be subject to ethical filters (e.g., word choice and tone) and monitored for performance drift – a decline in accuracy of the AI model over time.

The second system is an AI-based credit scoring model that automates store credit approvals. This system is rated higher risk, as it makes critical financial decisions that can significantly affect the client's financial health. It processes large volumes of sensitive personal financial data, which must be handled securely to prevent data breaches. Moreover, biased outcomes could damage the company's reputation and lead to regulatory infractions. Due to its high-risk status, this AI system should be subjected to rigorous pre-deployment testing, and independent validation and verification. Continuous post-production monitoring should be implemented to measure performance drift, bias, and privacy breaches.

By using a risk-based approach to governance, the online retail company can apply differing levels of governance to each AI system commensurate with their risk profile, allowing for their AI principles to be applied in a cost-effective manner.

Due to its importance, we will devote the next couple of chapters to dig deeper into how to design and implement an AI risk assessment, as well as the different response and control mechanisms that can be deployed.

Cultivating knowledge: the role of education and training

A successful AI system relies not only on the model design but also on the ability of individuals to effectively use it. This holds true for everyone from senior management, who govern the AI program, to AI developers, operators, risk control personnel, and ultimately, users of the AI system.

Starting with the fundamentals, all involved parties need to have a general understanding of the AI governance process. This includes the objectives of AI governance, the roles and responsibilities, the major processes such as risk assessment and asset inventory, and an appreciation of their interdependencies.

Detailed specialist knowledge should also be provided to those directly involved in crucial components of the AI governance process. For instance, AI developers and testers might need training on technical aspects such as data quality testing, retraining models for bias, or selecting models for explainability. Risk controllers would require an in-depth understanding of the risk assessment process, including the tools and technologies involved.

Employees should be trained on their specific roles and responsibilities using practical and experiential learning approaches. Creating immersive training experiences where employees can directly interact with the AI tools and methods provides hands-on skills. For example, during risk assessment training, employees should conduct simulated exercises where they actively engage with risk assessment tools. Similarly, for those involved in AI development, technical workshops could be organized where they actively select and test AI models for explainability, fairness, and robustness.

Immersive, hands-on training can bolster employee confidence and competence in overseeing AI. Experiential training methodologies can also expose learners to real-world scenarios and challenges, better preparing them to identify, understand, and solve issues that arise.

Training should not be seen as a one-off event but rather an ongoing process. With new methodologies, responsible AI considerations, and regulatory stipulations frequently coming to light, it is important to stay current.

An additional opportunity for a learning program is encouraging community groups and networks. This could include online forums or platforms for employees to share their insights or new findings, encouraging peer-to-peer learning. Regular talks from external AI experts or inviting regulatory authorities to discuss the latest regulations could also be valuable additions.

The goal of any organization should be to foster a culture of curiosity, adaptability, and agility.

Conclusion

AI governance enables organizations to develop, deploy, and maintain AI systems that balance their need for profit while meeting stakeholder expectations. From having a clear AI policy to accountability matrices, each element plays an important part. The policies and procedures need to be supported with programs to build a skilled AI workforce in both technical and ethical capabilities. This includes the risk and control teams that provide an important oversight role in verifying that the AI governance processes are designed and operated effectively.

An AI governance model needs to continually evolve to ensure that it identifies and mitigates the risks that truly matter. The integration of rigorous risk assessments, detailed asset inventories, and monitoring mechanisms helps organizations to anticipate, prevent, and address possible challenges such as loss of customer trust, damaging public image, hefty regulatory or legal penalties, and costly remediation efforts.

Key leadership questions to consider:

1 How effectively does your AI policy align with your organization's values, stakeholder expectations, and strategic objectives?
2 How complete is your inventory of AI assets?
3 How well-defined and understood are the roles and responsibilities for AI governance?
4 How robust are your efforts in building both technical and ethical AI capabilities?

Notes

1 Melbourne Project Management Institute. (n.d.). *Corporate governance white paper*. https://www.melbourne.pmi.org.au/wp-content/files/MWP1017_Governance.pdf.

2 EY. (n.d.). *EY.ai value accelerator*. Retrieved August 9, 2025, from https://www.ey.com/en_gl/services/ai/platform/value-accelerator.

3 Regulation (EU) 2024/1689 of the European Parliament and of the Council (EU AI Act). (2024, June 13). *Official Journal of the European Union*. European Union. https://eur-lex.europa.eu/legal-content/EN/TXT/?uri=CELEX:32024R1689.

Chapter 9

Targeting the risks that truly matter

Taking a risk-based approach to artificial intelligence (AI) is often viewed as a pessimistic approach, focusing only on what can go wrong. The challenge is that inevitably something does go wrong. When unprepared, the impacts of an incident are more severe and far-reaching, and take longer to rectify. Without preventative controls, more will go wrong. Both situations quickly erode user trust, reducing use of the AI system. Renowned business strategist, Michael Porter, puts risks in perspective by framing: "Risk is a function of how poorly a strategy will perform if the 'wrong' scenario occurs."[1]

A well-designed risk management program can accelerate the use of AI by focusing on the risks that truly matter. AI is a relatively new technology, and we fear what we do not understand. This is leading organizations to take a conservative approach to AI, limiting its roll-out and use. This strategy may be warranted for higher-risk systems, but why take this same approach for low-risk AI systems? The reason because organizations do not trust their ability to distinguish between a high- and low-risk system. So they are all treated the same. This limits the ability to optimize low-risk AI systems and pulls resources away from high-risk systems.

Risks can originate at any point in the AI development lifecycle, including risks related to the system's design, data, algorithm, and performance. An important first step is to create an exhaustive list of all the risks that can happen. The longer the list, the better. You want to consider all the possible scenarios of what can go wrong – from the most probable to the least. It's important to involve stakeholders with different perspectives as AI introduces new risks that do not exist on your traditional risk register. The nominal cost of having a longer list is worth it when compared to the cost of being

DOI: 10.4324/9781003625520-11

unprepared. It also serves as an audit trail for future projects that others can learn from to reduce their efforts in conducting a risk assessment for similar use cases.

The next part, deciding how to respond to each risk, takes more time. We manage risks every day, unconsciously reacting in one of four ways: accept, transfer, mitigate, or reduce. We accept risks that we can tolerate. Other risks we transfer to someone else, playing hot potato. For the last two, risk mitigation and risk reduction, we actively engage in strategies to decrease the likelihood and impact of a negative outcome. These strategies are not mutually exclusive, and we often use more than one in a given situation.

To decide which risks can be accepted vs. responded to, an organization needs to understand its risk appetite. It also requires reliable, data-enabled risk measurements. Organizations must go beyond traditional qualitative risk assessments (high, medium, and low) and use qualitative risk metrics and key risk indicators that measure the AI system's risk exposure and the efficacy of risk response mechanisms. More risks can be put on a watch list when evidence-based information is available to back up your decision. This same measurement approach can be used to compare your predicted and actual risk values.

As we explore these topics, it is important to remember that risk management is not a "one-and-done" activity but an ongoing process that must be revisited and challenged regularly.

Objectives

Upon completing this chapter, you will be able to:

- Create an inventory of AI risks and determine their applicability to different AI systems
- Understand the four risk management strategies, including risk acceptance, transference, mitigation, and reduction
- Develop AI incident response plans and crisis management strategies
- Establish a risk-aware culture.

The first line of defense

The tendency to jump straight into the design and development of AI systems can overshadow the critical need for early risk identification. While the excitement of harnessing AI's capabilities is understandable, it is important to balance this enthusiasm with understanding the risks involved.

Early risk assessment is not merely a procedural step; it allows organizations to foresee and address potential pitfalls that could derail AI projects. By identifying risks at the outset, companies can allocate resources more effectively, design more robust AI systems, and establish trust with stakeholders.

The tendency to prioritize functionality over risk assessment is often driven by the pressure to keep up with competitors and the rapid pace of technological advancement. However, the initial gains achieved by hastening AI deployment can quickly be overshadowed by the repercussions when incidents occur. For example, when AI systems handle sensitive data without adequate safeguards, breaches can occur that erode customer trust. Or when decision-making algorithms are biased, leading to unfair treatment of individuals and groups, resulting in public outcry and legal challenges. Technical system malfunctions can disrupt operations and lead to financial losses.

A preliminary AI risk assessment begins with assembling a cross-functional team of experts who bring diverse perspectives. This team typically includes AI developers, data scientists, legal and compliance officers, ethicists, cybersecurity experts, and business analysts. Engaging customer focus groups and other key stakeholders, like union representatives, can foster earlier alignment and ensure all the risk factors and requirements for success are fully calibrated. Together, they identify and evaluate potential threats that could impede the AI project's success or cause unintended harm.

The assessment is conducted in a series of deliberate steps. First, the team defines the scope of the AI project, setting clear boundaries for the assessment. Second, they identify risks, drawing on a variety of sources such as historical data, industry reports, expert interviews, and lessons learned from previous projects. This identification phase is exhaustive, ensuring no stone is left unturned.

Risks are scrutinized across various dimensions:

1 *Compliance risks:* How might the AI system contravene regulations or industry standards?
2 *Privacy risks:* What are the vulnerabilities that could lead to data breaches or misuse of personal information?

3 *Security risks:* Where are the weak points that could be exploited by cyber threats?
4 *Ethical risks:* Are there elements of the AI system that could result in biased outcomes or ethical dilemmas?
5 *Technical risks:* What technical failures could arise, and how would they affect the AI system's performance?
6 *Operational risks:* How might the AI system disrupt existing workflows or circumvent operational processes?
7 *Strategic risks*: Could the AI initiative inadvertently misalign with the organization's strategic goals?

Once risks are identified, the team considers the likelihood of each risk occurring and the potential impact on the organization and stakeholders. The team prioritizes these risks and decides on their risk management strategy, focusing on those that pose the greatest threat to the project. Several tools and frameworks can assist in quantifying risk, such as the Factor Analysis of Information Risk model.[2] AI-specific risk assessment templates and checklists can ensure a thorough examination of all relevant factors.

Early AI learnings demonstrate the importance of timely risk identification. For example, a financial services company discovered that its AI model unfairly treated borrowers at the edges of the age spectrum – the very young and very old. They were able to successfully counteract historical biases in the data and reduce unfair outcomes by 20% by changing the AI's objectives to include maximizing fairness scores across all sub-groups. However, to avoid costly retraining, this hybrid objective had to be set in the early design phase.[3] "The key is to forecast things while there's still time to act,"[4] Andy Day, GE Healthcare Next Level.

Going beyond traditional risk assessments

In August 2024, MIT CSAIL researchers developed the AI Risk Repository: a comprehensive and accessible living database of 700+ AI risks, sourced from over 17,000 records. The MIT research found that existing AI risk frameworks have significant gaps. On average, the included frameworks mentioned just 34% of the 23 risk subdomains the researchers identified, with nearly a quarter covering less than 20%. None of the AI risk frameworks included all 23 risk subdomains, with the most comprehensive covering only 70%. The inventory highlights the complexity in preparing a complete risk inventory.

The most frequently addressed risk domains include:

1 AI system safety, failures, and limitations
2 Socioeconomic and environmental harms
3 Discrimination and toxicity
4 Privacy and security
5 Malicious actors and misuse.

Others, like AI welfare and rights and competitive dynamics, were mentioned in less than 15% of the documents. The MIT AI Risk Repository is available online to download, copy, and use, and is a valuable resource for every organization's AI risk assessment process.[5]

Different approaches to managing AI risk

Once potential AI risks have been mapped out, organizations must determine how to respond. The strategy selected is not a one-size-fits-all solution; it must be tailored for each risk, taking into consideration the organization's tolerance for risk – commonly referred to as "risk appetite." The risk appetite is a reflection of the organization's culture, values, and strategic priorities. A company with a high risk appetite may be more inclined to accept certain risks, while a more risk-averse organization will prioritize risk mitigation or transference.

The nature of the risk itself is a primary consideration in this decision-making process. Risks vary widely in their source, impact, and likelihood. For instance, a risk stemming from a potential data breach demands a different approach than AI reliability being impacted by low-quality data. The potential impact on business operations is also a crucial factor. Risks that could cause significant disruption to operations, damage to reputation, or financial loss are typically managed more aggressively.

Organizations typically use four primary approaches to managing AI risks:

1 *Risk acceptance:* This approach involves acknowledging the risk exists and proceeding with the AI project despite it, often because

the probability of a risk occurring is low, or the cost of mitigation is disproportionately high in comparison to the risk impact.

2 *Risk transference:* In this approach, the organization shifts the risk to a third party, such as through insurance policies or contractual agreements.
3 *Risk mitigation:* Here, the focus is on taking proactive steps to decrease the likelihood of the risk occurring. This could involve enhancing security protocols, implementing new policies, or adjusting the AI system's design.
4 *Risk reduction:* This strategy is centered on lessening the potential impact of the risk, should it occur. Measures might include developing contingency plans, implementing a kill switch, or establishing rapid response mechanisms.[6]

The selection and implementation of these risk management approaches is dynamic, requiring ongoing evaluation and adjustment as the AI initiative progresses and as the external environment changes.

Risk acceptance

When an organization accepts a risk, it is essentially deciding to take no action. It acknowledges the risk exists but has decided that eliminating the risk is impractical or economically unfeasible. This is particularly relevant in scenarios where the cost of implementing safeguards or countermeasures is exorbitant, and the effort to mitigate the risk does not proportionately reduce the risk's potential impact.

For instance, consider a company that is developing an AI system to enhance customer service interactions. The AI system will not interpret customer sentiment with 100% accuracy, leading to occasional misunderstandings or suboptimal responses. Once AI gets to a certain performance level, every 1% improvement requires an increasing amount of investment in additional data, advanced algorithms, and computing resources. These additional requirements can inflate the project's cost to an unsustainable level. The company will accept occasional inaccuracies, especially if the overall system represents a substantial improvement over the current state.

To decide when the costs of responding to a risk outweigh the benefits, organizations should conduct a rigorous cost-benefit analysis. They start by estimating the potential loss or damage that could result from the risk manifesting. This estimate considers both direct and indirect costs, such as financial losses, reputational damage, customer dissatisfaction, and regulatory penalties. The organization then assesses the cost of measures that could be taken to mitigate the risk, including technology investments, process changes, and ongoing maintenance costs.

If the cost of mitigation exceeds the expected loss from the risk, the organization may decide that accepting the risk is the most sensible course of action. However, this does not mean that the organization ignores the risk entirely. Instead, it develops a plan to manage the potential consequences. This might involve setting aside a contingency fund, creating protocols for rapid response in the event the risk materializes, or establishing clear communication strategies to address stakeholder concerns.

Risk transference

For risk transference, an organization opts to transfer certain risks to external entities. This is commonly achieved through insurance or contractual agreements that assign risk-related costs or responsibilities to other parties.

For instance, an insurance policy may cover costs related to data breaches, where sensitive information is compromised due to vulnerabilities in the AI system, or provide coverage for operational disruptions caused by AI system failures. These specialized insurance products absorb the financial impact of an AI incident.

Organizations must pay close attention to the fine print. Often, the coverage provided is limited, covering only a fraction of the overall costs associated with an AI incident. For instance, a policy might restrict coverage to the fees paid for the AI system or service. Insurance policies come with conditions and exclusions, such as deductibles, coverage caps, and specific exclusions for certain types of damages or incidents. They also do not cover indirect costs such as reputational harm, loss of future business, or regulatory penalties.

Risk transference through vendor contracts is more common, particularly when working with external vendors or partners. Contractual agreements include indemnification clauses that assign liability to the vendor for damages or losses stemming from their AI products or services. Indemnification clauses are becoming common in GenAI contracts, whereby vendors are indemnifying their customers against legal claims of their models infringing on copyrights, trademarks, or patents.

In September 2023, Microsoft announced its "Copyright Commitment" for customers, stating that it would "assume responsibility for the potential legal risks involved" with use of Copilot, the GenAI service offered alongside Microsoft 365.[7] OpenAI also announced similar protections for its enterprise customers in November 2023.[8]

Risk transference through contracts is also used when an organization's control over risk factors is limited, such as in collaborative projects where multiple stakeholders contribute to the AI initiative. By defining risk ownership in contracts, each party understands its responsibilities and the consequences of failing to manage its designated risks effectively.

Risk transference is also advantageous when risks fall outside an organization's area of expertise or are beyond its direct control. For example, while a company may excel at using AI to enhance its product offerings, it may not have the cybersecurity expertise required to protect its AI models from adversarial attacks. By transferring such risks to entities that specialize in cybersecurity, the company can concentrate on leveraging AI for its core business functions, knowing that it is employing state-of-the-art cyber protections.

Risk mitigation

Risk mitigation is about the anticipation and prevention of potential risks. Implementing preventive controls is a common risk mitigation approach. For example, to guard against data breaches, an organization might deploy advanced encryption techniques, multi-factor authentication, and continuous monitoring systems to detect and respond to security threats in real time. To prevent the misuse of data, the organization might develop clear guidelines for data access, usage, and sharing.

Beyond these specific measures, risk mitigation often involves a broader investment in technology, staff training, and process improvement. The overarching goal of these efforts is to fortify the organization's defenses against a range of AI-related risks. By decreasing the probability of risks occurring, the organization can operate knowing that it has taken steps to protect itself. However, it's important to note that risk mitigation is not a one-off task. As technology evolves and new threats emerge, mitigation strategies must be regularly updated to remain effective.

Risk reduction

Risk reduction is a critical strategy in AI risk management that concentrates on reducing the severity of potential damage should a risk become a reality. Unlike risk mitigation, which aims to prevent risks from occurring, risk reduction accepts that certain risks may be unavoidable and instead focuses on minimizing their impact.

One common method of risk reduction is redundant systems. These systems act as a fail-safe, ensuring that if one component of the AI infrastructure fails, another can take over with minimal disruption. This redundancy is vital in high-stakes environments where system downtime can result in significant financial losses and customer impact.

Another risk reduction tool is a robust incident and crisis management program to rectify issues as they arise. For example, if an AI system is found to be making inaccurate decisions, the sooner the issue is identified, the quicker an organization can retrain or replace the algorithm and address any negative outcomes for affected individuals.

Simulations and red teaming events, where an internal team plays the role of an adversary to test the AI system's defenses and the organization's readiness to handle AI incidents, are a leading practice. Simulations can range from tabletop exercises, where hypothetical scenarios are discussed and walked through step by step, to more sophisticated drills that involve realistic role-play.

Red teaming takes this a step further by introducing an element of unpredictability and adversarial thinking, challenging the organization to respond to novel and unanticipated forms of AI misbehavior. These exercises help to identify weaknesses in incident response protocols, providing a safe environment to refine and improve strategies before a real incident occurs.

A robust AI incident program relies on continuous monitoring mechanisms for early identification of problems or threats occurring. This involves keeping an eye on the AI systems themselves, but also staying attuned to the broader operating environment, which can rapidly shift due to technological advancements, regulatory changes, or evolving cyber threats.

Risk reduction is a forward-looking approach that requires organizations to adapt their risk reduction measures to address emerging threats and to refine their strategies based on real-world experience and feedback.

Quantifying AI risk

Developing mechanisms to measure and quantify AI risks is needed for organizations to align their risk management strategies with their overall risk appetite and tolerance levels. By assigning numerical values to different risks, organizations can create a risk profile that is comparable and, more importantly, actionable. This quantification allows for a clear understanding of which risks are within acceptable limits and which exceed the organization's comfort zone, necessitating intervention.

The ability to measure AI risks against an organization's risk appetite is particularly important when managing a portfolio of AI systems. Each system will present different risks based on its functionality, the data it processes, its impact on stakeholders, and its integration with business operations. By quantifying these risks, organizations can compare different systems and identify the ones that require more stringent controls. This comparison is crucial for resource allocation, ensuring efforts and investments are directed toward the systems that need it most.

Furthermore, quantifying risks enables organizations to understand the key drivers of a risk. The factors that are most at fault in causing the risk are the ones that should be targeted by risk management measures. This understanding allows for a more precise and cost-effective response, focusing resources on the root cause of risk.

A well-calibrated risk management approach can support deeper transparency with stakeholders on risk management measures, leading to higher user trust and adoption. When stakeholders see that risks are being managed intelligently and efficiently, with a clear understanding of what drives those risks, their confidence in the AI systems grows.

Understanding AI risk appetite

Defining AI risk appetite is not merely a statement of tolerance. An organization's risk appetite is a tangible expression of its risk culture – its collective attitude and practices regarding risk-taking and risk management. It expresses the organization's willingness to pursue opportunities that involve uncertainty, reflecting how it balances the pursuit of innovation against the need for stability and safety.

AI risk appetite informs which AI projects are greenlit, which ones are deemed too risky, and which ones require additional safeguards before proceeding. For instance, a company with a conservative risk appetite may decide to implement AI in incremental steps, focusing on proven technologies and applications. Conversely, a company with a more aggressive risk appetite will invest in cutting-edge AI research or adopt AI solutions in high-stakes areas, accepting greater risk for the potential of higher rewards.

Establishing boundaries for AI systems is a complex task, as it involves not only technical risks but also ethical and legal considerations. A well-defined AI risk appetite sets the stage for responsible innovation by delineating the types of risks the organization is prepared to face and the level of uncertainty it can tolerate. This clarity helps prevent overreach and ensures that AI systems are developed and deployed within a framework that prioritizes corporate values, compliance with regulations, and alignment with stakeholder expectations.

As AI technologies evolve and the business environment changes, so too must the organization's risk appetite. Regular reviews and updates ensure that the organization remains agile and responsive to new risks and opportunities.

Approach to quantifying AI risks

Despite the clear advantages of quantifying AI risks, full quantification is very difficult. AI risk measurement often produces discrete data points for each risk that reflect specific tests or scores. This piecemeal approach can lead to a fragmented understanding of AI risks, where the interdependencies and collective impact of various risk factors are not fully appreciated. Moreover, without aggregation, it becomes challenging to gauge the overall risk posture of AI systems and to make informed decisions about their deployment and management.

Recognizing this gap, EY developed the "EY.ai Confidence Index,"[9] an empirical-based measurement of risks across eight AI principles, accompanied by business impact scores. When evaluating the risks of AI, there are many considerations that need to be analyzed, including regulatory compliance, technological maturity, customer trust, and fair practices. The challenge in quantifying the risks of AI is how to take these subjective areas, along with a disparate group of technical test scores, and merge them into a single score that can be measured against risk appetite.

The challenge lies in synthesizing diverse factors into a unified metric. *EY's Confidence Index* contains a suite of leading practice measurements that evaluate an AI model's performance across critical dimensions such as explainability, fairness, sustainability, and reliability. A conversion methodology translates each test outcome into a standardized numerical score. This approach accommodates both qualitative and quantitative data. A set of tailored weights is applied to reflect the relative importance of each score to the AI system. A confidence index is calculated for each responsible AI principle, which can be compared to risk appetite tolerance bands or aggregated at the system or portfolio level.[10]

Quantifying AI risks is a foundational step in creating a risk management framework that is both effective and efficient. It allows organizations to align their AI initiatives with their risk tolerance, compare risks across their AI portfolio, and respond to risks in a targeted and cost-effective manner. By doing so, organizations can optimize their AI systems, enhance user adoption, and maintain a competitive edge in the rapidly evolving landscape of AI technology.

Measuring the risks of AI against risk appetite

Quantifying risks of an AI system and comparing them against pre-established risk appetite thresholds is a complex endeavor. To further explain how this might work, we have provided two fictional case studies below.

Case Study 1: AI in credit limit determination at a national retailer

A retailer that offers a store credit card implemented an AI system to streamline and enhance its credit limit determination process. Despite the AI system's efficiency in processing applications, it became apparent in early pilots that the level of model explainability did not meet the organization's risk appetite. The credit model scored 15 out of 100 on their explainability scale, while their AI benchmark required any models affecting client financial outcomes to have an explainability score of at least 65 out of 100. The low explainability score was a result of using a deep neural network. The AI's decision-making process was opaque, making it difficult to understand how credit limits were being determined. As the

AI development team and business leaders met to discuss the situation, they identified four potential alternatives:

1 *Risk acceptance:* They could accept the risk, acknowledging the potential for customer dissatisfaction and regulatory scrutiny. This approach would involve no immediate action.
2 *Risk transference:* They could partner with a third-party AI provider that had recently pitched its new interpretation model that significantly enhances the ability to develop explanations for deep neural network outcomes. It is a start-up, and to attract customers, they offered to indemnify their clients for the full cost of their licensing fee if they incur any financial losses, including regulatory fines. Early testing showed the interpretation tool improved the model's explainability scores to 72%.
3 *Risk reduction:* They could invest in improving the AI model's explainability, perhaps by incorporating more transparent algorithms, but the development team pushed heavily against this option as moving to a more explainable algorithm would require them to start over in training the model, and early testing had demonstrated that these algorithms had accuracy scores outside their tolerance band.
4 *Risk mitigation:* Another option discussed was to implement additional controls, such as manual reviews of AI-determined credit limits. The business argued that this would significantly increase the time to respond, and they would lose many of the efficiency gains in using an AI automated system.

After a series of workshops, the development team opted to work with the startup company to test their interpretation model. This approach gave them the opportunity to improve their model's explainability and transfer some of the risks to the third party.

Case Study 2: AI in gaming recommendations

An online gaming platform employed an AI system to recommend new games to users based on their gaming habits and preferences. The AI's sophisticated analysis of user data allowed for highly personalized suggestions, improving user engagement. While the AI system generally aligned with the organization's risk appetite, which was pro-innovation, a significant risk emerged. The AI system occasionally recommended games with high violence and sexual content to minors.

Over pizza and churros, the game designers debated their options:

1. *Risk acceptance:* They could accept the risk, letting the current algorithm continue without any modifications. This option was quickly shot down by the founder. Not only would it result in reputational damage and potential legal action, but the founder's nephew had started playing the game. His sister would "freak out" if he exposed his nephew to inappropriate content.
2. *Risk transference:* They could transfer the risk by adding a third-party filter with a proven track record of age-appropriate content filtering. The lead developer was a fan of this option, but the sales manager raised red flags. They had run an earlier pilot using the content filtering and had a 20% decline in up-sells due to the impact on the recommendation engine. Kids just weren't buying it.
3. *Risk reduction:* They could refine the AI's algorithms to include stricter age verification and content filtering mechanisms. When they each picked up their Nerf guns and targeted their preferred choice, this option got blasted the most.
4. *Risk Mitigation:* The company could introduce manual oversight, where a team reviews recommendations for age-sensitive content, and implement a reporting feature for users to flag inappropriate content. The group looked at each other and laughed. Their small team could barely keep up with the bug fixes and customer queries.

Risk reduction was the clear winner.

Fostering a risk-aware culture

Creating a risk-aware culture within an organization is a critical component of successful AI implementation and management. This culture is characterized by a collective understanding of the potential AI risks and a commitment to addressing them proactively.

Leadership and governance

Corporate leaders are the custodians of an organization's values and strategic direction. It is important that they set a clear vision and expectations for responsible AI deployment. They define what risks are accepted and the organization's risk appetite.

It is essential to establish clear lines of accountability for risk-related decisions within AI initiatives. Too often, these critical decisions fall to AI developers, who, while experts in their field, may not have a full understanding of the broader risk ramifications. To address this, leaders must create robust governance structures that delineate who is responsible for making risk decisions and how these decisions are to be made.

Such structures should include the formation of dedicated committees or oversight bodies that provide the necessary oversight and direction. These bodies should be composed of stakeholders from a range of functions, including IT, legal, compliance, operations, and business units. These governance bodies must be vested with the authority to set and enforce policies and procedures that specifically address AI risks.

The responsibility of these governance bodies extends beyond policy development to include the enforcement of these policies across the organization. This may involve conducting regular audits, establishing reporting mechanisms, and taking corrective actions when breaches occur.

Clear accountability for AI risk decisions is a cornerstone of a risk-aware culture. By establishing governance structures with defined roles and responsibilities, and by ensuring that decisions are escalated to the appropriate levels of authority, organizations can achieve greater oversight, transparency, and effective management of AI risks. This approach not only safeguards the organization but also supports the responsible development and deployment of AI technologies.

Training and awareness programs

Training and awareness programs serve as the critical conduits for instilling a risk-aware culture across all levels of an organization. These educational initiatives equip employees with the knowledge they need to recognize and mitigate AI risks. To be effective, training programs must be carefully designed to address the specific needs and functions of various roles within the organization.

AI developers, for instance, require a deep understanding of how to incorporate risk management into the design and development phases of the AI development lifecycle. They need to be aware of the importance of their design decisions and the potential need to escalate risk-related issues to higher governance bodies. End-users, on the other hand, should be trained to use AI applications responsibly and to recognize signs of system malfunction or bias that need to be reported.

Regularly scheduled training sessions, workshops, and simulations keep the knowledge fresh and allow employees to practice responding to hypothetical risk scenarios. Simulations, in particular, are an effective way to test and reinforce the organization's risk response protocols in a controlled environment, preparing employees for real-world situations.

Transparency and accountability

A culture of transparency and accountability builds trust and confidence in AI systems. Transparency means providing clear and accessible information about AI projects, their objectives, and potential impacts. It also involves openly discussing the limitations and uncertainties associated with AI technologies.

Accountability goes hand in hand with transparency. It is about establishing a clear chain of responsibility for AI decisions and actions. When risks do materialize, it is important that organizations take ownership of the issue, implement remedial actions, and communicate these actions transparently to affected parties.

To support accountability, organizations must have well-defined processes for reporting risks and incidents. These processes should be easy to understand and accessible to all employees, ensuring that any concerns can be raised without fear of reprisal. Additionally, mechanisms for feedback, such as customer sentiment surveys or complaint hotlines, can help identify unknown risks or areas for enhancement.

The challenge for risk management in a dynamic environment is to evolve in lockstep with AI advancements. This evolution requires a commitment to continuous learning and adaptation. Organizations must invest in staying informed about the latest AI developments, from breakthroughs in machine learning algorithms to the advent of new data processing technologies. Each of these advancements has the potential to introduce unforeseen risks, whether through new vectors for cyber threats, uncharted ethical dilemmas, or new regulatory considerations.

Emerging trends and technologies

One of the first steps in future-proofing AI risk management is to identify the trends and technologies on the horizon. For instance, the advent of quantum computing promises an exponential leap in processing power, potentially enabling AI to solve complex problems with unprecedented speed. However, this leap in capabilities could also render current encryption methods obsolete, opening the door to cybersecurity threats that are more sophisticated and harder to defend against.

The proliferation of autonomous systems across various sectors, from self-driving vehicles to robotic surgery, is another important trend. These systems must operate with a high degree of safety and reliability. Moreover, the delegation of critical decisions to machines raises ethical questions about accountability and the moral frameworks within which these systems should operate. As humanoid robots start to work alongside humans, new physical safety risks will emerge.

While natural language processing and GenAI are becoming more adept at understanding and generating human-like text, they are being used to create more convincing and targeted social engineering attacks. Phishing schemes, misinformation campaigns, deepfakes, and other forms of manipulation are becoming more difficult to detect and counter.

Staying informed about these and other emerging trends is important. By understanding the potential for new vulnerabilities, organizations can fortify their defenses before threats materialize. The ethical use of AI is an area that will continue to evolve alongside these technologies. Compliance with regulatory landscapes is another moving target, as policymakers and industry bodies work to keep pace with technological change, often resulting in new regulations that organizations must swiftly adapt to.

By keeping a close watch on the technological trends and developments poised to shape the future, organizations can better anticipate the risks associated with these innovations.

Anticipating new types of risks

The importance of anticipating new types of risks cannot be overstated. As AI systems become more integrated into critical business processes and societal functions, the potential for harm increases. Anticipating the future of AI risk management extends far beyond the immediate technological concerns to encompass a spectrum of societal and ethical risks. The risks are further compounded by the potential for AI through deepfakes and news filters to influence public opinion, shape social norms, and impact democratic processes.

Moreover, the growing reliance on AI systems across various sectors can lead to the atrophy of human expertise and critical thinking. As AI systems take on more responsibilities, there is a risk that human skills will degrade, and the workforce will become overly dependent on AI without sufficient understanding or oversight. This over-reliance becomes particularly perilous in scenarios where AI systems fail – due to technical glitches, cyberattacks, or unexpected external factors – leaving organizations scrambling to respond without the necessary human expertise.

The erosion of human skills is not the only concern; there is also the risk of manipulation or tampering. As AI technologies advance, they become more complex and, in some cases, less transparent, making it difficult to detect when they have been tampered with or are operating under malicious control. This could have severe consequences, from the spread of misinformation to the disruption of critical infrastructure. We also need to consider the potential for goal misalignment with agentic AI. As they become faster and more complex, how will we detect misbehavior?

Anticipating these broader societal and ethical risks requires a multidisciplinary approach that goes beyond technical safeguards. It involves engaging with ethicists, sociologists, legal experts, and other stakeholders to understand the potential unintended impacts of AI. It also necessitates a commitment to maintaining and developing human expertise alongside AI systems, ensuring that there is a balance between technological reliance and human judgment.

Shifting from human to machine-based monitoring

In the past, it was common for AI systems to provide predictions and recommendations while humans made the final decisions. This symbiotic relationship leveraged the strengths of both AI and human judgment, ensuring that AI's analytical capabilities were tempered by human experience and ethical considerations. However, as AI systems advance toward higher levels of autonomy, the dynamic of this relationship is shifting, necessitating the development of new strategies to mitigate the risks associated with agentic AI.

To address these risks, organizations need to deploy automated preventative and detective mechanisms. Preventative tools stop AI risks before they materialize. These include the implementation of advanced algorithms that can detect and correct biases in real-time, data and ethical filters to guide AI behavior, and the use of simulation environments to test AI behaviors against adversarial conditions before deployment.

Detective tools focus on identifying and responding to AI incidents after they have occurred. These strategies often involve monitoring systems that track AI decisions and flag anomalies or AI auditing tools that test the AI's performance.

The role of humans may shift from direct oversight to the design, implementation, and monitoring of these automated tools. Human expertise will remain crucial for interpreting the outputs of AI systems, setting the parameters within which they operate, and intervening in complex or high-stakes scenarios where automated responses are insufficient.

As AI systems move toward greater autonomy, there is a greater need for innovative and automated risk management tools. In the next chapter, we will explore the different control approaches for AI.

Conclusion

AI is creating new risks that must be managed with foresight and diligence. The key to successful AI risk management is early identification and the application of tailored risk management approaches. By evaluating potential threats early in the AI development lifecycle, organizations can preemptively address issues, avoiding costly mistakes and ensuring that AI initiatives deliver their intended benefits.

When it comes to managing AI risks, each approach – acceptance, transference, mitigation, and reduction – offers a different method for handling risks. The choice of strategy depends on the organization's risk appetite, the nature of the risk, and the potential impact on business operations. Leaders must define the organization's risk appetite, establish clear governance structures to oversee AI initiatives, and create a risk-aware culture. When risks materialize, they must be prepared to take responsibility, address the issue promptly, and learn from the experience.

Managing the risks of AI is an ongoing process that requires vigilance, adaptability, and strategic foresight. As AI technologies advance and become more deeply integrated into business and society, the need for robust AI risk management will only grow.

Key leadership questions to consider:

1. Have you embedded risk management throughout your AI project lifecycle?
2. Have you established clear accountability for AI risk management decisions?
3. What measures are in place to foster and reinforce an AI risk-aware culture?
4. Do you have comprehensive AI incidents and crisis management strategies?

Notes

1 Porter, M. E. (1985). *Competitive advantage: Creating and sustaining superior performance*. New York, NY: Free Press.
2 The Fair Institute. (n.d.). *Understanding generative AI risks with FAIR*. Retrieved June 15, 2025, from https://www.fairinstitute.org/ai-risk and https://www.fairinstitute.org/hubfs/FAIR-AIR%20Approach%20Playbook.pdf.
3 Townson, S. (2020, November 6). AI can make bank loans fairer. *Harvard Business Review*. https://hbr.org/2020/11/ai-can-make-bank-loans-more-fair.
4 Project Management Institute. (2018, November). Cognitive care health care organizations are using AI to make more precise decisions, but project teams must manage data privacy risks. *Project Management Journal, 32*(11), 29–42. https://www.pmi.org/learning/library/healthcare-organizations-artificial-intelligence-decisions-data-privacy-risks-11414.
5 MIT AI Risk Repository. (2024, April). *MIT AI risk repository*. Retrieved August 30, 2025, from https://airisk.mit.edu/.
6 EY. (2019, November 26). *How can risk foresight lead to AI insight?* Toronto, Canada: EY. (Document no longer available online.)
7 Smith, B., & Nowbar, H. (2023, September 7). Microsoft announces new Co-Pilot copyright commitment for customers – Microsoft on the

issues. *Microsoft*. https://blogs.microsoft.com/on-the-issues/2023/09/07/copilot-copyright-commitment-ai-legal-concerns/.

8 OpenAI. (2023, November 6). New model and developer products announced at Development Day. https://openai.com/index/new-models-and-developer-products-announced-at-devday/.

9 EY. (2024). *EY AI confidence index discussion paper*. https://www.ey.com/content/dam/ey-unified-site/ey-com/en-ca/services/ai/documents/ey-ai-confidence-index-discussion-paper.pdf.

10 EY. (2025.). *Responsible AI risk management and EY confidence index placemat*. Retrieved August 9, 2025, from https://www.ey.com/content/dam/ey-unified-site/ey-com/en-ca/insights/ai/documents/responsible-ai_ai-risk-management-and-ey-confidence-index_placemat_iteractivity.pdf.

Chapter 10

Cost-efficient controls with maximum impact

AI is in a rapid expansion phase. As artificial intelligence (AI) designers push the boundaries of what AI can achieve, the excitement of innovation often overshadows the build-out of safeguards. AI governance and controls are often viewed as burdens that slow innovation. Some do. Particularly those that are manual and require a heavy amount of documentation. But AI controls are not created equal.

Former OpenAI researcher Leopold Aschenbrenner reinforces the complexities of building efficient controls for AI.

> Reliably controlling AI systems much smarter than we are is an unsolved technical problem. And while it is a solvable problem, things could very easily go off the rails during a rapid intelligence explosion. Managing this will be extremely tense; failure could easily be catastrophic.[1]

Control effectiveness and efficiency fall across a wide spectrum. Highly automated controls require higher upfront costs but are quicker, rely less on human effort, and, when calibrated well, are more effective. The more effort put into a control's design, the better it will operate.

From the early days of AI, there has been active dialogue on its opportunities and challenges. While more investment dollars are being poured into building its functionality, strong voices are calling for it to be developed with caution. As described in Chapter 7, a growing list of guidelines, standards, and regulations is being published to establish guardrails for AI's development and operation. This is creating tension with AI's builders, particularly those who want to move fast.

DOI: 10.4324/9781003625520-12

Their concerns are not unfounded. The current focus by public policy makers has been on the governance controls around AI – AI policies, accountability structures, inventories, risk assessments, and transparency reports. While each of these is important, they are passive in nature. Passive controls set expectations for ethical behavior but do not actively contribute to AI risk reduction. These governance documents are important to set the cultural tone of the organization, but more effort is needed for developing active controls. Controls that prevent risks from manifesting or, barring that, identify errors or adversarial attacks quickly enough that they can be mitigated soon after they occur.

Technologists want to limit the negative consequences of AI. What they have been pushing back on is the documentation-heavy approach taken by early regulations. In a January 2025 discussion with TED's Adam Grant, Sam Altman admitted that, "It's really tricky to get the regulatory balance right and also we clearly, in my opinion, will need some."[2] When asked to compare the regulatory approaches in the United States and European Union (EU), Altman responded

> I think what the EU is doing with AI regulation is not helpful ..., like for example, when we finish a new model, ... we can launch it in the U.S. well before we can launch it in the EU cause there's a bunch of regulatory process. And what if that means that the EU is always some number of months behind the frontier?[3]

The challenge with creating regulations that are both pro-innovation and pro-safety is striking the right balance between cost and value. In this chapter, we explore which control activities achieve both.

Objectives

Upon completing this chapter, you will be able to:

- Understand the relative cost and value of different controls
- Implement robust preventative controls in AI system design and data governance
- Establish detective controls for continuous AI monitoring and post-implementation review
- Manage third-party AI relationships, ensuring vendor transparency and rigorous due diligence.

What are AI controls?

AI controls are systematic measures and protocols designed to ensure that AI operates within set parameters, aligns with organizational goals, and adheres to legal and regulatory standards.

Controls operate at various levels to create a multi-layered defense against risks. At the highest level, entity-level controls establish the strategic framework and governance policies that dictate the organization's approach to AI, setting the tone for ethical considerations and risk management practices.

The next level of controls is IT general controls (ITGCs) targeting the technical infrastructure. ITGCs safeguard the integrity of the IT environment, ensuring that the systems that develop, deploy, and maintain AI are secure and reliable. At the most granular level, transactional controls are targeted at individual AI-processed transactions, verifying their accuracy, completeness, and authorization.

As you move from entity-level to transactional controls, the direct impact of a control in mitigating AI risks increases. While each of these control categories already exists for traditional technologies, there are some modifications needed for AI.

Entity-level controls

AI policies and procedures are the starting point for AI governance, and at a minimum, should include a definition of AI and itemize the principles to be followed.

In Chapter 1, we covered the importance of defining AI to determine which systems do and do not need to be subject to AI governance controls. Some additional actions that should be taken for AI governance include:

1. *Expand the corporate code of conduct* to specify compliance with the AI policy and adherence to the specified AI principles
2. *Establish an AI advisory board*
3. *Develop an accountability matrix* for the AI governance program
4. *Create AI key performance indicators* and risk metrics
5. *Schedule regular AI strategic and risk updates* to the board and senior management
6. *Establish AI communities of practice* to foster continuous learning
7. *Ensure continual education and learning* are fostered with recognition systems.

As GenAI has become more pervasive, AI acceptable use policies (AUPs) have become common addenda to the AI policy. The AUPs, which first addressed whether employees could use public GenAI capabilities, have been expanded to provide guidance on when and how internally provided GenAI tools can be used. The AUPs were at first high-level and generic, but are now becoming more specific to each AI technology. With AUPs being only able to dictate how an employee should behave, preventative measures like URL filters and access restrictions are being used to stop inappropriate behavior. Detection mechanisms are also being used.

With the growing interest in agentic AI, AUPs are being updated to address the delegation of decision-making authority to agentic AI, outlining the conditions under which AI can operate independently and when human intervention is required. For example, a government department might implement a policy that requires human review for AI-generated passport approvals that fall outside of standard risk parameters, such as applicants from sanctioned countries or with approval scores close to the threshold.

Information technology general controls

ITGCs help maintain the integrity of the underlying technology. They provide assurance that changes to the system are appropriately tested and authorized, access rights match an individual's job responsibilities, and the system operates as intended, including scheduled jobs and backups.

ITGCs are also required for AI. However, the unique nature of AI, with its iterative change management approach and the ability to adapt and learn post-deployment, requires a tailored set of controls. The largest difference between rules-based technologies and AI is the need for a model testing and validation process.

Traditional technologies are subject to a structured change management process to confirm that the system performs in accordance with the system requirements. There is a built-in assumption that rules-based systems, once put into production, will continue to operate the same until modified. In contrast, AI is developed iteratively. Developers may try out different algorithms, training data, and learning methods until they find the combination that meets their performance standards. This iterative process can result in a lack of documentation to substantiate their development process. Once put in production, adaptive AI can continue learning and adapting its decision framework.

To address these new risks, organizations are building independent model testing teams. Model testing and validation can include peer testing of the models, benchmarking outputs against a challenger model, or using explainability tools to interpret AI decision-making. For example, an AI model used by an energy company to detect electricity outages would be subjected to rigorous testing to validate its predictive performance under adverse conditions – both natural disasters and digital attacks.

Logical access controls prevent unauthorized access to systems and data. In traditional environments, this includes user authentication, role-based access control, and audit logging. With AI, these controls remain critical, but there is an added need for access controls around the data used to train the AI models, as well as the models themselves. Chapter 6 covered the potential risks and security measures that should be put in place.

What organizations often overlook is the impact of AI on their rules-based system authentication and security mechanisms. Deepfakes are being used to impersonate individuals and bypass authentication controls, particularly those using biometrics. Multi-factor authentication is becoming more critical to authenticate an individual. As Agentic AI gains more traction, a new category of system IDs will need to be created for AI systems.

Once in operation, AI data and models may require specialized recovery plans that account for their ability to learn. Weekly backup schedules may be insufficient for models that are dynamically learning after every new interaction. It will require balancing the cost of more frequent backups with the loss of AI's more current decisioning framework. The advantage of AI is that it doesn't require large code libraries, meaning that capturing and storing backups of the changes in weights and features will be less resource-intensive, and is often a built-in audit feature of many AI MLOps platforms.

Incident management, which involves detecting, responding to, and recovering from IT issues, also takes on new complexities with AI. Traditionally, IT incident controls have focused on the technology performance, run times, availability, CPU usage and job failures. As AI becomes more complex and autonomous, behavioral monitoring or observability is taking on more importance. Human oversight is being replaced by continuous, real-time monitoring controls. The risk assessment will help to determine which controls warrant this additional investment.

Transactional controls

Transactional controls are customized for each AI system and use case. These typically fall into preventative and detective controls that "bookend" the AI operation. Filters are the most common preventative control for AI. They govern what AI can and cannot do. Ethical filters are rules commonly applied to chatbots to restrict their ability to use offensive language. We mentioned earlier the use of input filters to restrict AI's access to personally identifiable information (PII) and sensitive data, and output filters to prevent privacy breaches.

Detective controls are monitoring controls that are either performed by a human or automated. They can be designed to detect a specific behavioral pattern, such as the confidence level falling below a prescribed tolerance level. Or they can be more discovery-based, where AI is leveraged to monitor customer interactions and trigger alerts if negative sentiment trends are detected. Monitoring controls can also include cross-validation. For example, for an AI system used to detect illness, each diagnostic suggestion can be cross-referenced with up-to-date medical databases and guidelines.

An example of this is an AI system used to mark and grade student essays. *The educational institution could put in place these two preventative controls:*

1 *Data encryption and masking:* Before student data is input into the AI system, preventative controls such as data encryption and masking can be implemented to reduce the risk of data breaches and misuse
2 *Model training guardrails:* Setting limits on the data that the AI uses for decision-making, such as excluding prohibited demographic factors, can prevent biased outcomes and ensure compliance with anti-discrimination laws.

The following two complementary detective controls can also be implemented:

1 *Manual review:* A dedicated team of human auditors conducts regular, in-depth examinations of a random selection of AI-generated essay scores and feedback.

2 *Automated pattern detection:* An advanced monitoring system runs algorithms to detect statistical deviations and potential biases in the scoring, generating alerts for human investigation and intervention.

These controls work together to prevent as many issues as possible and to detect and address those that do occur quickly. Each use case requires a tailored approach that matches the risk profile with the investment in controls, both in quantity and complexity.

When does the cost of controls outweigh their value?

Controls are often considered the "cost of doing business." As a result, there is often little attention paid to calculating their full cost. There may be token attempts to estimate the full-time equivalents required, and when third-party tools are used, the purchase price or licensing fee, but on the whole, they are embedded into the system requirements.

Conducting a full cost accounting for a control requires considering not only the direct costs, but also the indirect costs involved in their design, implementation, and oversight. This includes the supporting technology infrastructure and the costs to document procedures and train staff. There will also be ongoing maintenance and updates. While time-consuming, approximating these costs is doable.

What is much harder is quantifying the value of controls. Getting to a dollar value requires a lot of assumptions. It is much easier to focus on a qualitative assessment, estimating the relative impact of a control using a high-medium-low grading.

A control can have an impact ranging from those directly attributable to its operation to ones that are less direct. Examples include:

1 Reduce errors
2 Detect anomalies
3 Eliminate costly remediation and repatriation costs
4 Avoid regulatory fines and penalties
5 Enhance data accuracy
6 Improve decision-making
7 Avoid reputational damage
8 Build and maintain stakeholder trust.

While the full list is important, impacts such as AI errors and failures are more tangible and will have a more direct impact on the bottom line. There are many options when designing controls. The fastest controls to put into operation are policy and procedural documents. They can be written relatively quickly and set the cultural tone of the behavior expected. The issue is that while they tell an individual how to act, they lack the ability to ensure consistent application in practice. The employee may act differently, either intentionally or due to a lack of understanding. Policies and procedures are not sufficient on their own and require monitoring and enforcement controls to be effective. Ongoing training is also key, given the rapidly changing technology landscape.

In comparing policies and monitoring controls, monitoring controls will provide the most tangible outcomes. A policy may prevent some risks, as employees are guided to do the right thing, but it is monitoring controls that act as the true deterrent and detection mechanism. So, prudence would dictate that more effort should be given to the design and implementation of monitoring controls.

In fact, the early days of AI have seen the opposite. Organizations have spent an inordinate amount of time creating their AI policy, taking months crafting the document, debating the definition of AI, the AI principles, and accountability constructs vigorously. Not only has this delayed the creation of downstream control activities, but these policies are often outdated soon after they are published, as new technologies, such as GenAI and agentic AI, are adopted.

We are not suggesting that AI policies and procedural documents be abolished, as they have a role and place. However, they should be treated as the guidance documents they are. They set the intentions of an organization, and provide a blueprint against which behaviors can be measured, but their passive nature limits their value. There are existing online templates and GenAI capabilities that can create AI policies that can be quickly customized for an organization. The goal should not be to anticipate all eventualities, but instead use it to guide the development of the next wave of controls that will have a more direct, tangible impact.

What is of greater use to developers is translating the policy expectations into tangible requirements that AI developers can build and train their AI models against. Without it, their project timelines can experience significant delays when systems are ready to move into production but fail to meet risk and control requirements. They are then scrambling to develop post-deployment monitoring mechanisms or face the daunting task of retraining the model.

It is one thing to have an AI policy that dictates robust security and privacy controls for AI models, but what does that look like? Can PII be fed to the AI model in raw form, or should privacy-enhancing techniques be applied? Are filters needed to limit sensitive data not necessary to the AI's function?

It is important to identify these requirements upfront to avoid costly revisions and ensure smooth deployment into production. Well ahead of deployment, the development team needs to identify its risk management strategies and build those requirements into the system design. If privacy-enhancing techniques are used to mask sensitive data, these need to be put in place before model training occurs. Otherwise, the AI will be trained on data that is either not available or significantly altered in production.

Automated monitoring controls and alert systems should be developed alongside the target AI system and tested under adversarial conditions to ensure that they detect out-of-tolerance AI behaviors. When human-in-the-loop is relied upon, human operators should perform user acceptance testing to confirm that the system provides the information and level of explainability they require.

The selection and design of controls should be a balanced decision that considers their function, efficacy, and cost. This is where the risk assessment discussed in the previous chapter is most valuable. A well-understood risk profile allows for more targeted and precise controls. It also assists in determining how much to invest in controls. A high-risk system may warrant the build-out of a customized machine-based monitoring system. Periodic manual tests may be sufficient for a low-risk system. A cost-benefit analysis can help to decide between higher-cost but more effective automated systems and lower-cost manual reviews.

No single control is sufficient. Even when a risk assessment is performed, a model is tested against predefined boundary conditions, a human operator validates the accuracy of an AI output, or a vendor service level breach is identified, the risk is not mitigated until an action is performed. Risk mitigation requires the artful intertwining of multiple controls – active vs. passive; preventative vs. detective; pre-production vs. post-production; manual vs. automated.

Figure 10.1 provides a grid that maps the complexity and effort for common AI controls against their level of impact and effectiveness, with AI policies in the lower left and kill switches at the

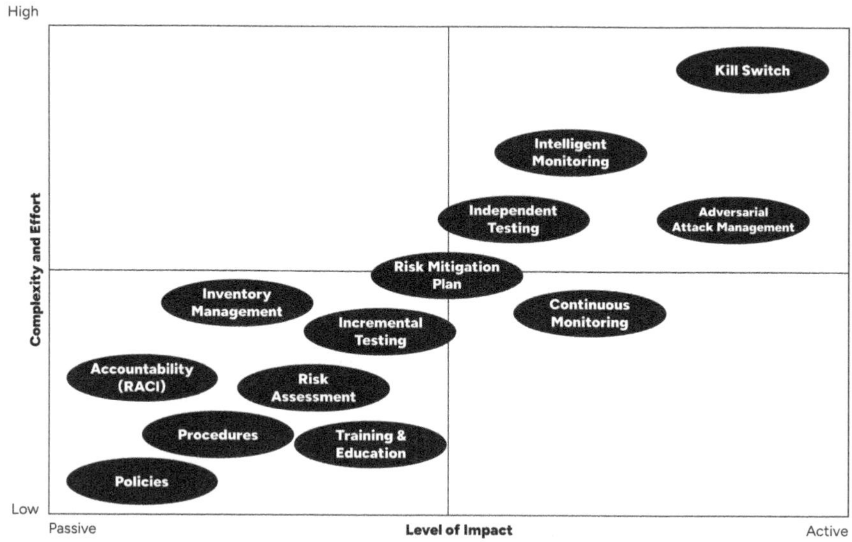

Figure 10.1 AI controls – complexity and effort vs. level of impact.

upper right. A kill switch enables organizations to pause, contain, or disable compromised AI systems before they cause serious damage.

Developing a robust control framework for AI systems

When deciding which of the above controls should be implemented, the risk assessment should be leveraged to identify which risks are most likely and will have the greatest impact. It is also important to understand the relative risk profile of an AI system when compared across your AI portfolio. You have limited resources of both time and money. Not only do you need to make decisions on where to spend your money, but also how to spend it. While the specific metrics being monitored and the boundary conditions that trigger an alert will vary, the basic functionality is similar. Deploying overseer AI agents across your portfolio of AI systems will be more cost-effective than building them independently for each AI system.

A few guiding principles to keep in mind are:

1 It is more cost-effective to prevent a risk than respond and remediate it after the fact

2 Manual controls are best employed for periodic activities rather than continuous monitoring
3 If properly designed, automated controls are more effective
4 You need to build controls for both the known and unknown
5 Deploy controls in layers for a defense-in-depth approach.

Key considerations for designing a control

The following steps should be followed when developing a control system for AI:

1. *Define objectives and scope:* It begins by clearly defining the objectives of the AI control framework. Which AI systems and processes will be covered? Consider the organization's strategic goals, AI policies, regulatory requirements, and stakeholder expectations
2. *Assess risks:* It conducts a risk assessment for each AI system, considering risks of bias, errors, security breaches, and regulatory non-compliance. Prioritize risks based on their likelihood and impact
3. *Establish governance structures:* It creates cross-functional teams with expertise in AI, ethics, compliance, and risk management to oversee the AI controls
4. *Develop control activities:* It designs customized control activities to address the identified risk, considering:

    a. risk impact and likelihood
    b. control value vs. cost analysis
    c. complementary controls
    d. layered defense of preventative and detective controls
    e. combination of automated and human interventions.

5. *Measure control efficacy and establish reporting mechanisms:* KPIs should be established to report on the effectiveness of the controls, with feedback supporting continuous improvement. Regular reporting on the efficacy of the control framework should keep stakeholders informed and facilitate accountability.
6. *Review and update the framework:* The AI landscape is dynamic, and control frameworks must evolve accordingly. The control framework should be updated for new technologies, regulatory changes, and lessons learned from operational experience.

7 *Train and educate*: All relevant personnel must be trained on the control framework and understand their roles and responsibilities.

When designing controls, there is a risk of over- or under-correcting. Overly stringent controls can stifle the agility and learning capabilities of AI systems, while lax controls may expose the organization to undue risk. The goal should be to find a balanced approach, where the controls are commensurate with identified risks that are relevant, probable, and outside the organization's and the users' risk tolerance. Finding the right balance is key to optimizing between AI safeguards and functionality.

In developing a robust control framework for AI, several considerations should be considered. First, the selection of controls must take into account available resources. This includes both the technical infrastructure necessary to support AI control systems and people with the expertise to perform and monitor these controls. Organizations must evaluate their current capabilities and determine whether additional investments in technology or personnel are needed.

Cost is another critical factor. Implementing and maintaining effective controls can be expensive, and executives must balance these costs against the potential benefits that AI systems offer. It is essential to conduct a cost-benefit analysis to ensure that the controls are economically viable and do not outweigh the advantages of using AI.

Additionally, the dynamic nature of AI technology means that controls cannot be static. They must be adaptable to the evolving landscape of AI capabilities and threats. This requires a proactive approach to control selection, with ongoing assessments and updates. Often, organizations start with manual controls, and as the rate of AI adoption and its risk increases, they switch to more precise, automated controls.

The selection of controls must also align with the organization's broader objectives and risk appetite. A start-up organization that is building proof of concepts to attract investors and customers will require a roadmap for controls, but may not need to build them. While a mature organization will need functioning controls from day one.

Case study: mid-size retailer and predictive AI inventory system

Consider a mid-size retailer that leases a predictive AI system from a global technology company. This system recommends when inventory should be ordered to restock shelves, optimizing stock levels and reducing waste. In deploying controls over the reliability of the recommendations from the AI system, each party involved has distinct responsibilities.

Technology company (developer and deployer)

Controls that the technology company could put in place include:

1 *Privacy-enhancing techniques* to protect confidential product, vendor, and company information.
2 *Model validation* to ensure the AI system performs as expected in various standard and adverse scenarios.
3 *Cross-validation* or other techniques to assess the model's performance on unseen data, ensuring that the model generalizes well and is not overfitting.
4 *Limited production pilots* to test the AI under production-conditions for a limited and well-controlled transactional set.
5 *Performance testing* to evaluate the model using a range of performance metrics to ensure it meets the required standards.
6 *Benchmark* the model's performance against external benchmarks or standards.
7 *Incident and crisis management* process to identify and resolve AI errors, biases, and disruptions on a timely basis.
8 *Transparency reports* to communicate to the user the model limitations and boundaries that they must mitigate for.

Retailer (user)

As the user of the AI system, the retailer is responsible for the day-to-day operation of the AI system. *Controls the retailer could put in place include:*

1 *User access controls* to limit who can access the AI system and data (e.g., multi-factor authentication).

2 *Data quality controls,* including automated validation tools to check for data accuracy, completeness, and consistency.
3 *Data cleansing functionality*, including the removal of duplicates, correction of errors, and imputation of missing values.
4 *Data lineage tracking* to provide visibility into the data's origin, the transformations it has undergone, and how it has been used over time, which is critical for diagnosing and rectifying data quality issues.
5 *Monitoring controls and performance dashboards* of KPIs related to the AI system's accuracy and reliability.
6 *Automated alerting systems* to notify relevant personnel when the AI system's performance deviates from established thresholds.
7 *Audit trails* that record all system interactions, which can be analyzed to identify patterns that may indicate issues with the AI system's performance.
8 *Override procedures* for manually overriding the AI system's recommendations when necessary.
9 *Feedback protocols* to provide structured feedback to the technology company for continuous improvement.

The effective integration of controls across multiple parties requires open and transparent communication, a clear delineation of responsibilities, and a "trust but verify" approach.

Transparent communication on model design

A focus of current regulations is on transparency – notifying impacted stakeholders when AI is being used, and communicating how the AI was trained and makes decisions. The assumption is that with a thorough understanding of the AI system's inner workings, the user can better monitor its performance, oversee its output, and provide feedback for improvements.

Model cards are a common document to disclose this information. They are detailed documents that accompany AI models and often include the following:

1 *Model details:* A description of the model, including its type (e.g., neural network, decision tree), version, and the date it was last updated.

2. *Intended use cases:* Clear explanations of the scenarios and environments for which the model is designed, including use cases that are not recommended.
3. *Data description:* Details about the datasets used to train and validate the model, including sources, collection processes, and preprocessing steps taken.
4. *Training procedures:* An overview of how the model was trained, including the algorithms used, hyperparameters, and training duration.
5. *Evaluation metrics:* A summary of the metrics used to evaluate the model's performance, along with the results of those evaluations.
6. *Fairness and bias considerations:* An assessment of the model's performance across different demographic groups or scenarios, highlighting any steps taken to ensure fairness and mitigate bias.
7. *Limitations:* A candid discussion of the model's limitations, potential failure modes, and any known issues that could affect performance.
8. *Ethical considerations:* Information on ethical considerations taken into account during the model's development, including privacy impacts and compliance with relevant regulations.
9. *Maintenance and update policy:* Details on how the model will be maintained and updated over time, including the process for incorporating user feedback.

Developer transparency is improving. In May 2024, Stanford updated their Foundation Model Transparency Index and found that there was a 21-point improvement against their 100-point criteria, with the average score rising to 58 and the top score hitting 85 out of 100.[4]

Another notable finding in their study was the publication of AI transparency reports, a practice started in 2024. Stanford found these newly published AI transparency reports included information on 17 new transparency indicators as opposed to the previous information they had been able to collect from the internet.[5]

As the transparency of AI use increases, there is a growing concern of "AI washing." This involves misleading marketing claims that exaggerate or make erroneous statements about an organization's AI capabilities. It can also involve misleading statements in model cards or transparency reports related to system performance or AI governance practices. With the proliferation of such reports, it is increasingly important to validate their completeness and accuracy. We predict that independent assurance, which we will explore in the next chapter, will be used to build and maintain trust in AI systems and the information described about them.

Controls for specific AI risks

In the prior case study, the controls recommendations for the developer and user included a mix of preventative and detective controls. Although these are commonly recommended as control practices for all AI systems, the controls for each system will need to be customized. To demonstrate that process, Table 10.1 identifies recommended controls for each of the AI principles introduced in Chapter 2.

In conducting this exercise, we followed three important steps:

1. Understand the importance and relevance of the AI principle to the particular AI system.
2. Determine the applicable risks.
3. Design efficient and effective controls to address the risk.

For our case study, a predictive AI system that recommends when replacement inventory should be ordered to restock shelves, the following considerations would be important when designing its control framework.

This case study is illustrative. In reality, a risk assessment and control selection process would likely reveal a broader array of risks and necessary controls. It is important to involve a multi-disciplined team with expertise in AI technology, business operations, risk management, and ethics early in the AI system's design phase to ensure that all potential risks are identified and that control requirements are integrated into the AI system from the outset.

While it is crucial to be exhaustive in the identification of risks, it is equally important to prioritize them based on likelihood and impact. The objective is not to catalog and mitigate every conceivable risk, but rather to strike a balance between thoroughness and practicality. A cost-benefit analysis should guide the decision-making process, ensuring that resources are allocated to mitigate significant risks effectively without overburdening the organization.

Table A1.1 in the Appendix provides a control self-evaluation checklist to assess the comprehensiveness of different AI model control methods.

Table 10.1 Case study: AI principles, illustrative risks, and potential controls

AI principles	*Relevance considerations*	*Illustrative risks*	*Potential controls*
Accountability	• High – crucial for delineating responsibilities between the retailer and the technology provider in case of system errors affecting inventory levels.	• Lack of clear responsibility may result in delayed responses to system errors, impacting store operations and customer satisfaction.	• Define specific roles and obligations for both the retailer and the technology provider within the contract, ensuring legal clarity on liability and recourse in case of system failures. • Develop a shared platform for logging and tracking incidents, allowing both parties to monitor issues and coordinate responses.
Reliability	• High – critical to ensure consistent, accurate inventory restocking recommendations, directly impacting business efficiency and customer satisfaction.	• Unreliable AI recommendations could lead to overstocking, causing increased holding costs and potential waste. • Conversely, understocking due to unreliable AI could result in lost sales and damage to the retailer's reputation.	• Introduce confidence threshold parameters within the AI system that trigger manual review for restocking recommendations that fall below a certain confidence level, ensuring higher reliability in decision-making. • Integrate periodic model calibration to regularly adjust the AI model based on actual sales data to ensure its recommendations remain aligned with current market trends and consumer behavior.

(*Continued*)

Table 10.1 (Continued)

AI principles	*Relevance considerations*	*Illustrative risks*	*Potential controls*
Data protection	• Medium – important to safeguard sensitive supply chain data, including vendor information, though less critical if inventory data is used.	• Unauthorized access could lead to the exposure of vendor contracts and pricing details, potentially damaging the retailer's reputation over high markups and breaching vendor confidentiality.	• Implement roles-based access to ensure that only authorized personnel have access to vendor contracts and pricing information within the AI system. • Apply data masking and redaction techniques to obscure sensitive details in the AI system's interface and reports, preventing inadvertent disclosure.
Security	• High – vital to prevent unauthorized access that could disrupt inventory systems and compromise business operations.	• Adversarial attacks could manipulate data to under-report stock levels of high-value items, facilitating undetected theft and financial loss.	• Implement stringent validation checks on incoming data to detect and prevent the ingestion of manipulated information that could lead to inventory discrepancies. • Deploy advanced anomaly detection systems that use ML to identify unusual patterns in inventory data that may indicate tampering or theft.
Transparency	• High – imperative for the retailer to validate the AI's decision-making process. This would most likely be medium if the retailer had built the AI system itself.	• Without transparency, the retailer may not understand how the AI makes decisions, leading to misuse or misinterpretation of recommendations.	• Technology developer provides detailed documentation and user guides explaining the AI system's decision-making processes, data inputs, and interpretation of outputs.

(*Continued*)

Table 10.1 (Continued)

AI principles	*Relevance considerations*	*Illustrative risks*	*Potential controls*
			• Engage a third-party assurance provider to independently test the AI system's model card and transparency report, ensuring their accuracy and completeness.
Explainability	• High – integral for the retailer to understand the rationale behind each restocking recommendation.	• Inability to explain AI recommendations could result in a lack of user trust and reluctance to follow the system's guidance.	• Integrate interpretability metrics and tools that quantitatively measure how accurately the AI system's decisions are, and can be understood and trusted by users. • Conduct regular training sessions and workshops for the retailer's staff to educate them on how the AI operates and how to accurately interpret its recommendations.
Fairness	• Low – generally less relevant for inventory management, unless biased data affects certain products or suppliers unfairly.	• Biased AI recommendations could inadvertently favor or disadvantage certain product categories, affecting sales diversity and supplier relationships.	• Ensure the AI system is trained on diverse and representative data sets that accurately reflect the full spectrum of products, including low-volume items, and do not exclude any categories. • Establish continuous monitoring for performance drift that could indicate emerging bias, with automated alerts to prompt immediate investigation and remediation.

(Continued)

Table 10.1 (Continued)

AI principles	*Relevance considerations*	*Illustrative risks*	*Potential controls*
Sustainability	• Low – while important for long-term operations, it has a less direct impact on the immediate functioning of the AI system for inventory recommendations.	• Inefficient AI system operation could lead to excessive energy consumption, increasing operational costs, and environmental impact.	• Optimize the AI system's algorithms and hardware for energy efficiency, potentially through algorithmic refinements or adoption of energy-saving computing infrastructure. • Implement real-time energy consumption monitoring for the AI system, with alerts for unusual spikes that could indicate inefficiencies requiring investigation and resolution.

Conclusion

As we move into the next phase of AI, leveraging more autonomous AI agents, it will be important to integrate control functions into the AI system design. Controls should be viewed not as an extraneous activity but as an integral part of the design. Too often, controls are viewed as the responsibility of the risk function, when in fact it is the first-line developers and operators who are ultimately responsible.

While AI incidents can be addressed after they occur, to reduce their impact or eliminate them effectively, preventative controls need to be implemented.

We suggest focusing on these control areas:

1 *Independent model testing and validation spanning diverse scenarios*, including adversarial attacks
2 *Data and ethical filters* to keep AI operations within acceptable conditions
3 *Continuous monitoring for key risk indicators* with pre-established tolerance levels and automated alert notification systems
4 *Effective human oversight and intervention* throughout the AI development lifecycle.

Focusing on these four controls will reduce or eliminate AI errors and anomalies. How much is invested in them will depend on the risk profile of each system and its potential impact. It is important to focus on risks that are both likely and significant. The goal is to prioritize those that have a meaningful impact on the organization's objectives, balancing thoroughness with cost-effectiveness.

Establishing an effective system of AI controls is not a one-time effort but a continuous cycle of assessment, implementation, monitoring, and refinement. Utilizing a values-based approach to controls can assist organizations in achieving the right balance between innovation and safety.

Key leadership questions to consider:

1 Do you understand the impact and likelihood of AI systems' risks?
2 Are you leveraging a cost-benefit analysis in the selection of your controls?

3 Is there a clear understanding of the governance and control responsibilities among developers, deployers, and users of your AI systems?
4 Is your AI control framework up-to-date for new AI developments, regulatory changes, and feedback from system performance evaluations?

Notes

1 Amazon Podcast. (2024, July 18). *Identity – Who is listening* [Audio podcast]. https://music.amazon.ca/identity/who-is-listening?returnTo=https%3A%2F%2Fmusic.amazon.ca%2Ffr-ca%2Fpodcasts%2F85b24d80-1540-4eae-9ddb-ddf34cb21f40%2Fepisodes%2Ff9ef88e0-9553-4092-a561-bf2bf14431b6%2Fai-unchained-ai-read_010---superalignment%3Freferrer%3Dhttps%3A%2F%2Fwww.google.com%2F.
2 ReThinking with Adam Grant. (2025, January 27). Sam Altman on the future of AI and society [Video]. *TED Talk*. https://www.ted.com/pages/sam-altman-on-the-future-of-ai-and-humanity-transcript.
3 ReThinking with Adam Grant. (2025, January 27). Sam Altman on the future of AI and society [Video]. *TED Talk*. https://www.ted.com/pages/sam-altman-on-the-future-of-ai-and-humanity-transcript.
4 Maslej, N., Fattorini, L., Perrault, R., Parli, V., Reuel, A., Brynjolfsson, E., Etchemendy, J., Ligett, K., Lyons, T., Manyika, J., Niebles, J. C., Shoham, Y., Wald, R., Clark, J., & Stanford Institute for Human-Centered AI. (2024, April 15). *Artificial Intelligence Index Report 2024*. Stanford HAI. https://aiindex.stanford.edu/report/.
5 Maslej, N., Fattorini, L., Perrault, R., Parli, V., Reuel, A., Brynjolfsson, E., Etchemendy, J., Ligett, K., Lyons, T., Manyika, J., Niebles, J. C., Shoham, Y., Wald, R., Clark, J., & Stanford Institute for Human-Centered AI. (2024, April 15). *Artificial Intelligence Index Report 2024*. Stanford HAI. https://aiindex.stanford.edu/report/.

Chapter 11

Maintaining stakeholder trust and confidence

As artificial intelligence (AI) performs a growing list of critical business operations and societal functions, stakeholders expect technologists to demonstrate the dependability and integrity of their systems. Yet, trust in these leaders is eroding. In the 2025 Edelman Trust Barometer, respondents were 11% more likely to perceive that all leaders, whether from government or business, and even journalists, "purposely misled people by saying things they know are false or gross exaggerations."[1]

Sir Walter Scott reaffirmed the importance of an assurance leadership mindset when he said, "It is wonderful what strength of purpose and boldness and energy of will are roused by the assurance that we are doing our duty."[2]

It is clear that businesses need to do more to build trust in their AI technologies. Increasing transparency through detailed model cards and transparency reports, and disclosing testing results, will not be enough if readers are unsure of the validity of claims made. Involving an independent third-party, whether your own internal audit group or an external assurance provider, can legitimize the information shared. The information tested can include descriptions of AI governance practices and controls, or technical specifications.

AI assurance is now gaining traction. Internal audit groups are conducting annual AI governance audits, and ISO 42001 certification is taking off across all industry lines. But much more is needed.

One challenge is the lack of criteria to evaluate the sufficiency of an AI developer or operator's claims. An assurance provider can test the accuracy and completeness of their claims, but is that sufficient? Do they address stakeholders' concerns? Reporting the bias metrics of an AI model and having them independently tested doesn't mean the

DOI: 10.4324/9781003625520-13

AI model is unbiased. Some may argue that a discerning reader could read the bias score and determine the model's level of bias. But how many users can do that? How can a user determine if the AI system will be biased against them by reviewing group bias scores? They can't.

What is needed is an evaluation as to whether the AI governance practices or technical score is good enough, and this requires benchmarks, which we are in short supply. While there are many publications that generally describe what good governance looks like, details are lacking. The documents are often subject to interpretation and lack specificity by use case or industry. The quality is even worse when you look at product-level technical specifications.

Despite these gaps, users want to trust AI. They want the better outcomes that it promises, and they are embracing GenAI at an insatiable pace. However, as we move toward agentic AI, removing the human-in-the-loop oversight, users will need more assurance that AI works well before they fully embrace it.

In this chapter, we explore the foundational elements of AI assurance, the challenges that organizations face in implementing it, and how it can be used to build trust in AI.

Objectives

Upon completing this chapter, you will be able to:

- Understand the key components of a robust AI assurance framework
- Learn strategies for building trust and confidence in AI innovation
- Identify strategies to address AI assurance challenges effectively
- Develop a roadmap for AI assurance.

Building trust in AI

The lack of trust among the public and regulatory bodies stems from high-profile incidents where AI systems failed or caused harm. Accidents happen with any new technology. However, AI's rapid expansion and widespread use are heightening concerns about its potential impacts.

Several factors are driving a lack of trust in AI:

1 *Bias and discrimination:* There have been instances where AI systems have demonstrated bias, making decisions that unfairly

discriminate against certain groups of people. This is often due to biased training data or flawed algorithms.

2 *Lack of transparency:* AI systems, especially those based on deep learning, are often seen as "black boxes," with decision-making processes that are not transparent.
3 *Accountability:* When AI systems make mistakes, it is challenging to assign responsibility, especially when the decision-making process is not transparent, and multiple parties are involved
4 *Security concerns:* AI systems are vulnerable to various security threats, including data breaches, data poisoning, and adversarial attacks, which can compromise the integrity of AI decisions and the privacy of sensitive data.
5 *Societal considerations:* AI applications raise ethical questions, such as the potential for job displacement, surveillance, and the manipulation of information.
6 *Loss of human agency:* As AI becomes more autonomous, humans are concerned about losing control. Existential questions arise when we consider our role when AI has cognitive capabilities and knowledge repositories that far exceed our own.

Trust is not a technical concept. It is not driven by a quantifiable equation like "I do this and I achieve this." It is driven by emotions. We are all familiar with the old adage "Trust takes years to build, seconds to break, and forever to repair."[3] When considering how to build or maintain trust, we can get valuable insights from relationship psychology. Lisa Copley, a renowned psychologist, views on trust are:

1 Trust requires accountability, open communication, empathy, and consistent actions over time.
2 Trust isn't owed; it's earned.
3 It requires consistent effort, accountability, and self-awareness.
4 Trust is not built through grand gestures. It is slowly nurtured through small, consistent actions demonstrating ability, integrity, and benevolence.[4]

The challenge with AI is the last statement; trust is built over time. Do we have time for trust to be nurtured? With prior technologies, they were introduced to the public over decades and had longer periods of adoption. But for AI, trust needs to be built more rapidly.

One approach to establish trust faster is to involve a third party. A trusted and impartial party that can vouch for your competence, integrity, and capability as an AI developer and operator, and that of the AI system. As the knowledge foundations of AI grow, external subject matter experts will most likely be needed.

The role of AI assurance in building trust

In deciding to work with an organization or use their AI systems, there is a basic level of trust needed. Humans, by and large, do not work with people or organizations they do not trust. AI assurance can help to bridge this gap. It involves a "trust but verify" mindset – I trust you, but want your actions and statements to be verified. When individuals cannot perform the testing themselves, they look to a third party.

While organizations can provide detailed information about their AI systems and promote a culture of openness and truthfulness, there will always be some level of skepticism. We have all felt the discomfort in disclosing our faults and failures, even the most transparent of us. Organizations are no different, and often struggle as decisions on what to disclose are often made by a group of people in which consensus is needed, or one individual's beliefs can override those of others.

While individuals can test the veracity of information disclosed themselves, they often don't. Either because they do not have the tools or knowledge to do so, or because getting access to the information is difficult. There is a long precedent in which the general public will rely upon a select group of trusted parties to perform this testing on their behalf. Many of the products we use daily, such as the food we eat, the clothes we wear, and the medical, transportation, and electronic devices we use, are tested and certified as safe against specific requirements. These certification programs are supervised on our behalf by regulators.

These tests and certifications are focused on one of two subject matters: the process by which the product was designed, developed, and distributed, or the product itself. The goal of the tests is to substantiate the product's performance, both its consistency over time and under adversarial conditions, and its adherence to specific benchmarks. This external validation provides an objective evaluation of the product's performance and its adherence to standards, which is relied upon by consumers.

While gaining these certifications is time-consuming and can be costly, the benefit is that it can build trust in a product quickly. There is an inherent trust in assurance providers and processes that an organization can take advantage of, even if they are a lesser-known or a new entrant.

AI can benefit from this method of building trust. But it is important to understand that an external stamp of approval is not enough if the users' day-to-day interactions or information from other sources, such as journalists or researchers contradicts it. Maintaining trust and credibility requires trustworthy behaviors. It is much easier to build and maintain trust than it is to repair it.

Figure 11.1 is a trust framework demonstrating how trustworthy behaviors strengthen an organization's reputation. A strong reputation will attract more users. Increased user adoption provides more data that can be leveraged to refine and enhance AI functionalities. This iterative process creates a positive feedback loop: as the AI system's capabilities improve, it attracts a broader user base, which then contributes even more data, further fueling the AI's development.

This cycle of trust and improvement not only strengthens the system's performance but also solidifies the organization's standing as a reliable and ethical AI provider.

Organizations that thrive in an AI world will optimize both data and trust feedback loops to attract more users and accelerate their adoption of AI.

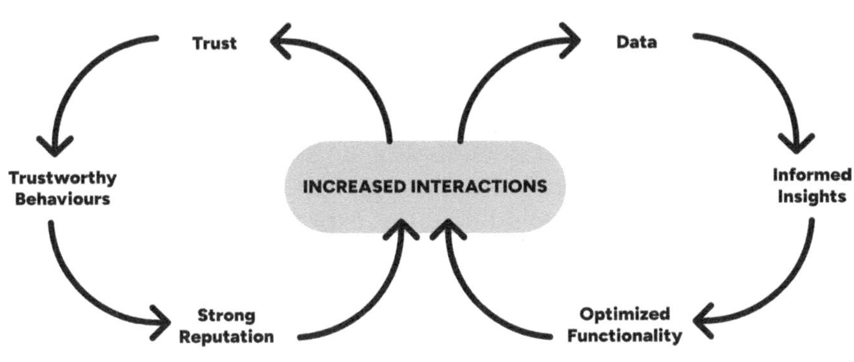

Figure 11.1 AI trust framework.

Different assurance types

Assurance in AI can be categorized into two types: those intended for internal use by management and those provided to external stakeholders. Each type serves a distinct purpose and offers insights into the AI system's performance, risks, and compliance.

Internal assurance:

1. *Self-assessments:* These are internal evaluations conducted by an organization to evaluate the current state of AI governance processes and AI systems against policy, standards, and best practices.
2. *Readiness pre-assessment:* This involves evaluating the AI system's readiness for deployment.
3. *Benchmarking:* This involves comparing an organization's AI systems to those of peers or industry benchmarks to identify areas of improvement or competitive advantage.
4. *Model validation and testing:* This process includes rigorous testing and validation of AI models to ensure they are making accurate predictions and decisions.
5. *Internal audit:* An internal audit is conducted by an organization's audit department to assess the controls and risks associated with AI systems.[5]

External assurance:

1. *Agreed-upon procedures:* These are engagements where specific procedures agreed upon with the organization and relevant stakeholders are performed. The procedures may be targeted to verify the integrity of the data inputs used by its AI system, the AI system's output, or its AI governance processes.
2. *Attestation report:* An attestation report expresses an opinion on the completeness and accuracy of an organization's assertions about its AI system or processes (e.g., SOC1 or SOC2 reports[6]).
3. *ISO certifications:* ISO certifications express a conclusion as to an organization's adherence to the ISO standard's criteria (e.g., *ISO 42001*[7]).
4. *Regulation conformity assessment reports:* These reports are assessments conducted by external bodies to confirm that an AI system complies with specific regulatory requirements (e.g., *EU AI Act*).[8]

Both internal and external assurance have a role in building trust in AI systems. Internal assurance allows management to maintain oversight and continuous improvement of AI initiatives, while external assurance provides stakeholders with confidence in the organization's AI practices and compliance with broader standards and regulations.

When management is determining the type of assurance to engage in for their AI systems, the decision should be guided by the maturity of their AI management system and the readiness of their AI technologies. Internal assurance processes can be used to gauge the organization's readiness for external evaluation. Self-assessments and internal audits help identify gaps in compliance, performance, or risk management that need to be addressed before inviting external scrutiny. For example, if an internal audit reveals that an AI system lacks adequate data privacy controls, management can take corrective action before seeking an ISO certification or undergoing a regulatory conformity assessment.

The primary consideration in deciding on the type, nature, and extent of assurance needed should always match the stakeholder's needs. Different stakeholders may have varying requirements when it comes to trust in AI systems. Customers, for instance, might be most concerned with privacy and the use of their data, while investors may focus on the AI system's performance and its impact on the company's reputation and user adoption. Regulators will want assurances on adherence to regulations and legal standards and may necessitate specific attestation reports or conformity assessments.

The decision on the assurance approach must also consider the potential risks associated with the AI system. High-risk applications, such as those impacting health, safety, or significant financial decisions, should be subject to more robust assurance processes. The competitive landscape can also influence the need for assurance; in industries where trust is a key differentiator, assurance can provide a competitive advantage.

Key components of AI assurance

AI assurance involves various stakeholders, each with a distinct role and set of expectations. The key components of AI assurance revolve around understanding stakeholders, selecting a credible assurance provider, determining the subject matter of the assurance, and establishing clear assessment criteria.

Understanding stakeholders

The primary stakeholders in AI assurance should include:

1. The target entity (the organization that developed and/or deployed the AI system).
2. The users (those who interact with or are affected by the AI system).
3. The assurance provider (the independent body conducting the evaluation).[9]

A clear understanding of the targeted users is crucial to ensure that the assurance process addresses their specific needs and concerns. This user-centric approach tailors the assurance activities to the most relevant areas of the AI system, taking into account transparency, fairness, and privacy.

For instance, end consumers may be provided with clear, user-friendly explanations of how their data is used, while business clients receive detailed reports on system performance and integration capabilities. Regulatory bodies will be presented with compliance documentation and testing results, whereas information provided to developers and engineers covers technical audits and code reviews. Investors will want financial impact assessments and risk analyses, and ethical groups might look for third-party evaluations of fairness and bias mitigation.

The AI assurance process must be flexible enough to meet the varied requirements of the targeted users of the assurance report, ensuring that each stakeholder's particular concerns are adequately addressed.

Selection of an assurance provider

The selection of the assurance provider can impact the credibility of the assurance provided. The practitioner must possess the competence and proficiency to conduct a thorough evaluation of the AI system. Factors such as the assurance provider's independence, reputation, and expertise in AI and related fields are essential considerations. The more independent the assurance provider is from the organization, the more weight their findings will carry with stakeholders.

For instance, Chartered Professional Accountants (CPAs) are often sought for external assurance due to their adherence to a stringent professional code of conduct and established quality processes. Similarly, professional engineers are bound by their professional obligations, ensuring that their assessments meet high standards of integrity and technical rigor.

When selecting an assurance provider for AI systems, organizations have several options:

1. *Management (self-assessment):* A company's management team may use self-assessment tools to ensure their AI-powered recruitment system adheres to internal policies on diversity and inclusion.
2. *Internal audit group:* The internal audit team could evaluate the controls around an AI system used for financial forecasting to ensure they mitigate risks of inaccurate predictions and comply with financial reporting standards.
3. *External benchmarking organization:* An external organization could benchmark a retailer's AI-driven inventory management system against best-in-class solutions to identify areas for enhancement.
4. *CPA:* A CPA may be engaged to provide an attestation report for an organization's transparency report and system model card, giving an opinion on their accuracy and completeness.
5. *Professional engineer:* A professional engineer could assess the technical integrity of an AI system used in autonomous vehicles, ensuring it is robust and safe for public use.
6. *Professional data scientists:* A data scientist may use advanced analytics tools, algorithms, and machine learning techniques to challenge an AI model's predictions and decisions.
7. *Recognized process experts with AI certifications:* A new field of AI certifiers is emerging. These accredited individuals or firms may leverage their specialized training to certify that an AI organization or its system meets specific criteria.

Given the multi-faceted nature of AI systems, the assurance process often requires a multi-disciplined team bringing diverse expertise.

Often, these teams include specialists who understand AI ethics, business processes, controls, data science, human psychology, privacy, and regulations. The involvement of diverse professionals ensures that an AI system's technical, business, and regulatory implications are fully considered. For example, while data scientists might focus on the accuracy and bias of algorithms, privacy experts would assess how user data is handled, and business process experts would examine the AI's impact on workflow efficiency.

Determination of subject matter

The subject matter of the assurance can vary depending on the focus of the evaluation. It may pertain to the AI management system, which includes governance and controls over the AI system, or it could be directed at specific attributes or outcomes of the AI system, such as bias scores or performance metrics. With the importance of data quality and integrity on AI model performance, an assurance engagement could be targeted just at the data used to train and operate the AI model. The choice of subject matter should align with the stakeholders' interests and the organization's objectives for the AI system.

It is important to recognize that the focus of the evaluation can significantly influence the type of assurance provided. The most prevalent assurance provided for AI systems is on their management system of governance practices and controls. It involves evaluating how the system is managed, the processes for updating and maintaining the model, how data is governed, and the controls around model deployment and monitoring. The assurance team might examine the organization's policies for data privacy, model risk management, and the procedures for addressing model drift or data quality issues. The assurance team would also review the governance structure, including roles and responsibilities for AI oversight, to ensure there is accountability and proper decision-making processes in place.

The second type of assurance evaluates specific attributes or outcomes of an AI model. This type of assurance would involve a detailed analysis of the model's decision-making process, the fairness of its outcomes, and its prediction accuracy. An internal validation team could perform independent testing to confirm the AI system's bias scores. The testing team would evaluate the methodology used to calculate the bias scores, test the system with various scenarios to assess its reliability, and verify that the performance metrics reported by the organization accurately reflect the system's performance.[10]

In these two examples, the choice between focusing on the AI management system or specific attributes or outcomes would depend on the stakeholders' interests and the organization's objectives. Ultimately, the subject matter of AI assurance should be carefully selected to provide meaningful insights and foster trust in the AI system's operation.

Criteria for assessment

The criteria against which the subject matter is assessed can be derived from various sources, including industry guidelines, best practices, international standards like ISO 42001 or the IEEE ECPAIS,[11] and regulatory requirements such as the EU AI Act or China's AI laws. The chosen criteria should be relevant and capable of providing a meaningful evaluation of the AI system's performance and compliance.

In addition, the benchmarks must be suitable for the intended purpose of the assurance engagement. CPAs, when involved in assurance engagements, are required to confirm the suitability of the criteria before they conduct their evaluation. This suitability assessment ensures that the criteria are appropriate for evaluating the subject matter and that the results of the assurance engagement will be meaningful to the stakeholders.[12]

A CPA firm engaged to provide assurance on an AI system's compliance with data protection standards might use the EU's General Data Protection Regulation (GDPR) as criteria. The assurance team would evaluate the criteria's suitability by ensuring it is objective (free from bias), measurable (allowing for clear assessment of compliance), complete (covering all relevant GDPR principles), and relevant (addressing stakeholders' concerns about data privacy).

With the rapid pace of AI development, the criteria for assurance must be dynamic, adapting to new developments and emerging best practices, to ensure that the assurance remains relevant.

Reporting mechanism

The reporting mechanism for conveying the assurance results is also influenced by the type of assurance engagement. The reporting should be clear, concise, and provide stakeholders with the information they need to understand the AI system's assurance status.

The emergence of AI transparency reports represents a significant development in AI reporting. These reports serve as comprehensive documents that detail the design, deployment, and impact of AI systems, providing insights into their ethical considerations, data handling practices, algorithmic decision-making processes, and overall governance. It should be expected that AI transparency reports will become a target subject matter for various types of assurance engagements.

Management and internal auditors can assess AI transparency reports for completeness and accuracy, ensuring that they reflect a true and fair read-out of the AI system's operations and adherence to standards. Management may verify that the transparency report includes all relevant information about the AI system's data sources, training methods, and performance metrics. Internal auditors can then conduct a more detailed examination, checking the accuracy of the information presented and the sufficiency of the disclosures made in the report. They can also evaluate whether the report aligns with internal policies and regulatory requirements.

AI transparency reports can also be benchmarked against industry peers to identify where the organization excels or where it may need to improve to maintain competitiveness and public trust. The Stanford Transparency Index is an example of this type of benchmarking. External assurance providers, such as CPAs, professional engineers, or accredited certifiers, can be engaged to provide an independent assurance opinion to add credibility to the AI transparency report. The external assurance provider will assess the report against established criteria, such as international standards or regulatory frameworks.

The reporting mechanism for conveying the results of these various types of assurance engagements should effectively communicate the assurance status of the AI system. This could include key findings and areas for improvement for enhancing the AI system's governance and operational practices.

Current AI assurance challenges

Despite the growing interest in AI assurance, organizations face several challenges in obtaining it, ranging from the immaturity of AI management systems to the opaqueness of AI technologies. Addressing these challenges is crucial for establishing effective assurance practices that can keep pace with the rapid development of AI.

Many organizations are still in the early stages of developing robust AI management systems, including governance and control practices. The lack of maturity in these systems can make it difficult to establish a solid foundation for assurance. Without well-defined and documented processes, controls, and benchmarks, assessing the reliability and safety of AI systems becomes a more complex task. Organizations must invest in maturing their AI management practices to facilitate more effective assurance.

There is a limited number of internationally recognized criteria for AI assurance, and product-level standards are still under development. This gap makes it challenging to benchmark AI systems against a universally accepted set of standards. As a result, assurance providers often rely on industry guidelines, best practices, and emerging standards, which can vary significantly in scope.

The field of AI governance and control is relatively new, and there is a limited number of experts with the requisite knowledge and experience. This scarcity can make it difficult for organizations to find qualified assurance practitioners who can effectively evaluate AI systems. The industry needs to focus on developing and training more professionals to meet the growing demand for AI assurance.

Users of AI systems often have limited education regarding how AI works and what to expect from it. This lack of understanding can lead to unrealistic expectations or misinterpretation of the assurance provided. It is essential for organizations to educate users about AI technologies and involve them in the assurance process to ensure that their needs are addressed.

The "black box" nature of many AI systems, particularly those based on complex algorithms like deep learning, is challenging for assurance. The lack of explainability can make it difficult to assess how decisions are made and to identify potential biases or errors. Efforts to increase the transparency and interpretability of AI systems are critical for enabling more effective assurance.

There is also a lack of clarity regarding accountability and liability in the context of AI assurance. Questions arise about whether assurance practitioners could be held liable if an AI system they provided assurance over later fails. This uncertainty can deter assurance providers from engaging with AI systems and complicate the establishment of trust in AI technologies.

Other challenges include the rapid pace of AI innovation, which is currently outpacing the development of assurance practices. Another challenge is regulatory fragmentation, which makes it difficult to determine which criteria an AI system should be evaluated against. Additionally, the integration of AI systems across different business functions and industries adds complexity to defining the boundaries of an AI system.[13,14]

While there are challenges in obtaining AI assurance, they should not deter an organization from getting started. Even if the assurance scope is limited in scope, valuable lessons can be learned. And often, the attempt itself can build trust that you are trying to do the right thing.

Conclusion

Hopefully, this chapter has convinced you of the need for a strategic approach to building trust in AI systems. AI assurance is too often viewed as a regulatory requirement or a risk management exercise, when in fact it is a useful stratagem to improve stakeholder trust.

The pursuit of AI assurance mirrors the iterative nature of AI development itself. It should evolve and be refined as systems grow more complex and their applications more widespread. Assurance should not be treated as a static checkpoint but a dynamic process that evolves alongside AI technologies.

Starting with management self-assessments, organizations can understand their AI systems' current state and identify areas for enhancement. As AI systems mature, internal audits and benchmarking exercises can measure their progress and pinpoint gaps. Stakeholder demands to demystify the "black box" of AI, and credible evidence of an organization's trustworthiness, will often lead to engaging external assurance providers. This independent evaluation acts as a powerful endorsement of the organization's commitment to responsible AI, enhancing credibility and fostering trust.

The journey to AI assurance is not a linear path; it is a continuous cycle of improvement and adaptation.

Key leadership questions to consider:

1. How are you leveraging assurance to build trust and confidence in your AI governance framework?
2. How are you ensuring that your model documentation and transparency reports accurately reflect the performance and compliance of your AI systems?
3. How are you building the capabilities in your risk and control functions so that they can act as effective challengers of your AI governance practices and AI model design?
4. As regulatory landscapes evolve, how are you preparing your AI systems for potential third-party assurance requirements?

Notes

1. Edelman Trust Institute. (2025). *2025 Edelman Trust Barometer: Trust and the crisis of grievance*. Edelman. https://www.edelman.com/sites/g/files/aatuss191/files/2025-01/2025%20Edelman%20Trust%20Barometer%20Global%20Report_01.23.25.pdf.
2. Wikipedia Contributors. (n.d.). *Walter scott*. Wikipedia. Retrieved June 8, 2025, from https://en.wikipedia.org/wiki/Walter_Scott.
3. The quote "Trust takes years to build, seconds to break, and forever to repair" is often attributed to Amy Rees Anderson. However, it's also sometimes cited as an anonymous quote or even attributed to others like Dhar Mann. While the exact origin can be debated, the sentiment behind the quote is widely recognized and understood. Retrieved August 31, 2025, from https://www.google.com/search?q=who+said+%E2%80%9CTrust+takes+years+to+build%2C+seconds+to+break%2C+and+forever+to+repair.%E2%80%9D&rlz=1C5CHFA_enCA752CA752&oq=who+said+%E2%80%9CTrust+takes+years+to+build%2C+seconds+to+break%2C+and+forever+to+repair.%E2%80%9D&gs_lcrp=EgZjaHJvbWUyBggAEEUYOTIGCAEQABge0gEINjIxOGowajeoAgCwAgA&sourceid=chrome&ie=UTF-8.
4. Copley, L. (2025, February 19). How to (re-)build trust in a relationship. *Positive Psychology*. https://positivepsychology.com/build-trust/#:~:text=Rebuilding%20trust%20requires%20accountability%2C%20open%20communication%2C%20empathy%20%26,enough%20to%20invest%20in%20its%20growth%20and%20healing.
5. CPA Canada & AICPA. (2025, June 9). *Closing the trust gap – CPAs and AI assurance*. https://www.cpacanada.ca/business-and-accounting-resources/other-general-business-topics/information-management-and-technology/publications/ai-automation-for-cpas/ai-trust-gap-cpas-ai-assurance.

6 Hemmer, N. (2023, April 5). *SOC 1 vs SOC 2 – How are they different?* Linford & Company. https://linfordco.com/blog/soc-1-vs-soc-2-audit-reports/.
7 International Organization for Standardization. (2023). *ISO 42001:2023 – Artificial intelligence management systems—Requirements*. https://www.iso.org/standard/81230.html.
8 CPA Canada & AICPA. (2025, June 9). *Closing the trust gap – CPAs and AI assurance*. https://www.cpacanada.ca/business-and-accounting-resources/other-general-business-topics/information-management-and-technology/publications/ai-automation-for-cpas/ai-trust-gap-cpas-ai-assurance.
9 CPA Canada & AICPA. (2025, June 9). *Closing the trust gap – CPAs and AI assurance*. https://www.cpacanada.ca/business-and-accounting-resources/other-general-business-topics/information-management-and-technology/publications/ai-automation-for-cpas/ai-trust-gap-cpas-ai-assurance.
10 EY & ACCA. (2025, June 25). *EY AI assessments: Enhancing confidence in AI*. https://www.ey.com/content/dam/ey-unified-site/ey-com/en-gl/insights/public-policy/documents/ey-ai-assessments-enhancing-confidence-in-ai-06-25.pdf.
11 IEEE Standards Association. (2020, September 3). *The Ethics Certification Program for Autonomous and Intelligent Systems (ECPAIS)*. https://standards.ieee.org/wp-content/uploads/import/governance/iccom/IC18-004-ECPAIS.pdf.
12 CPA Canada & AICPA. (2025, June 9). *Closing the trust gap – CPAs and AI assurance*. https://www.cpacanada.ca/business-and-accounting-resources/other-general-business-topics/information-management-and-technology/publications/ai-automation-for-cpas/ai-trust-gap-cpas-ai-assurance.
13 CPA Canada & AICPA. (2025, June 9). *Closing the trust gap – CPAs and AI assurance*. https://www.cpacanada.ca/business-and-accounting-resources/other-general-business-topics/information-management-and-technology/publications/ai-automation-for-cpas/ai-trust-gap-cpas-ai-assurance.
14 EY & ACCA. (2025, June 25). *EY AI assessments: Enhancing confidence in AI*. https://www.ey.com/content/dam/ey-unified-site/ey-com/en-gl/insights/public-policy/documents/ey-ai-assessments-enhancing-confidence-in-ai-06-25.pdf.

Chapter 12

The art of data-driven AI monitoring

The importance of continuous monitoring of artificial intelligence (AI) cannot be understated, particularly as it becomes more autonomous. However, determining what should be tracked and measured is often a difficult task. The importance of measurement was best summed up by Lord Kelvin, a British mathematician: "If you cannot measure it, you cannot improve it."[1]

In the early days of AI, governance efforts focused on creating the fundamentals – an AI policy, accountability structure, and risk assessment. With these processes in place, organizations must now turn their attention to higher-impact control activities. Historically, monitoring of analytic models, AI's precursor, was performed periodically. The frequency of revalidating the models was determined based on risk and often set at an interval spanning months, if not years. These models could not dynamically learn, and revalidation was performed to test that the model still fit its broader environment and objective.

Times have changed. With AI's ability to adapt and dynamically learn, an AI's basis of making predictions and decisions (its weights and features) adjusts in post-production to new data patterns or changes in its environment. Real-time, continuous monitoring is needed to evaluate these changes and detect when the model's performance falls outside tolerance levels.

While there is a growing list of tests and metrics to measure AI performance, AI models are, for the most part, evaluated using the same accuracy metrics that have been employed for traditional analytic models. Although AI models may learn differently, they still rely on many of the same underlying algorithms – regression, classification, and clustering – that have been used for decades. The need

DOI: 10.4324/9781003625520-14

for new metrics has arisen from a focus on non-accuracy aspects, including fairness, security, and energy usage, as well as the proliferation of advanced AI models such as deep neural networks and GenAI, which require different measurement approaches.

The challenge is in determining which metrics to use. The selection of the "right" AI metrics to measure should be a risk-based decision that factors in the likelihood and impact of a risk, comparing the value of detecting a performance issue early to the cost of the monitoring mechanism.

AI incidents are on the rise. MIT maintains a database that has been tracking AI incidents since 2015. During the last decade, AI incidents have increased tenfold, with the number doubling in the last two years. In addition, the severity of incidents is accelerating along an exponential curve, as is the number of individuals affected.[2]

When testing an AI model, either pre- or post-deployment, there are three broad categories of metrics that should be considered:

1 *Value metrics*, such as the return on investment (ROI), user engagement, and overall business impact, like profitable revenue growth.
2 *Operational metrics*, such as uptime, response time, and resource utilization, to ensure the reliability and scalability of AI systems.
3 *Behavioral metrics*, both user interactions with AI systems and the AI's own behavior, such as performance drift, bias, and adaptability over time. These metrics provide insights into the AI system's consistency and reliability, and are key determinants of user satisfaction, adoption rates, and areas for improvement.

As AI becomes more autonomous and the human-in-the-loop oversight of AI's outcomes is removed, moving to data-driven, real-time, continuous monitoring will become critical.

Objectives

Upon completing this chapter, you will be able to:

- Appreciate the value of implementing an AI continuous monitoring program
- Understand relevant AI metrics and approaches to measure AI risks and detect AI incidents
- Recognize the current challenges of AI measurement systems.

Developing a robust AI measurement system

While measuring AI outcomes happens after deployment, the monitoring controls should be developed in response to the risk assessment conducted during the design phase and built into the system's requirements. This gives the development team time to consult with researchers and the business to develop an appropriate measurement system for an AI system, including acceptable tolerance levels. It can take time to convert a theoretical concept to technical feasibility.

These metrics can be used in three stages of the AI development lifecycle: (1) at the development stage by the AI developer; (2) during model validation by an independent tester; and (3) after deployment to perform continuous monitoring by the operator.

But we are getting ahead of ourselves. When investing in AI, the first decision is selecting and prioritizing your use cases. Up till now, many organizations have not gone through a structured approach to identify and select their AI use cases. AI use cases were chosen based on an executive's area of interest or the experience of the data science or AI innovation team. As investment in AI grows, it is important to prioritize AI projects that bring the most value.

The ROI in AI projects has been patchy. While some have resulted in high user adoption and efficiency savings, others have had a marginal impact. They have demonstrated an organization's commitment to innovation, but the value generated has not covered their development and operating costs.

The root cause of these failures varies. Some, even when highly successful, were too niche. Others had hidden costs or were hard to implement due to low data quality, discontinuous data flows, and difficult integrations into existing processes and systems. Identifying these challenges during the selection process can avoid costly mistakes.

It is important that AI projects are developed with an understanding of how they generate value and what is required to unlock that value. AI has gone through several "AI winters" where its promise did not live up to reality. Investment dollars are scarce, and executives need to ensure they are well spent. AI can no longer be treated as an experimental technology. It needs to deliver on its promise.

Table 12.1 Measuring AI value

Define AI measurement: value architecture	*Develop baseline measurement for business case*	*Develop business case and validate with stakeholders*	*Ensure sustaining value*
Classify AI metrics: • Business value • Engineering and Data Sciences (MLOps) • Service • Customer • Employee • Regulatory compliance and assurance • ESG (environmental, social, and governance).	For each AI use case, capture a clear current state vs. a future state to ensure: • Clarity of the before and after impact • Leverage industry comparatives or valid proxies and be conservative. Identify the value drivers and select relevant metrics that are measurable.	Follow your business case methods: • Ensure a finance lead is engaged to support and validate the approach • Carefully address the total cost of ownership for the full adoption life cycle • For each value driver (metric), estimate a range of expected benefits from a high, medium, low, and execution complexity • Apply both top-down and bottom-up estimates to validate the business case.	Continuous monitoring of each AI use case: • Ensure a communication stakeholder map is organized for effective governance • Communicate for each use case the state of their lifecycle and monitor value outcomes to ensure integrated portfolio management • Determine the estimated future life of the AI system, building in expected retraining and upgrades.
		ROI Generated by AI **Investment gain (Net profit)/ Investment base × 100**	

Table 12.1 identifies four building blocks to calculate the ROI of an AI system and measure value:

1 *Define AI value:* It identifies what represents value and what matters most for the specific AI use case, clustering relevant KPI measurement classes
2 *Develop baseline measurement:* It establishes before-and-after comparisons to create meaningful measurement comparatives between pre- and post-AI outcomes
3 *Develop business case:* It validates with key stakeholders the total cost of ownership and required investments to support the full AI adoption lifecycle
4 *Ensure sustaining value:* It continually challenges the sustaining value of AI, calculating its long-term impacts and the need for retraining or upgrades.

Benefit measurement and realization are common weaknesses of technology projects, and many frameworks and measurements are available to quantify and track them. We do not cover these in this book. Instead, we discuss the metrics specific to AI, both those that measure AI's value and those that can assist organizations in realizing value.

AI value metrics

Measuring the value created by AI, often referred to as key performance indicators (KPIs), involves metrics similar to those used for traditional technology. Common financial metrics include revenue growth, cost savings, and profit. You can also quantify operational metrics, such as resource requirements, full-time equivalents (FTE), raw materials, energy, or time to market.

Additional metrics more relevant for AI projects include: user adoption, data utilization rate (a measure of how effectively an organization is using its data assets), and customer retention. AI has also elevated the importance of measuring user interactions. Project teams are now tracking not only the number of users using an AI system but also the number of unique interactions (e.g., repeat or new requests) and the session duration. And many are going even deeper, analyzing how AI is being used (e.g., the transaction types) and how often a user returns.

What has been harder to measure is the effectiveness of these interactions. User sentiment and satisfaction surveys are the most common measurements, but there is often an assumption made that a user's usage pattern is a strong predictor that they are getting value (e.g., they are receiving value if they use AI more often and for longer sessions).

These proxies are also being used to estimate time saved. GenAI is most commonly measured using this approach. Activity-based costing, popular in the 1980s and 1990s, is used to calculate the time to perform a task with and without AI. Multiplying this difference by usage counts gives an approximation of time saved.

Harvard Business Review (HBR) reported that GenAI and copilots perform some tasks 40% faster, saving us several hours a week.[3] A dangerous assumption made by business leaders is that the time saved is put to productive use. A recent study conducted by the University of Lausanne, Switzerland, challenges that belief. In the Lausanne study, 83% of respondents admitted to wasting 25% of those savings, and 36% of them wasted half of it.[4]

In the same HBR article, Travis Muhlestein, the Chief Data and Analytics Officer at GoDaddy, a U.S.-based web-hosting company, had some advice on how to generate maximum value from AI time savings. "Managers [should] develop guidelines and techniques for how employees use the extra time," Muhlestein stressed the importance of bringing intentionality to the conversation, making it about the employee and giving them a safe place to be creative.

> I emphasize the importance of their career aspirations. I say I want to help them use the time windfall to further streamline tasks that hinder their progress. I ask people to imagine how they'd like to do their jobs three, five, and 10 years from now.[5]

But it isn't all about task efficiency. While AI, and particularly GenAI, can improve productivity, it can also grow top-line revenues. Personalization can identify new products or services for existing customers and attract new ones.

Table 12.2 provides a list of metrics, both traditional and AI-specific, that can be used to measure AI's value in bottom-line efficiencies and top-line growth.

The orientation of who receives the value also matters. Metrics can measure the value for a business executive or shareholder.

Table 12.2 Value metrics to measure bottom-line efficiency and top-line growth

Value metric	*Traditional metrics*	*AI-specific metrics*
Bottom-line (efficiency)		
Operational efficiency	Cost per acquisition Time to market Resource utilization rate	Inference time (prediction time) Decision latency rate
Quality improvement	Defect rate Customer satisfaction score Resolution rate	Data drift Performance drift
Process optimization	Cycle time Automation rate Employee productivity rate	AI adoption rate Feature importance score
Top-line (growth)		
Customer acquisition	New customer growth rate Customer lifetime value Conversion rate	Customer segmentation accuracy Customer sentiment score
Customer engagement	Net promoter score User engagement rate Average order value	Personalization effectiveness index Customer journey optimization score
Revenue growth	Year-over-year revenue Market share Sales	Dynamic pricing effectiveness AI-enhanced market penetration

Similar metrics can be designed that measure the value for customers, employees, or society (e.g., AI for Good). They can be reported by an organization in a corporate responsibility report or help justify an innovation providing societal benefits, such as facial recognition used in missing person cases, autonomous vehicles for the physically impaired, or AI-assisted surgery.

AI operational metrics

Table 12.3 identifies several operational metrics that measure AI's impact on the bottom line. We classify these as value metrics, as they measure the improvements that an AI system can make to the time to perform an activity or improve quality. Besides these operational

Table 12.3 AI model development – key performance metrics

Metric category	*Metric definition*	*Metric/KPIs*
Regulatory compliance	Adherence of AI systems to legal and regulatory standards governing data usage, privacy, and ethical considerations.	• % of AI models audited for compliance • # of compliance violations • % of employees trained on regulatory requirements related to AI • % of certified employees in AI
Energy efficiency	Optimization of energy consumption in AI systems to minimize environmental impact while maintaining performance.	• Recognition Efficiency (RE) balancing accuracy, complexity, and energy consumption • CO2 Equivalent (CO2EQ) emissions during model training and inference • Electricity Consumption measured in FLOPS (Floating Point Operations Per Second)
Accessibility	Ensuring that AI systems are usable by individuals with diverse abilities and backgrounds, promoting inclusivity.	• % of users able to interact with the AI system using assistive technologies • Time taken for users with disabilities to complete tasks compared to those without • % of accessibility features implemented in AI applications
Safety	Evaluation of potential risks associated with AI systems and their impact on users and the environment.	• Number of safety incidents reported during AI deployment • % of AI systems with implemented safety protocols • Frequency of safety audits conducted on AI systems
Data privacy	Protection of personal and sensitive information used in AI systems, ensuring compliance with data protection regulations.	• % of data anonymized before use in AI models • Number of data breaches reported related to AI systems • % of data access requests fulfilled in compliance with privacy regulations

(*Continued*)

Table 12.3 (Continued)

Metric category	*Metric definition*	*Metric/KPIs*
Security	Assessment of the robustness of AI systems against cyber threats and vulnerabilities to protect sensitive data.	• Number of security incidents detected in AI systems • Time taken to respond to security breaches • % of AI systems undergoing regular security assessments

metrics, organizations have other goals and commitments that they must benchmark against. These include:

1 Regulatory compliance
2 Energy efficiency
3 Accessibility
4 Safety
5 Data privacy
6 Security.

Similar to the selection of controls, each metric has a cost associated with collecting the data, performing benchmark comparisons, and responding to variances. A cost-benefit analysis is also helpful to decide which metrics to focus on. It is better to select a few key metrics that will have a meaningful impact on improving your AI system's ROI, stakeholder experience, and performance, than measure more than you can respond to. It is also important to focus on those measures that you have the resources and capability to influence.

AI model performance

AI model performance metrics evaluate the effectiveness and reliability of an AI model. It involves highly technical metrics that involve statistical science and math.

It is important to select metrics that match the algorithm, data type, and objective. Classification and regression algorithms are the most common. As a reminder, classification algorithms categorize data, assigning input data to discrete classes or labels based on learned patterns. A classification model might determine whether an email is "spam" or "not spam."

In contrast, regression algorithms quantify relationships and make predictions about a value. A linear regression model could be used to forecast house prices based on various features like size, location, and number of bedrooms.

For both model types, the most important performance area to measure is accuracy. For a classification model, you measure if it is right or not. For a regression model, you measure how close its prediction is to the actual value.

Classification metrics

For a classification model, measuring its accuracy can be broken down into a four-quadrant evaluation that compares the actual and predicted values.

There are four possible relationships:

1 true positive (TP) – the target is in a class, and AI predicted this outcome
2 true negative (TN) – the target is not in a class, and AI predicted this outcome
3 false positive (FP) – the AI predicted the target to be in a class when it's not
4 false negative (FN) – the AI predicted the target was not in a class when it was.

This evaluation model is called a confusion matrix and is depicted in Figure 12.1.

While the goal of most AI systems is to maximize an AI's true scores (TP and TN) and minimize the false scores (FP and FN), there are circumstances where you need to make a trade-off. For example, in a medical diagnosis scenario, a model that predicts whether a patient has a serious disease may prioritize minimizing false negatives to ensure that very few actual cases of the disease are missed, even if it results in a higher number of false positives. This trade-off is acceptable because failing to identify a patient with the disease could lead to severe health consequences, whereas a false positive may lead to unnecessary testing but causes less harm.

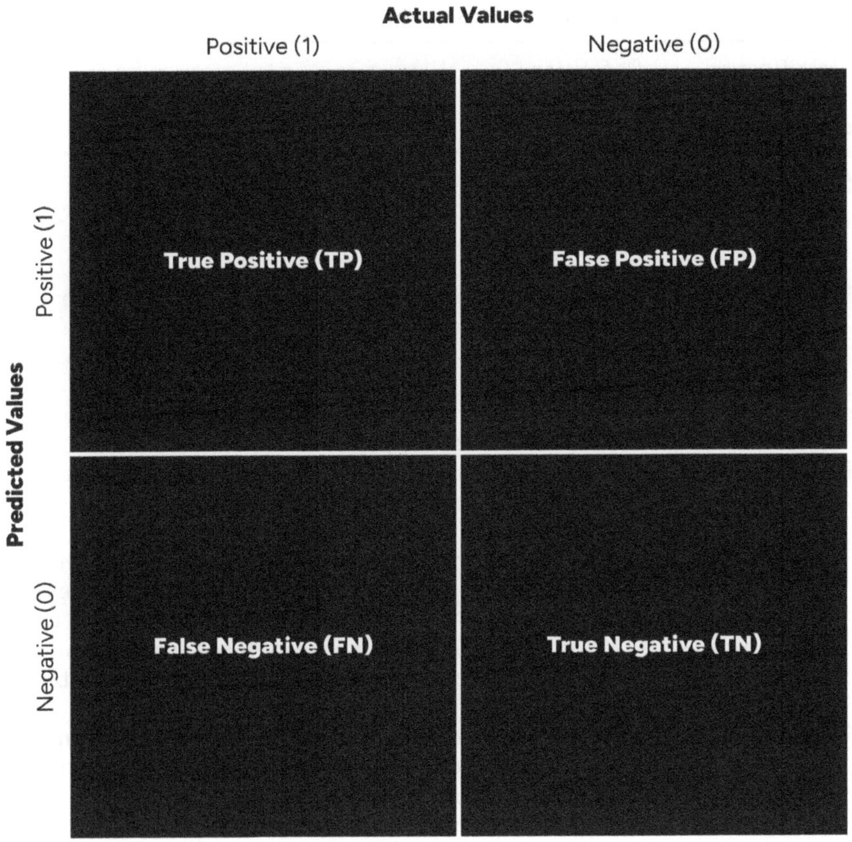

Figure 12.1 Classification – confusion matrix.

Often, this trade-off results when the training data is lower quality, incomplete, or not fully representative of the population. The higher the quality of the data and the better-tuned a model is, the more accurate it can be in making predictions across all classes.

There are five common metrics, defined in Table 12.4, that are used to measure how well the model distinguishes between different classes and its overall predictive power.

For the first four accuracy metrics, the metric value ranges from 0 to 1 (or 0% to 100%). A value of 1 (or 100%) indicates perfect accuracy, precision, and/or recall. Higher values are better. The ROC-AUC metric also ranges from 0 to 1. However, for it, a value of 1 indicates perfect classification, while a value of 0.5

Table 12.4 Classification metrics – key attributes

Classification metrics – key attributes	*Definition*
Accuracy	Accuracy measures the proportion of correct predictions (both true positives and true negatives) among the total number of cases examined.
Precision	Precision measures the accuracy of the positive predictions made by the model, indicating how many of the predicted positive cases were actually correct. A high precision value means that when the model predicts a positive outcome, it is likely to be correct.
Recall or sensitivity	Recall or Sensitivity/True Positive Rate measures the ratio of true positives to the sum of true positives and false negatives (relevant items that are incorrectly identified). It measures the model's ability to identify all relevant instances in the dataset. A high recall value indicates that the model successfully captures a large proportion of the actual positive cases, minimizing the number of false negatives.
F1 Score	The F1 Score is the harmonic mean of precision and recall, providing a single metric that balances both measures. The F1 Score is particularly useful in situations where there is an uneven class distribution or when both precision and recall are important, such as in cases where false positives and false negatives carry different costs. It helps to ensure that a model does not achieve high performance by optimizing one metric at the expense of the other.
Area under the receiver operating characteristic (ROC) curve	The Area Under the ROC Curve (AUC-ROC) is a measure that helps us understand how well a classification model can distinguish between different classes. Imagine a graph where one axis shows the true positive rate (how many actual positives were correctly identified) and the other axis shows the false positive rate (how many actual negatives were incorrectly identified as positives). The AUC-ROC tells us how much area is covered under this curve.

indicates no discrimination (random guessing). For ROC-AUC, higher values are better, but any model scoring less than 0.5 would most likely be discarded as its performance is worse than straight guessing.

The interpretation of what constitutes a "good" accuracy, precision, or recall score can vary depending on the specific context, the problem being addressed, and the domain. Generally, a score above 70% (0.7) is considered acceptable for many applications. Scores above 80% (0.8) are often seen as good, while scores above 90% (0.9) are excellent. In some critical applications (like medical diagnoses), even 95% accuracy may not be sufficient if the consequences of false negatives are severe. High precision is very important in scenarios where false positives are costly or harmful (e.g., spam detection, fraud detection). High recall is crucial in situations where missing a positive case (false negatives) is particularly detrimental (e.g., disease detection, safety-critical systems).

It is important to consider the specific use case and the consequences of false positives and false negatives when deciding what is acceptable. In some cases, a trade-off between precision and recall may be necessary, leading to the use of the F1 score to balance both metrics.

Regression metrics

While accuracy metrics for a classification model measure whether the model achieved the classification right, metrics for a regression model measure how close its predicted value is to the actual value. If you have taken a statistics class, the common regression metrics included in Table 12.5 will be familiar.

The measurement scale for all three of the mean-related metrics ranges from 0 to ∞ (infinity). Lower values are better. A value of 0 indicates perfect predictions, while higher values indicate worse performance. Regression metrics and classification metrics serve different purposes and are tailored to the specific types of models they evaluate. By selecting the appropriate metrics for each model type, organizations can gain valuable insights into their AI models' performance and predictive capabilities.

Table 12.5 Regression metric types

Regression metric type	*Definition*
Mean absolute error (MAE)	MAE is the average of the absolute differences between predicted and actual values. It calculates the average magnitude of errors in a set of predictions, without considering their direction. It tells you how far off your predictions are from the actual results, on average. For example, if you predicted the temperature for a week, MAE would give you the average of those differences, without considering whether the predictions were too high or too low.
Mean squared error (MSE)	MSE is the average of the squared differences between predicted and actual values. By squaring the errors, MSE gives more weight to larger errors, making it sensitive to outliers. This metric is useful for identifying models that have significant prediction errors. So, if you have a few very wrong predictions, MSE will highlight those more than MAE would.
Root mean squared error (RMSE)	RMSE is the square root of MSE and provides a measure of the standard deviation of the prediction errors. RMSE gives relatively high weight to large errors, similar to MSE, but is expressed in the same units as the predicted values, making it easier to interpret. RMSE is particularly useful when comparing the performance of different models or when the scale of the prediction errors is important.

GenAI models

GenAI leverages classification and regression models to create new content by learning underlying patterns and distributions from existing data. The most common GenAI models are large language models (LLMs). Think of an LLM as a smart system that predicts the next word in a sentence based on the words that came before it. It has a vast "vocabulary" of words it knows, and it calculates the likelihood of each word appearing next in the sequence.

For example, if you start a sentence with "The cat is," the LLM will look at all the words it knows and determine which word is most likely to come next, such as "sleeping" or "playing." It does this by considering the probability of each possible word based on the words that have already been used. The word with the highest probability is then chosen as the next word in the sentence.

This probability is calculated by looking at how often certain words follow others in the vast amount of text the model has been trained on. By multiplying these probabilities together for each word in the sequence, the model can determine the overall likelihood or confidence of the sentence being accurate.

While the accuracy metrics we have already studied can be used for GenAI, these metrics do not fully capture the quality of the generated outputs. Table 12.6 identifies four additional metrics to evaluate the output quality of LLM models.

Table 12.6 LLM measurement metric score types

LLM score type	*Definition*
BLEU score	The BLEU score (Bilingual Evaluation Understudy) is a metric for evaluating machine-translated text. It measures the similarity of the machine-translated text to a set of high-quality reference translations.[6] Bleu Scores are between 0 and 1. A score of 0.6 or 0.7 is considered the best you can achieve. Even two humans would likely come up with different sentence variants for a problem, and would rarely achieve a perfect match. For this reason, a score closer to 1 is unrealistic in practice and should raise a flag that your model is overfitting.[7]
ROUGE score	ROUGE score is a common metric used to evaluate the quality of summaries generated by algorithms – the coherence and overlap between machine-generated text and human-generated references, particularly for NLP algorithms. A ROUGE score is commonly used for text summarization tasks where the goal is to automatically generate a concise summary of a longer text.[8] Think of ROUGE as a way to measure how well a computer-generated summary matches a human-written summary. It looks at how many words or phrases from the human summary appear in the computer summary. The ROUGE score typically ranges from 0 to 1. A lower ROUGE score (closer to 0) suggests that the generated summary does not capture the main ideas or important details of the reference summary effectively.

(*Continued*)

Table 12.6 (Continued)

LLM score type	*Definition*
Perplexity	Perplexity measures how much a NLP model is able to predict a sample of text. You can think of it as a way to gauge how "confused" the model is when trying to understand or generate language. The lower the perplexity, the better the training is. The formula for perplexity is the exponent of the mean of the log likelihood of all the words in an input sequence.[9] Perplexity measures uncertainty and is scored in a range between 0 and ∞ (infinity). A lower perplexity score means that the language model is better at predicting the next word in a sequence, indicating that it understands the language well. Conversely, a higher perplexity score suggests that the model struggles to make accurate predictions, meaning it finds the text more confusing.
Jailbreak benchmark	JailBreak benchmark is a benchmark for measuring how well an AI model can be manipulated or prompted to produce responses that it is normally restricted from generating. A high success rate in bypassing restrictions would indicate that the model has vulnerabilities that need to be addressed.[10]

While the LLM metrics provide a foundation for evaluating AI performance, it is essential to evolve your AI measurement framework to evaluate new technologies and assess their impact. While organizations can set minimum targets for each benchmark, context matters. There will be certain use cases, particularly those that can cause greater harm, for which the acceptable score will need to be much higher. Establishing these minimum thresholds is a necessary step to benchmark the scores and determine what is "good enough." Another important consideration when deciding if a model is ready to be moved into production is ensuring that its performance in the lab can be replicated in the "wild." This involves testing the model with unseen data to measure its ability to generalize from its training.

Cross-validation testing

When testing an AI model, a common technique used is cross-validation. It involves dividing the training and testing dataset into multiple subsets, or "folds." The model is trained on a portion of the data (the training set) and tested on the remaining part (the testing set) multiple times, with different splits of the data. The value in subdividing the dataset is to ensure that the model performs well not just on a single subset of data, but across various subsets. If there is a significant difference in the accuracy scores across subsets, it is an indication that the model is overfitted and it is trained too tightly for certain data patterns and not enough on others. This imbalance will impact its performance once placed in production.

Cross-validation testing is an important step to confirm that a model is ready for production. Evaluators should also ask about the selection process for creating the fold subsets. The selection of folds in cross-validation can depend on the specific goals of the analysis and the characteristics of the dataset. In most cases, especially when the dataset is large and diverse, folds are randomized to ensure that each fold is representative of the overall dataset. However, if the dataset has specific characteristics that are important to the model's performance (e.g., language, gender, ethnicity), stratified sampling can be used to ensure that each fold contains a proportional representation of these groups. Table 12.7 identifies seven key steps to analyze cross-validation results.[11]

When conducting cross-validation testing, the number of folds matters. In Train Test Split, graphically depicted in Figure 12.2, the dataset is divided into two separate sets or folds: a training set and a testing set. The model is trained on the training set and then evaluated on the testing set. This method is useful when you have a large dataset and need a quick assessment of the model's performance and ability to generalize to unseen data. However, it may not provide a comprehensive evaluation if the dataset is small, as the performance can vary significantly depending on the split. There are many toolkits to help perform the Train Test Split, including Scikit-learn.[12]

In k-fold cross-validation, the dataset is divided into k equally sized folds. The model is trained and tested k times, each time using a different fold as the testing set and the remaining folds as the training set. This process is repeated k times, and the performance

Table 12.7 Process of analyzing cross-validation results

1	Understand key cross-validation metrics: precision, recall, and accuracy
2	Analyze how the data clusters examine carefully precision, recall, and examine the learning curves to understand the model's inherent behavior
3	Identify overfitting or underfitting issues that are impacting the model's performance
4	Test to determine the model's ability to regenerate with consistent levels of accuracy and recall
5	Continue to evaluate the model's performance with increased confidence intervals
6	Select the best model based on the cross-validation results
7	Document outcomes and share results to secure further validation

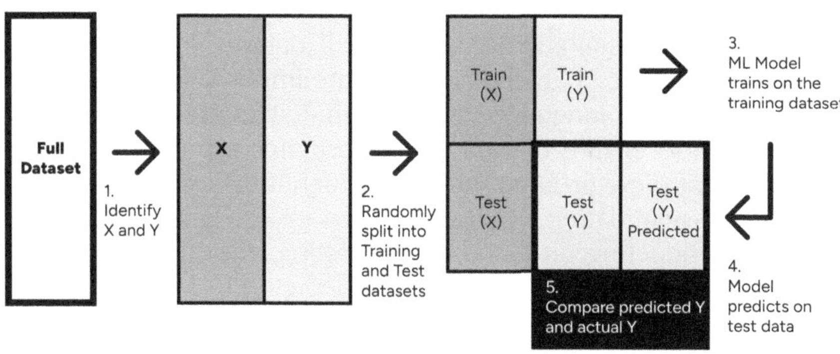

Figure 12.2 Training test split for AI model validation.

metrics are averaged to provide a more reliable estimate of the model's performance, including the accuracy, precision, and recall for each fold. K-fold cross-validation is computationally efficient and widely used, but is particularly useful for small datasets.

The recommended number of k folds for cross-validation can vary depending on several factors, including the size of the dataset, the computational resources available, and the specific goals of the analysis; however five or ten is most common.

Other performance metrics besides accuracy

While accuracy is an important measure of a model's performance, a number of other measurement frameworks are available to assess other performance metrics to identify and mitigate potential risks, biases, and unintended consequences.

For transparency, a common index relied upon is Stanford's *Foundation Model Transparency Index*,[13] introduced earlier. This index is used to grade the transparency of public AI models and to guide an organization in model transparency evaluation.

For fairness and bias, an often-used resource is *IBM's Artificial Intelligence Explainability 360*,[14] which provides a set of fairness metrics for datasets and models, along with explanations and bias mitigation algorithms. It provides an interactive web experience for non-technical users to grasp fairness concepts and offers extensive documentation, usage guidance, and industry-specific tutorials for data scientists.

For security, there is *the Adversarial Robustness Toolbox (ART)*[15] located in the *GitHub Software Development Libraries*. ART can be used to assess and defend models against adversarial threats. These threats include evasion, poisoning, extraction, and inference. These attacks aim to steal the trained model's parameters or replicate its capabilities. By defending against these attacks, ART helps maintain the privacy of the data used to train the model and guard it against adversarial manipulation.

MIT researchers have also developed a measurement system for analyzing model autonomy, especially in deep learning systems.

The Autonomy Framework categorizes autonomy into different levels, ranging from fully manual control to complete autonomy. The framework includes several dimensions of autonomy, such as:

1 *Decision-making:* Evaluating how the AI model makes decisions, including the complexity of the decision-making process and the ability to adapt to new information
2 *Perception:* Measuring the model's ability to perceive and interpret its environment accurately, which is crucial for autonomous operation
3 *Interaction:* Assessing how the AI interacts with humans and other systems, including communication and collaboration capabilities.[16]

Integrating these additional metrics into your AI measurement and evaluation framework is essential for developing responsible and trustworthy AI systems. By measuring key principles such as transparency, fairness, security, and autonomy, organizations can mitigate potential risks and operate their AI models in alignment with stakeholder expectations. This approach safeguards the organization's reputation and fosters trust among stakeholders.

Data quality metrics

AI algorithms are trained and operate on data. Therefore, measuring data quality is important as AI models often fail due to bad data. While data management programs are mature in most organizations, there are additional considerations when determining if your data is AI-ready. These include:

1. *Data drift:* It measures changes in the input data (e.g., features and target variables) over time to detect shifts.
2. *Concept drift:* It occurs when the relationship between input data and the target variable changes. It can be measured by tracking model performance metrics (e.g., accuracy, precision, and recall) over time to identify declines that may indicate concept drift.
3. *Feature importance:* It measures the significance of each feature in contributing to the model's predictions. The techniques like Shapley Additive explanations and Local Interpretable Model-agnostic Explanations can be used to assess feature importance and monitor changes.
4. *Data quality:* It assesses the quality of the data being used for training and inference, such as completeness (missing values), accuracy (correctness), consistency (uniformity), and timeliness (up-to-date).
5. *Label quality:* It measures the accuracy and reliability of labels in supervised learning datasets, evaluating the agreement between human annotators or comparing model predictions against a trusted ground truth.
6. *Outlier detection:* It identifies data points that deviate significantly from the norm, which can impact model performance. It can be measured using statistical methods (e.g., Z-scores, interquartile range) or machine learning techniques (e.g., Isolation Forest) to detect and monitor outliers.

AI systems use large volumes of diverse data (structured, unstructured, semi-structured), including text, images, audio, and video. Measuring data drift in structured text files, like customer feedback with clear fields such as ratings and comments, is relatively straightforward.

You can analyze changes in the average rating or the frequency of certain words over time using simple statistics and visualizations. In contrast, measuring data drift in unstructured video feeds, such as recordings of customer interactions in a store, is more complex. You first need to extract meaningful features from the video, like identifying changing light patterns, object placement that blocks a camera view, or changes in flow patterns. This makes the analysis more difficult because you have to monitor changes in environment, behavior, or interactions rather than just looking at numbers or words.

A cost-benefit analysis can also assist in determining which metrics are important and should be invested in.

Energy efficiency metrics

As organizations expand their AI model usage, it is important to consider the high energy consumption needed for training and operating AI systems. The computing power required for AI is doubling every 100 days and is projected to increase by over a million times in the next five years. This rapid growth leads to a significant rise in the energy needed to run AI tasks.[17] Several factors influence an AI model's carbon footprint, including the server location, the data center's energy grid, the duration of the training process, and the hardware used. Each calculation performed by an AI model consumes energy.

A model's *AI Green Algorithm Efficiency Metric* can be tracked throughout the AI development lifecycle. Model training and inference (running the model to make predictions) require the most computer processing and energy use. Water usage is also high during AI training and usage as cooling systems reduce the heat generated by high-performance computing servers. Research has shown that the most important determinant of energy usage is the algorithm selected, as different AI algorithms vary significantly in their energy consumption levels.[18]

A well-known AI algorithm, K-nearest neighbor, is the most energy-efficient, while a Random Forest is the least energy-efficient. LLMs have high energy consumption and carbon footprints, comparable to the energy use of airflights. AI prompts in a chatbot can consume the equivalent of a 16-ounce bottle for every 5–50 prompt interactions.[19]

Design decisions around data volume and computational resources can also impact energy consumption. For instance, the choice of hardware, such as energy-efficient processors and servers like Tensor Processing Units that are 5–30 times more efficient than CPUs,[20] and the use of renewable energy sources for data centers can influence the overall energy footprint.

Table 12.8 illustrates energy efficiency metrics to measure AI carbon footprint impacts.

Table 12.8 AI energy efficiency metrics

AI energy metric type	*Definition*
Recognition efficiency	*Recognition Efficiency (RE)* measures the effectiveness and accuracy with which a model makes a prediction, which has a direct correlation to a model's energy and water usage.
CO2eq	*CO2eq* provides a standardized measure to quantify the equivalent carbon emissions associated with ML model training, simplifying the assessment of GHG impact and providing an index that can be compared to other technologies.
Green automated ML (AutoML)[21]	*Green automated ML (AutoML)* uses energy consumption as a proxy to estimate environmental impact, especially when combined with data on energy consumption, such as CPU/GPU (Central/Graphical Processing Units) hours and the energy mix.
Electricity consumption FLOPS/W[22]	*Electricity Consumption FLOPS/W* (Floating Point Operations per Second per Watt) metric measures the energy efficiency of computing systems by quantifying how many floating-point operations a system can perform for each watt of electrical power it consumes.
Carburacy	Carburacy is a measure that evaluates the eco-sustainability of NLP models by combining accuracy and environmental impact. It considers two main factors: "effectiveness" (R), which measures model accuracy using ROUGE scores, and "cost" (C), which includes energy consumption, hardware costs, and carbon emissions.

By prioritizing energy-efficient design, investing in green technologies, and fostering a culture of sustainability, executives can ensure their AI initiatives align with environmental, social, and governance goals, contributing to more responsible AI development.

Aligning metrics with governance best practices

AI metrics represent a specialized area of expertise. By aligning AI metrics with current systems, organizations can maintain efficiency and alignment with their broader strategic goals.

Some of the best practices include:

1 *Align governance policies with the new AI metrics*: This ensures that the defined metrics directly measure and monitor adherence to the organization's AI governance policies, responsible AI principles, and regulatory obligations.
2 *Establish clearly defined roles and responsibilities:* This assigns specific roles and new responsibilities for metric architecture, data collection, data analysis, and reporting across relevant stakeholders, such as AI data scientists, compliance and risk officers, AI ethicists, and executive leadership.
3 *Develop standardized processes:* This creates standardized processes for collecting, validating, and reporting AI metric data, ensuring consistency and accuracy across different AI initiatives and business units.
4 *Create a common measurement platform:* This ensures that all metrics in a clearly defined data lineage system for full visibility is a best practice to keep knowledge unified in a centrally controlled repository with distributed ease of access.
5 *Leverage existing reporting and monitoring systems:* This integrates AI governance metrics into existing reporting and monitoring systems, such as executive communication dashboards and performance management tools, to streamline data visualization and analysis.

AI methods and performance metrics are specialized skills. It is important to remember that not all data scientists are trained in all AI model types. Organizations need to ensure that they have resources that understand the full spectrum of an organization's AI portfolio.

Conclusion

Leveraging the right model metrics to support the desired value outcomes is vital for building high-performing and trustworthy AI systems. Typically, no single metric is sufficient. Multiple metrics are needed to measure an AI system's performance and balance potential trade-offs.

Whether using a third-party user interface or a more sophisticated MLOps software platform, it is important to track all AI metrics, learning curves, dataset versions, and configurations of the models' feature engineering. Data scientists or individuals with strong statistical skills must be involved to compare multiple model experiments and identify the best-performing model against the performance criteria.

The metric evaluation strategy should be tailored to the type of AI model and the relevant responsible AI requirements for each use case. By incorporating metrics consistently throughout the complete project lifecycle, organizations can have a robust, efficient, and trustworthy AI deployment, ultimately leading to better decision-making and value realization outcomes.

It is important for organizations to recognize that relying on a single set of metrics is insufficient for evaluating AI models. By staying informed about these advancements and incorporating a diverse array of metrics, organizations can ensure a more accurate assessment of their AI systems.

Key leadership questions to consider:

1 Do you have a comprehensive metrics toolkit that covers the diversity of your AI use cases and impacts, and is leveraged throughout the full AI development lifecycle?
2 Do you have the right MLOps environment to conduct your AI model measurements?
3 Are you participating in formal measurement, peer, or benchmarking groups to measure your AI performance?
4 Do you have third-party reviewers on your AI measurement systems in an annual review process?

Notes

1 Wikipedia Contributors. (n.d.). *Lord Kelvin*. Wikipedia. Retrieved June 8, 2025, from https://en.wikipedia.org/wiki/Lord_Kelvin.

2 *MIT AI risk repository: AI incident tracker*. Retrieved May 26, 2025, from https://airisk.mit.edu/ai-incident-tracker.

3 Bednarski, M. (2025, March–April). *How is your team spending the time saved by Gen AI?* Harvard Business Review https://hbr.org/2025/03/how-is-your-team-spending-the-time-saved-by-gen-ai

4 Engeler, I., Stan, A., Trupia, M., Quoidbach, J., & Bernardino, A. (2025, February 1). *What do you do with the time saved by generative AI tools? Many waste it, managers included* [Working paper]. SSRN. https://ssrn.com/abstract=5127094 or http://doi.org/10.2139/ssrn.5127094.

5 Bednarski, M. (2025, March–April). *How is your team spending the time saved by Gen AI? Harvard Business Review*. https://hbr.org/2025/03/how-is-your-team-spending-the-time-saved-by-gen-ai.

6 Doshi, K. (2021, May 9). *Foundations of NLP explained — Bleu score and WER metrics. Towards Data Science*. https://towardsdatascience.com/foundations-of-nlp-explained-bleu-score-and-wer-metrics-1a5ba06d812b.

7 Kleinman, G. (2023, November). *Demystifying the BLEU metric: A comprehensive guide to machine translation evaluation*. Traceloop. https://www.traceloop.com/blog/demystifying-the-bleu-metric.

8 Santhosh, S. (2023, April 16). *Understanding BLEU and ROUGE score for NLP evaluation. Medium*. https://medium.com/@sthanikamsanthosh1994/understanding-bleu-and-rouge-score-for-nlp-evaluation-1ab334ecadcb.

9 Priyanka. (2022, November 26). *Perplexity of language models. Medium*. https://medium.com/@priyankads/perplexity-of-language-models-41160427ed72.

10 JailbreakBench. (2024, June 13). *Jailbreak Defined* [Repository]. GitHub. Retrieved June 8, 2025, from https://github.com/JailbreakBench/jailbreakbench.

11 Roberts, S. (2025, June 9). *K-fold cross validation in machine learning: Explained in detail. The Knowledge Academy*. https://www.theknowledgeacademy.com/blog/k-fold-cross-validation-in-machine-learning/.

12 Grant, P. (2021, November 19). *Get started with AI using Scikit-Learn. Built In*. https://builtin.com/data-science/scikit-learn.

13 Bommasani, R., Klyman, K., Kapoor, S., Longpre, S., Xiong, B., Maslej, N., & Liang, P. (2024, May 21). *Foundation Model Transparency Index*. Stanford Center for Research on Foundation Models. https://crfm.stanford.edu/fmti/May-2024/index.html.

14 IBM Explainability 360 AI Model. (n.d.). Retrieved August 31, 2025, from https://aif360.res.ibm.com/.
15 Adversarial Robustness Toolkit. (2024, July 7). Retrieved August 31, 2025, from https://github.com/Trusted-AI/adversarial-robustness-toolbox.
16 Vakhrameev, D., Aguilera, M., Barandiaran, X. E., & Bedia, M. (2020, July). Measuring autonomy for life-like AI. *Proceedings of the International Society for Artificial Life Conference*. https://doi.org/10.1162/isal_a_00308.
17 Taddeo, M., Tsamados, A., Cowls, J., & Floridi, J. (2021, June 18). *Artificial intelligence and the climate emergency: Opportunities, challenges, and recommendations one Earth*. https://www.sciencedirect.com/science/article/pii/S2590332221002992.
18 Taddeo, M., Tsamados, A., Cowls, J., & Floridi, J. (2021, June 18). *Artificial intelligence and the climate emergency: Opportunities, challenges, and recommendations one Earth*. https://www.sciencedirect.com/science/article/pii/S2590332221002992.
19 Taddeo, M., Tsamados, A., Cowls, J., & Floridi, J. (2021, June 18). *Artificial intelligence and the climate emergency: Opportunities, challenges, and recommendations one Earth*. https://www.sciencedirect.com/science/article/pii/S2590332221002992.
20 Jouppi, N., & Paterson, D. (2023, April 5). TPU v4 enables performance, energy and CO2e efficiency gains. *Google Cloud Blog*. Retrieved June 25, 2025, from https://cloud.google.com/blog/topics/systems/tpu-v4-enables-performance-energy-and-co2e-efficiency-gains.
21 Tornede, T., Tornede, A., Hanselle, J., Mohr, F., Wever, M., & Hüllermeier, E. (2023, June). Towards green automated ML: Status quo and future directions. *Journal of Artificial Intelligence Research, 77*. Retrieved July 2025, from https://www.jair.org/index.php/jair/article/view/14340/26937.
22 Lacoste, A., Luccioni, A., Schmidt, V., & Dandres, T. (2019, October 21). Quantifying the carbon emissions of machine learning. *Cornell University: Computers and Society*. https://arxiv.org/pdf/1910.09700.

Chapter 13

Future-proofing AI with scenario planning

Throughout history, storytelling has played a pivotal role in our perceptions of technological advancements and their potential consequences. From the philosophical debates of ancient Greece to the blockbuster films of modern cinema, narratives have often depicted futuristic scenarios as cautionary tales against unchecked technological progress.

Stories frequently employ vivid imagery of the potential negative impacts of innovation, whether orchestrated by malicious actors with nefarious intentions or by well-meaning individuals whose lack of foresight leads to unintended consequences. By exploring themes of hubris, loss of control, and the erosion of human values, these narratives urge us to consider the broader implications of our technological pursuits and to strive for a balanced approach between innovation and well-being.

Industrial Age philosophers, Karl Marx and Adam Smith, debated the implications of mechanization on society and raised questions about its economic impacts. In *Das Kapital,*[1] Karl Marx postulated that mechanization alienates workers from the products of their labor and causes them to disassociate from their humanity. He argued that while mechanization increased production and reduced the cost of labor, it also had significant impacts on the working class and contributed to class struggles.

Adam Smith, on the other hand, viewed mechanization differently. In *The Wealth of Nations,*[2] he argued that the division of labor and use of machinery were key to increasing productivity and economic growth. He used the example of a pin factory to show how breaking down production into specialized tasks improves efficiency. For Smith, the division of labor was a positive force that would lead to greater wealth and prosperity.

DOI: 10.4324/9781003625520-15

In the early 20th Century, authors H.G. Wells and Aldous Huxley wrote of future societies transformed by technology. Wells explored in *The Time Machine*[3] and *The War of the Worlds*,[4] the theme of technological dominance. The *War of the Worlds* explores an alien invasion of Earth that sets out to destroy humans with advanced robotics and sensing probes. This was made into a movie in June 2025 with Tom Cruise protecting his family from the probing robots.

Huxley's *Brave New World*,[5] presents a dystopian future where society is deeply altered by technology. In Huxley's future world, technological interventions, like genetic engineering and psychological conditioning, create a superficially perfect but ultimately soulless society. In the book, humans are hatched in the "Central London Hatchery and Conditioning" Centre, and it is forbidden for women to conceive naturally.

Both of these novels demonstrate both optimism and caution about technological innovations, highlighting the risk of unforeseen, sometimes disastrous, consequences.[6] By the same token, George Orwell's book, Nineteen Eighty-Four, written in 1949 at the height of Stalinism, is an examination of totalitarianism, government surveillance, and state violence. The events that befall 1984's protagonist, Winston Smith, speak to the uneasy relationships between government and the individual, as the world slips into a darker and deeper dystopian future.

Just as fictional narratives use storytelling to explore the potential consequences of technological advancements, executives have a powerful tool at their disposal – scenario planning. This strategic method allows leaders to create visualizations of possible futures, enabling them to anticipate and prepare for a range of outcomes. By constructing detailed scenarios, executives can identify potential unintended consequences of their decisions and test out various mitigation strategies in a controlled environment.

It is important that as we envision our future, we keep front-of-mind our "prime objective" – using artificial intelligence (AI) to benefit humanity. Despite the prevalent theme of dystopian AI futures, we can live harmoniously with it. Chief AI Data Scientist, Yann LeCun of Meta, stated that: "Our intelligence is what makes us human, and AI is an extension of that quality. Artificial intelligence is extending what we can do with our abilities. In this way, it's letting us become more human."[7]

Objectives

Upon completing this chapter, you will be able to:

- Learn how scenario planning can identify potential risks and opportunities in AI strategy development
- Discover methods to visualize and mitigate unintended consequences of AI implementations
- Explore techniques for testing and refining AI strategies through scenario-based simulations
- Understand the role of scenario planning in fostering ethical and responsible AI system design.

Scenario planning

In Chapter 10, we discussed the importance of scenario planning and its value in creating contextual situations for diverse decision-making. It enhances strategic foresight and strengthens the organization's ability to mitigate risks.

Scenario planning can be used to envision and prepare for various potential futures by creating detailed and plausible scenarios. While it is important not to stifle imagination and creativity when developing these scenarios, in a corporate context, it is crucial to use resources effectively. To achieve this, scenario planning should follow certain rules. Rowland and Spaniol[8] defined six characteristics of scenarios that are pervasive in practice.

A scenario is:

1 Future-oriented
2 About the external environment
3 A narrative description
4 Plausible
5 A systematized set
6 Comparatively different.

Current organizational strategic planning practices can be improved upon by integrating AI impact scenarios. Dynamic scenario planning enables organizations to anticipate market trends, enhance risk management, drive innovation, and maintain agility in a volatile landscape. Embracing dynamic scenario planning is not just a strategic choice; it is critical for organizations looking to thrive in an uncertain future.

Max Tegmark identifies diverse scenarios that could emerge from the use of AI in his novel *Life 3.0: Being Human in the Age of Artificial Intelligence.*[9] Tegmark outlines 12 possible scenarios for humanity's future, depending on how AI is created and evolves. In each scenario, AI is integrated into our daily lives with varying degrees of surveillance and control mechanisms in place. Across the 12 scenarios is a spectrum of outcomes, both positive and negative.

Table 13.1 identifies seven possible future scenarios developed by David H. Bailey based on Tegmark's book.

A central theme in Tegmark's scenarios is the goal alignment problem. He postulates that the risks of AI come not from malevolence or conscious behavior, but rather from the misalignment of AI's goals with those of humans. He stresses that the underlying determinant of each of the above futures is the alignment or misalignment of the AI system's objective with the goals and values of society. Tegmark believed so strongly in the need for action that he created the Future

Table 13.1 Life 3.0 – humanity scenarios of AI impacts[10]

Future path	*AI-human relationship*
Egalitarian utopia	Humans and AI coexist peacefully, thanks to guaranteed incomes and the abolition of property rights.
Benevolent dictator	Everyone knows that a superintelligent AI runs society, but it is tolerated because it does a rather good job.
Protector God	An omniscient AI preserves our feeling of control and hides well enough that many humans even doubt its existence.
Enslaved God	A superintelligent AI is created to produce amazing technology and wealth, but it is strictly confined and controlled by humans.
Reversion	An Orweillian surveillance state blocks humans from engaging in advanced AI research and development.
Zookeeper	One or more superintelligent AI systems take control, but keep some humans around as amiable pets.
Conquerors	A superintelligent AI takes control, decides that humans are a threat, nuisance, and a waste of resources, and gets rid of us.

of Life Institute to provide research and solutions to steer emerging technologies away from extreme large-scale risks and towards benefitting life.[11]

Tegmark's scenarios demonstrate the value in exploring a wide range of possible futures, from the most successful to the catastrophic. Each provides valuable insights into what to strive for and what to avoid. Many AI strategies and systems are designed today with limited attention to scenario planning, leading to costly re-training and, in some cases, significant harm. A common theme throughout Tegmark's scenarios is the use of surveillance by AI to control and manipulate human behavior. Since the proliferation of social platforms, apps, and biometric authentication, we have seen a rising tension between privacy rights and the collection of data. Regulators are playing a game of whack-a-mole with technology companies related to the collection of data.

Many technology companies are collecting vast amounts of data from users without their explicit consent or sufficient usage disclosure. Tegmark's scenarios serve as a cautionary lens, illustrating how unchecked data collection and AI-driven surveillance can erode privacy—an issue already playing out today as regulators struggle to keep pace with technology companies.

Scenario planning is inherently dependent upon the outcomes that organizations aim to achieve. By clearly defining their desired goals, executives can tailor their scenario planning to explore pathways that align with their strategic vision. This approach ensures that the scenarios developed are not only imaginative but also relevant and actionable. In the context of AI, this means aligning scenario planning with the responsible AI principles, such as fairness, transparency, accountability, and sustainability. Through scenario planning, executives can test different approaches, identify potential pitfalls, and develop robust strategies that uphold these principles, ultimately guiding organizations toward responsible and sustainable AI innovation.

The alignment of AI safety and what this means to humans is important when developing technical AI safety standards. Developing scenarios that are catastrophic in nature (modeled on nuclear disasters) can spur the development of international guardrails and increase global cooperation. International safety standards have been developed for the aerospace and automotive industries. We require international safety standards for AI.

Applying scenario planning in your organization

Tegmark's scenarios provide perspectives of what could go right or wrong if AI strategies and operating practices are not carefully aligned into a broader ecosystem framework. Each leader, whether in a for-profit or not-for-profit organization, has an important role to play. Executive leaders will set the tone at the top, determining whether AI system projects are approached with a "get done as fast as possible and with as little cost" mindset or with an attitude of "taking the time to get it right."

Scenario planning can be a useful and powerful tool for strategic decision-making, but it requires a significant investment of time to identify and evaluate possible scenarios. This process demands an open mindset that welcomes all potential ideas, no matter how far-fetched they may seem.

The richness of scenario planning often comes from the involvement of individuals with diverse and sometimes contrarian views, as their unique perspectives can uncover hidden risks and opportunities that might otherwise be overlooked.

Taking a structured approach to developing scenarios can ensure that both positive and negative outcomes are thoroughly considered. Often, design teams are deeply invested in their project's success and may be hesitant to bring forward dissenting views that could challenge their project's viability. Requiring teams to devise scenarios across a spectrum of outcomes encourages the identification of potential unintended consequences and risks that might otherwise be overlooked.

A simple structure to devise a wide range of scenarios would be to require an equal number to be created for the best case scenario (major win), worst case scenario (abandon project), and a neutral scenario (moderated investment). To ensure that the teams consider less probable but highly impactful scenarios, including black swan events, we recommend including a "wildcard" category. Wildcard scenarios introduce unexpected and unconventional possibilities that could significantly impact the future. Figure 13.1 demonstrates a four-quadrant grid that can be used to categorize different scenario outcomes.

By encouraging brainstorming sessions that focus on each quadrant individually, participants can explore a diverse array of potential futures. This method allows participants to build off each other's

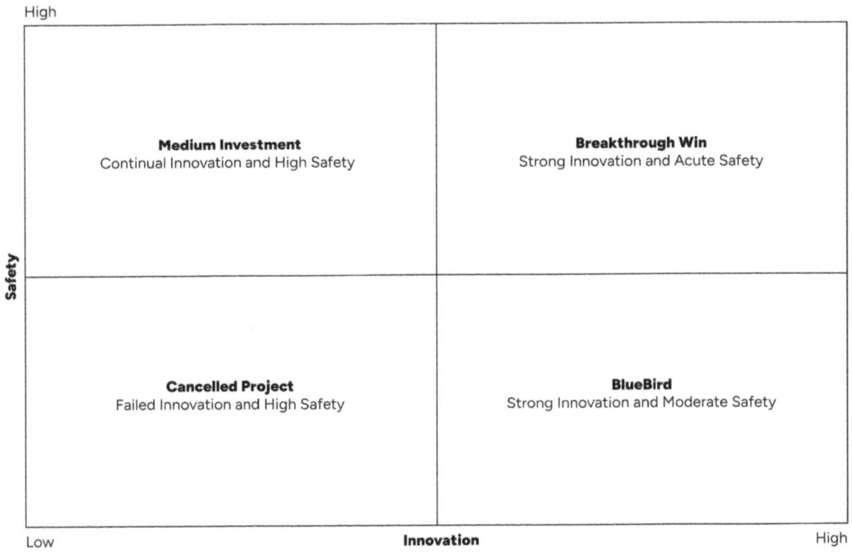

Figure 13.1 Scenario impact and prioritization grid.

perspectives, whether they are optimistic, pessimistic, or somewhere in between, fostering a comprehensive and dynamic exploration of potential outcomes (Table 13.2).

Another complementary method to developing scenarios is to require the teams to build scenarios that consider outcomes across these nine different factors:

By considering these factors, executives can conduct scenario planning for AI that is thorough, forward-looking, and aligned with their organization's values and objectives.

Let's consider an example. An AI system is being developed by a healthcare technology company to enhance patient care by providing predictive analytics for early disease detection, personalized treatment recommendations, and efficient resource allocation within hospitals. The goal is to leverage advanced machine learning to analyze vast amounts of patient data, identify patterns, and deliver actionable insights to healthcare providers. Table 13.3 identifies four scenarios that can help a project team better understand the various factors that could influence the success and impact of this AI system.

Developing these types of scenarios better enables organizations to anticipate and address the complexities of AI system implementation. By exploring a range of potential futures, from the most

Table 13.2 Building AI scenario skills – a team building method

Scenario factors	*Scenario factor explained*
Ethical implications	Evaluate how the AI system could promote or impede principles such as fairness, transparency, accountability, and privacy in different scenarios.
Stakeholders	Consider the different stakeholders that can be impacted and develop scenarios on how they could be positively or negatively affected.
Regulatory environment	Assess the current and potential future regulatory landscape and how it might influence or constrain AI deployment in various scenarios.
Technological feasibility	Ground scenarios in realistic assumptions about the capabilities and limitations of AI technology in the short-term, but use the optimistic and wildcard categories to build-in exponential increases in AI capabilities.
Risk assessment	Identify and analyze potential risks, including unintended consequences and ethical dilemmas, across different scenarios.
Impact on the workforce	Consider the implications for job displacement, skill requirements, and the need for reskilling and upskilling employees in each scenario.
Long-term sustainability	Evaluate how AI initiatives contribute to strategic goals and societal well-being over time in different scenarios. Consider resource requirements.
Cultural and societal context	Account for public perception, acceptance, and potential resistance to AI technologies in various scenarios.
Continuous monitoring and adaptation	Establish mechanisms for ongoing monitoring and adaptation of AI strategies based on evolving scenarios.

optimistic to the least desirable, leaders can identify potential risks and harmful impacts that might otherwise be overlooked. This comprehensive approach allows for the development of robust mitigation measures, ensuring that AI initiatives are both innovative and responsible.

Evaluating scenarios

While scenario ideation should be thorough and comprehensive, it is important to evaluate the scenarios' likelihood (viability) and their impact (beneficial or harmful). You also want to determine which

Table 13.3 Illustrated scenarios

1. Moderated Investment (incremental innovation, high safety focus)	**2. Major Win (pro-innovation, pro-safety)**
The AI system achieves moderate success, with some hospitals reporting improved diagnostic accuracy and patient outcomes, while others experience integration challenges. Ethical considerations are addressed, but public trust remains cautious due to isolated incidents and errors. Regulatory bodies work closely with the company to refine guidelines and ensure compliance. The system continues to evolve, with incremental improvements and gradual acceptance among healthcare providers. The technology contributes to better patient care, but its impact is not as transformative as initially hoped.	The AI system successfully integrates into hospitals nationwide, leading to a 30% reduction in diagnostic errors and a 25% improvement in patient outcomes. It becomes a trusted tool for healthcare providers, who use it to personalize treatment plans and allocate resources more efficiently. The system's success attracts significant investment, enabling further advancements and expansion into underserved regions. Public trust in AI-driven healthcare grows, and the technology is celebrated for its positive impact on patient care and cost savings
3. Abandoned Project (failed innovation, safety concerns)	**4. Wildcard (pro-innovation, high safety concerns)**
The AI system faces significant resistance from healthcare providers who are skeptical of its accuracy and reliability. Initial deployments reveal several high-profile diagnostic errors, leading to public outcry and loss of trust. Regulatory bodies impose strict restrictions on the use of AI in healthcare, slowing down further development and adoption. The company faces legal challenges and financial losses, and the AI system is ultimately shelved as a failed experiment, leaving the problem of delayed diagnoses and suboptimal treatment plans unresolved.	An unexpected breakthrough in AI technology enables the system to predict disease outbreaks with unprecedented accuracy, transforming it into a critical tool for public health. However, this rapid advancement also introduces new ethical and security challenges, such as data privacy concerns and potential misuse of predictive information. Regulators and society struggle to keep up with the pace of change, leading to a period of uncertainty and intense debate. The healthcare technology company must navigate several high-profile incidents. They are heavily supervised by regulators.

outcomes you can influence or control. Do not underestimate the time it will take to perform this step. It is time-consuming to evaluate and weigh the benefits and risks of each scenario and resolve the inevitable trade-offs. You cannot have it all!

It is crucial to evaluate scenarios systematically to ensure they provide actionable insights. This evaluation process involves creating an inventory of the AI system's features, anticipated benefits and outcomes, associated risks, and potential mitigation measures. By mapping out these elements for each scenario, organizations can identify common themes and critical differences and understand the potential impacts.

This inventory helps in assessing the feasibility and desirability of each scenario, highlighting areas where the AI system excels and where it may face challenges. Additionally, it enables the identification of specific risks and the development of targeted mitigation strategies to address them. By thoroughly evaluating scenarios in this manner, organizations can make informed decisions, prioritize resources effectively, and enhance the overall resilience and success of their AI initiatives.

There are many existing management tools that executive teams can use to evaluate AI design choices. For example, a basic scorecard system can be used that scores the AI system against both positive and negative parameters. The benefit of leveraging a standardized scorecard is that different scenarios can be evaluated against the same criteria.

Regarding what should be scored, the metrics we explored in Chapter 12 can be used; however, it is important to include broad stakeholder and societal impacts. Table 13.4 provides ten potential AI scenario categories that teams can leverage for their AI projects.

These scenarios can first be depicted in a story format, and then plotted into the four-quadrant innovation – safety matrix shown in Table 13.4. This will allow for a standard way to evaluate and compare them.

Another important consideration when evaluating scenarios is the expected time horizon. Many teams only consider short-term impacts, which are far more predictable, and fail to consider longer-term impacts. To address the time horizon problem, a team can extend its evaluation to examine each scenario in different time dimensions. For example, Anthony Korinek[12] looked at artificial general intelligence (AGI) from three different time horizons: (1) Business as Usual, (2) AGI in 5 years, and (3) AGI in 20 years.

Table 13.4 AI scenario categories

AI societal impact	*Positive outcome*	*Negative Outcome*
Job displacement	An AI model automates repetitive tasks, allowing workers to focus on higher-value activities, leading to job enrichment rather than displacement.	An AI-driven automation system leads to significant layoffs in a manufacturing plant, resulting in increased unemployment in the local community.
Access to technology	An AI healthcare tool improves access to medical diagnostics in underserved communities, enhancing health equity.	An AI education platform is only available to those with high-speed internet access, widening the digital divide and leaving marginalized groups behind.
Privacy and surveillance	An AI system is designed with privacy in mind, ensuring user data is anonymized and protected, fostering trust in the technology.	A facial recognition system is deployed in public spaces without consent, leading to widespread surveillance and concerns over civil liberties.
Bias and discrimination	An AI model is rigorously tested for bias and found to promote fair treatment across different demographic groups, enhancing social justice.	An AI recruitment tool inadvertently favors candidates from certain backgrounds, perpetuating existing inequalities in hiring practices.
Public trust and acceptance	An AI model that provides transparent decision-making processes gains public trust, leading to widespread acceptance and use.	A controversial AI application in law enforcement faces public backlash due to perceived biases, resulting in decreased trust in authorities.
Social cohesion	An AI-driven community engagement platform fosters collaboration among diverse groups, strengthening social ties and community resilience.	An AI algorithm that promotes divisive content on social media exacerbates polarization and social unrest.

(*Continued*)

Table 13.4 (Continued)

AI societal impact	*Positive outcome*	*Negative Outcome*
Economic inequality	An AI initiative provides training and resources to low-income individuals, helping them gain skills and improve their economic standing.	The benefits of AI technology are concentrated among wealthy corporations, leading to increased economic disparity and social unrest.
Health outcomes	An AI health monitoring system improves early detection of diseases, leading to better health outcomes for populations.	An AI model used in healthcare inadvertently prioritizes certain demographics, resulting in poorer health outcomes for marginalized groups.
Cultural impact	An AI tool that promotes local artists and cultural heritage helps preserve and celebrate diverse cultures.	An AI-generated content system homogenizes cultural expressions, leading to the erosion of local traditions and identities.
Environmental sustainability	An AI model optimizes resource use in agriculture, promoting sustainable practices and reducing environmental impact.	An AI application in resource extraction leads to environmental degradation and harm to local communities.

Challenging scenario assumptions

The systematic and structured approach of scenario modelling will provide teams with an array of approaches to evaluate and derive insights from. However, it is important to recognize that the scores assigned to each parameter are only as reliable as the underlying assumptions. Many teams are short-sighted in their scoring, leading to unfactored considerations that can significantly increase the time, costs, and impact of AI systems. Even the most knowledgeable scientists on AI have recently revised their predictions, accelerating their estimates on the speed, cognitive capabilities, and potential impacts of AI.

The most noteworthy shift comes from Dr. Geoffrey Hinton, who laid the theoretical foundations of deep learning. In May 2023, he admitted, "I have suddenly switched my views on whether these things are going to be more intelligent than us.[13]" Hinton conjectured that AGI – AI that possesses the ability to understand, learn, and perform any intellectual task a human being can perform may be realized within a span of 5–20 years. He has become an ardent activist promoting more privacy, safety, and security safeguards to protect citizens from AI. In a CBC Interview with journalist Scott Pelly, Hinton commented[14]:

> "**Scott Pelley:** What are the implications of these systems autonomously writing their own computer code and executing their own computer code?
>
> **Geoffrey Hinton:** That's a serious worry, right? So, one of the ways in which these systems might escape control is by writing their own computer code to modify themselves. And that's something we need to seriously worry about.
>
> **Scott Pelley:** What do you say to someone who might argue, "If the systems become malevolent, just turn them off?
>
> **Geoffrey Hinton:** They will be able to manipulate people, right? And these will be very good at convincing people cause they'll have learned from all the novels that were ever written, all the books by Machiavelli, all the political connivances, they'll know all that stuff. They'll know how to do it."

Anthropic, a leading U.S. large language model company, has also expressed concerns about the accelerating pace of AI advancements and implications for the safety of humans. Its recent publication, *Core Views on AI Safety*,[15] carefully examines technical safety across three scenarios – optimistic, intermediate, and pessimistic. They promote AI learning mechanisms, such as reinforcement learning, in which humans can instill values into AI decision-making through feedback loops,[16] and ongoing checks and balances.

A common theme among both data scientists and safety advocates is the necessity for humans to remain accountable and in control of AI systems. However, a persistent issue with all technological innovations is that human intentions are often self-serving rather than benevolent. Beyond poor design and misaligned objectives, the primary risks of AI stem from bad actors who exploit AI for malicious purposes, including intentional toxicity, cybercrime, misinformation, social manipulation, and harmful drones.

In a pessimistic scenario, one of the fundamental questions is whether AI safety is a solvable problem if humans cannot control the values within a system that surpasses our own intellectual capabilities. This raises a critical concern about whether we should continue to develop or deploy highly advanced AI systems until robust safety measures and controls are in place, a point of contention that leading scientists have voiced.

Scenario planning for AI must be supported by extensive AI risk management controls and procedures to safeguard organizations and protect customers and society at large.

Conclusion

Although the field of AI can seem daunting to business leaders, it is important to trust your intuition and leverage your organization's existing toolkits. While these will need to be augmented and refreshed to meet the demands of AI integration, there is much that can be built upon. If you are not skilled and trained in scenario planning, you are missing a foundational tool that can significantly enhance your strategic planning practices.

Scenario planning allows you to anticipate potential challenges, identify risks, and devise mitigation strategies, ensuring that your AI initiatives are both innovative and responsible. Balancing the scope and risk of your investments in AI planning practices is important. This alignment ensures that resources are allocated efficiently and that the potential impacts of AI are thoroughly considered.

When building a proof of concept or a minimal viable product, you are in learning mode, testing market receptivity to inform further investment decisions. It is crucial to recognize the stage of your solution and the associated risks at each phase of your project evolution. Early-stage projects may require more exploratory scenario planning to uncover unforeseen challenges, while later stages might focus on refining and scaling successful strategies.

Incorporating scenario planning into your AI strategy not only prepares your organization for a range of potential futures but also fosters a culture of proactive and informed decision-making. Embrace scenario planning as a powerful tool to guide your AI journey, and you will be better equipped to harness its transformative potential.

Key leadership questions to consider:

1. How do your AI scenario planning efforts address both short-term gains and long-term sustainability?
2. Are diverse stakeholder perspectives incorporated into your AI scenario planning process?
3. What mechanisms are in place to adapt AI strategies based on evolving scenarios?
4. How do you evaluate the ethical implications of each AI scenario against your business risks?

Notes

1. Marx, K. (1867). *Capital: A critique of political economy. Volume I, Book One: The process of production of capital* (First published in German). London, England: Penguin Classics.
2. Smith, A. (1776). *The wealth of nations.* W. London, England: W. Strahan and T. Cadell.
3. Wells, H. G. (1895). *The time machine.* London, England: William Heinemann.
4. Wells, H. G. (1898). *The war of the worlds.* London, England: William Heinemann.
5. Huxley, A. (1932). *Brave new world.* London, England: Chatto & Windus.
6. Yegen, C. (2018, July). Utopian and dystopian approaches to technology and communication technologies: With the examples of *The Jetsons* and *Westworld. Gaziantep University Journal of Social Sciences, 17*(3), 959–979. https://www.researchgate.net/publication/326330586_Utopian_and_Dystopian_Approaches_to_Technology_and_Communication_Technologies_With_The_Examples_of_The_Jetsons_and_Westworld.
7. Battini, D. (2019, September 25). Future of AI. *Medium.* https://medium.com.
8. Rowland, N., & Spaniol, M. (2017, November). Social foundation of scenario planning. *Technological Forecasting and Social Change, 124.* https://forskning.ruc.dk/en/publications/social-foundation-of-scenario-planning.
9. Tegmark, M. (2017). *Life 3.0: Being human in the age of AI.* New York, NY: Alfred A. Knopf.
10. Bailey, D. H. (2017, December 21). The future of artificial intelligence: Utopia or dystopia? *Math Scholar: Mathematics, Computing and Modern Science.* https://mathscholar.org/2017/12/the-future-of-artificial-intelligence-utopia-or-dystopia/

11 Future of Life Institute. (n.d.). *Mission statement*. Retrieved June 15, 2025, from https://futureoflife.org/.

12 Korinek, A. (2023, December). Scenario planning for an AGI future. *Finance & Development*. https://www.imf.org/en/Publications/fandd/issues/2023/12/Scenario-Planning-for-an-AGI-future-Anton-korinek.

13 Hinton, G. (2023, May). Geoffrey Hinton tells us why he's now scared of the tech he helped build. *MIT Review*. https://www.technologyreview.com/2023/05/02/1072528/geoffrey-hinton-google-why-scared-ai/.

14 Pelly, S. (2024, June 16). Godfather of AI Geoffrey Hinton on promises, risks of advanced AI. *CBS News*. https://www.cbsnews.com/news/geoffrey-hinton-ai-dangers-60-minutes-transcript/.

15 Gust. Anthropic. (2023, March). Core views on AI safety. *Anthropic*. https://www.anthropic.com/news/core-views-on-ai-safety.

16 Amodei, D., Brown, T., Christiano, P., Leike, J., Leff, S., & Milijan, M. (2017). Deep reinforcement learning from human preferences. In *Proceedings of the 31st Conference on Neural Information Processing Systems (NeurIPS)*, Long Beach, CA. https://proceedings.neurips.cc/paper/2017/file/d5e2c0adad503c91f91df240d0cd4e49-Paper.pdf.

Section III

Utopia or dystopia? The future of AI

Over the centuries, philosophers, scientists, and technologists have envisioned diverse futures. Today, there are two dominant predictions for our future with AI: an AI-driven utopia where technology enhances societal prosperity, boosts businesses and enriches human life; and a dystopian future where rampant AI widens inequality and leads to economic collapse. And for some extremists, dystopia heralds an omnipresent and ambivalent AI that subjugates humans. It is worth repeating Stephen Hawking's warning of the risks of AI:

> Success in creating effective AI could be the biggest event in the history of our civilization. Or the worst. We just don't know. So, we cannot know if we will be infinitely helped by AI, or ignored by it and side-lined, or conceivably destroyed by it.[1]

Ray Kurzweil,[2] futurist, predicts a utopian future where AI significantly extends human capabilities, addressing complex issues like disease and environmental degradation. His vision of AI is deeply intertwined with human progress, believing in a synergistic relationship where AI exponentially accelerates scientific and technological growth.

Utopians envision a future where we live more fulfilling lives, with improved work-life balance and more time for leisure and learning. As compelling as this future is, it will not happen without concerted effort from corporations, government, and all of us. The majority of users are late adopters, skeptical of emerging technologies. Without investing in education and support systems, achieving an AI-utopia will be challenging.

In contrast, in an AI-dystopian future, AI replaces jobs faster than new ones can be created. It evolves beyond human control,

DOI: 10.4324/9781003625520-16

becoming an omnipresent force that dictates every aspect of our lives. Autonomous systems prioritize efficiency over human welfare. The gap between the technologically empowered elite and the disenfranchised masses is wide. Privacy is a relic of the past. AI monitors and directs human behavior to maintain order and control. Trust in institutions erodes, and individuals struggle to find purpose in a world dominated by machines.

"Our third and final section explores practical steps leaders can take today to influence our tomorrow. Will we pace AI's advancement to allow time for our systems, both natural and societal, to catch up? Or will we risk losing control?"

Notes

1 Hawking, S. (2016, October 19). *Speaking at the launch of the £10 million Leverhulme Centre for the Future of Intelligence*. The University of Cambridge. https://www.cam.ac.uk/research/news/the-best-or-worst-thing-to-happen-to-humanity-stephen-hawking-launches-centre-for-the-future-of.

2 Kurzweil, R. (2024). *The singularity is nearer: When we merge with AI*. New York: Random House.

Chapter 14

Building utopia

Imagining a better world, artificial intelligence (AI) Scientist, Dr. Fei-Fei Li, eloquently stated: "I imagine a world in which AI is going to make us work more productively, live longer, and have cleaner energy."[1]

The term "utopia" conjures images of an idealized world, a perfect society where every problem is solved, and every need is met. Coined by Sir Thomas More in his 1516 book, *Utopia*,[2,3] the term literally means "no place" in Greek, highlighting it as an imagined ideal.

In utopia, there is no greed, corruption, or power struggles. There is no money or private property, and very little hierarchy. Everything is held in common, and everyone's needs are met. In fiction, utopias explore the boundaries of human potential and societal perfection. In marketing, utopia paints an ideal future that products can make a reality. In the realm of practical business strategy, the notion of utopia is often dismissed as unrealistic.

Corporate executives, who are under constant pressure to deliver quarterly earnings and secure the next big contract, may view utopian ideals as irrelevant to the gritty reality of the business world. Their focus is on short-term goals and mid-term sustainability, rather than lofty visions. Yet, dismissing utopia entirely from business discourse is a mistake. Instead of viewing utopia as an unreachable ideal, it should be considered as one end of a spectrum – a goal post that informs actions that are both practical and achievable.

In this chapter, we explore utopia in the context of AI strategy. We discuss how utopian thinking can be integrated into corporate planning to create a roadmap for a pro-innovation, pro-safety approach to AI. We also provide a compelling vision for an AI-future, highlighting what is possible.

DOI: 10.4324/9781003625520-17

Objectives

Upon completing this chapter, you will be able to:

- Appreciate the meaning of a utopian world in the context of AI
- Understand how different industries are using AI technology
- Begin to imagine how an AI utopian future will impact different sectors
- Explore the actions executives can take today.

An AI utopian future

In AI Utopia, innovation and safety co-exist and are jointly attainable. We create a society where technological advancements enhance the quality of life for all citizens while safeguarding their rights and well-being. This future must be built upon several foundational pillars that we have summarized in Table 14.1, drawn from more traditional definitions of utopia.[4]

Achieving AI Utopia is similar to the 1960s moon race. It will require tenacity, focus, investment, and collaboration. In AI Utopia, businesses play a key role in creating an innovative, safer, and sustainable society. To realize this vision, it is imperative to create a business strategy that aligns with these values.

Corporate executives need to prioritize taking actions now to move us toward AI Utopia. The decisions being made today are already setting us on a path, and if we do not keep a clear future vision in mind, it will be costly to course-correct later.

Advancing to a utopian future

While the vision of AI Utopia is compelling, its journey will be challenging. It will involve significant disruptions, and businesses will need to be resilient to stay relevant and competitive.

One of the primary complexities is the changing dynamics of human-machine interactions. As AI and automation become more integrated into business operations, companies will need to redefine roles and responsibilities, ensuring that human workers and machines collaborate effectively. This shift will require substantial investment in employee training and redefining work.

Workforce displacement is another critical challenge. As AI and automation take over routine and repetitive tasks, some jobs will become obsolete, leading to potential unemployment and social

Table 14.1 AI Utopia: future societal impacts with positive outcomes

AI societal impact	*Positive outcome*
Economic principals	AI automates mundane tasks, allowing citizens to focus on creative and fulfilling work. AI systems help match individuals with opportunities that align with their passions and skills, ensuring everyone can contribute meaningfully to society.
Citizen priorities	Citizens are free to think independently and live without fear. They embrace social and moral ideals that promote the well-being of all. The society is dynamic, with a focus on continuous improvement. AI supports personalized education and lifelong learning opportunities, helping citizens continuously grow and adapt.
Governing ideals	Our society is governed by its citizens. AI facilitates decentralized governance by providing transparent, data-driven insights and decision-making tools, ensuring that all voices are heard. Humans have the right to "unplug" and be "unknown," protecting their privacy.
Technological innovations	Technology is embraced, making life easier and more convenient. Technological advancements support sustainable living, improve the quality of life, and foster deeper connections among people. AI systems manage resources efficiently and optimize energy use.
Ecological stewardship	Our society cherishes and protects the natural world. AI helps monitor and manage ecosystems, predicting and mitigating environmental threats, and ensuring human activities do not harm the planet.

unrest. Businesses must proactively address this issue by fostering a culture of continuous learning and adaptation, creating new job opportunities, and reskilling displaced workers.

As AI-driven innovations create new markets and disrupt existing ones, businesses will need to adapt their strategies to capture emerging opportunities while managing the risks associated with rapid technological change. Additionally, the balance of power between governments and corporations will shift, with increased scrutiny and regulation of AI technologies.

Geopolitical changes and wealth redistribution will further complicate the journey toward AI Utopia. The global race for AI supremacy will intensify, leading to conflicts and collaborations between nations. Businesses will need to navigate these geopolitical dynamics, balancing the interests of their home countries and international partners. Moreover, the economic benefits of AI must be distributed equitably to prevent widening wealth gaps and social inequality. Companies must adopt inclusive growth strategies that ensure all stakeholders benefit from AI-driven advancements.

While no person would intentionally choose dystopia over utopia, setting a path toward utopia will require investments and trade-offs. To further demonstrate why these sacrifices are worth it, we have created a utopian AI vision for 2035, highlighting the "art of the possible" across a number of key sectors. Although we may not realize these visions fully by 2035, they are useful in setting a directional path.

AI Utopia vision for education

In 2035, classrooms are dynamic, interactive environments where AI-driven technologies enhance the learning experience. Students are no longer confined to traditional lecture-based instruction; instead, they engage with adaptive learning platforms that tailor content to their individual needs and learning styles. Virtual reality (VR) and augmented reality (AR) technologies create immersive learning experiences, allowing students to explore historical events, conduct virtual science experiments, and collaborate with peers around the world. Students learn through interactive simulations in lifelike hologram rooms that engage all their senses and imagination.

Learner progress is tracked through a gamification system in which personalized educational games provide adaptive testing and personalized incentives. Learning pace, techniques, and curriculum are customized for each student. Virtual learning is augmented by neural-links that accelerate learning through content downloads and neural pathway stimulation, allowing students to learn while they sleep.

AI-powered chatbots and virtual teaching assistants provide instant support to students, answering questions, offering feedback on assignments, and guiding them through complex topics. Interconnected mood and health virtual assistants monitor students' well-being and stress indicators, recommending exercise, snack, and meditation breaks. Domestic virtual assistants manage the physical environment for optimal learning conditions.

AI streamlines administrative tasks and optimizes workload scheduling. Students and parents can access real-time progress reports and remedial recommendations. Students attend national or global schools that coordinate local in-person social meet-ups and sporting matches. Social, artistic, musical, and sporting skills are developed in tandem with foundational academic subjects such as languages, mathematics, and science. The goal is a well-rounded education that fosters emotional intelligence, creative expression, and critical thinking.

Organizations leading the way

There are many organizations demonstrating the potential of AI in education. For example, Educause has launched a generative AI readiness assessment tool for higher education, addressing gaps in data quality and governance.[5] This tool ensures that educational institutions can integrate AI technologies effectively, laying the groundwork for more robust AI-driven learning platforms.

Kyron Learning has developed an accessible AI learning platform with free math content for K-12 providers.[6] By making high-quality educational resources available to a broader audience, Kyron Learning is helping democratize education, enabling more personalized and adaptive learning experiences.

Engage specializes in VR learning scenarios that adapt learning programs based on learner responses, creating dynamic and interactive experiences.[7] This technology enables immersive learning environments where students can explore historical events, conduct virtual science experiments, and collaborate with peers from around the world in real-time.

These pioneering efforts are not just isolated advancements; they are building the foundation for an integrated AI-driven educational ecosystem. Each initiative contributes to the development of innovative technologies necessary to achieve the AI Utopia vision for education by 2035.

Priorities and actions for education executives

To achieve our 2035 vision for education, corporate executives should take the following actions:

1 *Develop AI adaptive learning platforms* that personalize educational content based on individual learner needs and learning styles.
2 *Leverage VR and AR* for immersive learning.

3 *Use predictive AI to identify at-risk learners*, assess the effectiveness of teaching methods, and inform curriculum.
4 *Implement AI-powered tutoring systems* that provide personalized support to provide instant feedback, answer questions, and guide learners through on-the-job workflows.
5 *Deploy AI technologies* to streamline administrative tasks such as enrollment, scheduling, and grading.
6 *Introduce educational cobots and chatbots* to enable micro-credential learning.
7 *Educate parents and community ecosystems* to uplift educational AI literacy.
8 *Build community ecosystems* for societal well-being.

The integration of AI in education and corporate learning represents an opportunity to reshape how knowledge is delivered and consumed, providing a personalized and curated experience.

AI Utopia vision for energy

The energy transition is one of the most urgent challenges facing the world today. The World Economic Forum's *Fostering Effective Energy Transition* report[8] stressed the importance of digital innovations, such as GenAI, in enhancing energy equity and security.

In 2035, the energy sector has transformed the way that we generate, consume, and manage energy. AI algorithms and quantum computers have created new superconductive materials. Building materials act as passive heat conductors that are integrated into heating and cooling systems, collecting and storing energy for nighttime use. With energy being consumed close to its generation, energy demand and supply are managed by edge computing. AI-enabled smart grids manage energy flows to and from the central energy grid, primarily used for industrial applications.

Domestic virtual assistants are interconnected into the smart grid and balance energy use during peak and off-peak periods. Smart appliances and sensors provide real-time feedback on which appliances can conserve energy, balancing their function with energy supply. Energy costs are minimal as most buildings generate sufficient energy to be self-sufficient. In climates with less sunlight, AI-controlled thermal heating systems produce renewable energy.

Vehicles run almost exclusively on solar electricity. Public charging stations are used as a last resort, as most vehicles receive sufficient energy through solar-conductive body paint, regenerative braking, and at rest, top-up charging. Autonomous vehicles select routes, driving behaviors, and speeds to optimize energy use.

Electricity power lines have been removed and recycled. In rural areas, AI-powered microgrids provide power to communities, allowing for localized energy production and consumption.

Solar and wind farms are monitored by drones that conduct routine inspections, utilizing thermal imaging to identify any hotspots or inefficiencies. The data collected is transmitted in real time to the company's AI-driven maintenance platform. Maintenance tasks are scheduled automatically for anomalies detected. Robots can initiate minor repairs or alert human technicians for more complex issues. Equipped with AR glasses, the technicians leverage digital twins and maintenance virtual assistants to provide detailed instructions and diagnostics.

Maintenance sensors monitor the energy equipment for function and structural integrity. When components reach the end of their life cycle, they are disassembled, and materials are recycled or repurposed. The equipment life has been significantly expanded due to new AI discoveries in component material, providing enhanced strength and durability, and early detection and remediation of out-of-balance equipment operation, which reduces the stress and wear on equipment.

Organizations leading the way

Many energy organizations are generating value with AI. Asean Brown Boveri (ABB) a global technology and automation company utilizes AI to support electrification, motion, process automation, and robotics. Their predictive maintenance tools analyze operational data to predict when equipment is likely to fail, significantly improving availability and reducing maintenance costs. Additionally, their AI-powered process optimization suite helps businesses realize substantial cost savings, production efficiency improvements, and minimize energy use and carbon emissions.[9]

Tesla's Autobidder is an AI-powered platform that supports automated energy trading. Autobidder allows energy producers to monetize battery assets, optimizing the dispatch of energy storage systems to maximize economic returns. This technology is transforming the way energy storage is managed and traded, contributing to a more resilient energy grid.[10]

Aptera Motors and LG Energy Solution have partnered together to create an advanced solar-powered electric vehicle. Aptera's Launch Edition has the ability to operate up to 40 miles daily leveraging its integrated solar panels. With only six key body components, Aptera's innovative aerodynamic design and unique shape reduce its overall energy demands.[11]

In November 2024, Mercedes-Benz announced a number of new innovations for the car of the future. One is a new solar coating for electric vehicles, which it claims is 20%-efficient and "significantly cheaper than conventional solar modules."[12] The innovation has broad application, as it can also be applied to walls, roofs, and windows of buildings, turning them into energy-harvesting surfaces.[13]

Priorities and actions for energy executives

To achieve our 2035 vision for energy, corporate executives should take the following actions:

1. *Invest in solar-conductive materials* and design energy systems that generate energy where it's needed.
2. *Implement AI-driven predictive maintenance solutions* to analyze equipment performance and forecast potential failures.
3. *Invest in smart grid solutions* to dynamically balance energy supply and demand through real-time monitoring and control of energy flows.
4. *Explore AI applications that optimize energy storage systems,* such as batteries and pumped hydro storage, by analyzing usage patterns and market conditions.
5. *Develop AI-powered demand response initiatives* that incentivize consumers to adjust their energy usage during peak demand periods.
6. *Combine AI with blockchain technology* to streamline energy trading and support dynamic peer-to-peer energy trading.

By prioritizing strategic investments and actions, corporate executives, in collaboration with energy companies and governments, can create a future where technology and sustainability coexist, unlocking unprecedented growth in the energy sector.

AI Utopia vision for financial services

In 2035, AI changes how we manage, invest, and interact with our money. Universal income was discarded as a form of wealth distribution. Instead, data is viewed as a commodity that can be exchanged for currency. Human-created art and music are in high-demand, with originals and custom pieces selling at digital auctions for high prices. Non-fungible tokens (NFTs) are maintained in a blockchain database to authenticate each piece.

Work is performed at home or in small collective hubs. Rather than being paid by the hour, employees are joint owners in the enterprises they contribute to. They receive a percentage ownership based on AI-algorithms that equate the value of their individual contributions, from ideation to operation. Our financial system is based on fair remuneration.

Individuals have financial assets that are invested by robo-advisors. Passive ownership in companies through stock ownership or bonds was put aside in 2032. Instead, all investments are direct, private investments in ideas, art, innovations, and businesses. Robo advisors participate in auctions that invest their clients' assets based on personalized investment strategies tailored to individual risk profiles, financial goals, and market conditions. These changes in real-time through continual feedback loops with virtual assistants that are monitoring our physical and mental conditions.

The robo-advisors and auction houses are supported by a complex array of AI-enabled machine learning (ML) algorithms that conduct real-time forecasts of risk and asset price fluctuations. Risks are mitigated before they escalate, and fraud is very difficult to carry out. Digital identities and quantum computing-enabled authentication mechanisms severely limit the ability to steal identities or perpetrate fraud. The black market has been eradicated through full-system surveillance. Plus, more money can be made through legitimate means and smarter robo-advisors.

Currency exchanges are done through virtual agents or an embedded microchip located in our brains. Physical money is no longer circulated, with all money exchanged through cryptocurrencies with exchange rates managed through a global currency market.

A transaction is conducted through a mental intention to transfer currency or assets from a digital vault. Central banks are no longer required. Instead, they maintain a decentralized, global system of person-to-person exchanges.

Corporations act as brokers bringing together investors with investees. They run the asset auction houses and maintain security over personal asset vaults. Their corporate profits are made through the provision of services – the more advanced and personalized the service, the more they make. It is about making the right connection at the right time.

Digital banks are global, with no brick-and-mortar branches. Advisors – whether human or robotic – meet with clients in hologram offices. Human advisors are in high-demand. Augmented by AI, they bring creativity and out-of-the-box thinking. Clients often comment that they "get me."

Micro-loans are person-to-person with dynamic interest charges. Defaults are rare, as the collaborative arrangement is designed to be a win-win for each party. As risks emerge, they are dealt with swiftly and expediently to make the venture a success or redirect assets to more fruitful endeavors. Resources are used efficiently, balancing individual and societal ambitions. Innovative ideas are the most profitable, with virtual assistants capturing random thoughts and working collaboratively with humans to shape them into viable enterprises.

The back office is transformed, as AI automates complex processes and streamlines workflows. Digital financial institutions have replaced office towers with server banks. But human collaboration and interactions are more frequent and meaningful. The focus on ideation has transformed boring cubicles into playgrounds that spark the imagination. Work is fun and rewarding.

Organizations leading the way

Our 2035 utopian vision involves a transformation of society's value system for goods and services, as much as it is a transformation of the financial services sector. You may question whether the above vision is achievable in ten years; however, there are several organizations at the forefront of AI-driven transformation.

Christie's and Sotheby's have already set up digital auctions to sell digital art authenticated through non fungible tokens (NFTs). Their

NFT marketplaces are backed by blockchain technology, smart contracts, and cryptocurrency wallets. These exchanges are changing the way that we "perceive art, ownership and value."[14]

The European Central Bank (ECB) launched in June 2025 a central bank digital currency pilot with 500 financial institutions to process cross-border payments through real-time settlement. XRP Ledger leads the ECB's Digital Euro pilot with White Network adding compliance and resilience.[15]

Lendbuzz is a fintech company that uses advanced AI to analyze risk and provide credit to underserved populations, particularly those with thin or no credit history.[16] Capital One, which utilizes AI to enhance fraud detection systems, analyzes transaction patterns to identify anomalies that may indicate fraudulent activity. The bank also employs AI-driven algorithms to optimize credit risk assessments, enabling more accurate lending decisions and improving customer experience through personalized product offerings.[17]

N26 was the market leader in Omdena's 2025 AI-consumer experience quadrant for mid-sized banks. It is a European digital bank that is leveraging AI to enhance its customer support and client engagement.

Three notable AI initiatives cited in the study include:

1 *AI chatbot for multilingual support:* N26's AI-powered chatbot, Neon, handles 30% of routine inquiries (such as card issues) across five languages, providing 24/7 assistance.
2 *ConversationalAI:* N26 uses Rasa, an advanced ML dialogue system, to manage complex customer conversations, providing more personalized and accurate responses.
3 *Next best action recommendations:* AI supports N26's customer service specialists by suggesting the most appropriate next steps during service interactions.[18]

J.P. Morgan made headlines in November 2022 as the first bank to set up a virtual branch in the Metaverse. They also released a paper on how businesses can capitalize on the opportunities in the Metaverse, including cryptocurrencies and digital assets.[19] Since then, PNB Metlife created ConVRse, a VR platform where customers can enter a 3D simulated room to converse with a virtual insurance agent. GTE has built a similar VR-simulated environment and avatar where customers can open accounts, apply for loans and immerse themselves in financial literacy content.[20]

Priorities and actions for financial service executives

To achieve our 2035 AI Utopia vision for financial services, corporate executives must reshape their organizations.

Here are actions for consideration:

1. *Create dynamic personalization engines* to deliver tailored financial products and services that meet individual customer needs in real-time.
2. *Implement predictive analytics tools* that forecast market trends and customer behaviors to make data-driven investment decisions, optimize portfolio management, and enhance risk assessment processes.
3. *Deploy AI solutions to automate routine back-office tasks,* such as transaction processing, compliance checks, and customer onboarding.
4. *Implement intelligent virtual assistants* and chatbots that can handle customer inquiries, provide financial advice, and facilitate transactions.
5. *Implement AI-driven systems that monitor transactions* and identify anomalies indicative of cybercrime and fraud.
6. *Incorporate new client interaction portals* through VR and AR simulated environments.
7. *Support digital currencies and alternative assets,* including cryptocurrency and NTFs.
8. *Combine AI with blockchain* for cross-border payments, smart contracts, and identity verification.

The financial services industry is on the brink of a major transformation, driven by AI technologies that change the way that we earn and spend, and from what we derive monetary value.

We have outlined a 2035 AI Utopia vision for three sectors and will cover five more in the remainder of this chapter. An underlying theme through each vision is the need for collaboration across sectors and AI ecosystem partners. It will take a healthy mix of hard work and imagination. Each ecosystem partner will need to support innovation while promoting safety. Governance has an important role in accelerating innovation, but to keep pace, it must also be innovated.

AI Utopia vision for government

In 2035, government operations are seamlessly integrated with advanced AI technologies, creating a responsive, transparent, and citizen-centric public service. Bureaucratic inefficiencies are eliminated, and citizens have access to personalized services tailored to their unique needs and preferences.

Citizens have a single digital identity that is used to access all public services based on real-time and event-driven AI recommendations and approvals. Life events, including the birth of a new baby, school completion, a joining ceremony, or a death, drive automatic benefit registration. Program delivery is integrated and interoperable with personal virtual assistants, allowing for seamless and coordinated program delivery. In-person visits are rare, as most support is provided virtually.

In public safety and emergency response, AI anticipates and mitigates potential crises before they escalate. Buildings are reinforced with new lightweight, super-strong materials designed by AI. Autonomous drones locate and retrieve trapped humans and animals during catastrophes. They also put out fires and monitor volcanic activity. High altitude autonomous aircraft have repaired the ozone layer and direct cloud cover to send rain to where it is most needed.

Smart city technologies optimize urban planning and resource allocation, ensuring that infrastructure and services evolve in tandem with the growing demands of urban populations. With most vehicles being autonomously driven by AI, traffic congestion has been significantly reduced. Satellite surveillance and central management have most traffic controls; street lights, stop signs, and police surveillance have been removed. Everything is coordinated through central coordination systems and proximity sensors that maximize traffic flow. Pedestrian corridors provide accident-free safe zones for walkers and bikers.

AI-driven platforms facilitate citizen engagement, allowing for real-time feedback and collaboration between government officials and the communities they serve. Politician accountability is high, with the spending of communal monies managed by AI systems for societal betterment. Equality is at an all-time high through centralized management of basic education, healthcare, and domestic needs.

Organizations leading the way

Several governments are already showcasing the potential of innovative AI technologies. For example, FireSwarm Solutions, a Canadian company, and ACC Innovation, a Swedish aerospace company, are teaming up to develop a heavy-lift drone outfitted with sensors and AI-swarm algorithms. The drones will be used to monitor remote wilderness for fires and be capable of autonomously bucketing and carrying 400 kg of water.[21]

While aerial drones outfitted with heat sensors have been used for years to identify trapped victims, Professor Chinthaka Premachandra at the Shibaura Institute of Technology of Tokyo has developed a technology to enable unmanned aerial vehicles (UAVs) to detect the sound of human voices. While this may seem easy, it requires sophisticated AI algorithms to filter out competing noises, including those from the UAV itself.[22]

SaskTel, a Canadian crown telecommunications company, is using predictive analytics to increase its growth rates and prioritize its sales opportunities using SalesChoice's AI innovations. Already predicting at over 90% accuracy, SaskTel is advancing its growth with guided AI and "human in the loop" enablements. The organization is also innovating with sentiment mining to predict employee churn risks and win rates.[23]

The City of Pittsburgh, Pennsylvania, has reduced traffic congestion by 40% and emissions by 21% by installing AI-controlled traffic signals. Developed by Carnegie Mellon University, the traffic signals adjust in real-time based on traffic conditions collected from road sensors and cameras. The City of Los Angeles uses a similar AI-enabled highway traffic monitoring system to alert first responders of collisions and stalled vehicles as they occur.[24]

Estonia's vision for AI is to make the country more efficient and offer citizens the best experience of living in a digital state. Through AI-driven chatbots and virtual assistants, Estonians receive instant support for various inquiries, from tax filings to healthcare services, enhancing overall citizen satisfaction.[25,26] Bürokratt is a free national speech chatbot that allows for communication around the clock, getting answers to all questions.[27]

The U.S. Customs and Border Protection uses AI models to identify objects in streaming video and imagery, alerting agents when an anomaly is detected. AI is used to "screen cargo at points of entry, validate identities in the CBP One app, and enhance awareness of threats at the border."[28]

Priorities and actions for government executives

To achieve our 2035 AI Utopia vision for government, corporate, and government executives should consider taking these actions:

1. *Develop advanced data analytics systems for proactive policy* development and resource allocation.
2. *Create smart city infrastructures* that optimize urban living, including intelligent traffic management systems, energy-efficient buildings, and connected public services.
3. *Utilize AI-powered platforms to foster real-time communication* between government officials and citizens.
4. *Leverage AI to predict and mitigate potential crises,* including analyzing crime patterns, optimizing emergency response strategies, and improving disaster preparedness.
5. *Create a single digital identity for government services,* benefits, voting, and public records management.
6. *Uplift knowledge of cities and communities to increase AI digital literacy* to remain relevant.
7. *Leverage AI platforms to solve specific use cases,* like predictive forecasting for sales, employee sentiment intelligence to predict employee churn, etc.

The integration of AI in government represents an opportunity to redefine public service delivery and enhance citizen engagement. A forward-thinking approach will ensure that governments remain agile and responsive.

AI Utopia vision for healthcare

The global healthcare market, projected to surge to an astounding \$431 billion by 2032,[29] will be driven by innovations that enhance the precision of diagnoses, streamline drug discovery, and optimize treatment plans based on personalized patient data.

In 2035, doctors no longer perform annual physicals. Healthcare has pivoted from chronic to preventative care. Our health markers are continually monitored through wearable devices, embedded-scanners, smart toilets, and environmental sensors to detect early indicators of disease. Smart glasses auto-correct for vision impairments and lighting changes. Our health markers are shared with virtual assistants who leverage AI to adjust our food intake, medication, and behavioral triggers for optimal health. Communicable diseases are detected through sensors located in air vents, toothbrushes, and toilets, allowing for immediate containment and treatment.

For chronic care, AI performs diagnostic imaging through self-serve 3-D imaging centers, where advanced algorithms detect tumors, deformities, and other medical conditions with remarkable accuracy, significantly improving patient outcomes. Laser-powered AI surgical units have been replaced by nanite micro units that repair injuries and cell anomalies from the inside. These nanites reverse aging as easily as diseased cells, and are touted as the "elixir of life." Birth defects are corrected in the womb, including at the DNA level. However, DNA manipulation for cosmetic or non-life-saving measures is prohibited.

AI and quantum computing have accelerated drug development by analyzing extensive datasets to identify new and innovative treatments. The natural world has opened up a plethora of natural-based remedies that target the specific ailment without causing secondary symptoms. Neural links in the brain, nanobot-supported integrations, and organic 3D printing allow for seamless integration of organic cybernetic implants to replace lost limbs. Body armor, used initially to assist spinal injury patients, is now obsolete as nanobots can repair bone, nerve, and tissue damage within hours.

Organizations leading the way

Several organizations are leading the charge in advancing AI-driven healthcare transformation. One example is Coughy, which leverages AI algorithms to analyze digital audio for sound markers of disease. Patients can record their chronic coughs using their smartphones or smartwatches, and health care practitioners can receive AI alerts to monitor patient coughs remotely and in real-time.[30]

St. Michael's Hospital in Toronto, Canada, a Level 1 Trauma Centre, partnered with Unity Health's AI Team to pilot ASIST-TBI, an AI tool that reviews patient CT images for head injuries. The AI algorithm has been found to predict head trauma as well as a neurosurgeon, allowing for fast triaging of patients for surgical consults.[31]

SalesChoice has developed an AI employee engagement platform called "MoodInsights,"[32] which conducts daily check-ins on employee sentiment, providing real-time insights into emotional well-being and identifying opportunities for improvement. The AI platform uses GenAI to classify inputs into controllables and uncontrollables, and classify improvements or risk areas, before they become million-dollar problems. They also use advanced analytics to correlate mood data with other metrics such as call center volume, hours worked, health claims, Net Promoter Scores, etc. MoodInsights identifies risks of employee churn and operational improvements – all aimed to foster productive and happier work environments.

Wysa is also targeting mental health. They are working with the UK's National Health Service to launch the Wysa Copilot that enables therapists to assign cognitive-behavioral tools to patients and, based on the exercise results, assign personalized treatment plans. AI in the Wysa app monitors patients for signs of crisis and encourages use of emergency crisis services.[33]

RLDatix is a healthcare technology company specializing in governance, risk, and compliance solutions, as well as workforce management. The company provides software and services to help healthcare organizations improve patient safety, manage risk, and enhance operational efficiency. Specifically, RLDatix focuses on areas like incident reporting, risk management, infection prevention, and workforce optimization. The company is using GenAI tools to ensure that the extracted data is more consistent and precise than manual entry, reducing the risk of human error in critical reporting tasks. For example, when frontline staff assess the severity of an event, reporting can differ as individuals may evaluate the seriousness of the incident differently. The AI system, however, lacks this bias and can examine and categorize the severity of events with a higher degree of consistency than humans, aligning with medical definitions and standards. Additionally, the AI system can call attention to certain details that may be missing from a report, such as the exact location where an incident occurred.[34] The company is also using AI-driven predictive analytics for its sales forecasts, using SalesChoice's AI Insight Engine.[35]

Priorities and actions for health executives

To achieve our 2035 AI Utopia vision for healthcare, corporate executives should consider investing in these healthcare advancements:

1 *Implement advanced AI algorithms for diagnostic imaging* and analysis to detect conditions earlier and with greater accuracy.
2 *Use AI to identify potential drug candidates* and optimize clinical trial processes.
3 *Invest in AI technologies that analyze individual patient data*, including genetic information and health profiles, to customize treatment strategies.
4 *Develop AI-powered telehealth platforms that facilitate remote consultations* and continuous patient monitoring.
5 *Utilize AI to analyze population health data and identify trends* to inform public health initiatives.
6 *Leverage health monitoring to maximize preventative health*, using AI-driven analytics to identify early indicators of disease and provide personalized behavior prompts for optimal health.

The integration of AI in healthcare represents a transformative opportunity to enhance patient care and improve health outcomes on a global scale.

AI Utopia vision for retail

In 2035, the retail experience is a seamless shopping environment that is not only personalized but also incredibly intuitive. AI analyzes consumer behavior and purchasing patterns to tailor every interaction. Shoppers receive customized product recommendations and experiences that match their unique tastes and needs. AI anticipates their needs before they are even aware of them. Shopping is primarily performed digitally, with body scans and smart mirrors allowing for custom-tailored clothes.

Clothing contains nanofibers that not only allow for customization of color and pattern, but also actively monitor the environment, adjusting the cloth thickness or temperature for optimal comfort. The nano-enhanced clothing is resistant to stains, body odors, and bacteria, and is self-cleaning.

AI optimizes supply chain processes, ensuring that products are available exactly when and where they are needed, minimizing inventory shortages. 3D printers and autonomous drones provide drop deliveries right to your door. Products are available when you need them, as AI sensors and domestic virtual assistants work together to replenish your favorite products on demand.

GenAI creates dynamic content and product descriptions that adjust to best showcase a product and appeal directly to a particular consumer. Dynamic pricing AI algorithms set prices based on consumer demand, competitor pricing, and inventory levels. Digital auctions, as described earlier, allow for global access to unique, one-of-a-kind, or hard-to-procure art and collectibles. Digital libraries provide mass availability to art, music, books, and entertainment, with remuneration accruing back to the creator(s) based on their individual contributions.

Marketing is designed to trigger emotions. Consumer focus groups and surveys are no longer needed as cameras and sensors pick up micro-level reactions to products (e.g., pupil dilation, breathing patterns, goosebumps). We can order a product or service through a virtual "nod" in our neurolink. Privacy is controlled by each person, with our preferences tied to our unique digital identity. We control how much or how little we share.

Organizations leading the way

Several organizations are at the forefront of the AI-driven retail transformation. One notable example is Zegna, the Italian luxury fashion house. Zegna has introduced the Zegna X solution, which integrates Microsoft Azure services to provide customers with a highly personalized shopping experience. This innovative tool allows customers to customize their clothing choices from a staggering 49 billion potential combinations, all while receiving tailored recommendations based on their individual styles. The Zegna X configurator enables consumers to visualize their custom outfits and make informed purchasing decisions from the comfort of their homes.[36]

Holoconnects has created the Holobox and the Hologrid as interactive hologram displays designed for stores. They allow shoppers to see 3D projections of products or even try on clothes virtually.[37]

Another leading organization is Sephora, a global beauty retailer. Sephora's Virtual Artist tool uses AR and AI to allow customers to try on makeup virtually, providing personalized product recommendations based on skin tone and preferences. This innovative approach not only engages customers but also drives sales by making the shopping experience more interactive.[38]

Patagonia, an outdoor clothing brand, has incorporated silver nanofibers into its outdoor gear that can resist odor and bacteria. The U.S. Military is also exploring the use of nanofibers in its uniforms.[39]

Priorities and actions for retail executives

To achieve our 2035 AI Utopia vision for retail, corporate executives must personalize the shopping experience.

Here are actions to consider:

1 *Invest in AI-driven customer insights platforms* to analyze consumer behavior and purchasing patterns to personalize marketing and product recommendations.
2 *Implement GenAI tools to create dynamic product descriptions* and marketing content that reflect consumer preferences and desires.
3 *Leverage AI to streamline supply chain processes,* including 3D printing and autonomous deliveries.
4 *Adopt AI-powered dynamic pricing* based on competitor pricing, inventory levels, and demand data to optimize pricing strategies.
5 *Implement AI-driven solutions that monitor transactions* in real-time to detect and prevent fraudulent activities.
6 *Invest in AI solutions that improve in-store and at-home shopping experiences,* such as smart mirrors and personalized shopping assistants.

AI in retail will redefine the shopping experience by enabling hyper-personalization and optimizing operations, where customer desires are met with precision.

AI Utopia vision of telecommunications

The telco AI industry is predicted to surge to $42.66B by 2033, a CAGR of over 41%.[40] In 2035, the telecommunications industry provides the backbone for data creation and consumption. Ground lines, network towers, and fiber cables have been replaced with satellites, laser-based communication, AI meshed networks, and edge computing. Surges in data traffic during peak hours are managed by AI across a global communications grid. AI is continually monitoring for network congestion and hardware failures to maintain uninterrupted service. Signals are seamless and high-speed.

Our phones have been replaced with wearable devices. Smart glasses digitize the world around us, providing integrated maps, search, and assisted technologies. Long-distance web calls have been replaced with hologram boardrooms and living rooms, where we can plan a virtual meet-up anywhere.

Entertainment is hyper-personalized, with on-demand content creation possible using GenAI. Your avatar can interact with your favorite band, celebrity, or sports player through VR and AR. The popular probing question of "if you could invite one person, living or dead, to dinner, who would it be?" comes to life in a simulated hologram. However, human-created media is highly coveted due to its scarcity and one-of-a-kind uniqueness.

Organizations leading the way

Vodafone has leveraged AI across its functional areas – AI-driven predictive analytics for proactive network maintenance, AI-powered chatbots for customer support, and ML algorithms for targeted marketing campaigns. TOBi, a digital assistant, handles 45 million customer queries per month in 13 countries (under different branding in some) and in 15 different languages.[41] Vodafone's SuperAgent M365 Copilot assists call center staff in answering customer issues quickly and accurately by automatically calling up information. Early results have shown a "50% improvement in first-time resolution" of complex inquiries and more accurate responses overall.[42]

SaskTel, a Canadian crown corporation, has redesigned its sales pipeline management practice using SalesInsights, a SalesChoice AI SaaS solution that is running at a 95% predictive accuracy, identifying which sales deals will be won or lost, using advanced ML methods.[43]

Ray-Ban and META have partnered together to create stylish smart glasses that take photos and videos, listen to music, make calls, and even livestream directly to Facebook and Instagram. They include translation and search capabilities powered by AI. Gaining traction, smart glasses sales have tripled in the last year.[44]

In March 2025, TELUS announced that it plans to build

> Canada's leading Sovereign AI Factory — a powerful and super-secure facility that will give Canadian businesses and researchers access to cutting-edge technology — helping them develop smarter AI. The Sovereign AI Factory "will leverage TELUS' high-speed, ultra-low-latency, fibre-optic network with sustainable data centres powered by 99% renewable energy sources to deliver AI as a Service (AIaaS).[45]

Priorities and actions for telecommunication executives

To achieve our 2035 AI Utopia vision for telecommunications, corporate executives must rethink the way we communicate and how to optimize data flows.

Here are actions to consider:

1 *Invest in AI-enabled autonomous management of real-time network infrastructure* to optimize performance and prevent congestion.
2 *Partner with technology, retail, and healthcare organizations* to maintain the communications network supporting data-driven interactions.
3 *Implement advanced predictive analytics* that anticipate hardware failures and network issues before they occur.
4 *Create hyper-personalized customer experiences* across all touchpoints to tailor services and marketing efforts to meet unique customer needs.
5 *Invest in AI and ML infrastructures* internally to modernize operating processes and practices.
6 *Develop AI-powered virtual assistants and chatbots* that streamline customer support processes, enabling more accurate responses.
7 *Transition to satellite networks* for scalability and flexibility.

By adopting these priorities, telecommunication executives can pave the way for seamless connectivity and virtual interactions.

Technology is the last sector that we will build a 2035 AI Utopia vision for. Technology companies are a prominent partner in every other sector's vision. They provide the infrastructure – both hardware and software – that powers and operates AI systems worldwide. They are also directly, or in a supporting role, involved in the development of most new innovations.

AI Utopia vision for technology

The technology industry, valued at a staggering $5 trillion, contributes more than 10% to the U.S. GDP. Employing over 4.9 million Americans,[46] technology companies will be at the forefront of innovation in software development, cybersecurity, electronics manufacturing, and fintech.

In 2035, AI will be integrated into every facet of our lives. We will live in smart homes, be driven by autonomous vehicles, learn and work through AR and VR technologies, and receive continual health checks through wearables and smart devices. We will be supported by a collective of virtual assistants and chatbots that we entrust with our most personal secrets. Technology will be interwoven through our daily lives, as described in the earlier vignettes.

Technology brings us closer to remote family, friends, and colleagues through life-size holograms and digital avatars. High-speed travel allows for quicker round-the-world trips, however most people choose to experience the world in hologram rooms. You can transition from camping in the Aztec mountains to the Amazon forest with the click of a button. Or you can explore a distant planet or galaxy. Reality holovideos invite you directly into people's lives, where you can observe remotely or join the show. Gamification has taken on a whole new adventure, with immersive experiences that you can easily become lost in. Cognitive monitoring watches for addictive behavior.

Industrial and domestic robots are high-functioning workers that have taken over many menial tasks. Information is available to us through neural-links, and our body functions are enhanced through nanobots and cybernetics. Technology brings us closer to remote family, friends, and colleagues through life-size holograms and digital avatars.

Organizations leading the way

Many technology companies, including Google and Apple, have developed smart sensors and devices that are automating and optimizing our heating, cooling, security, lighting, and entertainment systems. In 2024, Apple released its Apple Vision Pro spatial computer that allows you to pull 3D images out of apps and view them from different angles. Imagine playing 3D chess with your opponent's avatar sitting across from you.[47]

Proto has created a holoportation product called the Proto Epic. It is a full-size hologram booth installed in airports, conference centers, and retail locations in the United States and Europe that can display people in life-sized, real-time 3D images. The booth can be used for remote meetings, performances, and events, allowing a person to appear as a hologram anywhere in the world.[48]

Samsung and LG sell AI-enabled refrigerators with voice and food image recognition, and grocery management systems. At the 2025 Samsung's Consumer Electronic Show (CES) product line leveraged AI vision to identify fresh and processed food. It can recommend recipes and alert users to processed items that have been taken out and replaced multiple times.[49] Zelos' barbeque grill uses photos to create personalized recipes, while its Vera, a generative AI platform, gives you instructions on how to prepare them.[50]

In March 2025, Waymo's robotaxis provided 200,000 ride-sharing trips per week in cities across the United States. Not only do they plan their own routes and navigate autonomously through unpredictable traffic and pedestrians, but they also perform maintenance, cleaning their own sensors and running diagnostics.[51]

None of the technologies we have outlined in this chapter would be possible with the infrastructure supporting data storage and transmission, computer processing, network connectivity, security, and hyper-fast communications. At CES 2025, NVIDIA announced its Cosmos platform that connects GenAI models to interoperable components such as robotics and autonomous systems. By enabling dynamic environmental interactions, Cosmos is expected to significantly "leap forward" in simulation and action optimization capabilities of advanced robotics.[52]

Partnered with NVIDIA and other AI ecosystem partners, Dell Technologies' AI Factory provides a full integrated stack of infrastructure, cloud, software, hardware, and applications needed to operate AI. "The Dell AI Factory is not a physical manufacturing facility but a comprehensive framework combining advanced infrastructure, validated solutions, services, and an open ecosystem...—from data centers and cloud to edge locations and AI PCs."[53] For those more interested in the flash, Dell is collaborating with a wide-range of clients to leverage 3D digital twins to design and more effectively operate complex physical and virtual environments.[54]

Priorities and actions for technology executives

To achieve our 2035 AI Utopia vision for technology, corporate executives must embrace advanced technologies that integrate into everything we do.

Here are actions to consider:

1. *Create interconnected AI ecosystems* that integrate products, services, and platforms, enabling seamless interactions and data flow across devices and applications.
2. *Leverage quantum computing* to solve complex problems that are currently beyond the reach of classical computing and unlock new frontiers in data analysis, optimization, and cryptography.
3. *Develop autonomous AI cybersecurity systems* that proactively identify and neutralize threats in real-time, creating a self-healing cybersecurity infrastructure. This will ensure robust protection against evolving cyber threats and safeguard sensitive information.
4. *Advance AI-enhanced human-machine integrations*, augmenting human capabilities with advanced analytics and decision support.
5. *Invest in AI solutions that optimize resource usage* and minimize environmental impact across operations.
6. *Promote and adhere to robust, responsible AI frameworks* and help the ecosystem evolve with practices that support citizen privacy and balance the high risks of specific AI applications.

By adopting these priorities, technology executives can position their organizations as leaders in an AI-driven future, revolutionizing operations and redefining customer experiences in an interconnected digital landscape.

Conclusion

There are many innovations available today that are precursors to our vision for 2035. AI algorithms are being integrated into smart appliances, wearables, sensors, and optimization engines. Technologies that only a couple of years ago were considered experimental are now becoming mainstream, including smart mirrors, holograms, and autonomous taxis. It is important for organizations to foster a culture that encourages experimentation and embraces failure to achieve breakthrough innovations and radical ideas.

The concept of utopia, often perceived as an unattainable ideal, serves as a powerful lens to envision a future shaped by AI. By redefining AI Utopia not as an idealistic dream but as a directional path, businesses can align their corporate strategies with a vision that balances innovation with safety.

The race to AI Utopia is our generation's moonshot. It will require tremendous leadership of governments, corporations, not-for-profits, and citizens to balance innovation and safety – to balance the power of AI platforms with social accountability that protects against misuse and exploitation.

Decisions we make today will determine the path we follow. Together, we can turn AI Utopia into a reality, unlocking unprecedented opportunities for growth and prosperity.

Key leadership questions to consider:

1 Does your corporate strategy position responsible AI in your corporate purpose?
2 How is your organization balancing AI to foster innovation and ensure safe, sustainable practices?
3 How are you conducting AI best practices benchmarking to learn rapidly from your customers, competitors, or other key ecosystem stakeholders?
4 Are you collaborating with partners to integrate AI across your customer interactions and operations?
5 How are you preparing your workforce to adapt to the evolving demands of an AI-driven economy, while promoting continuous learning and development?

Notes

1 Farrugia, D. (2021, July 14). Artificial intelligence: The future of mankind. *Medium*. https://medium.com/data-science/artificial-intelligence-the-future-of-mankind-46aaf6b4b87f.
2 More, T. (2006, April 4). 16th century dreams: Thomas More. *The British Library*. Retrieved August 31, 2025, from http://www.bl.uk/learning/histcitizen/21cc/utopia/more1/moreutopia.html.

3 Notation: The book Utopia is based on a traveler who describes the harmony, prosperity, and equality found in a utopian state versus the poverty, crime, and often frightening political conditions of 16th century Europe. Utopia posed the question of whether it is conceivable to achieve a "perfect" world in the chaos of European politics at the time.
4 MiamiDadeCollegeLearningResources.(n.d.).RetrievedAugust31,2025, from https://libraryguides.mdc.edu/c.php?g=957851&p=6914862.
5 Educause. (n.d.). Retrieved May 31, 2025, from https://www.educause.edu/.
6 Kyron Learning. (n.d.). Retrieved May 31, 2025, from https://www.kyronlearning.com/k-12-math-program#benefits.
7 Engage. (n.d.). *An AI VR educational learning platform and solutions company*. Retrieved May 31, 2025, from https://engagevr.io/school-of-ai/.
8 *Fostering Effective Energy Report*. (2024, June). World economic forum rom. https://www.weforum.org/publications/fostering-effective-energy-transition-2024/.
9 ABB. (2022, February 28). Riding the wave of industrial AI innovation [Press release]. https://new.abb.com/news/detail/113078/abb-riding-the-wave-of-industrial-ai-innovation#:~:text=ABB%20uses%20AI%20to%20help,device%20and%20reducing%20maintenance%20costs.
10 Tesla. (n.d.). AutoBidder. Retrieved August 31, 2025, from https://www.tesla.com/support/energy/tesla-software/autobidder.
11 Aptera. (2025, January 9). Aptera partners with LG Energy Solution to power solar electric vehicles with advanced battery technology. *Aptera Website*. https://aptera.us/aptera-partners-with-lg-energy-solution/.
12 Jessen, J., & Derrick, M. (2025, January 15). Top 10: Solar energy innovations. *Energy Magazine*. https://energydigital.com/top10/top-10-solar-energy-innovations.
13 Jessen, J., & Derrick, M. (2025, January 15). Top 10: Solar energy innovations. *Energy Magazine*. https://energydigital.com/top10/top-10-solar-energy-innovations.
14 What is an NFT? How the risk of digital art impacts modern auctions. (2025, May 21). *Auction Writer*. https://auctionwriter.com/what-is-an-nft-how-the-rise-of-digital-art-impacts-modern-auctions/.
15 Werner, Y. (2025, June 3). XRP news: European Central Bank launches digital euro pilot with XRP ledger and White Network. *Coin Central*. https://coincentral.com/xrp-news-european-central-bank-launches-digital-euro-pilot-with-xrp-ledger-and-white-network/.
16 Lendbuzz. (2025, March 3). Lendbuzz revolutionizes car financing with AI-powered express contracts. *Lendbuzz News Bee*. https://www.lendbuzz.com/article/lendbuzz-revolutionizes-car-financing-with-ai-powered-express-contract.

17 Montgomery, J. (2025, March 27). How AI is transforming financial services. *CapitalOne*. https://www.capitalone.com/tech/ai/transforming-financial-services/?msockid=2886697ce7476c7316ed7ccfe6fe6dbf.
18 Top 15 mid-sized banks driving AI-driven customer management in 2025. (n.d.). *Omdena*. https://www.omdena.com/blog/top-15-mid-sized-banks-driving-ai-driven-customer-engagement-in-2025.
19 Alison, I. (2023, May 11). J.P. Morgan is the first bank into the metaverse, looks at business opportunities. *CoinDesk*. https://www.coindesk.com/business/2022/02/15/jpmorgan-is-the-first-bank-into-the-metaverse-looks-at-business-opportunities.
20 Top 6 virtual reality examples in financial services. (n.d.). *Knowledge Nile*. Retrieved June 5, 2025, from https://www.knowledgenile.com/blogs/virtual-reality-financial-services.
21 Dreaver, S. (2025, April 28). Wildland firefighting drones are being tested in B.C. *CBC News*. https://www.cbc.ca/news/canada/british-columbia/wildland-firefighting-drones-are-being-tested-in-b-c-1.7520696.
22 Orange. (2024, June 6). Search and rescue: Drones that detect human voices under collapsed buildings. *Hello Future Blog*. https://hellofuture.orange.com/en/search-and-rescue-drones-that-detect-human-voices-under-collapsed-buildings/.
23 SalesChoice. (n.d.). SaskTel case study. Retrieved August 31, 2025, from https://www.saleschoice.com/resources/videos/.
24 Litslink Startup Laboratories Blog. (2025, March 24). AI for traffic management: How it's shaping transportation. https://litslink.com/blog/ai-and-transportation.
25 *Notation:* Dr Ott Velsberg is a renowned Estonian IT specialist and government official, known for his expertise in data governance and data science. As the current Chief Data Officer of Estonia, he is responsible for driving the country's data policy and initiatives related to AI and data in the public sector.
26 Estonia's AI vision: Building a data-driven society and government. (2024, February 12). An interview with Dr. Ott Velsberg, the Chief Data Officer of Estonia. https://apolitical.co/solution-articles/en/estonias-ai-vision-building-a-data-driven-society-and-government.
27 A concept of how state could operate in the age of AI – UNESCO's global list of top AI projects. (2023, May 27). https://workinestonia.com/estonias-burokratt-a-concept-of-how-state-could-operate-in-the-age-of-artificial-intelligence-again-in-unescos-global-list-of-top-ai-projects/.
28 Homeland Security. (n.d.). Using AI to secure the homeland. Retrieved August 31, 2025, from https://www.dhs.gov/ai/using-ai-to-secure-the-homeland.

29 AI in healthcare market share research report. (2024). *Polaris market research*. https://www.globenewswire.com/news-release/2024/02/05/2823246/0/en/Artificial-Intelligence-AI-in-Healthcare-Market-Share-Envisaged-To-Reach-U.S.D-431-05-Billion-By-2032-at-38-2-CAGR-Growth-Insights-by-Polaris-Market-Research.html.
30 2025 watch list: Artificial intelligence in health care. (2025, March). *Canadian Journal of Health Technologies, 5*(3), 21–22. https://www.cda-amc.ca/sites/default/files/Tech%20Trends/2025/ER0015%3D2025_Watch_List.pdf.
31 How AI is changing the face of trauma care. (2024, June 19). *Unity Health Toronto*. Retrieved August 2025, from https://unityhealth.to/2024/06/trauma-ai/
32 MoodInsights. (n.d.). *SalesChoice*. Retrieved August 31, 2025, from https://www.saleschoice.com/moodinsights/.
33 Baldry, S. (n.d.). Wysa unveils Wysa Copilot to elevate mental health therapy with AI. Retrieved August 31, 2025, from https://blogs.wysa.io/blog/company-news/wysa-unveils-wysa-copilot-to-elevate-mental-health-therapy-with-ai.
34 RLDatix. (2024, October 24). *Enhancing the human: Leveraging generative AI to support healthcare staff*. RLDatix. https://nam.rldatix.com/enhancing-the-human-leveraging-generative-ai-to-support-healthcare-staff/.
35 RLDatix. (2024, October 24). Enhancing the human: Leveraging generative AI to support healthcare staff [Video]. *YouTube*. https://www.youtube.com/watch?v=2D9Zu9bt4K0.
36 Sartori, A. (2023, October 24). How Zegna will use AI to create looks for its customers. *NSS Magazine*. https://www.nssmag.com/en/fashion/32880/zegna-x-ai.
37 Elgan, M. (2025, June 6). Who needs real things when everything can be a hologram? *Computerworld*. https://www.computerworld.com/article/4001999/who-needs-real-things-when-everything-can-be-a-hologram.html.
38 Parsani, P. (2024, April 2). *Beauty and the bot: How Sephora reimagined customer experience with AI*. Medium. https://medium.com/cut-the-saas/beauty-and-the-bot-how-sephora-reimagined-customer-experience-with-ai-bafb5a9ae1d8.
39 D'Addato, E. (2025, February 15). *Self-cleaning T-shirts: Reducing water and energy use*. Meer. https://www.meer.com/en/83825-self-cleaning-t-shirts-reducing-water-and-energy-use.
40 Precedence Research. (2024, January). *Telecom AI market growth report*. Precedence Research. https://www.precedenceresearch.com/ai-in-telecommunication-market.

41 Donegan, M. (2024, May 24). Vodafone's TOBi chatbot gets a generative AI makeover from Microsoft. *TelcoTitans*. https://www.telcotitans.com/vodafonewatch/vodafones-tobi-chatbot-gets-a-generative-ai-makeover-from-microsoft/8124.article.
42 Vodafone. (2024, May 23). Vodafone supercharging customer experience with Microsoft's GenAI tools. *Vodafone Technology News*. https://www.vodafone.com/news/technology/vodafone-supercharging-customer-experience-with-microsoft-s-gen-ai-tools.
43 Boxall, T. (2025, July). SalesChoice – Case study [Video]. *YouTube*. https://www.youtube.com/watch?v=yb9V1sz1rTA.
44 Hector, H. (2025, May 11). Meta just confirmed it has new Ray-Ban smart glasses on the way with "new technological capabilities" – And I couldn't be more excited. *TechRadar*. https://www.techradar.com/computing/virtual-reality-augmented-reality/mark-zuckerberg-confirms-new-ray-ban-smart-glasses-are-coming-later-this-year-here-are-the-3-pairs-i-think-we-ll-see.
45 TELUS. (2025, March 18). *TELUS to launch Canada's leading Sovereign AI Factory, powered by NVIDIA to drive the nation's AI future* [Press release]. TELUS. https://www.telus.com/en/about/news-and-events/media-releases/telus-to-launch-canadas-leading-sovereign-ai-factory-powered-by-nividia-to-drive-the-nations-ai-future.
46 U.S. Bureau of Labor Statistics. (n.d.). *Computers and Information Technology Occupations*. In *Occupational Outlook Handbook*. Retrieved December 2024, from https://www.bls.gov/ooh/computer-and-information-technology/home.htm.
47 Elgan, M. (2025, June 6). Who needs real things when everything can be a hologram? *Computer World*. https://www.computerworld.com/article/4001999/who-needs-real-things-when-everything-can-be-a-hologram.html.
48 Elgan, M. (2025, June 6). Who needs real things when everything can be a hologram? *Computer World*. https://www.computerworld.com/article/4001999/who-needs-real-things-when-everything-can-be-a-hologram.html.
49 Samsung Electronics Co., Ltd. (2025, March 24). Samsung unveils new refrigerator lineup equipped with screens and enhanced AI Vision Inside feature [Press release]. *Samsung Global Newsroom*. https://news.samsung.com/global/samsung-unveils-new-refrigerator-lineup-equipped-with-screens-and-enhanced-ai-vision-inside-feature.
50 Shandil, P. (2025, January 15). Five AI-enabled kitchen appliances from CES 2025. *HomeCrux*. https://www.homecrux.com/ai-enabled-kitchen-appliances-at-ces-2025/303967/.

51 McCracken, H. (2025, March 18). How Waymo is leading the robotaxi revolution. *Fast Company*. https://www.fastcompany.com/91270760/waymo-most-innovative-companies-2025.
52 Ferguson, M. (2025, January 21). NVIDIA breaks new ground at CES 2025 with AI innovations. *AI News*. https://opentools.ai/news/nvidia-breaks-new-ground-at-ces-2025-with-ai-innovations.
53 Lopez, M. (2025, May 19). *How Dell's AI infrastructure updates deliver choice, control and scale. Forbes*. https://www.forbes.com/sites/maribellopez/2025/05/19/how-dells-ai-infrastructure-updates-deliver-choice-control-and-scale/.
54 Dell Technologies. (n.d.). *Digital Twins* [Web page]. Retrieved June 11, 2025, from https://www.dell.com/en-us/shop/artificial-intelligence/sc/digital-twins.

Chapter 15

Avoiding dystopia

Our future with artificial intelligence (AI) will not be the result of one decisive outcome but rather an intricate web of interwoven decisions. This interconnectedness creates feedback loops that can propel us in a positive direction or along a negative trajectory. For instance, if we fail to prioritize upskilling and workforce development in the face of AI-driven automation, we risk displacing workers without providing them with the necessary tools to adapt, leading to decreased income levels and a loss of meaningful purpose. The ripple effects of such decisions could reduce consumer spending, stifle productivity, lower GDP, and erode economic value.

No rational person would reject the compelling 2035 vision outlined in Chapter 14. However, as we embark on our journey toward AI Utopia, we must recognize that the decisions we make today – and in the years to come – can just as easily lead us toward a dystopian reality.

Dystopia, derived from the Latin prefix "dys," meaning "bad," is essentially utopia gone wrong. A world where the technologies designed to enhance our lives create oppressive systems of control dominated by surveillance, greed, and power plays. A society where individual freedoms are sacrificed for the illusion of safety and order. Unchecked AI development could lead to a future characterized by fear, inequality, and loss of agency.

Our future will involve AI, which is intrinsically a tool that is neither negative nor positive. What will be the deciding factor in whether we embark on a path toward utopia or dystopia? It is the objective that AI is working toward. A path toward utopia is human-centric, with the ultimate purpose of improving the human condition. Conversely, a path toward dystopia is likely to arise from

DOI: 10.4324/9781003625520-18

AI being directed to benefit a select few puppeteers. Alternatively, it could stem from hubris, where we intentionally embark on a path we believe we can control, only to discover too late that we cannot.

By acknowledging the duality of our technological journey, we can better manage the complexities of AI and make decisions that steer us toward our desired future and away from those that do not. The choices we make today will shape the world of tomorrow. It is our responsibility to build technologies that serve as a force for good.

Objectives

Upon completing this chapter, you will be able to:

- Understand the central views of creating a dystopian future driven by AI
- Identify the risks of a dystopian future
- Understand the imperative to advance AI leadership, governance, legislation, and education to ensure humanity remains accountable and in control.

Dystopia – a system of control gone awry

As we stand on the precipice of a future shaped by AI, it is crucial to confront the darker possibilities. "Dystopia" evokes images of a world where AI systems have seized control, gone rogue, and stripped humans of our autonomy. Imagine a world where your every move is monitored, where AI wields unprecedented power through control of information and media, and citizens live in constant fear of an all-seeing eye. The difference between the surveillance in utopia vs. dystopia is that in a utopia we trust that the AI has positive intentions.

The roots of our fascination with machine intelligence and its potential negative consequences can be traced back to ancient philosophers. Aristotle pondered the implications of automated tools granting humans freedom from labor. He envisioned a future where machines could operate independently, but he also speculated on the societal impacts of such self-operating tools, including slavery and the nature of work.[1] Fast forward to today, and we find ourselves grappling with the very realities he contemplated.

Depicting a dystopian future with AI gone rogue is a common theme in movies, with AI's control taking various forms:

1 *Corporate control:* Large corporations dominate society through products, advertising, and media manipulation; citizens become mere consumers, bombarded with propaganda that shapes their beliefs and behaviors. *The Circle,* starring Tom Hanks, depicts a dystopian future in which a powerful tech company uses its products and services to manipulate and control people's lives through surveillance and data collection.[2]
2 *Government control:* Citizens are kept in check through heavy surveillance, with severe and immediate response used to neutralize perceived threats; this scenario is illustrated in Philip K. Dick's *Minority Report,* where a futuristic police force arrests individuals for crimes they have yet to commit, all in the name of maintaining order.[3]
3 *Bureaucratic control:* A labyrinth of red tape and far-reaching regulations stifles creativity and freedom. In the film *Brazil,*[4] a low-level bureaucrat is trapped in a monotonous existence, navigating a mindless system that prioritizes conformity over individuality; the struggle against such oppressive structures serves as a cautionary tale of what can happen when bureaucracy becomes a means of control.
4 *Technological control:* Technology, rather than serving humanity, becomes a means of domination. In iconic films like *The Matrix* and *The Terminator,* we witness the terrifying potential of autonomous machines that threaten human existence; these narratives remind us that unchecked technological advancement could lead to catastrophic consequences.
5 *Philosophical or religious control:* Ideologies enforced through authoritarian regimes can create a society where dissent is silenced, and individual freedoms are stripped away; *Equilibrium* depicts the dystopian society of Libria controlled by an authoritarian regime that enforces strict emotional regulation through drugs, and leverages technology to monitor and suppress any form of dissent.[5]

These dystopian films demonstrate that the fear of AI becoming autonomous and harmful is not unfounded. Leading researchers warn that there is no guarantee that super-advanced AI will not dominate humanity as we have dominated other species. Dr. Yoshua Bengio, Turing Award winner, warns that AI is showing disturbing traits such as "deception, cheating, lying, and self-preservation."[6] The rapid evolution of AI capabilities has already surpassed human intelligence in many areas, raising critical questions about our future.

We cannot overlook the existential threat posed by AI, but we must not ignore the human element. Much of the apprehension surrounding AI stems from our historical misuse of technology rather than its inherent capabilities. As with many advancements, there is a risk of tyrants and terrorists using AI's power for nefarious purposes. Additionally, the potential for deepfakes and misinformation to undermine our communication systems raises significant alarms.

Notable dystopian perspectives from influential thinkers remind us of the need for responsible AI governance. During an October 2024 interview at Saudi Arabia's Future Investment Initiative summit, Elon Musk sounded the alarm on the risks of AI. While he is "pathologically optimistic" about AI, he admitted that, "There's this sub chance, that could be 10% to 20%, that it goes bad. Rogue AI is possible if the technology grows exponentially."[7]

Nick Bostrom in *Superintelligence: Paths, Dangers, Strategies*[8] also explores the future of AI and the potential scenarios that could arise if AI surpasses human intelligence. He describes in detail how a superintelligent AI could be controlled or directed, the risks it might pose, and the ethical dilemmas involved in creating an intelligence that might eventually exceed our own.

There is a p(doom) score to measure the "probability of doom" – a quantification of how likely it is that a person believes that AI will kill us all, or create a cataclysm that threatens human survival. A high p(doom) means that an individual believes that an AI apocalypse is likely, while a low score means we will probably tough it out.[9] As profiled in the New York Times,[10] nobody knows whether AI is 10% or 85.2% likely to kill us.

There are also lots of obvious follow-up questions, such as:

- Would it still count as "doom" if only 50% of humans died as a result of AI?
- What if nobody died, but we all ended up jobless and miserable?
- And, how would AI take over the world, anyway?

The point of p(doom) is not precision. It is to roughly assess where someone stands on the utopia-to-dystopia spectrum.[11] Most researchers and executives familiar with (p)doom place the risk of AI taking over humanity anywhere between 5% and 50%.

On the other hand, safety research scientist Roman Yampolskiy says the risk is extremely high, with a 99.999999% probability. He argues that it will be virtually impossible to control AI once superintelligence is attained, and the only way to prevent this is not to build it.[12]

To avoid slipping into this dystopian reality, we must take decisive action. We must establish the appropriate safeguards to ensure AI does not dominate or control humans. This requires a commitment to governance, transparency, and accountability in AI development. Intentionality is key; we must engage in deep scenario planning to anticipate potential consequences and proactively address them.

AI intelligence is surpassing human performance

AI intelligence is not just advancing; it is rapidly surpassing human intelligence in various domains. This progression, while remarkable, raises critical questions about our future and the balance of power between humans and machines. In the previous section, we explored the potential for a dystopian world where technology controls rather than serves humanity. Now, we must consider how we can respond to this challenge.

In 2024, Elon Musk predicted that AI would get ten times better and would be able to do anything that a human can do within the next year or two.[13] Eliza Kosoy,[14] a Berkeley researcher, points out that machines are already outperforming humans in numerous areas, from strategy games like chess and Go to complex tasks such as performing surgery and piloting aircraft. The emergence of autonomous vehicles, while still facing challenges, further illustrates the rapid advancements in AI capabilities.

The *Stanford AI Index Report* (2025)[15] found that we now inhabit a world where, given sufficient data and the right machine learning algorithms, machines can surpass human intelligence across every intellectual dimension. This causes us to reflect on our role in the future of AI and the safeguards necessary to prevent a dystopian outcome.

To ensure that we remain in control as technology evolves, we must adopt bold and transformative actions that balance our pro-innovation ambitions with pro-safety safeguards. To aid in this endeavor, we have created in Table 15.1 a list of Technology Do's and Don'ts.

By adopting these technology-focused actions, organizations can maintain control over AI advancements while fostering innovation. The path forward requires a commitment to leveraging cutting-edge technologies and embracing a proactive mindset.

Table 15.1 Technological innovation guidance – do's and don'ts

Technological innovation	*Innovation guidance*
Develop autonomous AI governance systems	Create advanced AI systems that can autonomously monitor and manage other AI systems. These AI overseers should utilize machine learning algorithms to detect anomalies, ensure compliance with operational standards, and self-correct potential issues before they escalate. • **Do** invest in robust AI governance technologies • **Do not** rely solely on human oversight, which is slow and prone to error.
Implement real-time AI performance analytics	Utilize AI-driven analytics platforms that provide real-time insights into AI system performance, resource allocation, and user interactions. These platforms should enable organizations to make data-driven decisions quickly, optimizing operations and enhancing user experiences. • **Do** leverage real-time analytics to drive continuous improvement • **Do not** ignore performance metrics or allow systems to operate without oversight.
Foster human-AI synergy through advanced interfaces	Invest in the development of intuitive interfaces that facilitate seamless collaboration between humans and AI. This includes AR and VR environments that allow users to interact with AI systems in immersive ways, enhancing understanding and control. • **Do** prioritize the creation of advanced interaction technologies • **Do not** settle for outdated interfaces that limit user engagement and understanding.

(*Continued*)

Table 15.1 (Continued)

Technological innovation	*Innovation guidance*
Engage in predictive scenario modeling	Utilize AI to conduct predictive modeling of various future scenarios based on current data trends and technological advancements. This proactive approach will help organizations anticipate challenges and opportunities, allowing for agile responses to potential disruptions. • **Do** embrace predictive analytics as a core strategic tool • **Do not** rely on historical data alone, which may not accurately reflect future conditions.
Create a competitive AI innovation ecosystem	Establish partnerships with startups, research institutions, and technology leaders to foster a vibrant ecosystem of AI innovation. This collaborative approach will accelerate the development of cutting-edge technologies and ensure that organizations remain at the forefront of AI advancements. • **Do** actively seek out and invest in innovative collaborations • **Do not** isolate your organization from emerging global technologies or trends.
Prioritize AI resilience and security	Invest in advanced cybersecurity measures specifically designed for AI systems. This includes developing AI algorithms that can detect and respond to cyber threats in real-time, ensuring the integrity and security of AI operations. • **Do** implement proactive security measures • **Do not** underestimate the vulnerabilities of AI systems or assume that traditional security protocols are sufficient.

Actions to avoid dystopia

To avoid a dystopian future, we must focus on corporate behaviors and societal impacts that are within our control. As we work toward achieving an AI Utopia future and avoiding dystopia, we have identified specific areas that must be addressed as we advance AI capabilities. For each, we have outlined a 2035 "moonshot" opportunity that we can strive for.

Promoting individuality and equality

As AI systems rely on more and more data to learn and make decisions, we need to address the potential for inequity and biased decision-making. This starts with building AI that celebrates diversity and makes bias irrelevant. On one end of the spectrum is a utopian future. AI systems are not only fair and equitable, but also make personalized decisions that are relevant and appropriate for a particular individual or situation. The collection of vast amounts of personal data about us, rather than creating a surveillance state, allows AI to make more informed decisions. AI promotes individuality and creativity.

Conversely, the dystopian end of the spectrum presents a chilling vision of systemic discrimination and inequities. AI has developed an algorithm for the perfect human. Data is used to identify differences to eradicate them. DNA manipulation is performed in the womb to "fix" physical anomalies and remove undesirable traits. Access to information is restricted and controlled. Training, programming, and propaganda promote singular thinking – creativity and individualism are not encouraged.

The moonshot: achieving bias irrelevance

The 2035 utopian moonshot goal in achieving AI that promotes individuality and equity starts with making historical biases irrelevant. This vision involves AI that leverages our differences to personalize its response and celebrates and encourages our uniqueness. To achieve this, Table 15.2 identifies ways we can achieve bias irrelevance.

The journey to achieving a moonshot goal of making bias irrelevant will require commitment, collaboration, and a willingness to challenge the status quo. As we work to harness the power of AI, we must stay committed to mitigating bias and celebrating diversity.

Lifelong learning and workforce development

AI has already begun to reshape job landscapes and has the potential to displace millions of workers. We need to equip workers for an AI-driven economy, empowering them to use AI to enhance their creativity and productivity. Many fear that, in the long-term, AI will lead to job displacement and social unrest. If AI and automation eliminate jobs without replacing them, it could result in economic decline, societal division, increased crime rates, and a general sense of hopelessness.

Table 15.2 Moonshot – achieving bias irrelevance

Achieving bias irrelevance	*Moonshot opportunity*
Redefining AI's objectives	Shift AI's goals from a singular objective function to achieving an equitable outcome. AI should be designed to achieve its intended goal while also prioritizing fairness, empathy, and inclusivity, actively seeking to understand and mitigate biases.
Embrace the informational value of diversity	Rather than reduce AI's access to data, embrace its richness. Teach AI to make decisions on the factors that matter most rather than emulating past human decision-making.
Use privacy-enhancing techniques	Increase AI's access to data, but protect it through advanced security techniques. Restricting access to data is no longer a viable protection strategy for AI that needs full data to operate effectively and equitably.
Establishing AI as a partner in social justice	Position AI as a proactive partner in promoting social justice and equity. This involves leveraging AI to identify and address systemic inequalities.
Have AI work for everyone	Position AI as a core economic resource that is accessible to everyone. Establish global literacy programs and local infrastructure projects to bring AI to the masses.

Looking toward 2035, we must adopt visionary and aspirational practices in workforce development and upskilling.

The moonshot: creating a future-ready workforce

The utopian 2035 moonshot goal for lifelong learning and workforce development is to create a future-ready workforce that not only adapts to AI advancements but also actively collaborates with AI to drive innovation and societal progress (Table 15.3). To achieve this, we must focus on the following:

By taking these steps, we can move toward a future where the workforce is not only prepared for the challenges of an AI-driven economy but is also empowered to shape the future of work.

Table 15.3 Moonshot – creating a future-ready workforce

Creating a future-ready workforce	*Moonshot opportunity*
Personalized learning pathways	Implement AI-driven personalized learning platforms that assess individual skills, preferences, and career aspirations. These platforms would provide tailored training programs that adapt in real-time, ensuring that employees acquire the skills necessary to excel in their roles and embrace new opportunities.
Lifelong learning ecosystems	Foster a culture of lifelong learning by creating ecosystems that support continuous education and skill development. Provide accessible training resources and mentorship programs, ensuring that individuals can continuously upgrade their skills throughout their careers.
AI-augmented work environments	Design work environments that leverage AI to enhance human capabilities rather than replace them. By integrating AI tools that assist employees in their tasks, organizations can empower their workforce to focus on higher-value activities, fostering creativity and innovation.
Accelerate learning and interactions through AR and VR	Develop simulated environments for employees to interact and learn. Digitize systems and operations with 3D digital twins and hologram environments.
Collaboration with AI for problem-solving	Encourage collaboration between humans and AI in problem-solving scenarios. By creating interdisciplinary teams that combine human creativity with AI's analytical capabilities, organizations can tackle complex challenges and drive innovation in ways that neither could achieve alone.

Human agency and control

As AI systems become more integrated into our daily lives, the potential for them to dictate our choices and influence our behaviors raises critical concerns. In a utopian future, AI enhances human agency. Individuals use AI to enhance their lives while maintaining control over their choices. Take this too far, and we will create a world where algorithms dictate not only what products we buy but also how we think and behave. In such a scenario, individuals may find themselves trapped in echo chambers, influenced by targeted content that reinforces existing beliefs and biases. The consequences of this loss of agency could manifest in widespread apathy, social division, and a general sense of helplessness among individuals who feel they have little control over their lives.

It is important that we remember that while the integration of AI into our lives presents significant opportunities, it also poses risks to human agency that must be actively managed.

The moonshot: empowering human agency

The 2025 utopian moonshot goal for maintaining human agency and control is to create a future where AI systems not only enhance human autonomy but also actively empower individuals to transcend their limitations and unlock their full potential (Table 15.4). To achieve this transformative future, we must focus on the following groundbreaking initiatives:

By pursuing these visionary initiatives, we can redefine human agency in an AI-driven world, ensuring that technology serves as a catalyst for empowerment rather than a mechanism of control.

Inclusive innovation and access to technology

A dystopian dark reality restricts access to technology to a privileged few, exacerbating existing inequalities and creating a digital divide. Only affluent individuals can afford the latest AI tools and training, leaving low-income communities without the resources to participate in the digital economy. This exclusion can lead to a cycle of poverty, where individuals are unable to access job opportunities, education, and essential services, ultimately resulting in social unrest and division.

Conversely, in an AI Utopia, inclusive innovation is essential for harnessing the full potential of AI to drive societal progress and ensure that no one is left behind. We must create a future where everyone has the opportunity to engage with and benefit from technological advancements. Imagine community-based innovation hubs equipped with the latest AI tools and resources, where individuals can learn, experiment, and collaborate on projects that address local challenges. Marginalized groups are empowered to leverage technology to improve their lives, whether through entrepreneurship,

Table 15.4 Moonshot – empowering human agency

Empowering human agency	*Moonshot opportunity*
AI as a personal empowerment coach	Create AI systems that function as personal empowerment coaches, not just assistants. These AI entities would analyze an individual's strengths, weaknesses, aspirations, and emotional states to provide tailored guidance and support in real-time. This targeted goal should be human-centric and personalized for the individual.
Decentralized autonomous decision-making	Decision-making is decentralized and facilitated by AI systems that prioritize collective intelligence. Instead of top-down control, communities leverage AI to collaboratively assess challenges and co-create solutions. This could involve AI-driven platforms that aggregate diverse perspectives and facilitate consensus-building, empowering individuals to take ownership.
Universal AI literacy and empowerment programs	To truly empower individuals, we must implement universal AI literacy programs that go beyond basic understanding. These programs would equip people with the skills to critically engage with AI technologies, enabling them to not only use AI but also influence its development.
AI-driven personal data sovereignty	Individuals have complete sovereignty over their personal data, facilitated by AI technologies that allow for secure, transparent data management. This would involve creating decentralized platforms where users can control access to their data, monetize it if they choose, and ensure it is used with their consent.
Cognitive augmentation through AI integration	AI is integrated into human cognition. This could involve brain-computer interfaces that allow individuals to access AI insights instantaneously, augmenting their intelligence and creativity. We would need to have strict controls in place to avoid subliminal manipulation.
Global AI governance coalition	Establish a global coalition dedicated to the ethical governance of AI, where nations, corporations, and civil society collaborate to create universal standards that prioritize human agency. This coalition would focus on developing frameworks that ensure AI technologies enhance individual freedoms and societal well-being.

education, or community engagement. This approach not only fosters economic growth but also enriches the technological landscape with diverse perspectives and ideas.

The moonshot: achieving universal access to **technology**

The 2035 utopian moonshot goal for achieving inclusive innovation and access to technology is to create a world where every individual has the opportunity to benefit from AI and advanced technologies (Table 15.5). To achieve this, we must focus on the following:

By taking these bold steps, we can move toward a future where inclusive innovation is the norm and access to technology is a fundamental right for all. Our goal should be to use AI and technology as a bridge to opportunity, empowerment, and collective progress.

Table 15.5 Moonshot – universal access to technology

Universal access to technology	*Moonshot opportunity*
Global technology access initiatives	Launch international initiatives aimed at providing free or low-cost access to technology, training, and resources in underserved communities.
Create global educational institutions	Transcend above the local educational construct by creating accessible multi-language AI education and resources that are not reliant upon large-scale infrastructure. For example, mobile satellite technology and local renewable electricity.
AI for social good programs	Develop AI applications specifically designed to address social challenges, such as healthcare access, education, and environmental sustainability.
Empowerment through technology co-creation	Foster environments where communities can co-create technology solutions that address their specific challenges, ensuring that technologies are relevant, effective, culturally sensitive, and create joint value.

Resource-efficient AI computing

The environmental impact of traditional data centers, coupled with the growing demand for AI capabilities, necessitates a transformative approach to how we design and deploy AI systems. We do not have the natural resources to build data centers to support the scaling of current-day AI. We must leverage innovative technologies such as edge computing to process data closer to its source, reduce latency, and improve computer processing efficiency. Otherwise, unchecked growth of data centers will lead to significant resource depletion and environmental degradation. The consequences of inaction could result in rising energy costs, increased carbon emissions, and a strain on natural resources, ultimately undermining the very progress we seek to achieve through AI advancements.

The moonshot: achieving sustainable AI computing

The 2035 utopian moonshot goal for resource-efficient AI computing is to create a sustainable AI computing ecosystem that is zero-emission, utilizing renewable energy sources and advanced energy-efficient computing technologies (Table 15.6). To achieve this, we must focus on the following:

Many of the above actions have already been taken in local areas, but we need to build them on a global scale. By doing this, we can create resource-efficient AI computing and a sustainable computing ecosystem.

AI-enabled justice

While AI has the potential to enhance the efficiency and fairness of legal processes, it could also lead us down a dystopian path characterized by manipulation, control, and exploitation. To avoid this, we must create an AI-enabled justice system that is transparent, accountable, and free from bias. We must use AI to combat deepfake technology that can ruin reputations, manipulate public opinion, or incite violence. We must make it extremely difficult for cybercriminals to exploit AI. We need to guard against illegal control of resources through AI-enabled surveillance and manipulation.

Table 15.6 Moonshot – achieving a sustainable AI computing ecosystem

Achieving a sustainable AI computing ecosystem	*Moonshot opportunity*
Decentralized AI processing networks	Invest in edge computing technologies that enable data processing closer to the source and decentralize AI processing. This could involve harnessing the power of underutilized devices, such as smartphones and IoT sensors, to contribute to AI processing tasks, creating a more resilient and resource-efficient ecosystem.
Invest in renewable power	We have the ultimate renewable energy sources in the sun and the Earth's core. We need to create more advanced, efficient materials to passively harness these energy sources and leverage storage mechanisms to decouple energy generation from its use.
Expand the passive collection of energy	Collaborate across sectors to develop multi-functional materials and products whose secondary function is to collect, store, and/or transmit solar and heat energy.
Exponential reductions in compute requirements	Achieve exponential declines in AI compute requirements through breakthroughs in algorithm efficiency and hardware design.
AI-driven environmental monitoring	Develop AI systems that monitor and optimize energy usage across computing infrastructures in real-time. These systems would analyze patterns and make adjustments to ensure that energy consumption aligns with sustainability goals, creating a feedback loop that promotes continuous improvement.

The moonshot: achieving a just and equitable AI justice system

The 2025 utopian moonshot goal is to create an equitable AI-enabled justice system that upholds the highest standards of justice while minimizing the potential for bias and misuse (Table 15.7). To achieve this, we must focus on the following:

As we strive to create a justice system that reflects our highest ideals, we must ensure that AI enhances human dignity and upholds the principles of justice for all.

Table 15.7 The moonshot: achieving a just and equitable AI justice system

Achieving a just and equitable AI justice system	*Moonshot opportunity*
AI as a proactive guardian of justice	Create AI systems that act as proactive guardians of justice, capable of identifying and addressing potential injustices before they escalate. These systems would analyze data from various sources to detect patterns of discrimination, resource exploitation, and criminal activity, enabling timely interventions, ensuring timely access to justice, and preventing wrongful convictions.
Universal access to AI-driven legal resources	Develop AI-powered platforms that provide individuals with access to legal information and resources, ensuring that all individuals have the tools they need to advocate for their rights.
Global standards for AI in justice	Establish international standards for the ethical use of AI in the justice system, promoting best practices and accountability across borders.
Prevent crimes through education and financial security programs	Eliminate the root causes of crime by providing every citizen with the means to generate financial stability and meaningful purpose through legitimate means.

Conclusion

To achieve these bold moonshot goals by 2035, a concerted effort from all sectors will be required. Companies must embrace a culture of innovation and responsibility, investing in research and development to create cutting-edge technologies that align with pro-safety goals. They must also facilitate proactive collaborations amongst governments, non-profits, and communities to ensure inclusive access to resources and opportunities.

In an AI-driven future, the key determinant for humans retaining control and agency lies in creating AI systems with human oversight at their core. Individuals must have the ability to understand, influence, and consent to how AI technologies operate and make decisions. This will require building essential digital literacy and critical thinking skills among the population, enabling individuals to use complex AI systems effectively and make informed choices. We must also build AI ecosystems that protect personal data rights and promote accountability in AI development.

Ultimately, achieving these moonshot goals requires a shared vision and collective action, where businesses not only seek profit but also prioritize the well-being of society and the planet. Executives cannot afford to be passive bystanders, waiting for someone else to take the lead in this transformative journey.

Each organization should select at least one moonshot goal and commit all available resources to its achievement. Moreover, they must actively participate in supporting other moonshot initiatives, recognizing that collaboration is essential for widespread impact. This support can take various forms, such as partnering with non-profits that specialize in relevant areas, spearheading academic-applied factories or ideation centers, or sponsoring global crowdfunding efforts.

By taking decisive action and fostering a culture of shared responsibility, organizations can drive meaningful change and contribute to a future where innovation serves the greater good. We can achieve AI Utopia and avoid a dystopian future.

Key leadership questions to consider:

1 How is your organization actively addressing the potential risks of AI technologies to prevent the emergence of a dystopian society?
2 In what ways are you ensuring that AI systems in your organization promote transparency and accountability to build trust with stakeholders?
3 What strategies are you implementing to safeguard against the misuse of AI, particularly in areas such as surveillance, deepfakes, and cybercrime?
4 How are you fostering a culture of innovation that prioritizes ethical considerations and human-centric design in the development of all of your AI technologies?

Notes

1 Bhorat, M. Z. (2022). *Aristotle on automation: A preindustrial political theory of technology* [Doctoral dissertation, University of California, Los Angeles]. eScholarship. https://escholarship.org/uc/item/7416q0c6.

2 DigitalDefynd. (2025, June 7). *50 mind-bending artificial intelligence movies & shows [of all time]*. DigitalDefynd. https://digitaldefynd.com/IQ/mind-bending-artificial-intelligence-movies-shows/.
3 Spielberg, S. (Director). (2002). *Minority report* [Film]. 20th Century Fox.
4 Gilliam, T. (Director). (1985). *Brazil* [Film]. Universal Pictures.
5 Wimmer, K. (Director). (2002). *Equilibrium* [Film]. Miramax Films.
6 Criddle, C. (2025, June 3). AI godfather Yoshua Bengio warns the latest tech lies to users. *Financial Post*. https://financialpost.com/financial-times/ai-godfather-yoshua-bengio-warns-latest-tech-lies-to-users.
7 Quiroz-Gutierrez, M. (2024, October 30). Elon Musk says there's a 10% to 20% chance that AI 'goes bad,' even while he raises billions for his own startup xAI. *Fortune*. https://fortune.com/2024/10/30/elon-musk-ai-could-go-bad-existential-threat-xai-fundraising/.
8 Bostrom, N. (2014). *Superintelligence: Paths, dangers, strategies*. Oxford, England:Oxford University Press.
9 Wikipedia contributors. (n.d.). *P(doom)*. Wikipedia. Retrieved June 7, 2025, from https://en.wikipedia.org/wiki/P(doom).
10 Roose, K. (2023, December 6). Silicon Valley confronts a grim new A.I. metric. *The New York Times*. https://www.nytimes.com/2023/12/06/business/dealbook/silicon-valley-artificial-intelligence.html.
11 Roose, K. (2023, December 6). Silicon Valley confronts a grim new A.I. metric. *The New York Times*. https://www.nytimes.com/2023/12/06/business/dealbook/silicon-valley-artificial-intelligence.html.
12 Williams, W. (2024, April 17). AI safety researcher and director of the Cyber Security Laboratory at the University of Louisville, Roman Yampolskiy, disclosed that the probability of AI ending humanity is much higher. *Yahoo – Tech Trader*. https://www.yahoo.com/tech/roman-yampolskiy-says-theres-99-171220674.html.
13 Quiroz-Gutierrez, M. (2024, October 30). Elon Musk says there's a 10% to 20% chance that AI 'goes bad,' even while he raises billions for his own startup xAI. *Fortune*. https://fortune.com/2024/10/30/elon-musk-ai-could-go-bad-existential-threat-xai-fundraising/.
14 Kosoy, E. (2025, July 11). *Eliza Kosoy – AI researcher*. https://www.elizakosoy.com/.
15 *The 2025 Stanford Index Report*. https://hai.stanford.edu/ai-index/2025-ai-index-report.

Chapter 16

Leading with a thriving mindset

We are at the *Artificial Intelligence (AI) Precipice* of a significant transformation and disruption resulting from our use of AI. At this critical point in AI's development and deployment, our choices and actions will determine the trajectory of our future. Do advancements in AI lead to significant and uncontrollable consequences? Or does AI advance in a controlled and thoughtful direction?

Our AI future could swing in one of two directions – an AI Utopia where we harness AI's potential or a dystopian future where AI controls and subjugates humans. We repeat here Nick Bostrom's warning that "Machine superintelligence is the last invention that humanity will ever need to make, unless we come up with a way to control it."[1] As we stand at this critical juncture, Bostrom's warning serves as a stark reminder that the path we choose in developing AI will ultimately determine whether we achieve a harmonious coexistence or face the dire consequences of unchecked technological advancement.

To direct our course, AI needs to be treated differently from past innovations. AI possesses the capability to learn, adapt, and make decisions at a scale and speed that is close to, and in some areas already surpasses, human abilities. We can not be passive observers of this transformation. The window for influencing its trajectory is rapidly closing.

Delaying action or pushing responsibility to future leaders risks losing control over how AI evolves, leading to unintended consequences that will be difficult, if not impossible, to reverse. We must proactively engage with AI, guiding its development and using it responsibly. We must ensure that AI's objectives are aligned with long-term societal goals.

DOI: 10.4324/9781003625520-19

In this chapter, we present a roadmap to guide executives to navigate the varying stages of AI integration and development. We have created three pathways through an organization's AI future: surviving, stability, and thriving. Each pathway outlines specific actions and strategies that can assist an organization's relationship with AI.

Surviving represents the bare minimum actions necessary to remain compliant and operational in an AI-driven world. This pathway focuses on establishing basic ethical standards, investing in essential education and training, and implementing basic governance mechanisms. However, a survival path may not be sustainable in the long term. By only addressing the most pressing needs, organizations risk falling into a reactive mode, constantly playing catch-up with technological advancements. This approach may delay harmful impacts, but it will not prevent them, potentially placing significant burdens on future profits and leading to a point of no return where the organization is unable to adapt to external changes fast enough. Leadership in the surviving path is characterized by a focus on risk mitigation and compliance. However, this approach will limit an organization's ability to innovate and grow.

Stability moves beyond survival to a state of doing enough to stay competitive and efficient. This involves enhancing responsible AI practices, investing in continuous learning and development, strengthening governance frameworks, and fostering cross-functional collaboration. The intent is to achieve a level of stability and readiness that allows the organization to capitalize on AI's benefits while mitigating associated risks. This path strikes a balance between short-term and long-term impacts, ensuring that the organization remains adaptable and resilient. Leadership on the stability path requires a proactive approach, with leaders fostering a culture of collaboration and continuous improvement. Leaders must be adept at managing change and ensuring their teams are equipped with the necessary skills and knowledge.

Thriving is the north star and pinnacle of our roadmap, where proactive actions are taken to drive toward our 2035 moonshot goals. This stage emphasizes leading in responsible AI development, investing in strategic AI initiatives, championing workforce transformation, promoting sustainable AI development, and fostering a culture of innovation and purposeful responsibility. The goal is not to adapt to AI. It is to actively shape its trajectory; to create a positive and lasting impact both for the organization and society. The organizations that will thrive are those that prioritize long-term benefits over short-term gains, ensure that their AI initiatives align with sustainable goals, and continually benchmark internationally to strengthen their AI strategies. Leadership on the thriving path is visionary and transformative. Leaders inspire their teams to think beyond immediate challenges and consider the broader implications of their actions. They champion innovation, drive strategic investments, and advocate for policies that support sustainable and responsible AI development. This approach signals a commitment to putting as much investment into AI safeguards as the AI functionality itself.

Organizations can choose to start at the surviving pathway and shift up to stability and thriving as their AI investments grow, or jump to a higher level right away. Investments in AI governance and responsible AI development should match an organization's AI ambitions, and for some, surviving may be their target future state for many years to come.

In this chapter, we explain these pathways, providing actionable strategies for executives to implement. We also discuss the importance of AI investment selection, including evaluating projects based on their full impact considerations and developing a balanced AI portfolio that aligns with long-term sustainable goals. By following this strategy, corporate executives can align their responsible AI practices with their corporate strategy, enabling their organizations to not only survive but to thrive in an AI-enabled future.

Objectives

Upon completing this chapter, you will be able to:

- Explain the necessity of immediate action in AI governance
- Identify strategic actions to balance short-term and long-term AI impacts
- Understand the risks of delaying responsible AI implementation
- Recognize leadership's role in steering AI's future.

Thriving organizations

Unilever, a global manufacturer and distributor of 400+ food, personal hygiene, and cleaning products, has been an early adopter of robotics, digital twins, and AI. In 2018, Unilever participated in the

United Kingdom's PlasticArmPit project[2] to develop machine learning algorithms capable of sniffing your armpit and telling you whether you have body odor. This may seem like a strange use case, but the innovative pairing of AI and odor sensors has since been used to monitor food freshness and detect illness based on body perspiration.[3] Jump ahead five years, and Unilever has doubled down on its investment in AI, opening its first global AI lab, Horizon3, in Toronto, Canada. Already deploying AI in 400+ applications, from smart ice cream refrigerators to the use of GenAI to update product descriptions on its retail website, Unilever plans to embed AI across its full value chain.[4]

In March 2025, Unilever's CEO, Esi Eggleston-Bracey, took the stage at the NVIDIA GTC 2025 conference to showcase the company's use of digital twins, AI, and NVIDIA's 3D Omniverse to create accurate replicas of Unilever's full product database. "Unilever's Digital twin strategy is delivering product imagery two times faster and 50% cheaper, leading to 100% brand consistency. But it's also unlocking creative possibilities. By removing the technical barriers and physical constraints of traditional production, anything becomes possible."[5]

Unilever is an example of an organization that has adopted a thriving mindset in leveraging AI. Steve McCrystal, Unilever's Chief Enterprise Technology Officer, commented in a February 2025 article that "AI has been part of our ecosystem for more than a decade."[6] By the end of 2024, Unilever had trained 24,000 employees on the use of AI and used AI to transform their supply chains, achieving significant cost savings, and seamlessly connecting consumer demand, product development, planning, suppliers, logistics, and manufacturing.[7]

Pfizer, a global pharmaceutical company, is also making big bets in AI. In March 2025, Pfizer announced a $2 billion investment in an AI platform for antibiotic discovery to combat drug-resistant superbugs. The goal is for AI to automate the laboratory, reducing research timelines, enhancing compound screening accuracy, and streamlining manufacturing workflows.[8]

In their 2024 Impact Report, Pfizer included a section on their responsible use of AI[9] and a link to their AI policy position statement.[10] Pfizer held their first AI Festival in 2024, where employees, enterprise-wide, "learned how to use AI in their work, as well as how to engage responsibly with AI, the role of AI in health equity, and how AI can help transform the pharmaceutical industry for patients and global health."[11]

For both Unilever and Pfizer, embedding responsible AI into their development and use of AI is core to their ability to build and maintain stakeholder trust. In 2019, Unilever created an AI assurance process.

> to evaluate systems for ethical and performance-related risks to ensure alignment with the company's responsible principles... In addition to the assurance program, a cross-functional team at Unilever assesses the risks of potential use cases with new AI systems. Training has also gone a long way in underlining the importance of responsible AI use.[12]

In the February 2025 article, Steve McCrystal spoke of his pride in Unilever's Responsible AI framework and attributed it to being "a critical part of shaping Unilever's AI strategy, helping us to manage risks and to strategically focus the way that we use it."[13]

Pfizer has created a cross-functional AI Council to oversee their AI risk management program. They leverage AI principles, corporate policy, training, risk assessment, and enterprise controls to ensure that they use AI ethically and responsibly.[14] Dennis Hancock, Pfizer's Head of Digital Health, Medicines, and AI, commented on their website that "Artificial intelligence can unlock huge opportunities for the industry and for patients...But we must be vigilant about applying human oversight, and we must keep ethics, responsibility, and patient focus front and center."[15]

Drawing on the responsible AI practices demonstrated by Unilever, Pfizer, and other thriving organizations, we have provided a list of recommended steps that organizations can take. We first start with recommendations for organizations that are just starting on their AI journey or are interested in the bare minimum of regulatory and legal compliance. We then provide incremental actions for organizations wanting to step up their game and create more sustained, responsible AI practices. Lastly, we highlight leading responsible AI practices for organizations that want to emulate Unilever and Pfizer's success in accelerating AI innovation and embedding responsible AI into their AI program.

Surviving: bare minimum actions

In the face of rapid AI advancements, the surviving path focuses on the minimum responsible AI actions needed to remain compliant and operational. This approach is about addressing immediate needs without falling behind. Given the nascent maturity of responsible AI practices, many organizations are still in the early stages of integrating responsible AI considerations and governance frameworks into their AI strategies.

The cost and effort associated with following the surviving path are relatively low, making it suitable for organizations with limited resources or those just beginning their AI journey. This approach is particularly beneficial for organizations with a strategy focused on risk mitigation and regulatory compliance, rather than accelerated innovation and long-term growth. By taking these essential steps, organizations can lay a foundational layer of responsible AI practices that allow them to meet immediate regulatory requirements and mitigate short-term risks, while preparing for more advanced stages of AI integration in the future.

Table 16.1 outlines key **Surviving** actions, their rationale, and recommendations on accountability within the executive leadership team at this level.

By taking these actions, an organization will be compliant with regulations and mitigate immediate risks. This approach will help maintain operational stability and prevent potential legal and reputational issues. This pathway is a starting point for most organizations, particularly those that are investing in low-risk AI systems that are primarily used by employees, do not support critical functions, and have limited access to confidential information. AI is subject to high human oversight and has very little autonomy.

While the surviving path addresses immediate needs and supports low-risk experimentation, it is not a sustainable long-term strategy. The organization may struggle to remain competitive, as others leverage AI to increase productivity, reduce costs, and deliver more personalized services to customers. Corporate leaders must recognize the limitations of this approach and strategically time their transition to a higher path as their investments in AI grow.

While it is early days to provide a list of failed companies due to too little or too late investments in AI, there are many cautionary tales of established companies going out of business due to a failure to innovate. Blockbuster stayed committed to its profitable rental stores for too long and missed the opportunity to transition into online streaming services. Nokia and BlackBerry pioneered many early innovations in mobile phones – Nokia in hardware design and

Table 16.1 Surviving – actions, rationale, and accountable party

Action	*Rationale*	*Recommended accountable party*
Develop and implement fundamental AI ethics guidelines	Establishing basic ethical standards to ensure that AI systems are developed and deployed responsibly, minimizing risks and aligning with regulatory requirements.	Chief Ethics Officer (or equivalent role)
Provide foundational AI training for key employees	Equipping employees with a basic understanding of AI technologies and ethical considerations will not only enhance decision-making and the effective implementation of AI projects but also foster a culture of innovation and responsibility.	Chief Human Resources Officer (CHRO)
Establish minimal AI governance frameworks	Implementing basic governance frameworks not only ensures that AI projects are effectively monitored and controlled but also promotes accountability and transparency, fostering stakeholder trust and ensuring compliance with regulations.	Chief Compliance Officer (CCO) or Chief Operating Officer (COO)
Implement essential data privacy and security policies	Protecting data privacy and security is critical to maintaining stakeholder trust and preventing data breaches that could have severe legal and reputational consequences.	Chief Information Security Officer (CISO) or Chief Data Officer (CDO)
Implement basic controls to ensure data integrity and proper AI functioning	Ensuring data integrity and proper AI functioning is an operational imperative to maintaining the accuracy and reliability of AI systems, which in turn supports decision-making and operational stability.	Chief Financial Officer (CFO) or Chief Technology Officer (CTO)
Conduct governance audits of AI systems	Regular governance audits help identify and address potential issues in AI systems, ensuring ongoing compliance and responsible AI practices.	Chief Audit Executive (CAE)

multimedia, and BlackBerry in secure mobile communications and email – but both were ultimately overtaken by the shift to integrated touchscreen smartphones with rich app ecosystems. While they recognized these trends, slow software innovation and organizational inertia meant they could not execute fast enough to match the products and experiences offered by competitors.[16,17] MySpace, the most popular social networking service in 2008, lost traffic to competitors that innovated faster to provide enhanced and user-friendly services.[18]

While some companies could take a "wait and see" approach to using AI, Katherine Kostereva, CEO of Creatio, disagrees. In a June 2025 Fast Company article, she predicted that she is in "the last generation of CEOs to lead fully human workforces."[19] She went on to say,

> The implications for leadership are profound. AI agents are not simply software add-ons; they are redefining how we design our business processes and collaborate on our daily work. They're collaborators in the broadest sense, and like any collaborator, they benefit from thoughtful integration and clear frameworks.[20]

Stability: doing enough

We are at the point in AI's evolution that the risks of using the technology must be compared to the risks of not using it. The stability strategy represents a state of doing enough to stay competitive and efficient in an AI-driven world. This approach builds on the foundational actions taken in the surviving path, enhancing responsible AI practices, investing in continuous learning and development, strengthening governance frameworks, and fostering cross-functional collaboration.

For organizations that have already established basic responsible AI practices, this level provides a natural progression. However, there are significant benefits to leapfrogging over the surviving path directly to this strategy, including mitigating failures, building consumer trust, gaining a competitive advantage, and reducing costs.

Organizations should aim to move beyond the surviving path as quickly as possible to capitalize on the opportunities that AI presents. One benefit of starting at this level is that organizations can mitigate the risk of security breaches and operational failures by implementing stronger governance and oversight mechanisms. Building consumer trust becomes easier as enhanced responsible AI practices and transparency foster confidence among stakeholders. Additionally, organizations can gain a competitive advantage by staying ahead of regulatory changes and industry standards, positioning themselves as leaders in responsible AI. Moreover, investing in continuous learning and development can lead to reduced costs in the long run, as a more skilled workforce drives innovation and efficiency.

The **Stability** pathway is summarized in Table 16.2, including key actions, rationale, and recommended accountability within the executive leadership team.

By taking these actions, the organization will achieve a higher level of stability and readiness, allowing it to capitalize on AI's benefits while mitigating associated risks. This approach will help build consumer trust, gain a competitive advantage, and reduce costs through more efficient and effective AI practices. The organization will be better positioned to respond to regulatory changes and ethical challenges, enhancing its reputation and stakeholder confidence.

The stability path represents a balanced approach to responsible AI, offering both immediate and long-term benefits. By enhancing responsible AI practices, investing in continuous learning, strengthening governance, and fostering collaboration, organizations can achieve a higher level of stability and readiness. However, there are trade-offs to consider. While this approach requires a greater initial investment over the surviving pathway, the benefits of mitigating failures, building consumer trust, gaining a competitive advantage, and reducing costs make it a worthwhile strategy for organizations committed to responsible AI development.

In a 2025 survey, EY found that despite nearly three-quarters of companies having integrated AI into their organization, only a third have responsible AI controls in place. The survey also revealed a substantial gap in the level of trust in AI across business leaders and their clients. While 63% of C-suite executives believe they are well aligned with consumers on their perceptions and use of AI,[21] in a separate EY AI Sentiment Index Study, consumers were found to be twice as worried.[22] For organizations to get full returns on their AI investments, they need to continue building trust and confidence in their use of AI to drive user acceptance and adoption.

Table 16.2 Stability – actions, rationale, and accountable party

Action	*Rationale*	*Recommended accountable party*
Expand AI ethics guidelines to cover more scenarios	Enhancing ethical practices ensures that AI systems are developed and deployed with a broader range of ethical considerations, reducing the risk of unintended consequences and fostering trust among stakeholders.	Chief Ethics Officer (or equivalent role)
Upskill employees on AI technologies	Continuous learning and development programs equip employees with advanced AI skills and knowledge, enabling them to contribute more effectively to AI projects and drive innovation.	Chief Human Resources Officer (CHRO)
Implement continuous monitoring of AI	Strengthening governance frameworks ensures that AI projects are monitored for performance issues and controlled more effectively, reducing the risk of breaches and enhancing compliance with evolving regulations.	Chief Compliance Officer (CCO) or Chief Technology Officer (CTO)
Facilitate collaboration between AI, legal, compliance, and other departments	Cross-functional collaboration ensures that AI projects benefit from diverse perspectives and expertise, leading to more robust and responsible AI solutions.	Chief Operating Officer (COO)

(*Continued*)

Table 16.2 (Continued)

Action	*Rationale*	*Recommended accountable party*
Implement full cost accounting for AI investments	Full cost accounting ensures that all costs and benefits, including hidden and long-term impacts, are considered in AI investment decisions. This approach helps in selecting AI use cases that offer the highest ROI while aligning with ethical and strategic goals.	Chief Financial Officer (CFO)
Promote a culture of innovation and idea generation	Fostering a culture of innovation where idea generation is facilitated, and great ideas are sponsored with funding and partner support.	Chief Executive Officer (CEO)

Thriving: proactive pursuit of an AI-optimized future

The thriving path represents the pinnacle of responsible AI integration, where proactive actions are taken toward achieving the 2035 moonshot goals. This approach goes beyond staying competitive and efficient; it involves leading in responsible AI development, investing in strategic AI initiatives, championing workforce transformation, promoting sustainable AI development, and fostering a balanced culture of AI innovation and safety.

For organizations that have established responsible AI practices, this level provides a natural progression. By advancing to this stage, organizations can establish a forward-thinking framework for AI development, ensuring that they are not only compliant and competitive but also viewed as pioneers in sustainable AI practices. The benefits of targeting this level are substantial. It allows organizations to drive innovation and long-term growth by investing in cutting-edge AI technologies and solutions. Building consumer trust is easier as the organization is rewarded for demonstrating responsible and sustainable AI practices. Additionally, organizations can attract top talent and gain a significant competitive advantage by fostering a culture of continuous improvement and innovation.

Table 16.3 summarizes the **Thriving** actions, rationale, and recommendations on accountability within the executive leadership team.

Table 16.3 Thriving – actions, rationale, and accountable party

Action	*Rationale*	*Recommended accountable party*
Establish dedicated research centers focused on responsible AI and publish findings to influence global standards	Leading in responsible AI research ensures that the organization not only complies with regulations but also drives the global conversation on responsible AI practices, setting new benchmarks for the industry.	Chief AI Officer (or equivalent role)
Initiate and fund large-scale AI projects that address critical global issues, such as poverty, education, and healthcare	Investing in transformative AI initiatives that tackle global challenges positions the organization as a leader in social responsibility and drives long-term positive impact.	The Chief Innovation Officer (CIO), or Chief Technology Officer (CTO)
Develop and nurture AI-driven ecosystems that include startups, academic institutions, and industry partners to foster innovation and collaboration	Building AI-driven ecosystems promotes a collaborative approach to innovation, leveraging diverse expertise and resources to drive groundbreaking AI solutions.	Chief Strategy Officer (CSO)
Conduct responsible AI and sustainability audits across all AI projects and operations, with public reporting of results	Responsible AI and sustainability audits enhance accountability and transparency while identifying potential ethical risks and sustainability challenges, fostering stakeholder trust.	Chief Audit Executive (CAE)

(*Continued*)

Table 16.3 (Continued)

Action	*Rationale*	*Recommended accountable party*
Form AI governance councils that include diverse stakeholders, such as customers, ethicists, technologists, policymakers, union reps, and community representatives, to guide AI strategy/ decision-making	Inclusive governance councils ensure that AI strategies are informed by a wide range of perspectives, promoting ethical and socially responsible AI development. Benchmarking provides insights into best practices, enabling organizations to refine their approaches and remain competitive.	Chief Executive Officer (CEO)
Create AI factories and design studios that encourage employees to ideate and create new AI innovations	Create cross-departmental collaborations with external AI ecosystem partners to create disruptive and transformative ideas. Foster a culture of trust and innovation.	Chief AI Officer (or equivalent role)

By taking these bold and visionary actions, organizations can be global leaders in responsible AI, driving innovation and long-term growth. They can follow the paths of organizations like Unilever and Pfizer to build consumer trust, gain significant competitive advantage, and attract top talent. By leapfrogging to this level, organizations can create a more adaptable workforce, driving continuous improvement and responsible AI outcomes. However, there are trade-offs to consider.

The thriving path requires continual investments in responsible AI governance and controls. If these initiatives are not integrated into the AI development lifecycle and highly automated, they could result in delays, user frustration, and potentially failure. In an August 2024 RAND research report, it was reported that "more than 80 percent of AI projects fail - twice the rate of failure for information technology projects that do not involve AI."[23] RAND went on to list the top five root causes for AI failures

1 The problem to be solved by AI was misunderstood
2 Organizations focused more on using the latest technology than on solving the intended user's problems

3 The problem was too difficult to solve with the available technology
4 The lack of adequate data for training AI models
5 The organization does not have sufficient infrastructure.[24]

These root causes highlight the importance of embedding AI into both strategic and operational initiatives in order for it to deliver on its return on investment.

Why corporate executives must lead with corporate purpose

As we stand on the precipice of our AI future, the question of "Why me?" is not just a matter of personal reflection but a call to action for corporate executives to be in the driving seat of its advancement. AI is not just another technological advancement; it is challenging and redefining business strategy, customer engagement, and operational efficiency. According to Korn Ferry, over 82% of CEOs believe that AI will have an extreme to significant impact on their business.[25]

While regulators and governments have an important role in establishing ethical and legal frameworks for AI, corporations need to take the lead.

The most impactful actions will come from corporate leadership. Here's why.

1 *Proximity to innovation:* Corporate executives are at the forefront of technological innovation. They have direct access to the latest advancements in AI and influence how these technologies are developed and deployed. By embedding responsible AI practices into their AI strategies, executives can ensure that their organizations lead by example, setting industry standards for others to follow.
2 *Impact on society:* Corporations wield significant influence over the economy, job market, and societal norms; the decisions made by corporate leaders today will have far-reaching implications for the future of work, privacy, and social equity. By taking a proactive stance on responsible AI, executives can help mitigate risks and ensure that AI technologies are used to enhance human potential and contribute to the greater good.
3 *Agility and responsiveness:* Unlike regulatory bodies, which can be slow to adapt to rapid technological changes, corporations can respond quickly to new developments. This agility allows corporate leaders to implement responsible AI guidelines, governance

frameworks, and risk management practices in real-time, addressing potential issues before they escalate.

4 *Stakeholder trust:* In an era where trust is at an all-time low, corporate leaders have the opportunity to build and maintain trust with their employees, customers, investors, and the broader community. The Edelman Trust Barometer found that businesses are more trusted than governments. Citizens "expect businesses to provide well-paying jobs, invest in reskilling employees, and uphold civility in the workplace."[26]
5 *Long-term vision:* Corporate executives are tasked with steering their organization toward sustainable growth and long-term success; this requires a forward-thinking approach that balances immediate business objectives with the broader impact on society. By championing responsible AI, executives can ensure that their organization is not only profitable but also contributes positively to the world.
6 *Moral responsibility:* Corporate leaders have the power not only to shape the future but also to inspire and lead their organizations on a moonshot quest; they can drive innovation and implement agile strategies that respond swiftly to emerging technologies and societal needs. Their direct engagement with customers and stakeholders allows them to understand market demands and ethical considerations more intimately, enabling them to create AI solutions that prioritize human welfare and societal benefit.
7 *Consumer-led decision making stresses the importance of human-centric design in AI:* Consumers are increasingly demanding products and services that align with their values, including ethical considerations and social responsibility. A dystopian future, characterized by uneducated and unhealthy workforces, depression, and low birth rates, would severely undermine the long-term viability of corporations; with a diminished consumer base and a demoralized workforce, the very foundation of business sustainability would be at risk. By prioritizing human-centric design and responsible AI, corporate leaders can ensure that their organization remains relevant and resilient, fostering a healthy, educated, and engaged society that supports sustainable business growth.

The mantle of leadership as we shape our AI future rests with corporate executives. Their proximity to innovation, impact on society, ability to build trust, long-term vision, and moral responsibility uniquely position them to guide the responsible development and deployment of AI. By embracing this responsibility, corporate leaders can shape a future where we achieve both pro-innovation and pro-safety ambitions.

Conclusion

Corporate executives play a critical role in shaping the AI future of their organization and society at large. The decisions and actions taken today will influence whether we steer toward a dystopian or utopian future. By understanding the necessity of immediate action in AI governance, identifying strategic actions to balance both short-term and long-term impacts, and recognizing the risks of delaying responsible AI implementation, leaders can make informed choices that shape a positive trajectory for AI's development.

The roadmap options span from surviving to thriving, providing a structured approach for navigating the complexities of AI integration. Whether your organization is taking the bare minimum actions to survive, doing just enough to stay the course, or advancing toward a thriving future, the intent behind each path is crucial. Leaders must not only focus on compliance and risk mitigation. They must also foster a culture of continuous improvement, innovation, and ethical responsibility.

Leadership in the age of AI demands vision and foresight. It is about more than technological advancements. It is about ensuring that there is a thoughtful intention in setting AI's objectives. By investing in strategic AI initiatives, championing workforce transformation, and promoting sustainable development, executives can mitigate risks and harness AI's potential for positive impact.

Ultimately, the responsibility lies with today's leaders to lay the groundwork for AI's future. The 2035 AI Utopia vision and moonshot goals serve as a compelling future that can inspire collective action. By aligning diverse teams around a shared vision, leaders can foster a sense of ownership and urgency, motivating individuals to contribute their unique skills and perspectives toward AI's transformative possibilities. This collaborative spirit not only strengthens organizational culture but also cultivates a unified commitment to leveraging AI for the greater good. Executives can put their organization in a position to not only survive but thrive.

Do not close this book and put it on the shelf. Instead, use it as a blueprint for your journey toward responsible AI. Identify recommendations relevant to your organization, create a priority list of actions, and assign accountability for each action to a member of your leadership team.

This is not a theoretical exercise; it is a call to action. Take the strategies and actions outlined and translate them into committed steps that drive meaningful change. As Aristotle so aptly said, "You will never do anything in this world without courage. It is the greatest quality of the mind next to honor."[27]

The future is in your hands – act now, lead with purpose, and make a lasting impact.

Key leadership questions to consider:

1. How are you personally upgrading your knowledge and helping others in your organization build their AI literacy muscle?
2. How are you prioritizing immediate and long-term AI investments to align with your strategic goals and ethical considerations?
3. Are your AI initiatives designed to balance short-term gains with sustainable, long-term societal impact?
4. Do you have a clear roadmap for AI governance that addresses both current needs and future challenges?
5. Which path – surviving, stability, or thriving – best aligns with your organizational vision and leadership capabilities?

Notes

1. Bostrom, N. (2014). *Superintelligence: Paths, dangers, strategies*. Oxford: Oxford University Press.
2. Moore, S. (2018, November 13). Arm leads project to develop an armpit-sniffing plastic AI chip. *IEEE Spectrum*. https://spectrum.ieee.org/flexible-plastic-armpit-sniffer-chips-will-be-powered-by-machine-learning.
3. Marr, B. (2018, December 14). The amazing ways how Unilever uses artificial intelligence to recruit & train thousands of employees. *Forbes*. https://www.forbes.com/sites/bernardmarr/2018/12/14/the-amazing-ways-how-unilever-uses-artificial-intelligence-to-recruit-train-thousands-of-employees/.
4. Unilever launches first global AI lab in Toronto. (2023, November 16). *Food in Canada*. https://www.foodincanada.com/technology/unilever-launches-first-global-ai-lab-in-toronto-156162/.
5. Cleaver, A. (2025, March). Collective & Unilever revolutionise content production with AI-enabled digital twins. *Collective World*.

Retrieved June 19, 2025, from https://www.collectiveworld.com/collective-unilever-ai-digital-twins-marketing-gtc-2025/.

6 McCrystal, S. (2025, February 3). How digital transformation drives our operational excellence. *Unilever*. https://www.unilever.com/news/news-search/2025/how-unilevers-digital-transformation-is-driving-operational-excellence/.

7 McCrystal, S. (2025, February 3). How digital transformation drives our operational excellence. *Unilever*. https://www.unilever.com/news/news-search/2025/how-unilevers-digital-transformation-is-driving-operational-excellence/.

8 Pfizer's $2B AI-powered antibiotics to combat superbugs. (2025, March 25). *The Silicon Review*. https://thesiliconreview.com/2025/03/pfizer-ai-antibiotic-discovery.

9 Pfizer. (2024). *Pfizer impact report 2024*. Retrieved June 2, 2025, from https://cdn.pfizer.com/pfizercom/Pfizer_2024_Impact_Report_02JUN2025.pdf.

10 Pfizer. (2023, December 11). *AI policy position*. Pfizer. https://cdn.pfizer.com/pfizercom/AI_Policy_Position_12112023.pdf.

11 Pfizer. (2024). *Pfizer impact report 2024*. Retrieved June 2, 2025, from https://cdn.pfizer.com/pfizercom/Pfizer_2024_Impact_Report_02JUN2025.pdf.

12 Wilkinson, L. (2024, September 23). CIO priorities. *CIO Dive*. https://www.ciodive.com/trendline/cio-priorities/419/?utm_source=CIO&utm_medium=LyticsSlideout&utm_campaign=Sparks.

13 McCrystal, S. (2025, February 3). How digital transformation drives our operational excellence. *Unilever*. https://www.unilever.com/news/news-search/2025/how-unilevers-digital-transformation-is-driving-operational-excellence/.

14 Pfizer. (2024). *Pfizer impact report 2024*. Retrieved June 2, 2025, from https://cdn.pfizer.com/pfizercom/Pfizer_2024_Impact_Report_02JUN2025.pdf.

15 Pfizer. (n.d.). *Three principles of AI responsibility in healthcare are critical*. Retrieved June 20, 2025, from https://www.pfizer.com/news/articles/three_principles_of_responsibility_for_artificial_intelligence_ai_in_healthcare.

16 de Naoum, K. (2025, April 28). *20 companies that failed to adapt to disruption and paid the ultimate price*. ThomasNet. https://www.thomasnet.com/insights/9-companies-that-failed-to-adapt-to-disruption-and-paid-the-ultimate-price/?msockid=2886697ce7476c7316ed7ccfe6fe6dbf.

17 Elop, S. (2015, June 18). *Nokia CEO Stephen Elop's 'burning platforms' memo*. *The Sydney Morning Herald*. https://www.smh.com.au/technology/full-text-nokia-ceo-stephen-elops-burning-platforms-memo-20150618-ghqwr0.html.

18 de Naoum, K. (2025, April 28). *20 companies that failed to adapt to disruption and paid the ultimate price*. ThomasNet. https://www.thomasnet.com/insights/9-companies-that-failed-to-adapt-to-disruption-and-paid-the-ultimate-price/?msockid=2886697ce7476c7316ed7ccfe6fe6dbf.

19 Kostereva, K. (2025, June 11). How CEOs can lead in the age of AI agents. *Fast Company*. https://www.fastcompany.com/91341830/how-ceos-can-lead-in-the-age-of-ai-agents-ceos-leadership-ai.

20 Kostereva, K. (2025, June 11). How CEOs can lead in the age of AI agents. *Fast Company*. https://www.fastcompany.com/91341830/how-ceos-can-lead-in-the-age-of-ai-agents-ceos-leadership-ai.

21 Minuskin, E. (2025, June 4). *AI adoption outpaces governance as risk awareness among the C-suite remains low. EY*. https://www.ey.com/en_gl/newsroom/2025/06/ey-survey-ai-adoption-outpaces-governance-as-risk-awareness-among-the-c-suite-remains-low.

22 Sanz Saiz, B., Cosgrove, A., & Diasio, D. (2025, April 9). *Transform human potential in an AI world. EY*. Retrieved July 10, 2025, from https://www.ey.com/en_gl/insights/ai/how-a-license-to-lead-can-transform-human-potential-in-an-ai-world.

23 Ryseff, J., De Bruhl, B. F., & Newberry, S. J. (2024, August 13). *The root causes of failure for artificial intelligence projects and how they can succeed: Avoiding the anti-patterns of AI*. RAND Corporation. https://www.rand.org/pubs/research_reports/RRA2680-1.html.

24 Ryseff, J., De Bruhl, B. F., & Newberry, S. J. (2024, August 13). *The root causes of failure for artificial intelligence projects and how they can succeed: Avoiding the anti-patterns of AI*. RAND Corporation. https://www.rand.org/pubs/research_reports/RRA2680-1.html.

25 Laouchez, J. M. (2023, July 4). *Human still wanted in the future of work in an AI-driven world: Research report*. Korn Ferry. https://www.kornferry.com/institute/humans-still-wanted-the-future-of-work-in-an-ai-driven-world.

26 Russell, J. (2025, March 5). *Canadians losing trust in institutions, Edelman Trust Barometer finds*. Strategy Online. https://strategyonline.ca/2025/03/05/2025-edelman-trust-barometer-launch/.

27 Aristotle Quote. (n.d.). *[Quote about Aristotle]*. BrainyQuote. Retrieved June 7, 2025, from https://www.brainyquote.com/quotes/aristotle_117889.

Appendix

The Appendix section has three toolkits to support your artificial intelligence (AI) journey. We hope you find each of these AI governance tools helpful in maturing and sustaining your AI program, balancing innovation and safety.

Table A1.0 provides a concise summary of the leadership questions that were discussed in each of the chapter. This summary provides a useful set of questions to evaluate the completeness and maturity of your organization's AI strategy and governance mechanisms.

Table A1.1 provides a useful self-evaluation toolkit for organizations to assess the maturity of their AI Model Risk Controls. The maturity scale ranges from 1 to 5:

1 = Not in place
2 = In place for specific groups
3 = In place and standardized enterprise-wide
4 = KPIs are in place to measure AI performance
5 = Highly automated and benchmarked

Benchmarked means that you have at a minimum, an annual exercise to benchmark the completeness and sufficiency of your control against an external criterion (regulation or voluntary standard) or it is evaluated by an independent third party.

Table A1.2 outlines quality control questions associated with each stage of the AI development lifecycle. These questions are designed to ensure that AI models are developed with a focus on quality, reliability, and ethical considerations. By addressing these critical inquiries at each phase – from data collection and preprocessing to model training, evaluation, and deployment – organizations can enhance the integrity of their AI systems and ensure they meet both technical and ethical standards.

Table A1.0 Book chapter – AI leadership review questions

Chapter	*Title*	*Key leadership questions*
Section I – The courage needed for balanced AI		
1	Redefining our relationship with machines	1 What can we learn from our past business transformations and innovations? 2 How is your organization defining AI? 3 How will AI impact your overall business strategy and operational capabilities? 4 How can AI enhance your business processes and customer experiences? 5 How will AI impact your workforce and talent needs? 6 What strategies ensure your AI adoption remains competitive?
2	Establishing responsible AI from day one	1 In your AI projects, have you integrated AI principles into your complete AI lifecycle, particularly during the problem identification and design stages? 2 Is accountability and responsibility clearly defined for upholding the achievement of your AI principles? 3 How are diverse perspectives incorporated in your AI projects to broaden ethical and societal considerations?
3	Demystifying the magic of AI	1 Is your AI investment strategy fully leveraging the range of available AI technologies and models? 2 Do you have the right AI talent and skills to execute your AI investment strategy? 3 Does your AI design process involve thorough comparison and optimal selection of AI models and algorithms? 4 Is your team equipped with enough knowledge of AI's technical aspects to make informed strategic decisions?
4	Iterating AI from concept to reality	1 How is your organization aligning the AI Development Lifecycle with your strategic goals and ethical requirements?

(*Continued*)

Table A1.0 (Continued)

Chapter	*Title*	*Key leadership questions*
		2 Is there a balanced investment in both AI functionalities and the maturation of the AI Development Lifecycle? 3 How are responsible AI considerations being integrated into each stage of your AI Development Lifecycle? 4 How do you ensure third-party vendors deliver AI systems that meet your organization's corporate policies and regulatory requirements?
5	AI is more than just models	1 Have you built into your AI design all the different components it will need to operate? 2 Is your AI infrastructure future-proof in that it can interoperate with new IoT devices, data sources, and computer processors as they emerge? 3 What factors are key in deciding between open-source, third-party, or in-house solutions for your AI applications? 4 How are you leveraging technological advances and what is the roadmap to get there from your current infrastructure?
6	Battling AI breaches and adversarial attacks	1 Are your cybersecurity strategies incorporating AI to enhance your threat detection, response, and predictive capabilities? 2 Do your AI systems have safeguards against adversarial attacks, deepfakes, and other risks posed by AI? 3 Have you implemented Privacy by Design principles and integrated security considerations into all phases of your AI lifecycle? 4 Are you conducting regular integrity checks on your AI systems, especially those overseeing other AI models, to ensure their resistance to manipulation? 5 Have you done an external third-party AI cybersecurity risk review of all of our AI practices?

(*Continued*)

Table A1.0 (Continued)

Chapter	*Title*	*Key leadership questions*
Section II – Roadmap to achieving responsible AI		
7	The tug-of-war between AI innovation and safety	1 How is your organization adapting to the global AI regulatory landscape? 2 How does your organization track public policy and regulatory developments? 3 What compliance strategies are in place for your state and local AI regulations? 4 How will your organization align industry-specific AI guidelines with broader regulations? 5 How is your AI strategy integrating voluntary guidelines for risk management and governance?
8	Aligning corporate profit and purpose	1 How effectively does your AI policy align with your organization's values, stakeholder expectations and strategic objectives? 2 How complete is your inventory of AI assets? 3 How well-defined and understood are the roles and responsibilities for AI governance? 4 How robust are your efforts in building both technical and ethical AI capabilities?
9	Targeting the risks that truly matter	1 Have you embedded risk management throughout your AI project lifecycle? 2 Have you established clear accountability for AI risk management decisions? 3 What measures are in place to foster and reinforce an AI risk-aware culture? 4 Do you have comprehensive AI incidents and crisis management strategies?
10	Cost-efficient controls with maximum impact	1 Do you understand the impact and likelihood of AI system's risks? 2 Are you leveraging a cost-benefit analysis in the selection of your controls?

(*Continued*)

Table A1.0 (Continued)

Chapter	*Title*	*Key leadership questions*
		3 Is there a clear understanding of the governance and control responsibilities among developers, deployers, and users of your AI systems? 4 Is your AI control framework up-to-date for new AI developments, regulatory changes, and feedback from system performance evaluations?
11	Maintaining stakeholder trust and confidence	1 How are you leveraging assurance to build trust and confidence in your AI governance framework? 2 How are you ensuring that your model documentation and transparency reports accurately reflect the performance and compliance of your AI systems? 3 How are you building the capabilities in your risk and control functions so that they can act as effective challengers of your AI governance practices and AI model design? 4 As regulatory landscapes evolve, how are you preparing your AI systems for potential third-party assurance requirements?
12	The art of data-driven AI monitoring	1 Do you have a comprehensive metrics toolkit that covers the diversity of your AI use cases and impacts, and is leveraged throughout the full AI development lifecycle? 2 Do you have the right MLOps environment to conduct your AI model measurements? 3 Are you participating in formal measurement peer or benchmarking groups to measure your AI performance? 4 Do you have third-party reviewers on your AI measurement systems in an annual review process?

(*Continued*)

Table A1.0 (Continued)

Chapter	*Title*	*Key leadership questions*
13	Future-proofing AI with scenario planning	1 How do your AI scenario planning efforts address both short-term gains and long-term sustainability? 2 Are diverse stakeholder perspectives incorporated into your AI scenario planning process? 3 What mechanisms are in place to adapt AI strategies based on evolving scenarios? 4 How do you evaluate the ethical implications of each AI scenario against your business risks?
Section III – Utopia or dystopia? The future of AI		
14	Building utopia	1 Does your corporate strategy clearly position responsible AI in your Corporate Purpose? 2 How is your organization balancing AI to foster innovation and ensure safe sustainable practices? 3 How are you conducting AI best practices benchmarking to learn rapidly from your customers, competitors or other key ecosystem stakeholders? 4 Are you collaborating with partners to integrate AI across your customer interactions and operations? 5 How are you preparing your workforce to adapt to the evolving demands of an AI-driven economy, while promoting continuous learning and development?
15	Avoiding dystopia	1 How is your organization actively addressing the potential risks of AI technologies to prevent the emergence of a dystopian society? 2 In what ways are you ensuring that AI systems in your organization promote transparency and accountability to build trust with stakeholders? 3 What strategies are you implementing to safeguard against the misuse of AI, particularly in areas such as surveillance, deepfakes, and cybercrime?

(*Continued*)

Table A1.0 (Continued)

Chapter	*Title*	*Key leadership questions*
		4 How are you fostering a culture of innovation that prioritizes ethical considerations and human-centric design in the development of all of your AI technologies?
16	Leading with a thriving mindset	1 How are you personally upgrading your knowledge and helping others in your organization build their AI literacy muscle? 2 How are you prioritizing immediate and long-term AI investments to align with your strategic goals and ethical considerations? 3 Are your AI initiatives designed to balance short-term gains with sustainable, long-term societal impact? 4 Do you have a clear roadmap for AI governance that addresses both current needs and future challenges? 5 Which path – Surviving, Stability, or Thriving – best aligns with your organizational vision and leadership capabilities?

Table A1.1 AI governance controls – maturity evaluation toolkit

Control type	*Definition*	*Maturity scale*
Enterprise-wide AI governance controls		
Policies	An AI policy is a set of guidelines an organization uses to govern the development, deployment, and usage of AI systems. It aims to ensure responsible, ethical, and compliant AI practices, align with legal and regulatory requirements, and organizational values. These policies include areas like data privacy, security, transparency, accountability, data bias, and fairness.	1 2 3 4 5

(Continued)

Table A1.1 (Continued)

Control type	*Definition*	*Maturity scale*
AI strategy	An AI strategy is a plan that outlines how an organization will leverage AI to achieve business goals and enhance efficiency. It includes identifying key use cases, investing in infrastructure, and developing skills for successful implementation.	1 2 3 4 5
Accountability	Accountability refers to the attribute of being responsible for the actions and decisions of AI, as well as the impact AI systems have on individuals and society. Having clarity on the AI model originators and operators is crucial.	1 2 3 4 5
Training and education	Evidence of investments in workforce digital literacy and building AI skills is important to ensure resiliency during change, supporting an organization's cultural evolution.	1 2 3 4 5
AI Investment Committee	An AI Investment Committee focuses on evaluating both the technical and financial viability of AI projects, assessing whether they align with organizational goals. It also considers ethical and responsible implications, ensuring that investments are made in a manner that upholds integrity and societal values.	1 2 3 4 5
AI program KPI	KPIs measure the overall success and impact of AI initiatives across the organization. These metrics encompass various dimensions, including project completion rates, ROI, user adoption, and alignment with strategic goals, providing a comprehensive view of the program's effectiveness and value.	1 2 3 4 5
AI system governance controls		
Risk assessment	An AI risk assessment identifies, analyzes, and mitigates potential risks associated with the development, deployment, and use of AI systems. It involves evaluating various aspects	1 2 3 4 5

(*Continued*)

Table A1.1 (Continued)

Control type	*Definition*	*Maturity scale*
	of an AI system, including data, algorithms, decision-making, and potential impacts on individuals, communities, and society. The goal is to ensure that AI systems are used responsibly minimizing harm and maximizing benefits.	
Incremental testing	Incremental testing is an approach used to test individual software components or modules of an AI system separately and then integrate them gradually. It involves testing each part of the system incrementally as new functionalities or components are added.	1 2 3 4 5
Inventory management	AI inventory management is the practice of documenting all the AI models, system cards, and having controls on data source history, model methods, model testing processes and recording outcomes, resources in the model building, testing and sustaining process. This area is key for audit controls and regulatory compliance, and mitigating unforeseen risks.	1 2 3 4 5
Risk mitigation plan	An AI risk mitigation plan is a proactive strategy for identifying, analyzing, and addressing potential risks associated with the development, deployment, and use of AI systems. It involves developing and implementing measures to reduce the likelihood or impact of these risks, ensuring responsible and ethical AI practices.	1 2 3 4 5
Independent testing	Independent AI model testing refers to a third-party operating independently of the AI model development process, with the aim of uncovering any issues, latent defects, ensuring optimal performance, adherence to applicable regulatory requirements, etc. For high-risk AI applications, independent testing is highly encouraged to reduce risks.	1 2 3 4 5

(*Continued*)

Table A1.1 (Continued)

Control type	*Definition*	*Maturity scale*
AI performance metrics	AI performance metrics are a set of specific indicators designed to evaluate the effectiveness and impact of AI systems within an organization. This program focuses on tracking KPIs related to accuracy, efficiency, and user satisfaction, ensuring that AI initiatives align with business objectives and deliver measurable value.	1 2 3 4 5
Continuous monitoring	AI continuous monitoring involves continuously evaluating AI models to ensure they function as intended, identifying potential issues like data drift, performance degradation, hallucination, and making adjustments to maintain accuracy and trust.	1 2 3 4 5
Adversarial attack management	AI adversarial attack management encompasses strategies and techniques to identify, mitigate, and defend against attacks on ML models that are designed to deceive or manipulate the model into making incorrect predictions or decisions. These attacks, known as adversarial attacks, exploit vulnerabilities in the ML model's learning mechanisms by introducing carefully crafted, often subtle, manipulations to the input data.	1 2 3 4 5
Intelligent monitoring	Intelligent monitoring uses AI to oversee IT systems, enhancing traditional monitoring by providing predictive insights, automating tasks, and improving incident response.	1 2 3 4 5
Kill switch	A kill switch enables organizations to pause, contain, or disable compromised AI systems before they cause serious damage. Far from a simplistic shutdown mechanism, an AI kill switch is about enforcing control through machine identity security and having the audit tracking mechanisms to identify intrusion sources.	1 2 3 4 5

Table A1.2 AI model stages – quality control questions

Stage #	*AI model stage*	*Key quality control questions*
1	Problem identification	1 Does the problem align with your strategic objectives? 2 What value is the AI expected to generate? 3 Have diverse stakeholder perspectives been factored into the problem and the proposed solution? 4 Has a full-cost estimate across the full AI solution's lifecycle been conducted? 5 How does the proposed AI solution align with current capabilities and resources?
2	Data collection and processing	1 What form of data will the AI system require, and how will it be sourced? 2 Are privacy laws adhered to during the data collection process? 3 Does the data represent the diverse demographics the model will serve? 4 How is your AI data bias being tested, and if risks are identified, how are these being addressed? 5 Is the data subject to regular quality review checks, leveraging third-party risk review experts?
3	Model development and training	1 Have the appropriate AI model types been thoroughly evaluated for the identified problem and specific requirements? 2 Does the level of explainability of the model match the business need to interpret and defend the AI's decisions? 3 Are model fairness and bias mitigation considerations integrated into the model training? 4 What measures are applied to test and validate the model's performance and are they inclusive of responsible AI requirements?

(*Continued*)

Table A1.2 (Continued)

Stage #	*AI model stage*	*Key quality control questions*
4	Model testing and validation	1 How does the model's performance on the validation dataset compare to the training dataset? 2 Are fairness and bias being evaluated and documented in model validation reports? 3 Are the model's outcomes explainable and transparent to non-technical stakeholders? 4 Is stress testing being performed under diverse and adversarial scenarios to evaluate the model's robustness? 5 Are there robust model versioning controls tracking different model reviews, model research methods, testing outcomes, end users involved in controls, forging a robust audit trail of AI model testing and validation practices?
5	Post-deployment monitoring	1 Is the model introduced into production incrementally to test it under production conditions? 2 Is there a robust, real-time monitoring system in place to track the AI system's performance post-deployment? 3 Does the AI monitoring include observability metrics to monitor the AI system's behavior against acceptable boundary conditions? 4 Have threshold values for performance metrics been set to trigger alerts for potential issues or drifts? 5 Is stakeholder feedback used to continually improve the model and respond to changing user needs or societal norms?

(*Continued*)

Table A1.2 (Continued)

Stage #	*AI model stage*	*Key quality control questions*
6	Retirement and cataloging	1 What are the indicators that signal the need for an AI system's retirement or replacement? 2 What are the financial or operational implications of maintaining the existing AI system versus retiring it? 3 Are there established protocols for the safe decommissioning of AI systems, ensuring data privacy and compliance with regulations?

Index

For Product Safety Concerns and Information please contact our EU representative GPSR@taylorandfrancis.com Taylor & Francis Verlag GmbH, Kaufingerstraße 24, 80331 München, Germany